# EXERCISE-BASED INTERVENTIONS FOR MENTAL ILLNESS

## PHYSICAL ACTIVITY AS PART OF CLINICAL TREATMENT

---

*Edited by*

### BRENDON STUBBS

*Institute of Psychiatry, Psychology and Neuroscience, King's College London and Head of Physiotherapy, South London and Maudsley NHS Foundation Trust, London, United Kingdom*

### SIMON ROSENBAUM

*School of Psychiatry, Faculty of Medicine, University of New South Wales, Sydney, Australia and The Black Dog Institute, Sydney, Australia*

ELSEVIER

**ACADEMIC PRESS**

An imprint of Elsevier

Academic Press is an imprint of Elsevier
125 London Wall, London EC2Y 5AS, United Kingdom
525 B Street, Suite 1650, San Diego, CA 92101, United States
50 Hampshire Street, 5th Floor, Cambridge, MA 02139, United States
The Boulevard, Langford Lane, Kidlington, Oxford OX5 1GB, United Kingdom

Notices
Knowledge and best practice in this field are constantly changing. As new research
and experience broaden our understanding, changes in research methods,
professional practices, or medical treatment may become necessary.

Practitioners and researchers must always rely on their own experience and
knowledge in evaluating and using any information, methods, compounds, or
experiments described herein. In using such information or methods they should be
mindful of their own safety and the safety of others, including parties for whom
they have a professional responsibility.

To the fullest extent of the law, neither the Publisher nor the authors, contributors, or
editors, assume any liability for any injury and/or damage to persons or property as
a matter of products liability, negligence or otherwise, or from any use or operation
of any methods, products, instructions, or ideas contained in the material herein.

**Library of Congress Cataloging-in-Publication Data**
A catalog record for this book is available from the Library of Congress

**British Library Cataloguing-in-Publication Data**
A catalogue record for this book is available from the British Library

ISBN: 978-0-12-812605-9

For information on all Academic Press publications visit our website at
https://www.elsevier.com/books-and-journals

  Working together
to grow libraries in
developing countries

www.elsevier.com • www.bookaid.org

*Publisher:* Nikki Levy
*Acquisition Editor:* Nikki Levy
*Editorial Project Manager:* Karen Miller
*Production Project Manager:* Mohanambal Natarajan
*Cover Designer:* Christian Bilbow

Typeset by TNQ Technologies

*This book is dedicated to all the patients who teach us how little we actually know.*

# Contents

## 4. Schizophrenia and Exercise

SHUICHI SUETANI AND DAVY VANCAMPFORT

## 5. Exercise for Alcohol Use Disorders

MATS HALLGREN

## 6. Sedentary Behavior and Mental Health

LEE SMITH, MARK HAMER AND BENJAMIN GARDNER

## 7. Exercise for Older People With Mental Illness

LI-JUNG CHEN, PO-WEN KU AND KENNETH R. FOX

# List of Contributors

**Aniyizhai Annamalai**  Departments of Medicine and Psychiatry, Yale University, New Haven, CT, United States

**Alan P. Bailey**  Orygen, The National Centre of Excellence in Youth Mental Health and Centre for Youth Mental Health, University of Melbourne, Melbourne, VIC, Australia

**Paquito Bernard**  University of Quebec at Montreal, Montreal, QC, Canada; Mental Health University Institute at Montreal, Montreal, QC, Canada

**Solfrid Bratland-Sanda**  University College of Southeast Norway, Bø, Norway

**Javier Bueno-Antequera**  Universidad Pablo de Olavide, Seville, Spain

**Rebekah Carney**  Faculty of Biology, Medicine and Health, University of Manchester, Manchester, United Kingdom

**Li-Jung Chen**  Department of Exercise Health Science, National Taiwan University of Sport, Taichung, Taiwan

**Lydia Chwastiak**  Department of Psychiatry and Behavioral Sciences, University of Washington School of Medicine, Seattle, WA, United States

**Joseph Firth**  Division of Psychology and Mental Health, University of Manchester, Manchester, United Kingdom

**Kenneth R. Fox**  Centre for Exercise, Nutrition and Health Sciences, University of Bristol, Bristol, United Kingdom

**Benjamin Gardner**  Department of Psychology, Institute of Psychiatry, Psychology and Neuroscience, King's College London, London, United Kingdom

**Benjamin I. Goldstein**  Department of Psychiatry, University of Toronto, Toronto, ON, Canada

**Paul Gorczynski**  Department of Sport and Exercise Science, University of Portsmouth, Hampshire, United Kingdom

**Mats Hallgren**  Department of Public Health Sciences, Karolinska Institute, Stockholm, Sweden

**Mark Hamer**  School of Sport, Exercise, and Health Sciences, National Centre for Sport & Exercise Medicine—East Midlands, Loughborough University, Loughborough, United Kingdom

**Matthew P. Herring**  Department of Physical Education and Sport Sciences, University of Limerick, Limerick, Ireland; Health Research Institute, University of Limerick, Limerick, Ireland

**Po-Wen Ku** Graduate Institute of Sports and Health, National Changhua University of Education, Changhua, Taiwan

**Oscar Lederman** University of New South Wales, Sydney, Australia

**Jacob Meyer** Iowa State University, Ames, IA, United States

**Probst Michel** Rehabilitation Sciences, KU Leuven, Leuven, Belgium

**Diego Munguía-Izquierdo** Universidad Pablo de Olavide, Seville, Spain

**Alexandra G. Parker** Institute for Health and Sport, Victoria University, Melbourne, Victoria, Australia

**Chad D. Rethorst** Psychiatry, UT Southwestern Medical Center, Dallas, TX, United States

**Ahmed Jerome Romain** University of Montreal Hospital Research Centre, Montreal, QC, Canada

**Simon Rosenbaum** School of Psychiatry, Faculty of Medicine, University of New South Wales, Sydney, Australia; The Black Dog Institute, Sydney, Australia

**Felipe Barreto Schuch** Universidade La Salle, Canoas, Brazil; Escola de Educação Física, Fisioterapia e Dança, Porto Alegre, Brazil; Hospital de Clínicas de Porto Alegre, Universidade Federal do Rio Grande do Sul, Porto Alegre, Brazil

**Lee Smith** Cambridge Centre for Sport and Exercise Sciences Anglia Ruskin University, Cambridge, United Kingdom

**Robert Stanton** School of Health, Medical and Applied Sciences, Central Queensland University, Rockhampton, QLD, Australia

**Brendon Stubbs** Institute of Psychiatry, Psychology and Neuroscience, King's College London and Head of Physiotherapy, South London and Maudsley NHS Foundation Trust, London, United Kingdom; Physiotherapy Department, South London and Maudsley NHS Foundation Trust, London, United Kingdom

**Shuichi Suetani** Queensland Centre for Mental Health Research, The Park Centre for Mental Health, Wacol, QLD, Australia; Queensland Brain Institute, The University of Queensland, St Lucia, QLD, Australia; Metro South Addiction and Mental Health Service, Queensland Health, Brisbane, QLD, Australia

**Davy Vancampfort** KU Leuven Department of Rehabilitation Sciences, Leuven, Belgium; KU Leuven, University Psychiatric Center KU Leuven, Leuven-Kortenberg, Belgium

**Martha Ward** Departments of Psychiatry and Behavioral Sciences and Medicine, Emory University, Atlanta, GA, United States

# Foreword

"A healthy mind in a healthy body" is not a new concept. From Roman times, when this link was posited by the poet Juvenal, we have known that better mental functioning was linked to physical well-being. However, the past two centuries saw major developments in human society that has led to a growing disconnect between physical health and mental well-being.

First, the wide availability of labor-saving technology in industrialized societies meant that, for the first time in human history, many people experienced a great reduction in energy expenditure, reflecting major changes in physical activity at work, new modes of transport, and the rapid development of sport as an observed rather than a participatory recreational activity. More recently, technology has produced a plethora of devices that deliver the world directly to our digital devices, circumventing the need to get out and see the world in person. These changes in physical activity were accompanied by the development of cheap, mass-produced foods, which were often energy-dense and involved the addition of sugar and fat to improve taste. Given these circumstances, it is little wonder that developed societies have seen a massive increase in rates of overweight and obesity in the population at large.

Secondly, the early 20th century saw the rise of psychoanalytic conceptualizations of psychiatric illness, stressing the primary role of psychological factors in the development of mental illness. These new psychiatric paradigms had a major impact on psychiatric treatment practices in many developed world settings. This clinical focus on the unconscious mind, and identification of innate and interpersonal psychological constructs believed to give rise to mental illness, led to physical health issues being perceived as largely outside the purview of psychiatry, clinical psychology, and medicine. In the last 30 years we have also seen new pharmacological treatments become available for those with severe mental illness, such as schizophrenia and bipolar affective disorder. Many of the newer medications have a negative impact on cardiometabolic functioning, and as a consequence, we have seen even greater rates of obesity, overweight, and metabolic disturbances in people living with severe mental illness than what has occurred in the general population. People with severe mental are dying 15–20 years earlier than their peers without a mental illness, chiefly through premature death from preventable and manageable physical health comorbidities. This situation has been rightly termed a "scandal." While those with more severe and enduring mental illness have been the subject of considerable attention, the current volume also includes chapters dealing with common mental disorders that are frequently treated in primary care, as well as with substance use disorders that are frequently comorbid with other mental health issues.

The last decade has seen a renewed recognition of the interdependence of mental and physical well-being for people living with mental health problems. Many studies have evaluated the impact of exercise interventions as an adjunct to usual care and found substantial benefits in terms of reduced psychiatric symptoms, better quality of life, and improvement in markers of cardiovascular and metabolic health. Ensuring these research outcomes become part of routine care in all mental health service settings is the next goal.

The editors of this volume, Brendon Stubbs and Simon Rosenbaum, are global leaders in developing the evidence base for exercise interventions in people living with mental illness. They have assembled leading experts in the field to review what research tells us, and their contributions detail how these data can be translated into scalable, feasible, cost-effective elements of standard care that aims to improve both physical and mental health.

The clinical focus of the work contained herein is no accident. Brendon Stubbs is the head of physiotherapy at the Maudsley Hospital and a postdoctoral research physiotherapist at the Institute of Psychiatry, Psychology, and Neuroscience, Kings College London. Simon Rosenbaum is an exercise physiologist who obtained extensive clinical experience before moving into his current research academic role at University of New South Wales, Sydney, Australia. Together, they and the other high-caliber contributors to this volume are inspired to ensure that the holistic health benefits of physical activity interventions become as routine as psychotropic medications and psychotherapy in treating those dealing with mental health problems.

While everyone who reads this book will benefit greatly from the distilled wisdom contained in the chapters in this volume, perhaps the greatest insight that the astute reader will experience lies in the strategies outlined to address one of the great challenges outlined by many of the contributors—how can we get people living with mental illness to obtain the manifold benefits of meeting physical activity guidelines, when so many not burdened with mental illness fail to meet this benchmark? The specific answers to this question are clearly detailed in the work that follows. We are beginning to see evidence that astute managers of mental health services are shifting resources to address this critical goal. Some are employing new clinicians with specific training in exercise prescription, others are empowering those at the clinical coalface with the skills and confidence to make asking about exercise habits as routine as asking about current mood. Improving exercise uptake in mental health service providers is another key strategy—if you, as a mental health clinician, are doing it yourself and experience the positive benefits, you are going to be much more likely to be a passionate and effective advocate for exercise and physical activity in those you treat.

Reducing sedentary time and increasing exercise participation in those engaged with mental health services should be seen as key performance indicators for good psychiatric care, akin to reducing readmission rates or suicide attempts. Reading this book alone will not achieve this, but we are sure that many who are inspired by the strength of the evidence and how it is possible to translate the available information into feasible and effective clinical interventions will join the editors and contributing authors of this volume in taking up the challenge of implementing systemic changes in mental health service delivery for the benefit of everyone in the community who is impacted by mental health issues.

*Philip B. Ward, BMedSc, PhD*
*Christoph Correll, MD*

# Introduction

The quantity of scientific studies documenting the benefits of physical activity for people living with mental illness has rapidly increased in recent years. Coupled with this increase in the scientific literature, consistent and targeted advocacy from various groups around the world has resulted in a shift in perception and attitudes toward the benefits of physical activity, by which physical activity is now seen as a highly acceptable and efficacious component of care.

Despite quantifiable progress in our scientific understanding of this topic, implementation of clinical physical activity and exercise programs as a routine part of psychiatric care remains ad-hoc. This implementation gap between evidence and clinical services is not unique to exercise and mental health and affects all aspects of health care, with the uptake of evidenced-based interventions more broadly in routine practice widely recognized as being complex, problematic, and slow (Balas and Boren, 2000; Colditz et al., 2012). For example, it takes 17 years to turn 14% of research findings into clinical practice that actually benefit patient care (Balas and Boren, 2000; Green, 2008), and clearly, the field of physical activity and mental health is not immune from the same systemic barriers to implementation pervasive across all areas of medicine.

The aim of this book is to help bridge this implementation gap and facilitate the translation of knowledge from those conducting and generating scientific research to those either currently working at the "coal-face" on the front-line and students completing clinical training in various exercise-related disciplines such as physiotherapy, exercise physiology, kinesiology, and adapted physical activity.

Underpinning ongoing advocacy efforts to increase employment opportunities for exercise practitioners within mental health services is an assumption that those exercise practitioners are ready to meet the challenges that working with this vulnerable population presents. While training in cardiovascular, musculoskeletal, and neurological disorders is likely to be an established part of the curriculum for many exercise-based practitioners, training in psychopathology and exposure to the unique barriers experienced by people living with a mental illness may not be a standard part of training in all areas of the world. This book aims to help fill this gap by providing an applied summary of the evidence that we hope will be useful for clinicians and researchers alike.

Ensuring that exercise practitioners are confident and competent to work within mental health services is only half picture. Ongoing advocacy must also target the mental health professionals who, until recent years, may not have had significant exposure to exercise and diet-related practitioners being part of the multidisciplinary mental health team. Such a cultural shift in the fundamental makeup of a mental health service no doubt takes time to achieve, and just as exercise practitioners require training in mental health, for a truly multidisciplinary approach, mental health professionals need training and exposure to the fundamentals of physical activity, ideally as early as possible within their clinical training.

Working in mental health as an exercise practitioner offers a unique and rewarding path. While we may be some way off realizing our long-term vision of seeing "mental health physical therapy" or "mental health exercise physiology" jobs advertised as routine and rivaling the more traditional career paths for exercise practitioners, recent progress and trajectory suggest that this vision is increasingly within reach. We also hope this text can contribute to breaking down the stigma surrounding mental health issues and hopefully encourage more exercise-based practitioners to choose a career in mental health.

## WHY MENTAL HEALTH?

In 1954 the first director-general of the World Health Organization, Dr. Brock Chisholm, famously stated that *"without mental health there can be no true physical health."* Mental and substance use disorders are a global health priority and are collectively responsible for the leading cause of years lived with disability worldwide (Whiteford et al., 2013). More than one in five, or an estimated 30% of the population, will experience a common mental disorder (depression or anxiety) throughout their life-time (Steel et al., 2014), with mental ill-health consistently listed as the primary reason for presentation to general practice/primary care (Sauver et al., 2013). Treating mental ill-health costs an estimated £22.5 billion per year in the United Kingdom alone (McCrone, 2008), a figure likely to be considerably higher if indirect costs and costs associated with disability and loss of productivity are also included.

Mental illness encompasses a broad spectrum of disorders including depression, anxiety, and psychotic illness and which are typically classified according to the Diagnostic and Statistical Manual of Mental Disorders (DSM; American Psychiatric, 2013). Anxiety and depression are the most common type of mental illness, affecting up to 60% of people with cardiovascular disease (Yohannes et al., 2010) and between 15% and 25% of cancer patients (Chochinov, 2001; Slade et al., 2009). This is an important point, as clearly not all exercise practitioners will necessarily want to specialize in mental health, however, as clinicians working with people, and the overwhelming prevalence of mental illness among both the general population and those living with chronic disease, mental illness is something that clinicians will be exposed to either as the primary reason for referral or as an important comorbidity.

## MENTAL ILLNESS AND MENTAL HEALTH

It is important to consider the distinction between *mental illness* and *mental health*. Mental health is more than simply the absence of mental illness and is a positive concept related to the social and emotional well-being of individuals and communities. On the other hand, mental health is influenced by culture but generally relates to the enjoyment of life, ability to cope with stress and sadness, the fulfillment of goals and potential, and a sense of connection to others (Hunter Institute of Mental Health, 2015). Both constructs are highly relevant to clinicians, and physical activity can confer benefits regardless of a person's current mental health status.

A *mental illness* is a disorder diagnosed by a medical professional (typically a general practitioner or a psychiatrist, who is a medical doctor who has specialized in psychiatry) that significantly interferes with an individual's cognitive, emotional, or social abilities (Hunter Institute of Mental Health, 2015). Mental disorders encompass a wide variety of signs, symptoms, experiences, and disorders. For example, mental illnesses can include mood disorders (e.g., major depression and bipolar disorder), anxiety disorders (e.g., generalized anxiety disorder and social anxiety disorder), psychotic disorders (e.g., schizophrenia), personality disorders (e.g., narcissistic personality disorder and borderline personality disorder), and substance use disorders (e.g., alcohol dependence or abuse; see Fig. 1). While each mental disorder may be viewed in isolation, comorbidity with other mental disorders is common. The two continua model of mental illness and health states that both mental health and

FIGURE 1 Broad classifications of mental illness. *Adapted from DSM-V; American Psychiatric, A., 2013. Diagnostic and Statistical Manual of Mental Disorders (DSM-5®). American Psychiatric Pub.*

mental illness are related, but distinct dimensions: one continuum indicates the presence or absence of mental health, the other the presence or absence of mental illness (Westerhof and Keyes, 2010).

## INTEGRATING MIND AND BODY: MENTAL AND PHYSICAL ILL-HEALTH

Poor mental health is known to be associated with poor physical health in what can be described as a bidirectional relationship. For example, obesity increases the risk of developing depression (Luppino et al., 2010), and people living with chronic pain and musculoskeletal disorders are more likely to experience comorbid mental ill-health (Stubbs et al, 2016a,b). Likewise and highly relevant to exercise practitioners is that the physical health of people with established mental illness is significantly poorer than the general population (as is discussed in detail throughout the following chapters) culminating in a 10- to 15-year reduction in life expectancy (Olfson et al., 2015; Erlangsen et al., 2017; Hjorthoj et al., 2017; Walker et al., 2015). The cause of this premature mortality is multifactorial, with high rates of preventable cardiovascular and metabolic diseases key contributing factors (Suetani et al., 2015). For example, people with mental illness are at a significantly increased risk of developing diabetes compared with the general population (Vancampfort et al., 2016). Obesity, hypertension, and hypercholesterolemia are all significantly more prevalent and smoking rates are approximately 2—3 times that seen in the general population (Newcomer and Hennekens, 2007). Further contributing to this substantial inequality is the fact that more than one-third of all cigarettes smoked are smoked by a person with a mental illness (Lasser et al., 2000). More specific to the exercise practitioner, and despite the increasing recognition of the health benefits associated with being physically active, people with a mental illness are on average, considerably less likely to be physically active compared with the general population (Vancampfort et al., 2017; Stubbs et al, 2016c,d, 2017a,b). Despite ongoing international calls for unified, targeted campaigns to increases access to exercise services for this population (Rosenbaum et al., 2018; Pratt et al., 2016; Probst, 2012, 2017; Brand et al., 2016), and increasing policy-level recognition of the importance of physical activity as a component of treatment (Ravindran et al., 2016; The Royal Australian and New Zealand College of Psychiatrists, 2015), more action is required to translate the overwhelming evidence into practice.

# MENTAL ILLNESS IS ALL OF OUR BUSINESS

We wanted to equip you the reader with summaries of the evidence and ideas for implementation from world experts in their respective fields. In addition, we should reiterate that while this book focuses on the evidence for physical activity in the context of mental illness and mental health services, this is a topic of relevance to us all. Mental illness is common in society, and regardless of the setting we work in, understanding the benefits of exercise for multiple conditions will be of relevance regardless of the setting in which you work. For instance, recent meta-analyses have demonstrated that one-third of people with stroke have depressive disorders (Mitchell et al., 2017), one in five people with osteoarthritis will have depression or anxiety (Stubbs et al., 2016b), and elite athletes are also at increased risk of anxiety and depression (Rice et al., 2016). Thus we hope to convey the message that even if you do not work in mental health services, this book will contain information that may be of interest to you.

*Brendon Stubbs*
*Simon Rosenbaum*

## References

American Psychiatric, A., 2013. Diagnostic and Statistical Manual of Mental Disorders (DSM-5®). American Psychiatric Pub.

Balas, E.A., Boren, S.A., 2000. Managing clinical knowledge for health care improvement. In: Yearbook of Medical Informatics, 2000: patient-centered systems.

Brand, S., et al., 2016. The current state of physical activity and exercise programs in German-speaking, Swiss psychiatric hospitals: results from a brief online survey. Neuropsychiatric Dis. Treat. 12, 1309–1317.

Chochinov, H.M., 2001. Depression in cancer patients. Lancet Oncol. 2 (8), 499–505.

Colditz, G.A., Brownson, R., Proctor, E., 2012. The promise and challenges of dissemination and implementation research. In: Dissemination and Implementation Research in Health: Translating Science to Practice, pp. 3–22.

Erlangsen, A., et al., 2017. Cause-specific life-years lost in people with mental disorders: a nationwide, register-based cohort study. Lancet Psychiatry 87, 99–105.

Green, L.W., 2008. Making research relevant: if it is an evidence-based practice, where's the practice-based evidence? Family Pract 25 (Suppl._1), i20–i24.

Hjorthoj, C., et al., 2017. Years of potential life lost and life expectancy in schizophrenia: a systematic review and meta-analysis. Lancet Psychiatry 4 (4), 295–301.

Hunter Institute of Mental Health, 2015. Prevention First: A Prevention and Promotion Framework for Mental Health. Hunter Institute of Mental Health, Newcastle.

Lasser, K., et al., 2000. Smoking and mental illness: a population-based prevalence study. JAMA 284 (20), 2606–2610.

Luppino, F.S., et al., 2010. Overweight, obesity, and depression: a systematic review and meta-analysis of longitudinal studies. Arch. Gen. Psychiatry 67 (3), 220–229.

McCrone, P., 2008. Paying the Price: The Cost of Mental Health Care in England to 2026.

Mitchell, A.J., et al., 2017. Prevalence and predictors of post-stroke mood disorders: a meta-analysis and meta-regression of depression, anxiety and adjustment disorder. Gen. Hosp. Psychiatr. 47, 48−60.

Newcomer, J., Hennekens, C., 2007. Severe mental illness and risk of cardiovascular disease. J. Am. Med. Assoc. 298 (15), 1794−1796.

Olfson, M., et al., 2015. Premature mortality among adults with schizophrenia in the United States. JAMA Psychiatry 72 (12), 1172−1181.

Pratt, S.I., et al., 2016. Increasing US health plan coverage for exercise programming in community mental health settings for people with serious mental illness: a position statement from the Society of Behavior Medicine and the American College of Sports Medicine. Transl. Behav. Med. 1−4.

Probst, M., 2012. The international organization of physical therapists working in mental health (IOPTMH). Mental Health Phys. Act. 5 (1), 20−21.

Probst, M., 2017. Physiotherapy and Mental Health, in Clinical Physical Therapy. InTech.

Ravindran, A.V., et al., 2016. Canadian network for mood and anxiety treatments (CANMAT) 2016 clinical guidelines for the management of adults with major depressive disorder section 5. Complementary and alternative medicine treatments. Can. J. Psychiatry, p. 0706743716660290.

Rice, S.M., et al., 2016. The mental health of elite athletes: a narrative systematic review. Sports Med. 1−21.

Rosenbaum, S., et al., 2018. The role of sport, exercise, and physical activity in closing the life expectancy gap for people with mental illness: an international consensus statement by exercise and sports science Australia, American College of sports medicine, British association of sport and exercise science, and sport and exercise science New Zealand. Transl. J. Am. Coll. Sports Med. 12, 22−44.

Sauver, J.L.S., et al., 2013. Why patients visit their doctors: assessing the most prevalent conditions in a defined American population. In: Mayo Clinic Proceedings. Elsevier.

Slade, T., et al., 2009. 2007 National survey of mental health and wellbeing: methods and key findings. Aust. N.Z.J. Psychiatry 43 (7), 594−605.

Steel, Z., et al., 2014. The global prevalence of common mental disorders: a systematic review and meta-analysis 1980-2013. Int. J. Epidemiol. dyu038.

Stubbs, B., et al., 2016. The epidemiology of back pain and its relationship with depression, psychosis, anxiety, sleep disturbances, and stress sensitivity: data from 43 low-and middle-income countries. Gen. Hosp. Psychiatry 43, 63−70.

Stubbs, B., et al., 2016. Prevalence of depressive symptoms and anxiety in osteoarthritis: a systematic review and meta-analysis. Age Ageing 45 (2), 228−235.

Stubbs, B., et al., 2016. Physical activity levels and psychosis: a mediation analysis of factors influencing physical activity target achievement among 204 186 people across 46 low-and middle-income countries. Schizophr. Bull. p. sbw111.

Stubbs, B., et al., 2016. Physical activity and depression: a large cross-sectional, population-based study across 36 low- and middle-income countries. Acta Psychiatry Scand. 134.

Stubbs, B., et al., 2017. Physical activity and anxiety: a perspective from the world health survey. J. Affect. Disord. 208, 545−552.

Stubbs, B., et al., 2017. Physical activity levels and psychosis: a mediation analysis of factors influencing physical activity target achievement among 204 186 people across 46 low- and middle-income countries. Schizophr. Bull. 43 (3), 536−545.

Suetani, S., Whiteford, H.A., McGrath, J.J., 2015. An urgent call to address the deadly consequences of serious mental disorders. JAMA Psychiatry 72 (12), 1166 1167.

The Royal Australian and New Zealand College of Psychiatrists, 2015. Keeping Body and Mind Together: Improving the Physical Health and Life Expectancy of People with Serious Mental Illness. The Royal Australian and New Zealand College of Psychiatrists, Melbourne.

Vancampfort, D., et al., 2016. Diabetes mellitus in people with schizophrenia, bipolar disorder and major depressive disorder: a systematic review and large scale meta-analysis. World Psychiatry 15 (2), 166–174.

Vancampfort, D., et al., 2017. Sedentary behavior and physical activity levels in people with schizophrenia, bipolar disorder and major depressive disorder: a global systematic review and meta-analysis. World Psychiatry 16 (3), 308–315.

Walker, E.R., McGee, R.E., Druss, B.G., 2015. Mortality in mental disorders and global disease burden implications: a systematic review and meta-analysis. JAMA Psychiatry 72.

Westerhof, G.J., Keyes, C.L., 2010. Mental illness and mental health: the two continua model across the lifespan. J. Adult Dev. 17 (2), 110–119.

Whiteford, H.A., et al., 2013. Global burden of disease attributable to mental and substance use disorders: findings from the Global Burden of Disease Study 2010. Lancet 382 (9904), 1575–1586.

Yohannes, A., et al., 2010. Depression and anxiety in chronic heart failure and chronic obstructive pulmonary disease: prevalence, relevance, clinical implications and management principles. Int. J. Geriatr. Psychiatry 25 (12), 1209–1221.

# CHAPTER

# 1

# Exercise for the Prevention and Treatment of Depression

*Jacob Meyer[1], Felipe Barreto Schuch[2,3,4]*

[1] Iowa State University, Ames, IA, United States; [2] Universidade La Salle, Canoas, Brazil; [3] Escola de Educação Física, Fisioterapia e Dança, Porto Alegre, Brazil; [4] Hospital de Clínicas de Porto Alegre, Universidade Federal do Rio Grande do Sul, Porto Alegre, Brazil

## OUTLINE

*Exercise-Based Interventions for Mental Illness*
https://doi.org/10.1016/B978-0-12-812605-9.00001-0

1

## INTRODUCTION

Major depressive disorder (MDD) is a highly prevalent condition (lifetime prevalence of about 16% in Brazil and 19% in the United States; Andrade et al., 2003) with a strong social impact and is one of the leading medical conditions contributing to the global burden of disease. Estimates suggest that MDD accounted for 8.2% of the global years lived with disability in 2010 (Ferrari et al., 2013).

The primary symptoms of MDD include low mood and lack of interest/motivation in activities that used to be pleasant, along with fatigue, impairments in appetite, sleep, and cognition, and suicidal ideation with or without a plan or a suicide attempt (American Psychiatric Association, 2013) for a minimum period of 2 weeks. In addition, these symptoms result in a clinically significant impairment in social, occupational, or other areas of functioning and are not related to physiological effects of a substance or another medical condition (American Psychiatric Association, 2013).

The two main strategies for treating depression proposed by most guidelines are pharmacological antidepressants and psychotherapies (Malhi et al., 2015; National Collaborating Centre for Mental Health (UK), 2010). Although helpful, antidepressant medication and/or psychotherapy do not work for all people. For example, the STAR*D study (Sinyor et al., 2010), the largest open trial evaluating the effects of pharmacological antidepressants, psychotherapies, or the combination of both, revealed that the response rate following the first pharmacological attempt was less than 50%. This suggests that about half of patients did not experience significant symptom improvements after the first treatment. Interestingly the response rate dropped following each subsequent strategy adopted (switching to or combining with a second medication).

MDD is associated with poor cardiovascular and metabolic outcomes. Approximately 30% of people with MDD also have metabolic syndrome, which is 54% greater than people without MDD (Vancampfort et al., 2014; Vancampfort et al., 2016). Similarly the rate of type II diabetes mellitus in people with MDD is about 8%; again, this represents a roughly 50% higher rate than people without MDD (Vancampfort et al., 2014, 2016).

In sum, (1) depression is a highly prevalent condition that is associated with a high burden to society; (2) current treatments may not work for all people with MDD and may not address the poor physical health of this population. Therefore strategies that (1) help to decrease the incidence and prevalence of MDD and/or (2) effectively treat (or augment treatment of) the primary and secondary symptoms (e.g., poor physical health) of MDD are required.

Exercise training is one intervention that may act on these two fronts, simultaneously decreasing the risk of depressive episodes in people free from depression and reducing depressive symptoms in people with depression. In this chapter, we aim to discuss (1) the relationship between physical activity and depression prevalence and incidence; (2) evidence from meta-analyses and systematic reviews on the effects of exercise in reducing depressive symptoms; (3) how exercise can be used to manage depressive symptoms; (4) exercise prescription guidelines for people with depression; (5) mechanisms involved in the effects of exercise on depressive symptoms; and (6) barriers and facilitators to exercise among people with depression.

# RELATIONSHIP BETWEEN PHYSICAL ACTIVITY AND DEPRESSION

Substantial evidence supports the notion that physical activity and depression are closely related. This relationship has been primarily assessed through answering two questions. First, is physical activity related to the *prevalence* of depression? Stated another way, is physical activity participation associated with the likelihood of *current* depression? Second, is physical activity related to the *incidence* of depression—that is, does physical activity participation predict *future development* of depression? If either prevalence or incidence of depression is related to physical activity participation or exercise, this would provide initial evidence to pursue experiments to improve current or prevent future depression through manipulating exercise behavior.

## Physical Activity and the Prevalence of Depression

Cross-sectional studies revealed a clear relationship between greater amounts of physical activity and reduced *current* depressive symptoms in people without a diagnosis of depression. Two large epidemiological studies that assessed both physical activity and depressive symptoms were the National Health and Nutrition Examination Survey (NHANES; Farmer et al., 1988) and the National Comorbidity Survey (Goodwin, 2003; Camacho et al., 1991). From an early wave of NHANES (1982–84; 1900 healthy adults), Farmer et al. (1988) found that greater depressive symptoms were associated with little or no self-reported physical activity across gender and race. From the National Comorbidity Survey (1990–92; 5877 people aged 15–54 years), Goodwin found that regularly active adults had a 25%–38% reduced risk of having current major depression than adults who were not regularly active. Additionally, there appeared to be a dose-response relationship between self-reported physical activity and depression with a lower risk of depression in the regularly active (8.2%) compared with the occasionally active (11.6%), the rarely active (15.6%), and the never active (16.8%).

Even in patients with depression, more physical activity is significantly related to lower depression severity (Harris et al., 2006). In a 424-person cohort of depressed adults, Harris et al. found that greater physical activity was related to lower levels of concurrent depressive symptoms. This suggests that even in patients suffering from depression, those who engage in a more active lifestyle may have lower symptom burden even in the face of current clinical illness. These findings extend the previously found association between exercise and depressive symptoms in the general population to those who are clinically depressed.

## Physical Activity and the Incidence of Depression

Substantial evidence exists demonstrating that current physical activity or a higher level of cardiovascular fitness is protective against the *development* of depression (i.e., incidence; Strawbridge et al., 2002; Schuch et al., 2016a). Data from the Alameda County study show that people who are active are less likely to develop clinical depression over 5 years (Strawbridge et al., 2002). Farmer et al. also showed from NHANES that physical activity was an independent predictor of depressive symptoms 8 years later. A more recent finding from a health cohort of 33,908 Norwegian adults found that baseline regular leisure-time exercise was associated with a reduced risk of developing depression over the next 11 years (Harvey et al., 2018). The results from this study also suggested that a relatively small amount of physical activity (1 h/week) was sufficient to significantly attenuate the likelihood of developing depression. The finding that high physical activity participation is negatively associated with future subclinical depressive symptom severity and a lower risk of developing clinical depression has been consistent across the literature and is supported by many studies of high methodological quality (Mammen and Faulkner, 2013).

Given the observational nature of incidence and prevalence studies, it is important to also consider reverse causality. That is, does depression predict lower future physical activity? Less research has been done on this topic, but it does appear that the presence of subclinical depressive symptoms can predict whether someone will drop out of an exercise program (Swardfager et al., 2015). Furthermore, baseline depression can predict a subsequent inactive lifestyle or poor adherence to exercise following a heart attack or other cardiac event (Roshanaei-Moghaddam et al., 2009) and, in adolescents, can predict decreased future physical activity (Gunnell et al., 2016). Given that a major symptom of depression is no longer enjoying previously enjoyed activities and that low motivation is common in depressed patients, it is not surprising that people with more depressive symptoms or with clinical depression are less likely to be physically active. However, this is important to be aware of for clinicians and exercise specialists who are working with depressed patients, as there may be additional issues specific to this population to overcome when attempting to increase physical activity in MDD.

# EXERCISE AS A TREATMENT FOR MDD

## Evidence From Meta-Analyses

Numerous meta-analyses have summarized the effects of exercise on depressive symptoms in people with depression. Following an early meta-analysis by North and colleagues investigating the effect of exercise on depressive symptoms (North et al., 1990) at least 18 other meta-analyses have investigated this same topic (North et al., 1990; Bridle et al., 2012; Carter et al.; Cooney et al., 2013, 2014; Daley et al., 2009; Danielsson et al., 2013; Krogh et al., 2011; Kvam et al., 2016; Lawlor and Hopker, 2001; Radovic et al., 2017; Rethorst et al., 2009; Rimer et al., 2012; Schuch et al., 2016b,c; Silveira et al., 2013; Exercise Interventions for Mental Health, 2006; Brown et al., 2013; Rebar et al., 2015; Josefsson et al., 2014; Krogh et al., 2017). Of the 19 meta-analyses performed, all 19 have found evidence that exercise reduces depressive symptoms in people with depression, with effect sizes ranging from small to very large. However, the high heterogeneity (i.e., the difference in the size of the effects across the studies) and subanalyses selecting only the studies with lower risk of bias (Krogh et al., 2017) have sparked controversy regarding the true effect of exercise on depression.

High statistical heterogeneity can be a sign that the analysis may be comparing "apples and oranges," in other words, pooling studies that are not directly comparable in terms of participants, study design, and interventions (Purgato and Adams, 2012). While high statistical heterogeneity may serve as an alert regarding the comparability of the studies, this can be somewhat expected in this research topic and should not nullify the findings. There are a variety of potential reasons for high heterogeneity, including disparate definitions of both depression and exercise, as well as the challenges to assess effectiveness in exercise treatment trials. Depression is a heterogeneous disorder that includes people with different severities and clusters of symptoms, which could lead to differential effects of exercise. For example, the antidepressant effects of exercise in people with MDD diagnosed by a psychiatrist is large, representing 1.13 standard deviations, while the effects in people with elevated depressive symptoms without necessarily having a diagnosis of MDD is smaller at 0.80 standard deviations (Schuch et al., 2016b). Also, recent studies have shown that people with atypical depression, a subtype of MDD, benefit more from exercise than people with non-atypical MDD (Rethorst et al., 2016). Clearly, when different studies include different proportions of people with diagnosed depression or people with atypical depression, the effects can be different, generating heterogeneity. Second, exercise can be based on different intensities (e.g., low, moderate, or vigorous), and moderate or vigorous exercise programs have shown greater effects in interventions of 8–20 weeks length compared with lighter intensity programs. Third, the type of control group that serves as the comparison can modify the effect. For example, Stubbs et al. demonstrated that control groups in exercise trials often have large reductions in depressive symptoms on their own (Standardized mean difference (SMD) = −0.92; Stubbs et al., 2015). Therefore an exercise intervention may appear to be more or less effective depending on the control used for comparison (e.g., treatment as usual, antidepressants, psychotherapy, and so on).

Regarding the quality of the trials, a Cochrane meta-analysis by Cooney et al. (2013), the last update of the "Exercise for depression" series, found that for "studies with adequate allocation concealment, intention-to-treat analysis, and blinded outcome assessment, the pooled SMD for this outcome was not statistically significant (−0.18, 95% CI −0.47 to 0.11)" (page 2). This conclusion is aligned with three of the four previous versions of the "exercise for depression" Cochrane reviews (Cooney et al., 2013; Lawlor and Hopker, 2001; Rimer et al., 2012; Mead et al., 2009) and with one subsequent meta-analysis published in 2014 in the Journal of the American Medical Association, one of the most prestigious journals in medicine where the authors state: "analysis of high-quality studies alone suggests only small benefits," along with "no association of exercise with improved depression" (Cooney et al., 2014, p. 2433). Although the Cochrane reviews are highly publicized, they are not free from error. Ekkekakis and Honey (2015) conducted a very detailed critique of the Cooney and et al. (2013) study, identifying several methodological issues, such as errors in the inclusion and exclusion criteria, the uniformity of rules, the procedures followed in assessing methodological quality and reporting errors. Considering the issues raised by Ekkekakis and Honey (2015), Schuch et al. (2016b) updated the Cooney review, finding a significant SMD of 0.88 for depressive symptom reduction in "high-quality trials." Overall, it appears that exercise has a moderate-to-large effect on depression from meta-analyses, but that the heterogeneity in outcome and the discrepancy among trials should be considered in interpreting the results.

## Exercise for Symptom Management

Exercise has consistently been found to improve mood and well-being following a single exercise session (Yeung, 1996). This has led to the potential for exercise to be used in symptom management in depression. In other words, a single bout of exercise can elevate mood in patients who are depressed and, when a patient is undergoing a period of heightened symptoms, they may be able to use exercise as a tool for short-term symptom relief.

In 2005, Bartholomew et al. found that participants receiving treatment for MDD had improved positive well-being and vigor after a moderate-intensity treadmill session that did not occur after a quiet rest session. This adds to evidence from a Master's thesis by Nelson and Morgan (1994) in which depressed female students ($n = 6$) exercised at 40%, 60%, and 80% of their estimated maximum capacity with results not supporting a dose-response relationship between exercise intensity and mood improvements. Each of the three sessions produced significant improvements in mood that were indistinguishable from each other. A similar assessment by Bodin and Martinsen (2004) found that martial arts exercise led to a significant improvement in self-efficacy and positive affect and a decrease in state anxiety across the session while similar changes did not occur following a cycling session. This study suggested that during-exercise mood may be related to the exercise stimulus itself, although they did not follow the participants to assess the duration or strength of postexercise changes in mood. Taken together, these studies found significant improvements in mood during and after a single session that lasted to each study's final assessment and could have led to improvements beyond 1 h, although there were no further assessments.

A more recent examination of this effect was performed by Meyer et al. (2016), who found that, in 24 women with major depression, a 20-min cycling bout at light, moderate, or hard intensity (rating of perceived exertion (RPE) of 11, 13, or 15) resulted in a significant decrease in depressed mood that was greater than the effect of sitting quietly (i.e., control condition). Indeed, this effect lasted 30 min (the final assessment point) and could have lasted longer. This second study provides additional support that the intensity of exercise is not critically important in the antidepressant response to a single session, corroborating the findings from Nelson and Morgan (1994). The larger sample size, control condition, and clinical diagnosis in this study's population also strengthen the evidence that exercise intensity likely has a small effect, if any, on the acute antidepressant effect to a single exercise session in depression.

A further article by Meyer et al. (2016) highlights another aspect related to exercise intensity—the potential usefulness of preferred exertion or exercising at an intensity that the patient chooses. In a separate session the investigators allowed participants to manipulate the workload themselves across a 20-min cycling session in a "preferred" intensity condition. The authors aimed to determine if the affective response to an acute session was different if (1) the exerciser chose how hard they would work (i.e., self-selected intensity), or if (2) they performed exercise at a similar intensity that was prescribed to them. They compared the response to the preferred session with the light, moderate, or hard intensity session (RPEs of 11, 13, or 15) that was closest in terms of average RPE to the exercise that they did during their preferred session (i.e., if the participant exercised at a high intensity during the preferred session, then their response to that session was compared with their response to the hard intensity prescribed session). This allowed the investigators to attempt to see what would have happened if they were prescribed a very similar intensity to what they would have chosen, which allowed them to try to isolate the affective effect of getting to choose the intensity. They found a slightly greater decrease in depressed mood after the closest prescribed session than to the preferred session with a small effect favoring the prescribed comparison session (Cohen's $d = 0.38$ for difference in depressed mood at 30 min postexercise). Depressed patients may experience a more beneficial acute mood effect from a single exercise session that is prescribed to them than one in which they are allowed to choose the intensity, although the difference was small and not statistically significantly different. On the other hand, Callaghan et al. (2011) evaluated the effect of a preferred exertion aerobic *exercise training program* in conjunction with psychosocial support in depressed women. In contrast to the results from the acute study, this enhanced exercise intervention resulted in decreased symptoms of depression, suggesting that preferred exertion might be useful in a treatment context. Overall, there is potential that working with an exercise practitioner or a fitness professional for external prescription and oversight of exercise may be helpful for depressed patients, although both preferred and prescribed intensities were still effective at improving mood in the acute study indicating any exercise is better than nothing.

Together, these results suggest that exercise intensity is not critically important acutely, for symptom management, but that exercise of even a light intensity can produce meaningful short-term improvements in mood in this population. A walk around the block or a walk during a lunch break may be sufficient to acutely alleviate depressive symptoms, which may be particularly important at times when symptoms or feelings of hopelessness are especially strong. Future work should determine if the duration of exercise influences the strength or duration of mood improvements postexercise or if the mode of exercise relates to the antidepressant response in patients suffering from depression. As typical antidepressant medications take weeks or months for clinical effects to occur, acute exercise appears a promising as needed, pro re nata, or PRN remedy in depression, providing short-term symptom relief that may not currently be achieved through traditional medication.

## Exercise Training for Depression: Historical Development and Potential Prescriptions

Exercise is routinely performed to increase physical fitness or improve cardiovascular health. When those are the goals of an exercise training program, decades and even centuries of work have identified near-optimal training programs to produce the desired improvements. Far less work has been done to optimize exercise training to specifically improve depression. Although exercise training has not been used as a front-line treatment, it is recommended in a number of national guidelines (Ekkekakis and Murri, 2017). The utility of exercise for the treatment of depression has been evaluated in a variety of ways, from initially determining its potential for treating depression to comparison with other treatments and even as an adjunct treatment to antidepressants or other treatments.

Initial research to determine an effect of exercise training on clinical depression was designed to assess its comparative effectiveness to other treatments. Early work in the 1970 and 1980s led by Greist (1979) and Klein (1984) showed comparable treatment efficacy for aerobic exercise training in depressed patients compared with time-limited or time-unlimited psychotherapy or with meditation or group therapy, respectively. In each of these studies, exercise treatment (i.e., running) was as effective for reducing depressive symptoms as the comparison psychotherapy treatments. This pair of studies provided the first controlled evidence that exercise training could be a successful clinical intervention for the treatment of depression. With group sizes of less than 30 in both studies, this provided initial evidence that exercise could be an effective treatment for depression, but replication of this effect in larger samples and broader populations was required.

Egil Martinsen, through a series of studies (Martinsen et al., 1985, 1989), in the 1980s, found that exercise was effective for improving depression and fitness, but that the improvement in fitness was not a critical component of the overall antidepressant effect of the treatment. His results showed that nonaerobic forms of exercise could be helpful for patients, and the focus did not need to be on improving cardiorespiratory fitness for improvements in depressive symptoms to occur. This pioneering work demonstrated that metabolic changes or adapting the aerobic system might not be a mechanism through which exercise training improves depression leading to new potential types of exercise (e.g., resistance training) as options for therapy and the pursuit to identify alternative mechanisms.

Much of the research looking at exercise for the treatment of depression has focused solely on aerobic exercise and increasing cardiorespiratory fitness, although Martinsen's research suggested that this may not be the only effective mode of exercise for depression. Indeed, Singh et al. conducted two randomized controlled trials evaluating the use of progressive resistance exercise training for treating depression. The first trial (Singh et al., 1997) compared resistance training in 32 older adults with major or minor depression with an attention control group and found significantly greater improvements in depression and quality of life in the resistance exercise group, with the added finding that intensity of training significantly predicted the decrease in depression scores. This trial was then followed up by a second trial (Singh et al., 2005) that included a low-intensity resistance training group (20% maximum load compared with 80% maximum load) and a general practitioner care control group in 60 older adults. This study found a response rate (decrease $\geq$50% in depressive symptoms) of 61% in participants in the high-intensity group and 29% in participants in the low-intensity group. Again, strength gain was associated with the reduction in depressive symptoms along with a variety of other quality of life improvements. Taken together, the results suggest that resistance training could also be used as treatment for clinical depression (at least in older patients), with strength gain potentially important for decreasing depression.

James Blumenthal was the first to compare exercise training to pharmacotherapy in the 1990 and 2000s, demonstrating similar effectiveness of exercise training and sertraline over 16 weeks in a series of studies. The first study (Blumenthal et al., 1999) randomized 156 men and women (aged >50 years) to an aerobic exercise training program, antidepressants (sertraline), or a combination of exercise and antidepressants for 16 weeks. There was no differential effect on the groups at the end of the 16 weeks, but those who were taking medications had a quicker initial response. The follow-up study provided a more robust assessment of the effect of exercise on depression by improving on the design of the initial trial with a placebo group. In the second study (Blumenthal et al., 2007), the investigators randomized 202 participants to 16 weeks of home-based aerobic exercise, supervised group exercise, sertraline, or a placebo pill. The results demonstrated a significant effect on the likelihood of remission of both home-based (38%) and supervised group–based (46%) exercise over placebo (26%) that was comparable with the effect of the sertraline group (44%), but only when early responders were removed. They concluded that exercise training either at home or in a group setting was superior to placebo and comparable with current antidepressant treatments for depression.

Based on the understanding that exercise appeared as effective as currently available treatments, the next step was to determine the optimal prescription of exercise for depression. In the first assessment of aerobic exercise dose, Dunn et al. (2005) evaluated the dose-response relationship of both the frequency of activity (three or five times per week) and the amount of exercise based on energy expenditure (7 or 17.5 kcal/kg/week). Their results showed no significant effect of frequency of activity, but that the amount/dose of activity that was performed was influential on the resulting level of symptom reduction. There was a 30% reduction in depression scores in the lower dose group which was comparable to their stretching control group (29% decrease) with the higher dose having a greater response (47% decrease). The higher dose was of a similar amount to the 150 min of moderate-to-vigorous physical activity guidelines and showed that exercising at that level could result in a large decrease of symptoms in patients with mild to moderate depression.

Trivedi et al. (2011) then provided the next step by showing that exercise training can be an effective augmentation or supplemental therapy for patients with treatment-resistant depression. This study found that if patients ($n = 126$) were provided with 12 weeks of structured exercise training at either a low dose (4 kcal/kg/week) or a high dose (16 kcal/kg/week), they had an increased rate of depression remission. Again, this study supported the notion that a higher dose of exercise can provide a greater effect (although, from this study, only in women without a family history of mental illness and for men with or without a family history). This extended the results from the Dunn et al. study to show that exercise was not only effective in treating initial depression but that it could be added to other treatments to increase the likelihood of remission and that, in both scenarios, a higher amount of exercise may be more effective for treating depression.

In summary, exercise is an effective treatment for depression that is comparable to other treatments, including antidepressant medications and comes with an extremely favorable side effect profile compared with pharmacotherapy. Rethorst and Trivedi (2013) provide an excellent primer for prescribing exercise for depression noting that either aerobic or resistance training can be effective, with three to five sessions per week, sessions lasting 45–60 min at 50%–85% of maximum heart rate for aerobic training or three sets of eight repetitions at 80% of one repetition maximum for resistance training, which last at least 10 weeks (Table 1.1). This chapter provides useful advice for prescribing exercise to depressed patients along with practical considerations for promoting exercise as a treatment option in this population. It is unclear if there is a threshold of exercise that would be required to elicit an antidepressant response or if it's simply that the more one does, the better for improving depression symptoms.

**TABLE 1.1**    Recommendation for Prescribing Exercise for Patients With Major Depressive Disorder

| Exercise Domain | Recommendation |
| --- | --- |
| Modality | Aerobic or resistance training |
| Session frequency | 3–5 exercise sessions/week |
| Session duration | 45–60 min |
| Exercise intensity | 50%–85% maxHR (aerobic) or 80% 1-RM (resistance) |
| Intervention duration | At least 10 weeks |

*maxHR*, maximum heart rate; *1-RM*, one repetition maximum; maximum weight that can be lifted in a single repetition for a given exercise. Exercise intensity for resistance training is typically quantified by percent of 1-RM, along with number of sets and repetitions.
*Reproduced with permission from Rethorst and Trivedi, 2013*

## Potential Mechanisms

A number of experts in the field of psychobiology, exercise psychology, and psychopathology have suggested mechanisms that may underlie the antidepressant effect of exercise. Of primary difficulty in finding out how exercise influences depression is the lack of a clinical, biological signature of depression. That is, there is no single abnormality or altered physiological system that occurs in depression, rather it is a heterogeneous disease characterized by symptoms that can be present in people with a variety of neurobiological dysregularities.

For example, the hypothalamic-pituitary-adrenal (HPA) axis produces cortisol in response to stress, and it has been hypothesized that exercise influences depression through normalization of the HPA axis (Phillips, 2017). Similarly, chronic subclinical inflammation has been implicated in depression, and exercise training can reduce this via repeated acute temporary increases in inflammation following each exercise session leading to an overall decrease in chronic inflammation (Pedersen and Hoffman-Goetz, 2000). An emerging concern in depression is a low-level of neurotrophins—a protein family that promotes nerve cell growth and survival—which are increased by exercise (English et al., 2014), potentially in relation to treatment. As a result of decreased neurotrophins the hippocampus and other brain areas may atrophy in depression, and exercise appears to be able to reverse this through an increase in hippocampal volume (Ernst et al., 2006). A further biological concern in depression is alteration in the storage and production of monoamines and some data support that storage or production of monoamines can be improved by exercise in animal models (Dishman, 1997). A review of these and other neurobiological mechanisms and an assessment of their support in the research literature has been published by Schuch et al. (2016d).

Exercise likely influences many of the abnormalities that have been found in subsets of depressed patients and evaluating the effect of exercise on the more prominent psychobiological correlates of depression may be helpful in two ways. First, it could improve our understanding of how exercise influences mood and well-being in general, allowing for targeted exercise prescriptions to maximize the mechanisms of action. Second, understanding the psychobiological effects of exercise can also lead to understanding more about the systems that are involved in depression potentially leading to broader investigations of biomarkers and pathways identified through exercise—depression interactions. The broad neurobiological effects of exercise are impressive compared with drugs that typically target a single system and the lack of negative side effects with exercise support its high potential as a strong therapeutic option.

## Barriers/Facilitators

Lifestyle modifications or changing behavior patterns, such as beginning an exercise program, are challenging in any population. For example, about 60.5% of patients who received a recommendation to exercise self-reported participating in an exercise program. However, only 49% of patients had exercised in the past year (Woolf et al., 2017).

Previous studies have investigated factors related to barriers or facilitators to physical activity. Firth et al. (2016), identified that in people with severe mental illness, low mood and stress were the most prevalent barriers to physical activity, followed by a lack of support. Vancampfort et al. (2015), found similar results showing that higher levels of depressive symptoms and also higher body mass index, the presence of physical comorbidity, and lower self-efficacy were linked to lower physical activity (PA). Some strategies may help patients and serve as facilitators to increasing PA engagement. First, there is no one-size-fits-all prescription, so considering preferences and previous experiences are key issues in promoting PA. Vancampfort et al. (2015) suggest that autonomous motivation may "hold the key" to adoption and maintenance of PA behavior in people with severe mental illness. Autonomous motivation includes the motivations that lead someone to be active due to reasons from within the person, reflecting the person's interests and values, which would lead to people adopting and maintaining exercise when they find the activity that they do to be enjoyable or challenging. Second, every progress, even if it is minimal, should be acknowledged and commended. Despite evidence supporting a dose-response relationship, people with depression usually have low cardiorespiratory fitness, so immediately starting with high volumes or intensities of exercise would be unrealistic. Therefore aiming for feasible and achievable goals and increasing them in a sustainable way can increase the chance of successfully adopting and maintaining an exercise program. Lastly, Schuch et al. (2016e) found that depressed people who have higher levels of social support are more likely to have symptom improvements in response to exercising, thus encouraging patients to exercise with friends or family may increase the chance of adoption and maintenance of exercise over the long term and also increase the chance of success in reducing symptoms.

## SUMMARY AND FUTURE DIRECTIONS

Depression is a prevalent and costly disorder that is having an increasingly damaging effect on the world's population. Both cross-sectional and longitudinal studies suggest that higher levels of exercise are associated with a decreased risk of current and future depression. Meta-analyses and guidelines indicate that exercise training is a potential treatment for depression with a large mean effect size of 0.88 from high-quality trials (Schuch et al., 2016b). Exercise also can exert powerful acute effects on mood and should be considered as a symptom management tool for short-term mood improvement. A number of potential mechanisms have been proposed to explain the effect of exercise on depression, although limited human experimental data address the issue of mechanism. Low mood and lack of motivation are barriers to engagement in PA. Strategies that may help to overcome these barriers include choosing enjoyable activities, establishing achievable goals, and considering the dose-response relationship in designing the training program. This field would benefit from future investigations designed to determine the minimal dose necessary to achieve antidepressant benefits and the relative importance of the components of an exercise prescription (frequency, intensity, time, and duration). Overall, higher amounts of physical activity participation can reduce the risk of developing depression in healthy people, and exercise is an effective treatment for MDD, which underlines the critical relationship between a healthy lifestyle and positive well-being.

## References

American Psychiatric Association, 2013. Diagnostic and Statistical Manual of Mental Disorders. American Psychiatric Publishing.

Andrade, L., et al., 2003. The epidemiology of major depressive episodes: results from the International Consortium of Psychiatric Epidemiology (ICPE) Surveys. Int. J. Methods Psychiatr. Res. 12, 3–21.

Bartholomew, J.B., Morrison, D., Ciccolo, J.T., 2005. Effects of acute exercise on mood and well-being in patients with major depressive disorder. Med. Sci. Sports Exerc. 37, 2032–2037.

Blumenthal, J.A., et al., 1999. Effects of exercise training on older patients with major depression. Arch. Intern. Med. 159, 2349−2356.

Blumenthal, J.A., et al., 2007. Exercise and pharmacotherapy in the treatment of major depressive disorder. Psychosom. Med. 69, 587−596.

Bodin, T., Martinsen, E.W., 2004. Mood and self-efficacy during acute exercise in clinical depression. A randomized, controlled study. J. Sport Exerc. Psychol. 26, 623−633.

Bridle, C., Spanjers, K., Patel, S., Atherton, N.M., Lamb, S.E., 2012. Effect of exercise on depression severity in older people: systematic review and meta-analysis of randomised controlled trials. Br. J. Psychiatry J. Ment. Sci. 201, 180−185.

Brown, H.E., Pearson, N., Braithwaite, R.E., Brown, W.J., Biddle, S.J.H., 2013. Physical activity interventions and depression in children and adolescents: a systematic review and meta-analysis. Sports Med. Auckl. N.Z. 43, 195−206.

Callaghan, P., Khalil, E., Morres, I., Carter, T., 2011. Pragmatic randomised controlled trial of preferred intensity exercise in women living with depression. BMC Publ. Health 11, 465.

Camacho, T.C., Roberts, R.E., Lazarus, N.B., Kaplan, G.A., Cohen, R.D., 1991. Physical activity and depression: evidence from the Alameda county study. Am. J. Epidemiol. 134, 220−231.

Carter, T., Morres, I.D., Meade, O., Callaghan, P., 2016. The effect of exercise on depressive symptoms in adolescents: a systematic review and meta-analysis. J. Am. Acad. Child Adolesc. Psychiatry. https://doi.org/10.1016/j.jaac.2016.04.016.

Cooney, G.M., et al., 2013. Exercise for depression. Cochrane Database Syst. Rev. 9, CD004366.

Cooney, G., Dwan, K., Mead, G., 2014. Exercise for depression. J. Am. Med. Assoc. 311, 2432−2433.

Daley, A., Jolly, K., MacArthur, C., 2009. The effectiveness of exercise in the management of post-natal depression: systematic review and meta-analysis. Fam. Pract. 26, 154−162.

Danielsson, L., Noras, A.M., Waern, M., Carlsson, J., 2013. Exercise in the treatment of major depression: a systematic review grading the quality of evidence. Physiother. Theory Pract. 29, 573−585.

Dishman, R.K., 1997. Brain monoamines, exercise, and behavioral stress: animal models. Med. Sci. Sports Exerc. 29, 63−74.

Dunn, A.L., Trivedi, M.H., Kampert, J.B., Clark, C.G., Chambliss, H.O., 2005. Exercise treatment for depression: efficacy and dose response. Am. J. Prev. Med. 28, 1−8.

Ekkekakis, P., Honey, I., 2015. Shrunk the pooled SMD! Guide to critical appraisal of systematic reviews and meta-analyses using the cochrane review on exercise for depression as example. Ment. Health Phys. Act. 8, 21−36.

Ekkekakis, P., Murri, M.B., 2017. Exercise as antidepressant treatment: time for the transition from trials to clinic? Gen. Hosp. Psychiatry. https://doi.org/10.1016/j.genhosppsych.2017.04.008.

English, A.W., Wilhelm, J.C., Ward, P.J., 2014. Exercise, neurotrophins, and axon regeneration in the PNS. Physiology 29, 437−445.

Ernst, C., Olson, A.K., Pinel, J.P.J., Lam, R.W., Christie, B.R., 2006. Antidepressant effects of exercise: evidence for an adult-neurogenesis hypothesis? J. Psychiatry Neurosci. 31, 84−92.

Exercise Interventions for Mental Health, 2006. A quantitative and qualitative review. In: Clinical Psychology: Science and Practice. Wiley Online Library, Stathopoulou. Available at: http://onlinelibrary.wiley.com/doi/10.1111/j.1468-2850.2006.00021.x/full.

Farmer, M.E., et al., 1988. Physical activity and depressive symptoms: the nhanes I epidemiologic follow-up study. Am. J. Epidemiol. 128, 1340−1351.

Ferrari, A.J., et al., 2013. Burden of depressive disorders by country, sex, age, and year: findings from the global burden of disease study 2010. PLoS Med. 10, e1001547.

Firth, J., et al., 2016. Motivating factors and barriers towards exercise in severe mental illness: a systematic review and meta-analysis. Psychol. Med. 46, 2869–2881.

Goodwin, R.D., 2003. Association between physical activity and mental disorders among adults in the United States. Prev. Med. 36, 698–703.

Greist, J.H., et al., 1979. Running as treatment for depression. Compr. Psychiatry 20, 41–54.

Gunnell, K.E., et al., 2016. Examining the bidirectional relationship between physical activity, screen time, and symptoms of anxiety and depression over time during adolescence. Prev. Med. 88, 147–152.

Harris, A.H.S., Cronkite, R., Moos, R., 2006. Physical activity, exercise coping, and depression in a 10-year cohort study of depressed patients. J. Affect. Disord. 93, 79–85.

Harvey, S.B., et al., 2018. Exercise and the prevention of depression: results of the HUNT cohort study. Am. J. Psychiatry 175, 28–36.

Josefsson, T., Lindwall, M., Archer, T., 2014. Physical exercise intervention in depressive disorders: meta-analysis and systematic review. Scand. J. Med. Sci. Sports 24, 259–272.

Klein, M.H., et al., 1984. A comparative outcome study of group psychotherapy vs. Exercise treatments for depression. Int. J. Ment. Health 13, 148–176.

Krogh, J., Nordentoft, M., Sterne, J.A.C., Lawlor, D.A., 2011. The effect of exercise in clinically depressed adults: systematic review and meta-analysis of randomized controlled trials. J. Clin. Psychiatry 72, 529–538.

Krogh, J., Hjorthøj, C., Speyer, H., Gluud, C., Nordentoft, M., 2017. Exercise for patients with major depression: a systematic review with meta-analysis and trial sequential analysis. BMJ Open 7, e014820.

Kvam, S., Kleppe, C.L., Nordhus, I.H., Hovland, A., 2016. Exercise as a treatment for depression: a meta-analysis. J. Affect. Disord. 202, 67–86.

Lawlor, D.A., Hopker, S.W., 2001. The effectiveness of exercise as an intervention in the management of depression: systematic review and meta-regression analysis of randomised controlled trials. Br. Med. J. 322, 763.

Malhi, G.S., et al., 2015. Royal Australian and New Zealand College of Psychiatrists clinical practice guidelines for mood disorders. Aust. N.Z. J. Psychiatry 49, 1087–1206.

Mammen, G., Faulkner, G., 2013. Physical activity and the prevention of depression: a systematic review of prospesctive studies. Am. J. Prev. Med. 45, 649–657.

Martinsen, E.W., Medhus, A., Sandvik, L., 1985. Effects of aerobic exercise on depression: a controlled study. Br. Med. J. Clin. Res. Ed. 291, 109.

Martinsen, E.W., Hoffart, A., Solberg, Ø., 1989. Comparing aerobic with nonaerobic forms of exercise in the treatment of clinical depression: a randomized trial. Compr. Psychiatry 30, 324–331.

Mead, G.E., et al., 2009. Exercise for depression. Cochrane Database Syst. Rev. Online 3, CD004366.

Meyer, J.D., et al., 2016. Psychobiological responses to preferred- and prescribed-intensity exercise in MDD. Med. Sci. Sports Exerc. https://doi.org/10.1249/MSS.0000000000001022.

Meyer, J.D., Koltyn, K.F., Stegner, A.J., Kim, J.-S., Cook, D.B., 2016. Influence of exercise intensity for improving depressed mood in depression: a dose-response study. Behav. Ther. 47, 527–537.

National Collaborating Centre for Mental Health (UK), 2010. Depression: The Treatment and Management of Depression in Adults (Updated Edition). British Psychological Society.

Nelson, T.F., Morgan, W.P., 1994. Acute effects of exercise on mood in depressed female students. Med. Sci. Sports Exerc. 26, S156.

North, T.C., McCullagh, P., Tran, Z.V., 1990. Effect of exercise on depression. Exerc. Sport Sci. Rev. 18, 379–415.

Pedersen, B.K., Hoffman-Goetz, L., 2000. Exercise and the immune system: regulation, integration, and adaptation. Physiol. Rev. 80, 1055–1081.

Phillips, C., 2017. Physical activity modulates common neuroplasticity substrates in major depressive and bipolar disorder. Neural Plast. 2017, e7014146.

Purgato, M., Adams, C.E., 2012. Heterogeneity: the issue of apples, oranges and fruit pie. Epidemiol. Psychiatr. Sci. 21, 27–29.

Radovic, S., Gordon, M.S., Melvin, G.A., 2017. Should we recommend exercise to adolescents with depressive symptoms? A meta-analysis. J. Paediatr. Child Health 53, 214–220.

Rebar, A.L., et al., 2015. A meta-meta-analysis of the effect of physical activity on depression and anxiety in non-clinical adult populations. Health Psychol. Rev. 0, 1–78.

Rethorst, C.D., Trivedi, M.H., 2013. Evidence-based recommendations for the prescription of exercise for major depressive disorder. J. Psychiatr. Pract. 19, 204–212.

Rethorst, C.D., Wipfli, B.M., Landers, D.M., 2009. The antidepressive effects of exercise: a meta-analysis of randomized trials. Sports Med. Auckl. N.Z. 39, 491–511.

Rethorst, C.D., Tu, J., Carmody, T.J., Greer, T.L., Trivedi, M.H., 2016. Atypical depressive symptoms as a predictor of treatment response to exercise in major depressive disorder. J. Affect. Disord. 200, 156–158.

Rimer, J., et al., 2012. Exercise for depression. Cochrane Database Syst. Rev. CD004366. https://doi.org/10.1002/14651858.CD004366.pub5.

Roshanaei-Moghaddam, B., Katon, W.J., Russo, J., 2009. The longitudinal effects of depression on physical activity. Gen. Hosp. Psychiatry 31, 306–315.

Schuch, F.B., et al., 2016a. Are lower levels of cardiorespiratory fitness associated with incident depression? A systematic review of prospective cohort studies. Prev. Med. 93, 159–165.

Schuch, F.B., et al., 2016b. Exercise as a treatment for depression: a meta-analysis adjusting for publication bias. J. Psychiatr. Res. 77, 42–51.

Schuch, F.B., et al., 2016c. Exercise for depression in older adults: a meta-analysis of randomized controlled trials adjusting for publication bias. Rev. Bras. Psiquiatr. Sao Paulo Braz. 1999 (38), 247–254.

Schuch, F.B., et al., 2016d. Neurobiological effects of exercise on major depressive disorder: a systematic review. Neurosci. Biobehav. Rev. 61, 1–11.

Schuch, F.B., Dunn, A.L., Kanitz, A.C., Delevatti, R.S., Fleck, M.P., 2016e. Moderators of response in exercise treatment for depression: a systematic review. J. Affect. Disord. 195, 40–49.

Silveira, H., et al., 2013. Physical exercise and clinically depressed patients: a systematic review and meta-analysis. Neuropsychobiology 67, 61–68.

Singh, N.A., et al., 2005. A randomized controlled trial of high versus low intensity weight training versus general practitioner care for clinical depression in older adults. J. Gerontol. Ser. A 60, 768–776.

Singh, N.A., Clements, K.M., Fiatarone, M.A.A., 1997. Randomized controlled trial of progressive resistance training in depressed elders. J. Gerontol. Ser. A 52A, M27–M35.

Sinyor, M., Schaffer, A., Levitt, A., 2010. The sequenced treatment alternatives to relieve depression (STAR*D) trial: a review. Can. J. Psychiatry Rev. Can. Psychiatr. 55, 126–135.

Strawbridge, W.J., Deleger, S., Roberts, R.E., Kaplan, G.A., 2002. Physical activity reduces the risk of subsequent depression for older adults. Am. J. Epidemiol. 156, 328–334.

Stubbs, B., et al., 2015. Challenges establishing the efficacy of exercise as an antidepressant treatment: a systematic review and meta-analysis of control group responses in exercise randomised controlled trials. Sports Med. 1–15. https://doi.org/10.1007/s40279-015-0441-5.

Swardfager, W., et al., 2015. Depressive symptoms predict non-completion of a structured exercise intervention for people with Type 2 diabetes. Diabet. Med. n/a. https://doi.org/10.1111/dme.12872.

Trivedi, M.H., et al., 2011. Exercise as an augmentation treatment for nonremitted major depressive disorder: a randomized, parallel dose comparison. J. Clin. Psychiatry 72, 677–684.

Vancampfort, D., et al., 2014. Metabolic syndrome and metabolic abnormalities in patients with major depressive disorder: a meta-analysis of prevalences and moderating variables. Psychol. Med. 44, 2017–2028.

Vancampfort, D., et al., 2015. What are the factors that influence physical activity participation in individuals with depression? A review of physical activity correlates from 59 studies. Psychiatr. Danub. 27, 210–224.

Vancampfort, D., et al., 2016. Diabetes mellitus in people with schizophrenia, bipolar disorder and major depressive disorder: a systematic review and large scale meta-analysis. World Psychiatry 15, 166–174.

Vancampfort, D., Stubbs, B., Venigalla, S.K., Probst, M., 2015. Adopting and maintaining physical activity behaviours in people with severe mental illness: the importance of autonomous motivation. Prev. Med. 81, 216–220.

Woolf, B.A.R., Williams, J.V.A., Lavorato, D.H., Bulloch, A.G.M., Patten, S.B., 2017. A comparison of recommendations and received treatment for mood and anxiety disorders in a representative national sample. BMC Psychiatry 17, 155.

Yeung, R.R., 1996. The acute effects of exercise on mood state. J. Psychosom. Res. 40, 123–141.

# Exercise for the Management of Anxiety and Stress-Related Disorders

Matthew P. Herring[1,2]

[1] Department of Physical Education and Sport Sciences, University of Limerick, Limerick, Ireland; [2] Health Research Institute, University of Limerick, Limerick, Ireland

*Exercise-Based Interventions for Mental Illness*
https://doi.org/10.1016/B978-0-12-812605-9.00002-2

19

Individuals commonly state that exercise helps them feel calmer, and, indeed, the available research supports the anxiety-reducing effects of exercise training among even otherwise healthy adults and adults with a diverse range of chronic illnesses. Importantly, although exercise was once believed to actually elicit anxiety in clinical populations and comparatively less is known regarding exercise effects among clinical populations, a rapidly growing body of literature supports both the benefits and prescription of exercise training for individuals with anxiety or stress-related disorders. Following an overview of what anxiety and anxiety and stress-related disorders are, how we believe they develop, and how best to measure anxiety, this chapter summarizes the available evidence of the effects of exercise training on anxiety among healthy adults, chronically ill adults, and individuals diagnosed with an anxiety or stress-related disorder to inform exercise prescription among these groups and provides a brief discussion of plausible mechanisms of the anxiolytic effects of exercise training.

# ANXIETY: WHAT IS IT AND WHY DO WE CARE?

## Definition and Conceptualizations

Anxiety is characterized by unpleasant feelings of apprehension and thoughts of worry that are frequently combined with autonomic nervous system activation. This definition conveys two critical points: (1) anxiety includes cognitive and emotional components and is often accompanied by physiological changes; and (2) these cognitive and emotional components distinguish anxiety from more diffuse, nonspecific arousal. Though anxiety can be an adaptive response to an objective or perceived threat, it can be maladaptive if the anxiety becomes severe and chronic (Barlow, 2002). For example, anxiety is a normal, evolutionarily adaptive response to real or perceived danger but is considered a maladaptive disorder when symptoms or behaviors become severe enough, particularly in the absence of threatening stimuli, to cause interference and/or impairment.

## Etiology and Development

An understanding of the prevailing etiological models for anxiety and stress-related disorders, particularly the neurobiological factors which may underlie their development, is critical to the establishment of a biologically plausible framework by which exercise may improve symptoms. To establish biological plausibility, exercise effects should be coherent with existing theory/knowledge about both how anxiety and stress-related disorders develop and biological adaptations to exercise training. Several models have been hypothesized to explain the etiology and expression of anxiety and stress-related disorders. Though no single model can adequately explain the development of anxiety disorders, evidence supports the involvement of genetic, biological, behavioral, and environmental factors (Smoller, 2015; O'Connor et al., 2000a; Bandelow et al., 2016).

A direct genetic abnormality for anxiety and stress-related disorders has not been confirmed, but some individuals may be more susceptible, particularly in the context of increased and/or excessive stress. The "diathesis–stress" hypothesis essentially proposes that genetics and adversity independently and interactively increase the liability to psychopathology (Smoller, 2015). Although a recent consensus statement concluded that, at present, none of the putative genetic or neuroimaging biomarkers is sufficient and specific as a diagnostic tool, the available pharmacogenetic studies point to the potential influence of serotonin transporter (*SLC6A4*), serotonin 1A (*HTR1A*), serotonin 2A (*HTR2A*), monoamine oxidase (*MAOA*), catechol-O-methyltransferase (*COMT*), and corticotropin-releasing hormone type 1 receptor (*CRHR1*) gene variants on interindividual differences in treatment response among individuals with panic disorder (PD), social phobia, and generalized anxiety disorder (GAD) (Bandelow et al., 2016). Importantly, these findings underscore the potential importance of monoaminergic systems in the development and treatment of anxiety and stress-related disorders and may be particularly important to exercise effects in anxiety and stress-related disorders, given recent evidence of significant associations of variants in serotonin and dopamine receptors (HTR2A, HTR2C, and DRD4) with exercise adherence and tolerance among 885 young adults (Herring et al., 2014a).

Existing models for the development of anxiety have focused on the cognitive and neurobiological aspects of anxiety (O'Connor et al., 2000a). Cognitive models have focused on threat-related cognitive biases in information processing (Ouimet et al., 2009). These models propose that pathological anxiety results from impaired cognitive appraisals, including overestimation of the intensity of feared events, underestimation of coping ability, or catastrophic misinterpretation of physiological/somatic symptoms related to anxiety (e.g., misinterpreting increased heart rate as a potential cardiac event; O'Connor et al., 2000a). Neurobiological models have focused on the neurocircuitry and neurobiology that underlie anxiety, including activity in the amygdala, anterior cingulate cortex, prefrontal cortex, and insular cortex and associated monoaminergic neurotransmitter activity (Shin and Liberzon, 2010). Integrative models which consider both approaches may ultimately prove to be more useful by accounting for neurobiological or neurophysiological aspects of emotional disturbance within cognitive models of anxiety (Clark and Beck, 2010). Prevailing models hypothesize that anxiety and stress-related disorders result from dysregulation of neurotransmitter systems, including serotonin, norepinephrine, dopamine, and γ-aminobutyric acid (GABA). Emerging evidence supports the potential interactive influence of other neurobiological factors, including inflammatory markers. For example, higher interleukin-6 has been reported among clinically anxious adults, independent of depression and neuroticism (O'Donovan et al., 2010).

Distinguishing between state and trait anxiety is also useful (Spielberger, 1966), particularly in the context of how acute and chronic exercise may influence state and trait anxiety. State anxiety is conceptualized as transient feelings of tension and worry, the intensity of which can fluctuate from moment-to-moment. Trait anxiety is conceptualized as an individual's predisposition to appraise a stimulus as threatening, has a biological basis, and is relatively stable over time; however, trait anxiety is sensitive to change in response to even short-term targeted interventions (Schwartz et al., 1999; Sklan et al., 2004). For example, interventions designed to reduce trait anxiety symptoms, including cognitive and behavioral therapies (Mitte, 2005), chronic massage (Moyer et al., 2004), and relaxation training (Manzoni et al., 2008), produce moderate-to-large reductions in trait anxiety scores.

## Anxiety and Stress-Related Disorders

Anxiety disorders are debilitating conditions characterized by excessive, chronic maladaptive anxiety symptoms that are often accompanied by strong autonomic nervous system activation, anxiety-related cognitions, and altered behavior (e.g., avoidance). Through the Fourth Edition of the Diagnostic and Statistical Manual of Mental Disorders (*DSM-IV*) (Association and Association, 2000), pathological anxiety was classified into six disorders: specific phobia, social phobia or social anxiety disorder (SAD), GAD, PD (with or without agoraphobia), obsessive–compulsive disorder (OCD), and posttraumatic stress disorder (PTSD). These widely used criteria for diagnosis were revised in May 2013 when *DSM-5* (APA, 2013) was published. OCD and PTSD were reclassified as obsessive–compulsive and related disorder and trauma- and stressor-related disorder categories, respectively, separate from the anxiety disorders; four anxiety disorders were added, including selective mutism, substance-induced anxiety disorder, anxiety disorder attributable to another medical condition, and separation anxiety disorder (in adults), and agoraphobia was decoupled from PD (APA, 2013). As we will address later in the chapter, because exercise training may improve common, overlapping symptoms of anxiety, OCD, and stress-related disorders through its effects on similar underlying neurobiological pathways, for the purpose of this chapter, we have addressed anxiety disorders, OCD, and PTSD together. Table 2.1 provides a brief description of anxiety disorders, OCD, and PTSD.

Anxiety disorders are the most prevalent type of psychiatric disorders with estimated global prevalence, adjusted for methodological differences between studies, of 7.3% (Baxter et al., 2013). However, lifetime prevalence rates of any anxiety disorder as high as 40% and 26% have been reported among US women and men, respectively (Kessler et al., 2012). Fig. 2.1 illustrates 12-month prevalence rates for anxiety disorders, OCD, and PTSD estimated from the National Comorbidity Survey Replication and Adolescent Supplement (Kessler et al., 2012). Estimates ranged from 1.2% for separation anxiety disorder and OCD to 7.4% for SAD and 12.1% for specific phobia. Though most individuals may experience a traumatic event at some point in their lifetimes, the lifetime prevalence of PTSD has been estimated at 5.7%–7% (Kessler et al., 2012; Kessler and Wang, 2008).

Anxiety disorders are also the most frequent mental health disorders in children and adolescents, with estimated worldwide-pooled prevalence

**TABLE 2.1**    Brief Descriptions of Primary Anxiety Disorders, OCD, and PTSD Based on *DSM-5* (American Psychological Association, 2013)

| Disorder | Primary Characterizations |
| --- | --- |
| Specific phobia | Marked fear or anxiety about specific object or situation that almost always provokes immediate fear or anxiety that is disproportional to actual danger, is avoided or endured with intense fear or anxiety, and lasts 6 months or more |
| Social anxiety disorder | Marked fear or anxiety about one or more social situations in which an individual may be scrutinized by others that almost always provoke fear or anxiety that is disproportional to the actual threat posed by the situation, is avoided or endured with intense fear or anxiety, and lasts 6 months or more |
| Generalized anxiety disorder | Excessive worry about a number of events or activities that occurs on more days than not for at least 6 months that is difficult to control, is associated with at least three associated symptoms, including restlessness, fatigue, difficulty concentrating, irritability, muscle tension, and disturbed sleep, and that causes significant distress or impairment |
| Panic disorder | Repeated unexpected panic attacks, or abrupt surges of intense fear or discomfort that strike without warning or obvious source, crescendo within minutes, are accompanied by somatic symptoms (e.g., accelerated heart rate, sweating, trembling, fear of losing control, shortness of breath, and so on), and lead to a month or more of persistent concern about additional attacks or their consequences and/or significant maladaptive change in behavior related to attacks |
| Obsessive–compulsive disorder | Presence of obsessions, compulsions, or both that are time-consuming and cause significant distress/impairment; obsessions are recurrent and persistent thoughts, urges, or images that are intrusive and unwanted, distressful, and cause the individual to attempt to ignore, suppress, or neutralize (most often with compulsion); compulsions are repetitive behaviors or mental acts that an individual feels driven to perform in response to obsession which are aimed at preventing or reducing anxiety and/or distress |
| Posttraumatic stress disorder | Exposure to actual or threatened death, serious injury, or sexual violence that results in significant impairment characterized by hyperarousal, intrusive re-experiencing, negative cognitions and mood, and persistent avoidance of stimuli associated with traumatic events. |

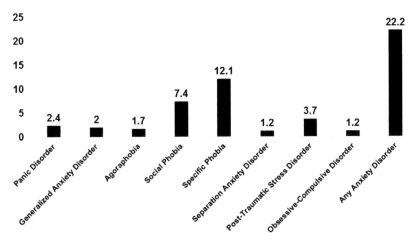

FIGURE 2.1 Twelve-month prevalence estimates for anxiety disorders, obsessive–compulsive disorder (OCD), and posttraumatic stress disorder (PTSD). *Data from Kessler, R. C., Petukhova, M., Sampson, N. A., Zaslavsky, A. M., & Wittchen, H. U. (2012). Twelve-month and lifetime prevalence and lifetime morbid risk of anxiety and mood disorders in the United States. Int. J. Methods Psychiatr. Res. 21(3), 169–184.*

of 6.5% (Polanczyk et al., 2015). These disorders represent the earliest forms of psychopathology (Beesdo et al., 2009), with the earliest age of onset found for separation anxiety disorder and specific phobia (Kessler et al., 2012). In addition, people aged 15–24 years experience episodes of anxiety 40% more often than people aged 25–54 years (Kessler et al., 2007). Recent evidence suggests that women are approximately 1.5–2 times more likely to be diagnosed with an anxiety condition (Bandelow and Michaelis, 2015), and limited evidence supports higher prevalence rates of anxiety disorders among non-Hispanic whites compared to other race/ethnicity groups (Breslau et al., 2005; Himle et al., 2009). A recent large systematic review of 48 reviews concluded that there is compelling evidence of substantial prevalence of anxiety disorders, particularly among women (5.2%–8.7%), young adults (2.5%–9.1%), individuals with chronic diseases (1.4%–70%), and individuals from Euro/Anglo cultures (3.8%–10.4%; Remes et al., 2016).

Anxiety disorders are also associated with significant economic and personal burden. In 2010, anxiety disorders globally accounted for 390 disability-adjusted life years per 100,000 persons, making them the sixth leading cause of disability worldwide (Baxter et al., 2014). Financial burdens result from direct treatment costs and various indirect costs (e.g., reduced work productivity; DuPont et al., 1998; Greenberg et al., 1999). Personal impairments among persons with an anxiety disorder included reduced health-related quality of life (Sareen et al., 2006), increased disability (Kroenke et al., 2007; Ludman et al., 2006; Sareen et al., 2005), increased absenteeism from work (Stein et al., 2005), and increased use of health care resources (Marciniak et al., 2005; McLaughlin et al., 2006). Individuals with an anxiety disorder also report significantly more medically unexplained physical symptoms compared to individuals without an anxiety disorder (Katon et al., 2007).

## Traditional Treatment of Anxiety and Stress-Related Disorders

There are well-established pharmacological and cognitive-behavioral treatments for anxiety and stress-related disorders (Puetz et al., 2015; Bandelow et al., 2007; Hoffman et al., 2008; Hoskins et al., 2015), but more than 40% of patients report no current treatment (Kroenke et al., 2007). Some are not interested in treatment, others have difficulty complying with treatment, and others have financial or other barriers that result in no or suboptimal treatment (Kessler et al., 2001). Pharmacotherapy has drawbacks including well-established negative side effects, including nausea and sexual dysfunction (Corona et al., 2009). In addition, because the symptom profiles of anxiety and stress-related disorders are hetero-geneous, pharmacotherapy may improve some symptoms but worsen others. SSRIs have shown efficacy for anxiety symptom improvement (Chessick et al., 2006; Hackett et al., 2003), but often exacerbate sleep disturbances (Schweitzer, 2005; Morehouse et al., 2011) and weight gain (Fava, 2000). Behavioral treatments have also demonstrated efficacy (Chambless et al., 1998; Hofmann et al., 2012), but logistical barriers associated with those treatments include the expense and the need for extensive specialized training among practitioners. Widespread access to cognitive-behavioral therapy (CBT) is currently unavailable and would require pervasive policy changes (McCrone et al., 2004). Thus there is a continued need for effective, accessible, low-cost remedies for anxiety and stress-related disorders, including exercise.

## Measurement of Anxiety Symptoms and Anxiety and Stress-Related Disorders

Research evidence regarding the development and treatment of anxi-ety and stress-related disorders is only as rigorous as the measurement on which the evidence is based. Thus a clear understanding of the tools available to screen for, diagnose, and assess symptom severity of anxiety and stress-related disorders is critical. Before discussing the relevant evidence of exercise effects on anxiety and stress-related disorders, the following section will briefly highlight different measurement tools.

### Diagnostic Interviews

Trained health care professionals, including clinical psychologists and psychiatrists, diagnose anxiety disorders based on well-defined diagnostic criteria and responses to standardized questions presented during interviews. For example, the Anxiety Disorders Interview Schedule for DSM-5, Adult Version (ADIS-5) is a structured diagnostic interview schedule that examines current episodes of anxiety disorders and is designed to allow for differential diagnosis among the anxiety disorders (Brown and Barlow, 2013). Each section of the ADIS-5 contains questions designed to determine if an individual meets criteria for a specific disorder, the focal concern associated with individual symptoms, and the relation of each symptom to symptoms previously reported in other sections (Brown and Barlow, 2013). After initial screening questions linked to key features of each disorder that are dichotomously rated (i.e., yes/no), symptom severity ratings are assigned for each disorder; for example, the symptom severity of GAD is assessed using a 9-point (0—8) Likert-type scale, and these severity ratings allow discrimination between principal diagnoses (Brown and Barlow, 2013).

### Diagnostic Screeners

However, from a research standpoint, it may be especially advantageous to improve efficiency in recruiting individuals likely to be diagnosed with an anxiety or stress-related disorder with the use of diagnostic screeners. These inventories are designed for clinical practice and research to facilitate efficiency in conducting initial diagnostic evaluations. For example, the Psychiatric Diagnostic Screening Questionnaire is a brief, psychometrically strong, self-report scale designed to screen for the most common *DSM-IV* disorders, which has shown good sensitivity (i.e., most actual cases are detected) and high negative predictive value (i.e., most identified noncases are indeed noncases; Zimmerman and Mattia, 2001a,b).

### Measures of Anxiety Symptoms

Valid and reliable measurement of general, nonpathological symptoms of anxiety is also of critical importance. For this purpose, self-report questionnaires measure the severity or intensity of anxiety symptoms across specified recall timeframes (i.e., right now, the past week including today, generally, etc.). Some commonly used instruments include the widely used 20-item State (STAI-Y1) and Trait (STAI-Y2) subscales of the State-Trait Anxiety Inventory (Speilberger et al., 1983), the 21-item Beck Anxiety Inventory (Beck et al., 1988), the 7-item anxiety subscale of the Hospital Anxiety and Depression Scale (Zigmond and Snaith, 1983), and the 5-item tension subscale of the Profile of Mood States—Brief (McNair et al., 1992).

### Disorder-Specific Symptom Inventories

Given the heterogeneous symptom profiles among anxiety disorders, OCD, and PTSD, disorder specific inventories are beneficial in assessing levels of hallmark symptoms specific to each disorder. For example, the 16-item Penn State Worry Questionnaire assesses pathological worry, the hallmark of GAD, and appears to be GAD specific (Meyer et al., 1990; Molina and Borkovec, 1994). Other disorder-specific inventories include the GAD-7 (Spitzer et al., 2006), the Liebowitz (1987) Social Anxiety Scale, the Panic and Agoraphobia Scale (Bandelow, 1995), the Yale-Brown Obsessive-Compulsive Scale (Goodman et al., 1989), and the PTSD Checklist (Civilian and Military Versions; Weathers et al., 1993; Wilkins et al., 2011).

# EXERCISE EFFECTS IN ANXIETY AND STRESS-RELATED DISORDERS

## Exercise Effects on Anxiety and Among Patients With Anxiety and Stress-Related Disorders

The Scientific Advisory Committee for the *2008 Physical Activity Guidelines for Americans* concluded that minimal evidence was available to support that physical activity or exercise protected against the onset of any anxiety disorder or reduced symptoms among patients with an anxiety disorder (Committee, 2008). Compared to what is known regarding the antidepressant effects of exercise, some key figures in exercise psychology, including Bill Morgan, Rod Dishman, and Patrick O'Connor, have previously postulated that the comparative lack of research into exercise effects among patients with an anxiety or stress-related disorder prior to the past two decades may stem from a misconception within the medical literature of the 1960s and early 1970s that physical activity may induce panic among people with anxiety neurosis (Morgan, 1979; O'Connor et al., 2000a; Buckworth, 2013). This misconception stemmed from a single study by Pitts and McClure (1967) in which 13 of 14 people with anxiety neurosis at rest experienced a panic attack following infusion of sodium DL-lactate. This led some to believe that exercise would induce panic because exercise increases lactate to a greater degree than sodium DL-lactate infusion. However, subsequent reports by Grosz and Farmer (1972) and Morgan (1979) detailed why exercise would not induce panic but infused lactate would. Infused lactate induces anxiety as a function of metabolic alkalosis and associated hyperventilation (Maddock et al., 1991), whereas elevated lactate induced by exercise results in metabolic acidosis. To that end, a review of 15 studies, O'Connor, Smith, and Morgan reported that only five panic attacks were found during 444 exercise bouts performed by 420 patients with PD (O'Connor et al., 2000c). However, across the past two decades a growing body of evidence, particularly from randomized controlled trials (RCTs), indicates that exercise training can improve anxiety symptoms among healthy adults, chronically ill patients, and patients with an anxiety or stress-related disorder.

### Exercise Effects on Anxiety

As shown in Table 2.2, at least nine meta-analytic reviews have supported the effects of acute and chronic exercise on anxiety symptoms among otherwise healthy adults, with effect sizes ranging from small to moderate, and have included measures of state and trait anxiety, within- and between-subjects designs, and focused on traditional (e.g., aerobic and resistance exercise) and alternative (e.g., tai chi and qigong) forms of exercise.

Similar findings have been reported among youth and adolescents; however, as Table 2.3 illustrates, there is a comparatively limited amount of evidence for the anxiolytic effects of exercise among children and adolescents.

The available experimental evidence demonstrates that anxiety symptoms are transiently reduced by approximately ¼ to ½ standard deviation in response to a single bout of exercise (Morgan, 1979; O'Connor et al., 2000b; Petruzzello et al., 1991; Petruzzello, 2012; Ensari et al., 2015). In practical terms, based on an estimated age-related normative score of ∼39 and standard deviation of ∼12 for a college-aged female (Speilberger et al., 1983), these effect sizes would correspond to a 3−6 point, or ∼7.7%−15.4%, reduction in state anxiety score in response to a single bout of exercise. A recent meta-analytic update of 36 RCTs of acute exercise effects on state anxiety published from 1991 to 2016 showed a small but statistically significant mean improvement (Hedges' $g = 0.16$) in state anxiety in response to a single bout of exercise compared with control conditions (Ensari et al., 2015). Though the magnitude of improvement in state anxiety after a single bout of exercise appears largest for individuals experiencing high anxiety, even persons with below average anxiety often report feeling less anxious after acute exercise (Motl et al., 2004).

The available evidence from RCTs also supports small-to-moderate anxiolytic effects of exercise training on comorbid anxiety symptoms among patients with a diverse range of chronic illnesses. As shown in Table 2.4, at least five meta-analyses have reported small-to-moderate, but

**TABLE 2.2**   Quantitative Reviews of Exercise Effects on Anxiety Among Primarily Healthy Adults

| Author(s) | Year | Focus of Review | k | Mean ES |
|---|---|---|---|---|
| Petruzzello, Landers, Hatfield, Kubitz, and Salazar | 1991 | Primarily healthy adults | 207 (state) 62 (trait) | 0.24 (state) 0.34 (trait) |
| Long and van Stavel | 1995 | Primarily healthy adults | 26 (within) 50 (between) | 0.45 0.36 |
| Wipfli, Rethorst, and Landers | 2008 | Primarily healthy adults | 49 | 0.48 |
| Conn | 2010 | Primarily healthy adults | 19 | 0.22 |
| Yin and Dishman | 2014 | Tai Chi & Qigong in primarily healthy adults | 11 (Tai Chi) 12 (Qigong) | 0.34 0.72 |
| Wang, Chan, Ho, Chan, Ng, and Chan | 2014 | Qigong in primarily healthy adults | 4 | 0.75 |
| Ensari, Greenlee, Motl, and Petruzzello | 2015 | Primarily healthy adults | 36 (state) | 0.16 |
| Rebar, Stanton, Geard, Short, Duncan, and Vandelanotte | 2015 | Meta-meta-analysis of metas of nonclinical samples | 306 (4 metas) | 0.38 |
| Gordon, McDowell, Lyons, and Herring | 2017 | Resistance exercise training in healthy and ill adults | 31 | 0.31 |

statistically significant mean effects are ranging from 0.28 to 0.40 among patients, including those with Fibromyalgia and Cardiovascular Diseases.

In the largest and most comprehensive meta-analysis to date, 75 effects were derived from 40 RCTs of exercise training among a myriad of chronically ill patients. As shown in Fig. 2.2 a small but statistically significant mean reduction in anxiety symptoms ($\Delta = 0.29$) was found along with small-to-moderate reductions across individual patient groups (Herring et al., 2010).

**TABLE 2.3** Quantitative Reviews of Exercise Effects on Anxiety Among Youth and Adolescents

| Authors | Year | Type of Review | Sample (Years) | Types of Research Designs | Mean ES |
|---|---|---|---|---|---|
| Ahn and Fedewa | 2011 | k = 25 | 3.67–17.66 | RCTs (16) Non-RCTs (9) | RCTs: ES = 0.35 Non-RCTs: ES = 1.51 |
| Wipfli, Rethorst and Landers | 2008 | k = 3 | <18 | RCTs | ES = 0.19 |
| Larun, Nordheim, Ekeland, Hagen, Heian | 2006 | k = 6 | 11–19 | RCTs | ES = 0.48 |
| Calfas and Taylor | 1994 | k = 20 | 11–21 | Quasi-experimental; CS | ES = 0.15 |
| Petruzzello, Landers, Hatfield, Kubitz, and Salazar | 1991 | k = 3 | <18 | Longitudinal | ES = 0.47 |

**TABLE 2.4** Quantitative Reviews of Exercise Effects on Anxiety Among Chronically Ill Patients

| Author(s) | Year | Focus of Review | k | Mean ES |
|---|---|---|---|---|
| Kugler, Seelback, and Kruskemper | 1994 | Cardiovascular disease patients | 13 | 0.31 |
| Rossy, Buckelew, Dorr, et al. | 1999 | Fibromyalgia patients | 5 | 0.38 |
| Puetz, Beasman, and O'Connor | 2006 | Cardiovascular disease patients | 19 | 0.40 |
| Herring, O'Connor, and Dishman | 2010 | Chronically ill patients | 75 | 0.29 |
| McDowell, Cook, and Herring | 2017 | Fibromyalgia patients | 25 | 0.28 |

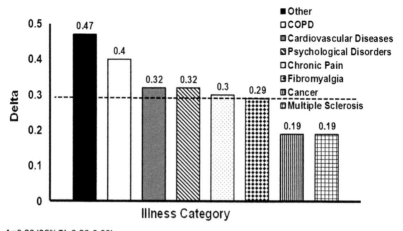

--- Δ=0.29 (95%CI: 0.23-0.36)

FIGURE 2.2    Mean effect of exercise training on anxiety symptoms across chronic illnesses. *Data from Herring, M. P., O'Connor, P. J., & Dishman, R. K. (2010). The effect of exercise training on anxiety symptoms among patients: a systematic review. Arch. Intern. Med. 170(4), 321–331.*

In addition, a meta-regression analysis, which examined the influence of potentially important participant and trial characteristics on the anxiolytic effects of exercise, showed larger anxiety reductions for exercise programs lasting up to 12 weeks, using session durations of at least 30 min, and an anxiety recalls time frame greater than the past week. Importantly, the findings also showed that, at the time, only one RCT of exercise training effects among anxiety disorder patients had been conducted, though there had been a handful of placebo-controlled trials (Herring et al., 2010).

### Exercise Effects Among Patients With Anxiety and Stress-Related Disorders

Compared to the large body of experimental literature regarding the effects of exercise training on depressive symptoms and disorders, the available evidence regarding the effects of exercise training among individuals diagnosed with an anxiety or stress-related disorder remains limited. Four of five recently published reviews have concluded that the limited available evidence suggests that exercise training may be an effective adjuvant or adjunct therapy for clinically significant anxiety (Jayakody et al., 2013; Asmundson et al., 2013; Herring et al., 2014b; Stubbs et al., 2017). Conversely, a recent meta-analysis of seven RCTs of aerobic exercise effects on patients with a *DSM-IV* defined anxiety disorder concluded that aerobic exercise training (AET) is not an effective

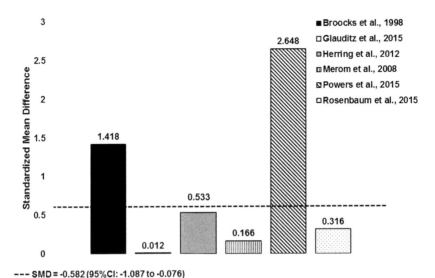

**FIGURE 2.3**  Mean effect of exercise training on anxiety symptoms among adults with an anxiety or stress-related disorder. *Data from Stubbs, B., Vancampfort, D., Rosenbaum, S., Firth, J., Cosco, T., Veronese, N., Salum, G. A., & Schuch, F. B. (2017). An examination of the anxiolytic effects of exercise for people with anxiety and stress-related disorders: a meta-analysis. Psychiatry Res. 249, 102–108.*

treatment for anxiety disorders when time spent exercising was accounted for by the control condition (Bartley et al., 2013). However, a more recent meta-analysis was conducted to address methodological shortcomings of this prior analysis, particularly the comparison of exercise with control conditions with known anxiolytic effects (i.e., mindfulness, nonaerobic physical activity; Stubbs et al., 2017). Stubbs et al. (2017) conducted a meta-analysis of six RCTs of the effects of exercise training among 262 adults with an anxiety or stress-related disorder. Exercise training resulted in a significant moderate-sized improvement in anxiety symptoms (standardized mean difference $= -0.58$, 95% CI: $-1.0$ to $-0.76$, $P \leq .02$). Fig. 2.3 illustrates effect sizes reported across the six RCTs.

These findings support that exercise is effective for improving anxiety symptoms among people with a diagnosed anxiety and/or stress-related disorder. Following a summary of the evidence from early studies of mixed samples of anxiety disorder patients, the available evidence of exercise effects for each anxiety or stress-related disorder is presented.

### Early Studies

In an early study, 44 inpatients with a *DSM-III* anxiety disorder completed aerobic exercise, usually walking or jogging, for five weekly 60-min sessions for 8 weeks (Martinsen et al., 1989b). All patients showed improvements except those diagnosed with social phobia. Improvements persisted among patients with GAD and agoraphobia without panic attacks at a 1-year follow-up (Martinsen et al., 1989b). However, one key limitation of this study was the lack of a control comparison.

A second early study investigated the effects of aerobic and nonaerobic exercise among 79 inpatients with various *DSM-III-R* anxiety disorders (Martinsen et al., 1989a). Patients were randomly assigned to aerobic or nonaerobic exercise for three 60-min sessions per week for 8 weeks. Patients in both exercise groups showed comparable significant reductions in anxiety independent of changes in aerobic capacity (Martinsen et al., 1989a), suggesting that increased aerobic fitness is not necessary to elicit improved anxiety. Limitations included the absence of a control group and concomitantly administered treatments.

In a third early study, walking was compared to jogging in 52 inpatients over an 8-week exercise training protocol and at a 6-month follow-up. Persistent anxiety reductions were reported 6 months after 8 weeks of AET. Improvements were not significantly different between jogging and walking (Sexton et al., 1989). However, lack of a control group in this study prevents the ability to draw meaningful conclusions.

### Studies of Mixed Samples of SAD, GAD, and PD Patients

The effect of adding a moderate-intensity home-based exercise program to 8–10 weeks of group CBT was examined in an RCT of 74 patients who were diagnosed with SAD, GAD, or PD (Merom et al., 2008). The addition of 30-min bouts of moderate-intensity walking exercise up to a goal of 150 min per week to CBT significantly reduced (effect size (ES) = 1.36) anxiety symptoms compared to the CBT control condition (Merom et al., 2008).

### Specific Phobias

Epidemiological studies suggest that physically active people are at reduced risk for specific phobias (Goodwin, 2003; Ströhle et al., 2007). However, at present, there appear to be no published RCTs or other investigations that have examined the influence of exercise training on persons with a principal diagnosis of specific phobia.

### SAD Patients

There is a small body of literature regarding the influence of exercise training on SAD. However, available evidence is difficult to interpret due to lack of a control group (Martinsen et al., 1989b; Jazaieri et al., 2012), small samples of SAD patients (Martinsen et al., 1989a; Julian et al., 2012), and the inability to isolate exercise effects from the combined effects of other established therapies (Merom et al., 2008; Phongsavan et al., 2008). The most recent evidence stems from a study of unmedicated patients (n = 56) with SAD who were randomly assigned to an 8-week intervention that involved either aerobic exercise or mindfulness-based stress reduction (MBSR). Exercise participants were asked to complete at least two individual and one group exercise session each week. The MBSR group completed a 2.5-h group class once per week, a 1-day retreat, and daily practice. The improvements in social anxiety symptoms immediately (ES range of 0.51–0.70) and 3-months (ES range of 0.49–0.54) following the exercise intervention were comparable to those found for MBSR (Jazaieri et al., 2012). Brain imaging data were obtained in response to a self-referential encoding task and tasks involving attention to autobiographical negative social anxiety-related memories. Exercise and MBSR training were associated with equivalent reductions in self-reported emotional reactivity in response to the negative social anxiety-related memories, and both groups had similar patterns of change in brain responses measured with functional magnetic resonance imaging (fMRI; Goldin et al., 2012a). Exercise and MBSR training also were associated with similar improvements in self-endorsement of negative social traits and increases in positive social traits, but the brain neural fMRI responses to these activities after exercise training differed from those found for MBSR (Goldin et al., 2012b). Importantly, accurate interpretation of the effects of exercise training, per se, is precluded based on these findings because of the absence of a control group that did not receive treatment.

### GAD Patients

One small RCT has examined the effects of 6 weeks of either resistance exercise training (RET) or AET on GAD remission and associated signs and symptoms (Herring et al., 2011, 2012). This trial has been characterized as a high-quality trial, demonstrating low risk of bias (Stubbs et al., 2017), but is currently the only RCT to focus on exercise training among patients with a principal diagnosis of GAD.

Thirty sedentary women, aged 18–37 years, diagnosed by clinicians blinded to allocation with a primary *DSM-IV* diagnosis of GAD and not engaged in treatment other than stabilized pharmacotherapy, were randomly allocated to RET, AET, or waitlist control (WL). RET involved two weekly sessions of lower body weightlifting which began at 50% of one-repetition maximum and progressed by 5% weekly. AET involved two weekly sessions of leg cycling matched with RET on body region, positive work completed during sessions, the time actively engaged in exercise (not simply the duration of the exercise session), and weekly load progression.

Importantly, high adherence (100%) and compliance to the prescribed exercise dose (>99%) and the absence of adverse events supported that exercise training was well-tolerated. Remission rates were 60%, 40%, and

30% following RET, AET, and WL, respectively. The number needed to treat three for RET suggested that, on average, for every 10 GAD patients who would perform a similar program of 6 weeks of RET, three additional remissions would be expected compared to untreated patients (Herring et al., 2012). To confirm the magnitude and consistency of these findings, a large amount of additional data is needed.

However, compared to WL, exercise training significantly reduced worry symptoms, the hallmark of GAD, and resulted in moderate-sized improvements (Hedges' $d \geq 0.40$) in trait anxiety and concentration along with other symptoms that co-occur with GAD including depression, feelings of energy and fatigue, and pain intensity. Although differences between AET and RET were not hypothesized because exercise conditions were matched on multiple features of the exercise stimulus, RET resulted in significant remission and larger magnitude effects for nine secondary outcomes (Herring et al., 2011, 2012). One factor that may have contributed to the better outcomes for RET is that the AET sessions were perceived as significantly less intense (rating of perceived exertion (RPE) = 9; "very light") than the RET sessions (RPE = 14; "somewhat hard" and "hard").

In addition to improvements in associated signs and symptoms of GAD, exercise training has also resulted in improved quality of life and sleep among GAD patients. Both RET and AET resulted in significant improvements in physical and mental dimensions of quality of life, particularly physical function, physical and emotional role impairments, and vitality (Herring et al., 2016), and sleep outcomes, including aspects of sleep initiation and continuity (Herring et al., 2015). Findings also suggested that improved sleep may be associated with reduced clinical severity among GAD patients.

Overall, improvements in response to exercise training among GAD patients have been of comparable magnitude to the effects of other empirically supported treatments for GAD, including pharmacotherapy, relaxation therapy, cognitive therapy, and CBT (Chessick et al., 2006; Hackett et al., 2003; Gould et al., 2004; Hofmann et al., 2010).

### OCD Patients

Three quasi-experimental studies have examined the effect of exercise training on OCD symptoms. A 6-week exercise training program was associated with reduced Yale-Brown Obsessive Compulsive Scale symptoms from the severe to moderate range among 11 OCD patients (Lancer et al., 2007). Similarly, a 12-week pilot trial examined the effect of the addition of AET to regular care on OCD symptoms among 15 patients diagnosed with OCD who had received at least 3 months of either pharmacological treatment or CBT (Brown et al., 2007). Patients completed three to four weekly sessions of 20–40 min of moderate-intensity aerobic exercise for 12 weeks. The authors reported that OCD symptom severity was significantly reduced by a large mean effect of ES = 1.69, and clinically meaningful reductions were demonstrated for 69% and 50% of patients at posttreatment and at a 6-month follow-up, respectively (Brown et al., 2007). More recently, a 12-week pilot study examined the feasibility and preliminary efficacy of adding a 12-week customized exercise training program, individualized for each patient based on peak heart rate during maximal exercise testing, to standard CBT among 11 patients with OCD (Rector et al., 2015). Very large improvements ($d = 2.55$) that exceeded the effects typically observed following CBT were reported, demonstrating the potential utility of exercise training to augment CBT for OCD. Although these preliminary studies lacked a true control group, the results suggest both the potential efficacy of exercise training and the need for well-designed RCTs.

One small randomized trial has investigated the effects of yoga among OCD patients (Shannahoff-Khalsa et al., 1999). Twelve patients practiced a version of kundalini yoga and were compared to 10 patients assigned to mindfulness meditation. At 3 months, those engaged in yoga improved more than the meditation group on the Yale-Brown Obsessive Compulsive Scale (34.8% reduction vs. 13.9%). However, one limitation of yoga studies is that both the absolute and relative (to maximum capacity) exercise dose is uncertain, and the relative contribution of the potential relaxation and meditative components of yoga beyond that of increased energy expenditure is unclear. Thus, though we continue to better understand whether yoga does or does not influence anxiety, it still is not possible to document dose—response effects.

Abrantes et al. (2012) recently reported the rationale and protocol for an National Institutes of Health—funded RCT testing the efficacy of 12 weeks of moderate-intensity aerobic exercise for OCD severity, anxiety, depression, quality of life, fitness, and cognition among 102 OCD patients currently engaged in pharmacotherapy and/or CBT. The authors postulated that exercise may provide a valuable treatment augmentation for patients with OCD, particularly among those with residual symptoms (Abrantes et al., 2012). Findings from this rigorously designed trial are forthcoming and should add needed information to this area of the literature.

### PTSD Patients

There are several rationales for why exercise may be particularly helpful for PTSD, including positive effects of exercise on associated symptoms of PTSD, including depression (Dunn et al., 2005), insomnia (Youngstedt, 2005), cognitive dysfunction (Kramer and Erickson, 2007), and fatigue (Puetz et al., 2008). However, the available evidence is limited, with only a handful of uncontrolled studies and only two published RCTs of exercise training effects among individuals with PTSD.

Three studies without control groups published by Motta et al. (2012) have reported reduced PTSD symptom severity, along with improved anxiety and depressive symptoms, following exercise training (Manger and Motta, 2005; Newman and Motta, 2007; Diaz and Motta, 2008). For example, 26 PTSD patients engaged in a 10-week program of aerobic exercise for 30 min at 60%−80% maximal heart rate ($HR_{max}$) for 2−3 days per week. Nine participants who met a liberal adherence criterion of 12 exercise bouts during the 10-week period showed significant improvements in PTSD symptom severity and improvements persisted at 1-month follow-up (Manger and Motta, 2005). In a second study, 15 adolescent females with PTSD living in a residential treatment facility were assessed (Newman and Motta, 2007). Eleven participants met the adherence criterion, averaging 22 bouts of 20 min of aerobic exercise across an 8-week intervention. The authors reported improved PTSD severity which persisted at 1-month postintervention (Newman and Motta, 2007). A third study similarly showed improved PTSD severity among 12 institutionalized female adolescents with PTSD in response to three weekly sessions of 25-min of aerobic exercise at 60%−90% $HR_{max}$ performed for 5 weeks (Diaz and Motta, 2008). These studies, conducted primarily with children and adolescents, were limited by small, heterogeneous samples, lack of a control condition, and/or low adherence rates. Nonetheless, this preliminary evidence suggested that exercise may be an effective treatment for PTSD and established a foundation on which more rigorous RCTs could be based.

To date, two RCTs have allowed rigorous examination of the effects of exercise training among individuals with PTSD. In a pilot RCT, Powers et al. (2015) randomized nine young adults with PTSD to complete either 12 sessions of prolonged exposure therapy alone or 12 sessions of prolonged exposure plus 30 min of moderate-intensity treadmill exercise at 70% of age-predicted $HR_{max}$ prior to each prolonged exposure session. The addition of exercise resulted in a significantly larger improvement in PTSD symptoms ($d = 2.65$). However, though these findings provide initial support that exercise may augment exposure therapy among patients with PTSD, the very small sample size and the low exercise dose somewhat caution against overinterpretation of the findings.

The most methodologically rigorous RCT to date examined the effects of a 12-week aerobic and RET intervention designed in accordance with American College of Sports Medicine guidelines, which consisted of a weekly supervised exercise session, two unsupervised home-based sessions, and a pedometer-facilitated walking program among 81 patients with PTSD (Rosenbaum et al., 2014). Both groups included in the intervention received usual care that involved a combination of psychotherapy, pharmacotherapy, and group therapy; though these interventions involved stimuli which may improve symptoms of PTSD, access to the treatments was equal for the exercise and control groups. Adherence to

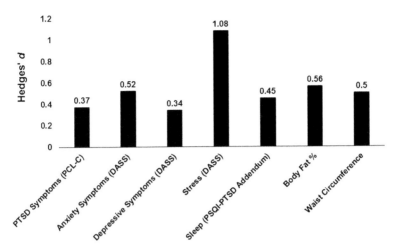

**FIGURE 2.4**   Mean effect of exercise training on symptoms among adults with posttraumatic stress disorder (PTSD). *Data from Rosenbaum, Sherrington, & Tiedemann. (2015). Acta Psychiatr. Scand. 131(5), 350–359.*

the supervised exercise sessions was 58%, quantified as mean attendance, and less than 20% of participants returned exercise diaries; thus the actual total exercise dose in which participants engaged is unknown. Nonetheless, the authors reported significant improvements in PTSD symptom severity and symptoms of anxiety, depression, stress, and PTSD-related sleep disturbance in the intervention group compared to the control group (Rosenbaum et al., 2014). As shown in Fig. 2.4, these significant improvements correspond to small-to-moderate magnitude changes for PTSD symptom severity, symptoms of anxiety and depression, and PTSD-related sleep disturbance, and a large improvement in stress ($d = 1.08$). These improvements are comparable to exercise-induced improvements among patients with SAD (Jazaieri et al., 2012) and GAD (Herring et al., 2011) and provide some of the first rigorous evidence to support the efficacy of even low-to-moderate doses of exercise training to improve symptoms among adults with PTSD. Importantly, given the high prevalence of cardiometabolic issues among individuals with mental health disorders, this trial provided important evidence of the concurrent benefit of exercise for symptoms of PTSD and metabolic outcomes, showing significant concurrent improvements in body fat and waist circumference (Fig. 2.4; Rosenbaum et al., 2014).

### PD Patients

Broocks et al. (1998) conducted the first randomized, placebo-controlled trial of 10 weeks of AET among PD patients. Forty-six outpatients diagnosed with moderate-to-severe *DSM-III-R* PD with or without agoraphobia were randomized to either 10 weeks of three to four weekly sessions of walking/running a four-mile (6.4 km) route, 112.5 mg per day of clomipramine, a tricyclic antidepressant, or placebo. Both exercise and antidepressant medication significantly improved anxiety symptoms compared to placebo, suggesting that exercise training may be as effective as pharmacotherapy. PD patients who completed exercise training reported large reductions in anxiety (ES = 1.10) compared to patients who took daily placebo pills. The clomipramine group demonstrated lower attrition and resulted in quicker improvements in anxiety symptoms (Broocks et al., 1998). Because of the strong placebo-controlled research design, this investigation provided strong evidence that exercise training can attenuate anxiety symptoms among PD patients.

A follow-up study with 75 PD patients compared the effects of 10 weeks of (1) exercise + 40 mg per day of paroxetine (a selective serotonin reuptake inhibitor), (2) exercise + placebo, (3) relaxation + placebo, or (4) relaxation + paroxetine (Wedekind et al., 2010). Comparable, large improvements in clinician- and self-derived symptoms were found for all the groups. Therefore adding antidepressant medication did not augment the anxiety improvements associated with regular exercise and exercise training showed similar effects to relaxation in reducing anxiety.

The therapeutic effects of 12 weeks of AET for PD patients also have been compared to CBT (Hovland et al., 2013). Patients were randomized to 12 weeks of three weekly group-exercise sessions focused on cardiorespiratory fitness and muscular strength (n = 17) or once weekly CBT (n = 19). Both treatments significantly improved symptoms, though CBT provided greater symptom alleviation than exercise immediately following treatment and at 6- and 12-month follow-ups for outcomes other than state anxiety, depressive symptoms, and quality of life.

The most recent RCT of exercise effects examined whether 8 weeks of AET involving three weekly 30-min sessions of treadmill running at 70% of $VO_{max}^2$ would more positively augment CBT treatment than very low−intensity, primarily flexibility-based exercise among 47 PD patients (Gaudlitz et al., 2015). Anxiety symptoms were significantly improved in both groups, but there were no significant differences between the treadmill running and very low intensity flexibility group following training. The authors reported a significant, moderate-sized difference in anxiety symptoms between the groups at 7-month follow-up. Though these findings provide support for the additive benefit of exercise when combined with CBT, some caution should be taken when interpreting these findings given the lack of a nonexercise control group and potentially important, albeit statistically nonsignificant, baseline differences between groups in total physical activity and anxiety symptoms (i.e., the exercise group was less physically active and less anxious at baseline). Nonetheless, the collective evidence to date clearly supports the need for larger trials aimed at determining the generalizability of the positive effects of exercise training for patients with PD.

## Plausible Mechanisms of the Anxiolytic Effects of Exercise

There are several mechanisms by which exercise training could reduce anxiety. Detailed presentations of these possibilities have been presented by others (Shin and Liberzon, 2010; DeBoer et al., 2012; De Chiara et al., 2010; Dietrich et al., 2005; Dishman et al., 2012; Fuss et al., 2010; Greenwood and Fleshner, 2011; Hare et al., 2012; Sciolino and Holmes, 2012; Sylvester et al., 2012). The following sections provide a brief snapshot of the most prominent psychological and neurobiological mechanisms that have been suggested to underlie exercise effects on anxiety.

### Self-Concept/Self-Esteem

Increased physical activity has been associated with increased physical self-esteem in randomized trials (Elavsky, 2010), and impaired self-esteem has been associated with elevated anxiety symptoms (Bos et al., 2010); thus it is possible that exercise training could improve anxiety via increased physical self-esteem or self-concept. One correlational study of 1036 young women showed that physical activity had inverse, indirect associations with symptoms of SAD, GAD, and OCD that were expressed through positive associations with specific and global physical self-concept and self-esteem (Herring et al., 2014c). Though cross-sectional, these findings support that physical activity might reduce the risk of anxiety disorders among young women by positive influences on physical self-concept and self-esteem.

### Exposure

Exposure therapy is a key tenet of CBT for some anxiety and stress-related disorders. Anxiety symptoms can be elicited during exercise such that exercise can be used to expose people to anxiety symptoms in a controlled, safe environment. Exercise may relieve anxiety by teaching persistence in the presence of negative somatic symptoms that individuals may fear and have learned to avoid (Smits et al., 2008; Stathopoulou et al., 2006). The addition of neutral or positive social interactions with exercise-induced anxiety symptoms also may allow individuals to "unlearn" links between their anxiety symptoms and conditioned stimuli that contribute to social or other phobias (Smits et al., 2008).

### Expectation/Placebo Effect

Exercise training may improve anxiety because people expect that it will help. A recent meta-analysis suggested that approximately half of the observed psychological benefits of exercise training may be attributable to the placebo effect (Lindheimer et al., 2015). Research on the placebo effect is limited by the lack of an adequate placebo condition for exercise training, supporting the need for creative research aimed at a better understanding of the placebo effect and its influence on the anxiolytic effects of exercise training.

### Adaptations in the GABA Neurotransmitter System

The most commonly prescribed antianxiety drugs target the effects of GABA. Limited evidence supports that exercise-induced adaptations in GABA could result in reduced anxiety. Chronic activity wheel running in rats can increase GABA levels, decrease the number of $GABA_A$ receptors in the corpus striatum, and increase open-field locomotion (Dishman et al., 1997). These findings are consistent with an anxiolytic effect according to the limbic-motor integration model of locomotor behavior proposed by Mogenson and Yang (1991).

### Adaptations in the Norepinephrine Neurotransmitter System

Norepinephrine likely plays a complex role in anxiety, as it can both increase and decrease anxiety. Norepinephrine is a modulatory neurotransmitter that usually is coreleased with the inhibitory peptide/trophic factor galanin. Rodent research suggests that regular physical activity enhances galanin and inhibits norepinephrine activity (Dishman, 1997; Soares et al., 1999; Van Hoomissen et al., 2004). These changes have been linked to reduced anxiety-like behavior in rodents (Sciolino and Holmes, 2012) and could plausibly contribute to reduced anxiety after exercise training.

### Adaptations in the Serotonin Neurotransmitter System

Excessive CNS release of serotonin (5-hydroxytryptamine, 5-HT) is anxiogenic. Available evidence has suggested that regular physical activity has effects on the brain that include (1) reductions in 5-HT levels in the central amygdala (Hovatta et al., 2010), (2) reductions in messenger RNA for the $5\text{-HT}_{1a}$ transporter, and (3) increases in the number of $5\text{-HT}_{1a}$ autoreceptors, which inhibit the release of 5-HT (Greenwood and Fleshner, 2011; Dishman, 1997). These adaptations in the serotonin system are associated with greater social exploratory behavior in rodents; thus, the animals exhibit less anxiety-like behavior when they are regularly physically active (Greenwood et al., 2012).

## Exercise Prescription, Dose, and Compliance

The available evidence has primarily focused on moderate-intensity exercise effects in anxiety and stress-related disorders, particularly moderate-intensity, continuous AET (i.e., walking, running, cycling). This highlights a critical need to examine understudied exercise modes, such as RET and sprint interval training, and dose—response relations. Though a recent meta-analysis of 31 effects derived from 16 RCTs of RET reported that RET significantly reduced anxiety symptoms by a small but statistically significant mean effect $\Delta$ of 0.31 (Gordon et al., 2017), only one RCT of GAD patients and one RCT of PTSD patients have examined RET. Only one RCT among GAD patients has directly compared the effects of RET and AET matched on meaningful features of the exercise stimulus, showing larger symptom improvements in response to RET (Herring et al., 2012). However, these findings may have been due partly to differences in perceived exertion between AET and RET. Though dose—response relations have not been rigorously examined, the available evidence suggests that moderate-intensity exercise can be prescribed to improve symptoms among anxiety and stress-related disorders, and it is possible that meeting and exceeding recommended levels of physical activity will convey greater benefits.

To this end, there also is a critical need to better monitor exercise intensity and quantify total exercise dose among patients with anxiety and stress-related disorders. Previous evidence supports the use of continuous heart rate monitoring during aerobic exercise sessions such that intensity minutes, based on individualized exercise prescriptions (i.e., 30 min per session at 65%—85% heart rate reserve), can be summed across all prescribed exercise sessions to empirically define and assess compliance with prescribed exercise dose using a heart rate physical activity score (Miller et al., 2014). This approach could be an important step toward enhancing both the viability of exercise prescription and the monitoring and promotion of compliance and adherence among individuals with anxiety or stress-related disorders.

Though modest to high adherence and compliance to exercise have been reported in some previous studies of individuals with anxiety and stress-related disorders, poor adherence, particularly noncompliance with prescribed exercise dose, is a critical limitation of exercise interventions, including interventions among people with anxiety and stress-related disorders. A recent review of nongenetic and genetic predictors of exercise adherence (Herring et al., 2014a) highlighted that (1) age, education, gender, ethnicity, previous physical activity, dietary habits, smoking, occupation, and social support have been associated with adherence; (2) higher body weight and body fat are frequently associated with nonadherence; (3) perceived self-efficacy is among the most consistent and strongest predictors of both exercise adoption and adherence; (4) social support and perceived barriers to exercise, particularly perceived lack of time and injury/illness, can strongly influence exercise behavior; and (5) exercise intensity and perceived effort have both been found to be negatively associated with exercise adoption and adherence. Exercise undertaken at an individual's preferred intensity has resulted in higher compliance rates compared to prescribed intensity (Callaghan et al., 2011); however, recent evidence has shown that prescribed intensity resulted in a significant, almost fourfold larger improvement in depressed mood among young adults with major depressive disorder (Meyer et al., 2016). Moreover, Herring et al. (2014a) highlighted how nonadherence and adherence may be considered part of a continuum of behavior that would include both compulsive and addictive behaviors, including potential exercise dependence. Regardless, it is clear that practitioners prescribing exercise to individuals with anxiety and/or stress-related disorders should be prepared for nonadherence and should remain aware that, though no single variable adequately predicts exercise adherence, assisting individuals in taking personal responsibility in exercise prescription, exercise program implementation, and monitoring of compliance with exercise dose, identifying modifiable barriers and developing strategies to overcome barriers, and promoting enhanced self-efficacy and self-motivation may facilitate adherence.

## SUMMARY

The available evidence from RCTs supports that exercise training can improve anxiety symptoms among healthy adults, chronically ill patients, and patients with PD. Preliminary evidence supports that exercise training improves symptoms among patients with GAD, SAD, OCD, and PTSD. The effects of exercise training appear to be comparable to other empirically supported treatments for PD and GAD. Collectively, the evidence has primarily focused on moderate-intensity exercise, highlighting a critical need to examine dose—response relations, better quantify total exercise dose, and empirically define and assess compliance with prescribed exercise dose. Well-designed RCTs are needed among understudied anxiety disorders, including specific phobias, SAD, OCD, and PTSD. Large trials aimed at determining the magnitude and generalizability of exercise effects appear to be warranted for PD, GAD, and PTSD. Future well-designed RCTs are also needed that focus on understudied exercise modalities, including RET, and the elucidation of plausible mechanisms of the anxiolytic effects of exercise training.

## References

Abrantes, A.M., Mclaughlin, N., Greenberg, B.D., Strong, D.R., Riebe, D., Mancebo, M., Rasmussen, S., Desaulniers, J., Brown, R.A., 2012. Design and rationale for a randomized controlled trial testing the efficacy of aerobic exercise for patients with obsessive-compulsive disorder. Ment. Health Phys. Act. 5, 155—165.

APA, 2013. Diagnostic and Statistical Manual of Mental Disorders: DSM 5. Books4US.

Asmundson, G.J.G., Fetzner, M.G., Deboer, L.B., Powers, M.B., Otto, M.W., Smits, J.A.J., 2013. Let's get physical: a contemporary review of the anxiolytic effects of exercise for anxiety and its disorders. Depress. Anxiety 0, 1–12.

Anh, S., Fedewa, A.L., 2011. A meta-analysis of the relationship between children's physical activity and mental health. J Pediatr Psychol. 36 (4), 385–397.

Association A.P., Association A.P., 2000. DSM-IV-TR: Diagnostic and Statistical Manual of Mental Disorders, Text Revision, vol. 75. American Psychiatric Association, Washington, DC.

Bandelow, B., 1995. Assessing the efficacy of treatments for panic disorder and agoraphobia. II. The panic and agoraphobia scale. Int. Clin. Psychopharmacol. 10, 73–82.

Bandelow, B., Baldwin, D., Abelli, M., Altamura, C., Dell'osso, B., Domschke, K., Fineberg, N., Grünblatt, E., Jarema, M., Maron, E., 2016. Biological markers for anxiety disorders, OCD and PTSD-a consensus statement. Part I: neuroimaging and genetics. World J. Biol. Psychiatry 17, 321.

Bandelow, B., Michaelis, S., 2015. Epidemiology of anxiety disorders in the 21st century. Dialogues Clin. Neurosci. 17, 327.

Bandelow, B., Seidler-Brandler, U., Becker, A., Wedekind, D., Rüther, E., 2007. Meta-analysis of randomized controlled comparisons of psychopharmacological and psychological treatments for anxiety disorders. World J. Biol. Psychiatry 8, 175–187.

Barlow, D.H., 2002. Anxiety and its Disorders: The Nature and Treatment of Anxiety and Panic. The Guilford Press, New York.

Bartley, C.A., Hay, M., Bloch, M.H., 2013. Meta-analysis: aerobic exercise for the treatment of anxiety disorders. Prog. Neuropsychopharmacol. Biol. Psychiatry 45C, 34–39.

Baxter, A., Scott, K., Vos, T., Whiteford, H., 2013. Global prevalence of anxiety disorders: a systematic review and meta-regression. Psychol. Med. 43, 897–910.

Baxter, A., Vos, T., Scott, K., Ferrari, A., Whiteford, H., 2014. The global burden of anxiety disorders in 2010. Psychol. Med. 44, 2363–2374.

Beck, A.T., Epstein, N., Brown, G., Steer, R.A., 1988. An inventory for measuring clinical anxiety: psychometric properties. J. Consult. Clin. Psychol. 56, 893.

Beesdo, K., Knappe, S., Pine, D.S., 2009. Anxiety and anxiety disorders in children and adolescents: developmental issues and implications for DSM-V. Psychiatr. Clin. N. Am. 32, 483–524.

Bos, A.E.R., Huijding, J., Muris, P., Vogel, L.R.R., Biesheuvel, J., 2010. Global, contingent and implicit self-esteem and psychopathological symptoms in adolescents. Personal. Individ. Differ. 48, 311–316.

Breslau, J., Kendler, K.S., Su, M., AGUILAR-Gaxiola, S., Kessler, R.C., 2005. Lifetime risk and persistence of psychiatric disorders across ethnic groups in the United States. Psychol. Med. 35, 317–327.

Broocks, A., Bandelow, B., Pekrun, G., George, A., Meyer, T., Bartmann, U., Hillmer-Vogel, U., Rüther, E., 1998. Comparison of aerobic exercise, clomipramine, and placebo in the treatment of panic disorder. Am. J. Psychiatry 155, 603–609.

Brown, R.A., Abrantes, A.M., Strong, D.R., Mancebo, M.C., Menard, J., Rasmussen, S.A., Greenberg, B.D., 2007. A pilot study of moderate-intensity aerobic exercise for obsessive compulsive disorder. J. Nerv. Ment. Dis. 195, 514–520.

Brown, T.A., Barlow, D.H., 2013. Anxiety and Related Disorders Interview Schedule for DSM-5, Adult and Lifetime Version: Clinician Manual. Oxford University Press.

Buckworth, J., 2013. Exercise Psychology, Human Kinetics.

Calfas, K.J., Taylor, W.C., 1994. Effects of physical activity on psychological variables in adolescents. Pediatr Exerc Sci. 6 (4), 406–423.

Callaghan, P., Khalil, E., Morres, I., Carter, T., 2011. Pragmatic randomised controlled trial of preferred intensity exercise in women living with depression. BMC Public Health 11, 465.

Chambless, D., Baker, M.J., Baucom, D., Beutler, L., 1998. Update on empirically-validated therapies, II. Clin. Psychol. 51, 3–16.

Chessick, C.A., Allen, M.H., Thase, M., Batista Miralha Da Cunha, A.B., Kapczinski, F.F., DE Lima, M.S., Dos Santos Souza, J.J., 2006. Azapirones for generalized anxiety disorder. Cochrane Database Syst. Rev. 3.

Clark, D.A., Beck, A.T., 2010. Cognitive theory and therapy of anxiety and depression: convergence with neurobiological findings. Trends Cognit. Sci. 14, 418–424.

Committee P.A.G.A., 2008. Physical Activity Guidelines Advisory Committee Report, 2008. US Department of Health and Human Services, 2008, Washington, DC.

Conn, V.S., 2010. Anxiety outcomes after physical activity interventions: meta-analysis findings. Nurs Res. 59 (3).

Corona, G., Ricca, V., Bandini, E., Mannucci, E., Lotti, F., Boddi, V., Rastrelli, G., Sforza, A., Faravelli, C., Forti, G., Maggi, M., 2009. Selective serotonin reuptake inhibitor-induced sexual dysfunction. J. Sex. Med. 6, 1259–1269.

De Chiara, V., Errico, F., Musella, A., Rossi, S., Mataluni, G., Sacchetti, L., Siracusano, A., Castelli, M., Cavasinni, F., Bernardi, G., Usiello, A., Centonze, D., 2010. Voluntary exercise and sucrose consumption enhance cannabinoid CB1 receptor sensitivity in the striatum. Neuropsychopharmacology 35, 374–387.

Deboer, L.B., Powers, M.B., Utschig, A.C., Otto, M.W., Smits, J.A.J., 2012. Exploring exercise as an avenue for the treatment of anxiety disorders. Expert Rev. Neurother. 12, 1011–1022.

Diaz, A.B., Motta, R., 2008. The effects of an aerobic exercise program on postraumatic stress disorder symptom severity in adolescents. Int. J. Emerg. Ment. Health 10, 49–60.

Dietrich, M.O., Mantese, C.E., Porciuncula, L.O., Ghisleni, G., Vinade, L., Souza, D.O., Portela, L.V., 2005. Exercise affects glutamate receptors in postsynaptic densities from cortical mice brain. Brain Res. 1065, 20–25.

Dishman, R.K., 1997. Brain monoamines, exercise, and behavioral stress: animal models. Med. Sci. Sports Exerc. 29, 63–74.

Dishman, R.K., Berthoud, H.-R., Booth, F.W., Cotman, C.W., Edgerton, V.R., Fleshner, M.R., Gandevia, S.C., Gomez-Pinilla, F., Greenwood, B.N., Hillman, C.H., Kramer, A.F., Levin, B.E., Moran, T.H., Russo-Neustadt, A.A., Salamone, J.D., Van Hoomissen, J.D., Wade, C.E., York, D.A., Zigmond, M.J., 2012. Neurobiology of exercise. Obesity 14, 345–356.

Dishman, R.K., Renner, K.J., Youngstedt, S.D., Reigle, T.G., Bunnell, B.N., Burke, K.A., Yoo, H.S., Mougey, E.H., Meyerhoff, J.L., 1997. Activity wheel running reduces escape latency and alters brain monoamine levels after footshock. Brain Res. Bull. 42, 399–406.

Dunn, A.L., Trivedi, M.H., Kampert, J.B., Clark, C.G., Chambliss, H.O., 2005. Exercise treatment for depression: efficacy and dose response. Am. J. Preven. Med. 28, 1–8.

Dupont, R.L., Rice, D.P., Miller, L.S., Shiraki, S.S., Rowland, C.R., Harwood, H.J., 1998. Economic costs of anxiety disorders. Anxiety 2, 167–172.

Elavsky, S., 2010. Longitudinal examination of the exercise and self-esteem model in middle-aged women. J. Sport Exerc. Psychol. 32, 862–880.

Ensari, I., Greenlee, T.A., Motl, R.W., Petruzzello, S.J., 2015. Meta-analysis of acute exercise effects on state anxiety: an update of randomized controlled trials over the past 25 years. Depress. Anxiety 32, 624–634.

Fava, M., 2000. Weight gain and antidepressants. J. Clin. Psychiatry 61, 37–41.

Fuss, J., Ben Abdallah, N.M.B., Hensley, F.W., Weber, K.-J., Hellweg, R., Glass, P., 2010. Deletion of running-induced hippocampal neurogenesis by irradiation prevents development of an anxious phenotype in mice. PLoS One 5, 1–9.

Gaudlitz, K., Plag, J., Dimeo, F., Ströhle, A., 2015. Aerobic exercise training facilitates the effectiveness of cognitive behavioral therapy in panic disorder. Depress. Anxiety 32, 221–228.

Goldin, P., Ziv, M., Jazaieri, H., Hahn, K., Gross, J.J., 2012a. MBSR vs aerobic exercise in social anxiety: fMRI of emotion regulation of negative self-beliefs. Soc. Cognit. Affect. Neurosci. 1–8.

Goldin, P.R., Ziv, M., Jazaieri, H., Gross, J.J., 2012b. Randomized controlled trial of mindfulness-based stress reduction versus aerobic exercise: effects on the self-referential brain network in social anxiety disorder. Front. Hum. Neurosci. 6, 1–16.

Goodman, W.K., Price, L.H., Rasmussen, S.A., Mazure, C., Fleischmann, R.L., Hill, C.L., Heninger, G.R., Charney, D.S., 1989. The Yale-Brown obsessive compulsive scale: I. Development, use, and reliability. Arch. Gen. Psychiatry 46, 1006–1011.

Goodwin, R.D., 2003. Association between physical activity and mental disorders among adults in the United States. Prev. Med. 36, 698–703.

Gordon, B.R., McDowell, C.P., Hallgren, M., Meyer, J.D., Lyons, M., Herring, M.P., 2018. Association of efficacy of resistance exercise training with depressive symptoms: meta-analysis and meta-regression analysis of randomized clinical trials. JAMA Psychiatry 75 (6), 566–576.

Gordon, B.R., Mcdowell, C.P., Lyons, M., Herring, M.P., 2017. The effects of resistance exercise training on anxiety: a meta-analysis and meta-regression analysis of randomized controlled trials. Sports Med 47 (12), 2521–2532.

Gould, R.A., Safren, S.A., Washington, D.O.N., Otto, M.W., 2004. A meta-analytic review of cognitive-behavioral treatments. In: Heimberg, R.G., Turk, C.L., Mennin, D.S. (Eds.), Generalized Anxiety Disorder: Advances in Research and Practice. Guilford Press, New York, NY, US.

Greenberg, P.E., Sisitsky, T., Kessler, R.C., Finkelstein, S.N., Berndt, E.R., Davidson, J.R., Ballenger, J.C., Fyer, A.J., 1999. The economic burden of anxiety disorders in the 1990s. J. Clin. Psychiatry 60, 427–435.

Greenwood, B.N., Fleshner, M., 2011. Exercise, stress resistance, and central serotonergic systems. Exerc. Sport Sci. Rev. 39, 140–149.

Greenwood, B.N., Loughridge, A.B., Sadaoui, N., Christianson, J.P., Fleshner, M., 2012. The protective effects of voluntary exercise against the behavioral consequences of uncontrollable stress persist despite an increase in anxiety following forced cessation of exercise. Behav. Brain Res. 233, 314–321.

Grosz, H.J., Farmer, B.B., 1972. Pitts' and McClure's lactate-anxiety study revisited. Br. J. Psychiatry 120, 415–418.

Hackett, D., Haudiquet, V., Salinas, E., 2003. A method for controlling for a high placebo response rate in a comparison of venlafaxine XR and diazepam in the short-term treatment of patients with generalised anxiety disorder. Eur. Psychiatry 18, 182–187.

Hare, B.D., D'onfro, K.C., Hammack, S.E., Falls, W.A., 2012. Prior stress interferes with the anxiolytic effect of exercise in c57bl/6j mice. Behav. Neurosci. 126, 850–856.

Herring, M., Sailors, M., Bray, M., 2014a. Genetic factors in exercise adoption, adherence and obesity. Obes. Rev. 15, 29–39.

Herring, M.P., Jacob, M.L., Suveg, C., Dishman, R.K., O'Connor, P.J., 2012. Feasibility of exercise training for the short-term treatment of generalized anxiety disorder: a randomized controlled trial. Psychother. Psychosom. 81, 21–28.

Herring, M.P., Jacob, M.L., Suveg, C., O'Connor, P.J., 2011. Effects of short-term exercise training on signs and symptoms of generalized anxiety disorder. Ment. Health Phys. Act. 4, 71–77.

Herring, M.P., Johnson, K.E., O'Connor, P.J., 2016. Exercise training and health-related quality of life in generalized anxiety disorder. Psychol. Sport Exerc. 27, 138–141.

Herring, M.P., Kline, C.E., O'Connor, P.J., 2015. Effects of exercise on sleep among young women with Generalized Anxiety Disorder. Ment. Health Phys. Act. 9, 59–66.

Herring, M.P., Lindheimer, J.B., O'Connor, P.J., 2014b. The effects of exercise training on anxiety. Am. J. Lifestyle Med. 8, 388–403.

Herring, M.P., O'Connor, P.J., Dishman, R.K., 2010. The effect of exercise training on anxiety symptoms among patients: a systematic review. Arch. Intern. Med. 170 (4), 321−331.

Herring, M.P., O'Connor, P.J., Dishman, R.K., 2014. Self-esteem mediates associations of physical activity with anxiety in college women. Med. Sci. Sports Exerc. 46 (10), 1990−1998.

Himle, J.A., Baser, R.E., Taylor, R.J., Campbell, R.D., Jackson, J.S., 2009. Anxiety disorders among African Americans, blacks of Caribbean descent, and non-Hispanic whites in the United States. J. Anxiety Disord. 23, 578−590.

Hoffman, D.L., Dukes, E.M., Wittchen, H.U., 2008. Human and economic burden of generalized anxiety disorder. Depress. Anxiety 25, 72−90.

Hofmann, S., Asnaani, A., Vonk, I., Sawyer, A., Fang, A., 2012. The efficacy of cognitive behavioral therapy: a review of meta-analyses. Cognit. Ther. Res. 36, 427.

Hofmann, S.G., Sawyer, A.T., Witt, A.A., Oh, D., 2010. The effect of mindfulness-based therapy on anxiety and depression: a meta-analytic review. J. Consult. Clin. Psychol. 78, 169−183.

Hoskins, M., Pearce, J., Bethell, A., Dankova, L., Barbui, C., Tol, W.A., Van Ommeren, M., De Jong, J., Seedat, S., Chen, H., 2015. Pharmacotherapy for post-traumatic stress disorder: systematic review and meta-analysis. Br. J. Psychiatry 206, 93−100.

Hovatta, I., Juhila, J., Donner, J., 2010. Oxidative stress in anxiety and comorbid disorders. Neurosci. Res. 68, 261−275.

Hovland, A., Nordhus, I.H., Sjøbø, T., Gjestad, B.A., Birknes, B., Martinsen, E.W., Torsheim, T., Pallesen, S., 2013. Comparing physical exercise in groups to group cognitive behaviour therapy for the treatment of panic disorder in a randomized controlled trial. Behav. Cognit. Psychother. 41, 408−432.

Jayakody, K., Gunadasa, S., Hosker, C., 2013. Exercise for anxiety disorders: systematic review. Br. J. Sports Med. 0, 1−11.

Jazaieri, H., Goldin, P.R., Werner, K., Ziv, M., Gross, J.J., 2012. A randomized trial of MBSR versus aerobic exercise for social anxiety disorder. J. Clin. Psychol. 68, 715−731.

Julian, K., Beard, C., Schmidt, N.B., Powers, M.B., Smits, J.A.J., 2012. Attention training to reduce attention bias and social stressor reactivity: an attempt to replicate and extend previous findings. Behav. Res. Ther. 50, 350−358.

Katon, W., Lin, E.H.B., Kroenke, K., 2007. The association of depression and anxiety with medical symptom burden in patients with chronic medical illness. Gen. Hosp. Psychiatry 29, 147−155.

Kessler, R.C., Angermeyer, M., Anthony, J.C., De Graaf, R., Demyttenaere, K., Gasquet, I., De Girolamo, G., Gluzman, S., Gureje, O., Haro, J.M., Kawakami, N., Karam, A., Levinson, D., Medina Mora, M.E., Oakley Browne, M.A., Posada-Villa, J., Stein, D.J., Adley Tsang, C.H., Aguilar-Gaxiola, S., Alonso, J., Lee, S., Heeringa, S., Pennell, B.E., Berglund, P., Gruber, M.J., Petukhova, M., Chatterji, S., Ustün, T.B., 2007. Lifetime prevalence and age-of-onset distributions of mental disorders in the World Health Organization's World Mental Health Survey Initiative. World Psychiatry 6, 168−176.

Kessler, R.C., Bergiund, P.A., Bruce, M.L., Koch, J.R., Laska, E.M., Leaf, P.J., Manderscheid, R.W., Rosenheck, R.A., Walters, E.E., Wang, P.S., 2001. The prevalence and correlates of untreated serious mental illness. Health Serv. Res. 36, 987−1007.

Kessler, R.C., Petukhova, M., Sampson, N.A., Zaslavsky, A.M., Wittchen, H.U., 2012. Twelve-month and lifetime prevalence and lifetime morbid risk of anxiety and mood disorders in the United States. Int. J. Methods Psychiatr. Res. 21 (3), 169−184.

Kessler, R.C., Wang, P.S., 2008. The descriptive epidemiology of commonly occurring mental disorders in the United States. Annu. Rev. Public Health 29, 115−129.

Kramer, A.F., Erickson, K., 2007. Capitalizing on cortical plasticity: influence of physical activity on cognition and brain function. Trends Cognit. Sci. 11, 342−348.

Kroenke, K., Spitzer, R.L., Williams, J.B.W., Monahan, P.O., Löwe, B., 2007. Anxiety disorders in primary care: prevalence, impairment, comorbidity, and detection. Ann. Intern. Med. 146, 317–325.

Kugler, J., Seelbach, H., Kruskemper, G.M., 1994. Effects of rehabilitation exercise programmes on anxiety and depression in coronary patients: a meta-analysis. Br J Clin Psychol. 33 (3), 401–410.

Lancer, R., Motta, R., Lancer, D., 2007. The effect of aerobic exercise on obsessive-compulsive disorder, anxiety, and depression: a preliminary investigation. Behav. Ther. 30 (53), 57–62.

Larun, L., Nordheim, L.V., Ekeland, E., Hagen, K.B., Heian, F., 2006. Exercise in prevention and treatment of anxiety and depression among children and young people. Cochrane Database Syst Rev. 3. CD004691.

Liebowitz, M.R., 1987. Social Phobia. Karger Publishers.

Lindheimer, J.B., O'Connor, P.J., Dishman, R.K., 2015. Quantifying the placebo effect in psychological outcomes of exercise training: a meta-analysis of randomized trials. Sports Med. 45, 693–711.

Long, B.C., van Stavel, R., 1995. Effects of exercise training on anxiety: A meta-analysis. J Applied Sport Psychol. 7 (2), 167–189.

Ludman, E., Katon, W., Russo, J., Simon, G., Von Korff, M., Lin, E., Ciechanowski, P., Kinder, L., 2006. Panic episodes among patients with diabetes. Gen. Hosp. Psychiatry 28, 475–481.

Maddock, R.J., Carter, C.S., Gietzen, D.W., 1991. Elevated serum lactate associated with panic attacks induced by hyperventilation. Psychiatry Res. 38, 301–311.

Manger, T.A., Motta, R.W., 2005. The impact of an exercise program on posttraumatic stress disorder, anxiety, and depression. Int. J. Emerg. Ment. Health 7, 49–57.

Manzoni, G.M., Pagnini, F., Castelnuovo, G., Molinari, E., 2008. Relaxation training for anxiety: a ten-years systematic review with meta-analysis. BMC Psychiatry 8, 1–12.

Marciniak, M.D., Lage, M.J., Dunayevich, E., Russell, J.M., Bowman, L., Landbloom, R.P., Levine, L.R., 2005. The cost of treating anxiety: the medical and demographic correlates that impact total medical costs. Depress. Anxiety 21, 178–184.

Martinsen, E.W., Asle, H., Solberg, O., 1989a. Aerobic and non-aerobic forms of exercise in the treatment of anxiety disorders. Stress Med. 5, 115–120.

Martinsen, E.W., Sandvik, L., Kolbjornsrud, O., 1989b. Aerobic exercise in treatment of nonpsychotic mental disorders an exploratory study. Exerc. Ment. Health 43, 521–529.

Mccrone, P., Knapp, M., Proudfoot, J., Ryden, C., Cavanagh, K., Shapiro, D.A., Ilson, S., Gray, J.A., Goldberg, D., Mann, A., Marks, I., Everitt, B., Tylee, A., 2004. Cost-effectiveness of computerised cognitive-behavioural therapy for anxiety and depression in primary care: randomised controlled trial. Br. J. Psychiatry J. Ment. Sci. 185, 55–62.

Mclaughlin, T.P., Khandker, R.K., Kruzikas, D.T., Tummala, R., 2006. Overlap of anxiety and depression in a managed care population: prevalence and association with resource utilization. J. Clin. Psychiatry 67, 1187–1193.

Mcnair, D.M., Droppleman, L.F., Lorr, M., 1992. Edits Manual for the Profile of Mood States: Poms, Edits.

Mcdowell, C.P., Cook, D.B., Herring, M.P., 2017. The effects of exercise training on anxiety in Fibromyalgia patients: a meta-analysis. Med Sci Sports Exerc. 49 (9), 1868–1876.

Merom, D., Phongsavan, P., Wagner, R., Chey, T., Marnane, C., Steel, Z., Silove, D., Bauman, A., 2008. Promoting walking as an adjunct intervention to group cognitive behavioral therapy for anxiety disorders—a pilot group randomized trial. J. Anxiety Disord. 22, 959–968.

Meyer, J.D., Ellingson, L.D., Koltyn, K.F., Stegner, A.J., Kim, J.-S., Cook, D.B., 2016. Psychobiological responses to preferred-and prescribed-intensity exercise in MDD. Med. Sci. Sports Exerc. 48 (11), 2207–2215.

Meyer, T.J., Miller, M.L., Metzger, R.L., Borkovec, T.D., 1990. Development and validation of the penn state worry questionnaire. Behav. Res. Ther. 28, 487—495.

Miller, F.L., O'Connor, D.P., Herring, M.P., Sailors, M.H., Jackson, A.S., Dishman, R.K., Bray, M.S., 2014. Exercise dose, exercise adherence, and associated health outcomes in the TIGER study. Med. Sci. Sports Exerc. 46, 69.

Mitte, K., 2005. Meta-analysis of cognitive-behavioral treatments for generalized anxiety disorder: a comparison with pharmacotherapy. Psychol. Bull. 131, 785—795.

Mogenson, G.J., Yang, C.R., 1991. The contribution of basal forebrain to limbic-motor integration and the mediation of motivation to action. Adv. Exp. Med. Biol. 295, 267—290.

Molina, S., Borkovec, T., 1994. The Penn State Worry Questionnaire: Psychometric Properties and Associated Characteristics.

Morehouse, R., Macqueen, G., Kennedy, S.H., 2011. Barriers to achieving treatment goals: a focus on sleep disturbance and sexual dysfunction. J. Affect. Disord. 132, 14—20.

Morgan, W.P., 1979. Anxiety reduction following acute physical activity. Psychiatr. Ann. 9, 36—45.

Motl, R.W., O'Connor, P.J., Dishman, R.K., 2004. Effects of cycling exercise on the soleus H-reflex and state anxiety among men with low or high trait anxiety. Psychophysiology 41, 96—105.

Motta, R.W., Mcwilliams, M.E., Schwartz, J.T., Cavera, R.S., 2012. The role of exercise in reducing childhood and adolescent PTSD, anxiety, and depression. J. Appl. Sch. Psychol. 28, 224—238.

Moyer, C.A., Rounds, J., Hannum, J.W., 2004. A meta-analysis of massage therapy research. Psychol. Bull. 130, 3—18.

Newman, C.L., Motta, R.W., 2007. The effects of aerobic exercise on childhood PTSD, anxiety, and depression. Int. J. Emerg. Ment. Health 9, 133—158.

O'Connor, P., Raglin, J., Martinsen, E., 2000a. Physical activity, anxiety and anxiety disorders. Int. J. Sport Psychol. 31, 136—155.

O'Connor, P.J., Raglin, J.S., Martinsen, E.W., 2000b. Physical activity, anxiety and anxiety disorders. Int. J. Sport Psychol. 31, 136—155.

O'Connor, P.J., Smith, J.C., Morgan, W.P., 2000c. Physical activity does not provoke panic attacks in patients with panic disorder: a review of the evidence. Anxiety Stress Coping 13, 333—353.

O'donovan, A., Hughes, B.M., Slavich, G.M., Lynch, L., Cronin, M.-T., O'farrelly, C., Malone, K.M., 2010. Clinical anxiety, cortisol and interleukin-6: evidence for specificity in emotion—biology relationships. Brain Behav. Immun. 24, 1074—1077.

Ouimet, A.J., Gawronski, B., Dozois, D.J.A., 2009. Cognitive vulnerability to anxiety: a review and an integrative model. Clin. Psychol. Rev. 29, 459—470.

Petruzzello, S.J., 2012. The ultimate tranquilizer? Exercise and its influence on anxiety. In: Acevedo, E.O. (Ed.), The Oxford Handbook of Exercise Psychology. Oxford University Press Inc, New York, NY.

Petruzzello, S.J., Landers, D.M., Hatfield, B.D., Kubitz, K.A., Salazar, W., 1991. A meta-analysis on the anxiety-reducing effects of acute and chronic exercise. Outcomes and Mechanisms. Sports Med. 11, 143—182.

Phongsavan, P., Merom, D., Wagner, R., Chey, T., Von Hofe, B., Silove, D., Bauman, A., 2008. Process evaluation in an intervention designed to promote physical activity among adults with anxiety disorders: evidence of acceptability and adherence. Health Promot. J. Aust. 19, 137—143.

Pitts Jr., F.N., Mcclure Jr., J.N., 1967. Lactate metabolism in anxiety neurosis. N. Engl. J. Med. 277, 1329—1336.

Polanczyk, G.V., Salum, G.A., Sugaya, L.S., Caye, A., Rohde, L.A., 2015. Annual research review: a meta-analysis of the worldwide prevalence of mental disorders in children and adolescents. J. Child Psychol. Psychiatry 56, 345—365.

Powers, M.B., Medina, J.L., Burns, S., Kauffman, B.Y., Monfils, M., Asmundson, G.J., Diamond, A., Mcintyre, C., Smits, J.A., 2015. Exercise augmentation of exposure therapy for PTSD: rationale and pilot efficacy data. Cognit. Behav. Ther. 44, 314–327.

Puetz, T.W., Beasman, K.M., O'Connor, P.J., 2006. The effect of cardiac rehabilitation exercise programs on feelings of energy and fatigue: a meta-analysis of research from 1945 to 2005. Eur J Prev Cardiol 13 (6), 886–893.

Puetz, T.W., Flowers, S.S., O'Connor, P.J., 2008. A randomized controlled trial of the effect of aerobic exercise training on feelings of energy and fatigue in sedentary young adults with persistent fatigue. Psychother. Psychosom. 77, 167–174.

Puetz, T.W., Youngstedt, S.D., Herring, M.P., 2015. Effects of pharmacotherapy on combat-related PTSD, anxiety, and depression: a systematic review and meta-regression analysis. PLoS One 10, e0126529.

Rector, N.A., Richter, M.A., Lerman, B., Regev, R., 2015. A pilot test of the additive benefits of physical exercise to CBT for OCD. Cognit. Behav. Ther. 44, 328–340.

Remes, O., Brayne, C., Linde, R., Lafortune, L., 2016. A systematic review of reviews on the prevalence of anxiety disorders in adult populations. Brain Behav. 6.

Rossy, L.A., Buckelew, S.P., Dorr, N., Hagglund, K.J., Thayer, J.F., McIntosh, M.J., Hewett, J.E., Johnson, J.C., 1999. A meta-analysis of fibromyalgia treatment interventions. Ann Behav Med 21 (2), 180–191.

Rosenbaum, S., Tiedemann, A., Sherrington, C., Curtis, J., Ward, P.B., 2014. Physical activity interventions for people with mental illness: a systematic review and meta-analysis. J. Clin. Psychiatry 75, 964–974.

Sareen, J., Cox, B.J., Clara, I., Asmundson, G.J.G., 2005. The relationship between anxiety disorders and physical disorders in the U.S. National Comorbidity Survey. Depress. Anxiety 21, 193–202.

Sareen, J., Jacobi, F., Cox, B.J., Belik, S.L., Clara, I., Stein, M.B., 2006. Disability and poor quality of life associated with comorbid anxiety disorders and physical conditions. Arch. Intern. Med. 166, 2109–2116.

Schwartz, C.E., Snidman, N., Kagan, J., 1999. Adolescent social anxiety as an outcome of inhibited temperament in childhood. J. Am. Acad. Child Adolesc. Psychiatry 38, 1008–1015.

Schweitzer, P.K., 2005. Principles and Practice of Sleep Medicine. Elsevier, Philadelphia.

Sciolino, N.R., Holmes, P.V., 2012. Exercise offers anxiolytic potential: a role for stress and brain noradrenergic-galaninergic mechanisms. Neurosci. Biobehav. Rev. 36, 1965–1984.

Sexton, H., Maere, A., Dahl, N.H., 1989. Exercise intensity and reduction in neurotic symptoms. A controlled follow-up study. Acta Psychiatr. Scand. 80, 231–235.

Shannahoff-Khalsa, D.S., Ray, L.E., Levine, S., Gallen, C.C., Schwartz, B.J., Sidorowich, J.J., 1999. Randomized controlled trial of yogic meditation techniques for patients with obsessive-compulsive disorder. CNS Spectr. 4, 34–47.

Shin, L.M., Liberzon, I., 2010. The neurocircuitry of fear, stress, and anxiety disorders. Neuropsychopharmacology 35, 169–191.

Sklan, E.H., Lowenthal, A., Korner, M., Ritov, Y., Landers, D.M., Rankinen, T., Bouchard, C., Leon, A.S., Rice, T., Rao, D.C., Wilmore, J.H., Skinner, J.S., Soreq, H., 2004. Acetylcholinesterase/paraoxonase genotype and expression predict anxiety scores in health, risk factors, exercise training, and genetics study. Proc. Natl. Acad. Sci. U.S.A. 101, 5512–5517.

Smits, J.A.J., Berry, A.C., Rosenfield, D., Powers, M.B., Behar, E., Otto, M.W., 2008. Reducing anxiety sensitivity with exercise. Depress. Anxiety 25, 689–699.

Smoller, J.W., 2015. The genetics of stress-related disorders: PTSD, depression, and anxiety disorders. Neuropsychopharmacology 41, 297–319.

Soares, J., Holmes, P.V., Renner, K.J., Edwards, G.L., Bunnell, B.N., Dishman, R.K., 1999. Brain noradrenergic responses to footshock after chronic activity-wheel running. Behav. Neurosci. 113, 558–566.

Speilberger, C.D., Gorsuch, R., Lushene, R., Vagg, P., Jacobs, G., 1983. Manual for the state-trait anxiety inventory. Consulting Psychologists, Palo Alto, CA.

Spielberger, C.D., 1966. Theory and Research on Anxiety. Academic Press, New York.

Spitzer, R.L., Kroenke, K., Williams, J.B., Löwe, B., 2006. A brief measure for assessing generalized anxiety disorder: the GAD-7. Arch. Intern. Med. 166, 1092−1097.

Stathopoulou, G., Powers, M.B., Berry, A.C., Smits, J.A.J., Otto, M.W., 2006. Exercise interventions for mental health: a quantitative and qualitative review. Clin. Psychol. Sci. Pract. 13, 179−193.

Stein, M.B., Roy-Byrne, P.P., Craske, M.G., Bystritsky, A., Sullivan, G., Pyne, J.M., Katon, W., Sherbourne, C.D., 2005. Functional impact and health utility of anxiety disorders in primary care outpatients. Med. Care 43, 1164.

Ströhle, A., Höfler, M., Pfister, H., Müller, A.G., Hoyer, J., Wittchen, H.U., Lieb, R., 2007. Physical activity and prevalence and incidence of mental disorders in adolescents and young adults. Psychol. Med. 37, 1657−1666.

Stubbs, B., Vancampfort, D., Rosenbaum, S., Firth, J., Cosco, T., Veronese, N., Salum, G.A., Schuch, F.B., 2017. An examination of the anxiolytic effects of exercise for people with anxiety and stress-related disorders: a meta-analysis. Psychiatry Res. 249, 102−108.

Sylvester, C.M., Corbetta, M., Raichle, M.E., Rodebaugh, T.L., Schlaggar, B.L., Sheline, Y.I., Zorumski, C.F., Lenze, E.J., 2012. Functional network dysfunction in anxiety and anxiety disorders. Trends Neurosci. 35, 527−535.

Rebar, A.L., Stanton, R., Geard, D., Short, C., Duncan, M.J., Vandelanotte, C., 2015. A meta-meta-analysis of the effect of physical activity on depression and anxiety in non-clinical adult populations. Health Psychol Rev. 9 (3), 366−378.

Van Hoomissen, J.D., Holmes, P.V., Zellner, A.S., Poudevigne, A., Dishman, R.K., 2004. Effects of beta-adrenoreceptor blockade during chronic exercise on contextual fear conditioning and mRNA for galanin and brain-derived neurotrophic factor. Behav. Neurosci. 118, 1378−1390.

Wang, C.W., Chan, C.H., Ho, R.T., Chan, J.S., Ng, S.M., Chan, C.L., 2014. Managing stress and anxiety through qigong exercise in healthy adults: a systematic review of meta-analysis of randomized controlled trials. BMC Complement Altern Med 14 (1), 8.

Weathers, F.W., Litz, B.T., Herman, D.S., Huska, J.A., Keane, T.M., 1993. The PTSD Checklist (PCL): Reliability, Validity, and Diagnostic Utility. Annual Convention of the International Society for Traumatic Stress Studies, San Antonio, TX. San Antonio, TX.

Wedekind, D., Broocks, A., Weiss, N., Engel, K., Neubert, K., Bandelow, B., 2010. A randomized, controlled trial of aerobic exercise in combination with paroxetine in the treatment of panic disorder. World J. Biol. Psychiatry 11, 904−913.

Wipfli, B.M., Rethorst, C.D., Landers, D.M., 2008. The anxiolytic effects of exercise: a meta-analysis of randomized trials and dose-response analysis. J Sport Exerc Psychol 30 (4), 392−410.

Wilkins, K.C., Lang, A.J., Norman, S.B., 2011. Synthesis of the psychometric properties of the PTSD checklist (PCL) military, civilian, and specific versions. Depress. Anxiety 28, 596−606.

Yin, J., Dishman, R.K., 2014. The effect of Tai Chi and Qigong practice on depression and anxiety symptoms: a systematic review and meta-regression analysis of randomized controlled trials. Ment Health Phys Act 7 (3), 135−146.

Youngstedt, S.D., 2005. Effects of exercise on sleep. Clin. Sports Med. 24, 355−365.

Zigmond, A.S., Snaith, R.P., 1983. The hospital anxiety and depression scale. Acta Psychiatr. Scand. 67, 361−370.

Zimmerman, M., Mattia, J.I., 2001a. The psychiatric diagnostic screening questionnaire: development, reliability and validity. Compr. Psychiatry 42, 175−189.

Zimmerman, M., Mattia, J.I., 2001b. A self-report scale to help make psychiatric diagnoses: the Psychiatric Diagnostic Screening Questionnaire. Arch. Gen. Psychiatry 58, 787−794.

# Bipolar Disorder and Physical Activity

*Davy Vancampfort[1,2], Benjamin I. Goldstein[3]*

[1] KU Leuven, Department of Rehabilitation Sciences, Leuven, Belgium; [2] KU Leuven, University Psychiatric Center KU Leuven, Leuven-Kortenberg, Belgium; [3] Department of Psychiatry, University of Toronto, Toronto, ON, Canada

## OUTLINE

# INTRODUCTION

Mood fluctuations are common in everyone's life, particularly when faced with stressful events. When mood changes are more distinct and persistent and result in significant distress or impairment, there might be an underlying affective disorder. Affective disorders can be classified along a spectrum defined by the extent and severity of mood change, from unipolar to bipolar disorder (BD)-II to BD-I (American Psychiatric Association, 2013). Those with unipolar disorder present with depressive episodes only, and individuals with BD-II or BD-I show increasingly pronounced episodes of mood elevation. In this chapter, we first briefly introduce the current clinical understanding of BD and explore the physical health status of people living with BD. We will then provide the current evidence base for the relationship between BD and physical activity and present the most important published trials, including a physical activity component before concluding with some future directions for this field.

# CLINICAL FEATURES

BD, previously known as manic-depressive disorder, is a severe and chronic mood disorder characterized by episodes of mania or hypomania and alternating or intertwining episodes of depression (American Psychiatric Association, 2013). Manic or hypomanic episodes are states of elevated mood and increased energy/motor drive, accompanied by a constellation of other symptoms such as impulsivity and reduced need for sleep, that differ in severity and duration. Although a manic episode impairs social or occupational functioning and might lead to hospital admission, in a hypomanic episode, a disturbance in functioning may be noticed by others but does not typically cause severe impairment (American Psychiatric Association, 2013). About three of four patients with an acute manic episode also present with psychotic symptoms (Goodwin and Jamison, 2007).

Bipolar depressive episodes share the same diagnostic criteria as unipolar depression but may have distinguishing characteristics. For example, bipolar depression usually has an earlier age of onset, has more frequent and briefer episodes, has an abrupt onset and offset, and is often linked to comorbid substance misuse (Grande et al., 2016). Next to this, higher rates of psychomotor retardation, greater difficulty thinking, more early morning awakening, more morning worsening of mood, and more frequent psychotic symptoms are observed in bipolar depression relative to unipolar depression (Mitchell et al., 2008). Diagnostic and Statistical Manual of Mental Disorders, Fifth Edition, criteria for a major depressive episode are however the same for bipolar and unipolar depression (American Psychiatric Association, 2013).

In order to be diagnosed with BD-I, at least one manic episode must be present, although major depressive episodes are typical but not needed for the diagnosis. Patients with BD-II have at least one hypomanic episode and one major depressive episode. Finally a cyclothymic disorder is given when the hypomanic and depressive periods do not fulfill criteria for hypomania or major depression for at least 2 years (American Psychiatric Association, 2013).

## EPIDEMIOLOGY, BURDEN, AND RISK FACTORS

In a worldwide mental health survey (Merikangas et al., 2011) the prevalence of BDs was consistent across cultures and ethnic groups, with a lifetime prevalence of 0.6% for BD-I and 0.4% for BD-II. The prevalence rates remained stable between 1990 and 2013 (Ferrari et al., 2016). Also, the burden of disease did not change over time. According to the World Health Organization global burden of disease study, BD ranks within the top 20 causes of disability among all medical conditions worldwide and sixth among the mental disorders (Whiteford et al., 2013). The functional disability of BD includes high unemployment rates, high dependence on public assistance, low annual income, decreased work productivity, poorer overall functioning, and lower quality of life. Next to this, psychosocial functioning appears to be significantly impaired in individuals who are in acute depressive or manic/hypomanic episodes while depressive symptoms induce the most enduring functional deficits. However, functional impairments persist even after significant mood symptoms have remitted. Adults with BD demonstrate also significantly poorer cognitive functioning in most domains compared with healthy controls, and it appears that neurocognition is the best predictor of community functioning (Best et al., 2017).

Therefore knowledge of the risk factors for developing BD is essential in order to reduce the burden of BD for patients, family members, and the society as a whole. A multifactorial model in which genes and environment interact is currently thought to best fit the disorder (Grande et al., 2016). BD has without a doubt a strong genetic background. Twin studies have suggested a monozygotic concordance rate of 0.43, and population-based family risk studies have estimated a heritability rate of about 58% (Song et al., 2015; Kieseppä et al., 2014). Environmental risk factors can be grouped in three clusters based on timing and postulated mechanism of action: neurodevelopment (e.g., maternal influenza during pregnancy and indicators of fetal development), substances (e.g., cannabis, cocaine, and other drugs like opioids, tranquilizers, stimulants, and sedatives), and physical/psychological stress (parental loss, adversities, abuses, and brain injury; Marangoni et al., 2016).

# PHYSICAL HEALTH OF PEOPLE WITH BIPOLAR DISORDER

People with BD have approximately a 10 years reduced life expectancy compared with the general population (Kessing et al., 2015). The underlying causes for this increased risk for premature mortality are multifactorial (Hayes et al., 2015). However, natural causes account for a substantial proportion of this premature mortality, and increased comorbid cardiovascular disease (Goldstein et al., 2015a) is a significant risk factor. Data from National Epidemiologic Survey on Alcohol and Related Conditions, for example, show that individuals with BD-I ($n = 1411$) have an almost five times higher risk for developing cardiovascular diseases than age-, race-, and gender-matched controls without BD (n = 34,851; Goldstein et al., 2009). A cross-sectional analysis of medical records of 314 primary care practices in Scotland (Smith et al., 2013) furthermore showed that compared with controls (n = 1,421,796), BD patients (n = 2582) were significantly less likely to have 0 recorded physical conditions and significantly more likely to have 1 of the 32 most common physical conditions, two physical comorbidities, and three or more physical comorbidities.

Cardiovascular disease risk factors such as obesity, hypertension, dyslipidemia, and dysglycemia are also associated with functional impairment, unemployment, more depressive and manic episode, suicide attempts, higher treatment costs, and more hospitalizations (Swartz and Fagiolini, 2012). As such a greater understanding of the associations between cardiovascular disease risk and BD may be advantageous in terms of improving both medical and psychiatric outcomes (Goldstein et al., 2015b).

Although shared pathophysiological mechanisms such as inflammation and endothelial dysfunction (Dargél et al., 2015; Goldstein and Young, 2013) contribute significantly to this high cardiovascular risk profile, poor lifestyle habits, including higher prevalence of smoking and high rates of substance abuse (Waxmonsky et al., 2005) and sedentary behavior (Vancampfort et al., 2016a,b), and lower levels of physical activity (Janney et al., 2014) play a prominent role. The relationship between BD and poor physical health is further complicated by the pharmacological treatment which can predispose the individual to cardiovascular risk factors such as obesity (Correll et al., 2015).

## Current Treatments for Bipolar Disorder

Current treatment strategies include mainly antidepressant, antipsychotic, and mood-stabilizing medications (Grande et al., 2016). Guidelines such as UK National Institute for Health and Care Excellence (Kendall et al., 2014) or German S3 guidance (Pfennig et al., 2013) recommended recently to add psychosocial interventions in the treatment. However, as indicated in the previous sections, BD is among the most burdensome psychiatric disorders and, even when treated using available medications and psychotherapies, is characterized by high rates of relapse, comorbidities, and functional impairments.

# PHYSICAL ACTIVITY AND BIPOLAR DISORDER

In recent years, interest has particularly grown in the efficacy and effectiveness of physical activity as a complementary intervention in the treatment of severe mental illness (Rosenbaum et al., 2014). People with BD are known to be a sedentary population. A recent meta-analysis demonstrated that people with BD spent in total 613.3 min (95% confidence interval [CI] = 389.9−836.6 min) or more than 10 h during waking hours being sedentary (Vancampfort et al., 2016a), which is, for example, substantially higher than levels reported in older people (>60 years; mean = 5.3 h/day; Harvey et al., 2014). A lack of physical activity is also evident in youth with BD, among whom only 1 in 20 meets recommendations for (vigorous) physical activity benchmarks (Jewell et al., 2015). Motivating people with BD toward an active lifestyle is therefore an important aspect of the multidisciplinary treatment and should be started as early as possible.

There are, to date, five reviews (Thomson et al., 2015; Souza de Sa Filho et al., 2015; Kucyi et al., 2010; Sylvia et al., 2010; Melo et al., 2016) on the effects of physical activity, and particularly its structured form, exercise. The overarching conclusions are that given the high rate of medical comorbidities experienced by people with BD, it is possible that exercise is a potentially useful and important intervention with regard to general health benefits; however, further research is required to elucidate the impact of exercise on mood symptomology.

Single bouts of aerobic exercise can inform our understanding of potential mechanisms underlying the benefits of longer exercise interventions. Recent research (Subramaniapillai et al., 2016) demonstrated that adolescents with BD experience similar exercise-induced emotional benefits as their healthy peers following a 20-min bout of moderate intensity exercise (heart rate goal of 60%−80% of the age estimated maximum [220−0.7 × age]). In another study of the same research group (Metcalfe et al., 2016), it was shown that 20-min bouts of aerobic exercise also impacts neural deactivation deficits in attention and activation deficits in inhibition. These findings are of high interest as the data show that one potential mechanism to explain the protective role of physical activity for severe mood fluctuations may be related to the association between physical activity participation and the functional connectivity of the brain (Douw et al., 2014). Functional connectivity can be defined as the temporal dependence of neuronal activity patterns of anatomically separated brain regions (Aertsen et al., 1989). For example, evidence suggests that cardiorespiratory fitness, which improves following physical activity adoption and maintenance, is associated with better functional connectivity between the different regions of the brain (Douw et al., 2014). It has been demonstrated recently (Brady et al., 2017) that bipolar mood states are associated with highly significant alterations in this functional connectivity, and altered activities in neural networks may be biomarkers of BD diagnosis and mood state that are accessible to neuromodulation and are promising novel targets for scientific investigation and possible clinical intervention. A better functional connectivity due to a better cardiorespiratory fitness may be potentially explained by mechanisms such as (1) the enhancement of the endothelial function and decrease arterial stiffness, oxidative stress and vascular inflammation (Davenport et al., 2012) and (2) the improvement of oxidative capacity, promoted by the improvement of the mitochondrial function and angiogenesis, allowing more exchange of neurotrophic factors, such as brain-derived neurotrophic factor (Erickson et al., 2012). However, more experimental research is urgently needed to clarify the role and underlying mechanisms of exercise as a strategy to regulate mood-related symptoms.

## EXAMPLES OF TRIALS INCLUDING A PHYSICAL ACTIVITY COMPONENT IN PEOPLE WITH BIPOLAR DISORDER

There have been several notable clinical trials in this field. In this section, we will briefly present some of these.

Gillhoff et al. (2010) were the first to compare the effects of a multimodal lifestyle intervention, with standard care on the body mass index (BMI) of people with BD using a randomized controlled trial design. The 5-month intervention included three modules focusing on nutrition, motivation, and physical activity (a personalized gym program). There was no additional information regarding the frequency of the program nor about the intensity or type of exercises. The primary finding of this study was a significant mean decrease of 0.3 kg/m² (95% CI = −0.7 to 0.06) in BMI in the multimodal lifestyle intervention ($n = 26$), whereas the control group receiving standard care ($n = 24$) showed an increase of 0.5 kg/m² (95% CI = 0.01−0.8) ($n = 24$). Looking at potential predictors, it emerged that this decrease was only observed in women and not in men. It was hypothesized that due to social desirability, women showed a higher drive for thinness compared with men and therefore may have been more motivated to adhere to the lifestyle intervention. There were however no changes in cardiovascular and metabolic syndrome measures over time (Gillhoff et al., 2010).

In the Self-Management Addressing Heart Risk Trial, Kilbourne et al. (2013) reported beneficial physical and mental health effects of a "Life Goals Collaborative Care" (LGCC) program compared with treatment as usual. LGCC is a psychosocial intervention designed to improve medical and psychiatric outcomes for persons with mood disorders through personal goal-setting aligned with wellness (health behavior change) and symptom coping strategies and supported through collaborative care (care coordination). Mixed-effects analyses comparing changes in 24-month outcomes among patients in LGCC ($N = 57$) versus enhanced usual care ($N = 59$) groups revealed that patients receiving LGCC had reduced systolic ($\beta = -3.1$, $P = 0.04$, Cohen's $d = -0.22$, i.e., a small effect) and diastolic blood pressure ($\beta = -2.1$, $P = 0.04$, Cohen's $d = -0.23$, i.e., a small effect) as well as reduced manic symptoms ($\beta = -23.9$, $P = 0.01$). It had however no significant impact on other primary outcomes (total cholesterol, physical health-related quality of life; Kilbourne et al., 2013).

Frank et al. (2015) compared the efficacy of an integrated risk reduction intervention (IRRI) in comparison to a control condition in BD-I patients with a BMI above 25 kg/m$^2$. The control condition included psychiatric care with medical monitoring for a 6-month period. Both conditions involved psychiatric treatment, assessment, and symptom monitoring conducted by a psychiatric nurse, but only those in the IRRI received lifestyle coaching. This included the development and maintenance of an individualized lifestyle plan. The lifestyle coach provided support and encouragement to the patient for making progress toward specific goals, including improving sleep and increasing physical activity using a pedometer. IRRI ($n = 58$) was associated with a significantly greater rate of decrease in BMI versus the control condition ($n = 56$; Cohen's $d = -0.51$, 95% CI $= -0.91$ to $-0.14$, i.e., a moderate effect).

In summary, the presented trials demonstrate that a multimodal intervention including a physical activity component and focusing on developing relevant, individualized goals within a collaborative care network leads to beneficial lifestyle changes positively affecting physiological measures. The evidence for mood and cognitive changes and functional improvements following these interventions is still too limited to make any firm conclusions.

## FUTURE DIRECTIONS

In spite of the promising results outlined previously, several critical issues regarding physical activity and BD remain unanswered. Future research should in particular focus on the evidence for physical activity in regulating mood fluctuations and improving cognitive functioning. Research involving acute bouts of exercise might assist in elucidating any underlying neurobiological mechanisms.

Another significant challenge is to establish and evaluate the efficacy and (cost-) effectiveness of lifestyle physical activity and/or structured exercise programs that are embedded in routine clinical practice and that benefit people with BD in the long term. To achieve this, novel approaches are needed to overcome issues related to motivational deficits, cost-effectiveness, accessibility, and time. The use of m-health technologies provides a unique opportunity for continuing motivational support in people with severe mental illness (Naslund et al., 2015). One of the next steps in the development of physical activity interventions therefore involves examining the potential of mobile technology and social media to augment face-to-face interventions and enhance treatment effects beyond the end of an intervention. In order to capture changing processes involved in physical activity adoption, adherence, lapse, and drop-out behaviors, physical activity research in people with BD requires the use of an experimental approach and a qualitative methodology (i.e., process evaluation).

Next to this future research should explore in more detail reasons why people with BD are less physically active and strategies to overcome any barriers should be investigated. The current evidence is mainly based on cross-sectional studies highlighting the need for longitudinal research comparing manic versus depressive patients and young versus chronic patients. If the ultimate purpose of this kind of physical activity research is to inform and motivate policy changes that will improve the mental and physical health of people with BD, merely documenting the relation of intrapersonal, interpersonal/cultural, physical environment, and policy variables to physical activity behavior is however insufficient. Environmental and policy change research is needed and should include assessments of broader health outcomes, such as changes in prevalence of chronic comorbidities, service utilization, as well as the economic costs and benefits of proposed policy changes.

In particular, the efficacy and (cost-)effectiveness of integrating clinicians with expertise in exercise prescription (e.g., physical therapists and exercise physiologists) and training in psychopathology in multidisciplinary mental health teams will be an important future step (Stubbs et al., 2014). One way of ensuring future integration of these experts is through educating the existing mental health workforce. Therefore there is a clear need for the development of education modules and minimal educational standards outlining the role of physical activity in the treatment of BD to be delivered across a range of disciplines, including psychiatry, psychology, mental health nursing, occupational therapy, and social work. Furthermore, it is imperative that students studying physical therapy receive training in psychopathology. While integration of clinicians with expertise in exercise prescription and educating the existing mental health workforce are commonplace in some European countries, it is still often neglected in other parts of the world (Probst, 2012).

## CONCLUSIONS

We are optimistic that the rapidly increasing evidence base for the importance of physical activity in the treatment of people with BD will, in due course, lead to a sustainable health policy change where physical activity interventions are incorporated into routine management. We are convinced that such change is essential in reducing the differential mortality and morbidity gaps and improving the mental and health-related quality of life of this vulnerable population.

## References

Aertsen, A., Gerstein, G., Habib, M., Palm, G., 1989. Dynamics of neuronal firing correlation: modulation of "effective connectivity". J. Neurophysiol. (Bethesda). 61, 900–917.

American Psychiatric Association, 2013. Diagnostic and Statistical Manual of Mental Disorders (DSM-5). American Psychiatric Association, Washington, DC.

Best, M.W., Bowie, C.R., Naiberg, M.R., Newton, D.F., Goldstein, B.I., 2017. Neurocognition and psychosocial functioning in adolescents with bipolar disorder. J. Affect. Disord. 207, 406–412.

Brady Jr., R.O., Tandon, N., Masters, G.A., Margolis, A., Cohen, B.M., Keshavan, M., Öngür, D., 2017. Differential brain network activity across mood states in bipolar disorder. J. Affect. Disord. 207, 367–376.

Correll, C., Detraux, J., De Lepeleire, J., De Hert, M., 2015. Effects of antipsychotics, antidepressants and mood stabilizers on risk for physical diseases in people with schizophrenia, depression and bipolar disorder. World Psychiatr. 14, 119–136.

Dargél, A.A., Godin, O., Kapczinski, F., Kupfer, D.J., Leboyer, M., 2015. C-reactive protein alterations in bipolar disorder: a meta-analysis. J. Clin. Psychiatr. 76, 142–150.

Davenport, M.H., Hogan, D.B., Eskes, G.A., Longman, R.S., Poulin, M.J., 2012. Cerebrovascular reserve: the link between fitness and cognitive function? Exerc. Sport Sci. Rev. 40, 153–158.

Douw, L., Nieboer, D., Van Dijk, B.W., Stam, C.J., Twisk, J.W., 2014. A healthy brain in a healthy body: brain network correlates of physical and mental fitness. PLoS One 9, e88202.

Erickson, K.I., Miller, D.L., Weinstein, A.M., Akl, S.L., Banducci, S., 2012. Physical activity and brain plasticity in late adulthood: a conceptual and comprehensive review. Ageing Res. 3, 6.

Ferrari, A.J., Stockings, E., Khoo, J.P., Erskine, H.E., Degenhardt, L., Vos, T., Whiteford, H.A., 2016. The prevalence and burden of bipolar disorder: findings from the Global Burden of Disease Study 2013. Bipolar Disord. 18, 440–450.

Frank, E., Wallace, M.L., Hall, M., Hasler, B., Levenson, J.C., Janney, C.A., Soreca, I., Fleming, M.C., Buttenfield, J., Ritchey, F.C., 2015. An integrated risk reduction intervention can reduce body mass index in individuals being treated for bipolar I disorder: results from a randomized trial. Bipolar Disord. 17, 424–437.

Gillhoff, K., Gaab, J., Emini, L., Maroni, C., Tholuck, J., Greil, W., 2010. Effects of a multimodal lifestyle intervention on body mass index in patients with bipolar disorder: a randomized controlled trial. Prim. Care Companion J. Clin. Psychiatry 12, e1–e8.

Goldstein, B.I., Carnethon, M.R., Matthews, K.A., Mcintyre, R.S., Miller, G.E., Raghuveer, G., Stoney, C.M., Wasiak, H., Mccrindle, B.W., 2015a. Major depressive disorder and bipolar disorder predispose youth to accelerated atherosclerosis and early cardiovascular disease: a scientific statement from the American Heart Association. Circulation 132, 965.

Goldstein, B.I., Fagiolini, A., Houck, P., Kupfer, D.J., 2009. Cardiovascular disease and hypertension among adults with bipolar I disorder in the United States. Bipolar Disord. 11, 657−662.

Goldstein, B.I., Schaffer, A., Wang, S., Blanco, C., 2015b. Excessive and premature new-onset cardiovascular disease among adults with bipolar disorder in the US NESARC cohort. J. Clin. Psychiatr. 76, 163−169.

Goldstein, B.I., Young, L.T., 2013. Toward clinically applicable biomarkers in bipolar disorder: focus on BDNF, inflammatory markers, and endothelial function. Curr. Psychiatr. Rep. 15, 425.

Goodwin, F.K., Jamison, K.R., 2007. Manic-Depressive Illness: Bipolar Disorders and Recurrent Depression. Oxford University Press.

Grande, I., Berk, M., Birmaher, B., Vieta, E., 2016. Bipolar disorder. Lancet 387, 1561−1572.

Harvey, J.A., Chastin, S.F., Skelton, D., 2014. How sedentary are older people? A systematic review of the amount of sedentary behavior. J. Aging Phys. Activ 23, 471−487.

Hayes, J., Miles, J., Walters, K., King, M., Osborn, D., 2015. A systematic review and meta-analysis of premature mortality in bipolar affective disorder. Acta Psychiatr. Scand. 131, 417−425.

Janney, C.A., Fagiolini, A., Swartz, H.A., Jakicic, J.M., Holleman, R.G., Richardson, C.R., 2014. Are adults with bipolar disorder active? Objectively measured physical activity and sedentary behavior using accelerometry. J. Affect. Disord. 152, 498−504.

Jewell, L., Abtan, R., Scavone, A., Timmins, V., Swampillai, B., Goldstein, B.I., 2015. Preliminary evidence of disparities in physical activity among adolescents with bipolar disorder. Ment. Health Phys. Act. 8, 62−67.

Kendall, T., Morriss, R., Mayo-Wilson, E., Marcus, E., Jones, S., Group, G.D., 2014. Assessment and management of bipolar disorder: summary of updated NICE guidance. BMJ 349.

Kessing, L.V., Vradi, E., Andersen, P.K., 2015. Life expectancy in bipolar disorder. Bipolar Disord. 17, 543−548.

Kieseppä, T., Partonen, T., Haukka, J., Kaprio, J., Lönnqvist, J., 2014. High concordance of bipolar I disorder in a nationwide sample of twins. Am. J. Psychiatr. 161 (10), 1814−1821.

Kilbourne, A., Goodrich, D., Lai, Z., Post, E., Schumacher, K., Nord, K., 2013. Randomized controlled trial to reduce cardiovascular disease risk for patients with bipolar disorders: the Self-management Addressing Heart Risk Trial (SMAHRT). J. Clin. Psychiatr. 74 (7), e655−662.

Kucyi, A., Alsuwaidan, M.T., Liauw, S.S., Mcintyre, R.S., 2010. Aerobic physical exercise as a possible treatment for neurocognitive dysfunction in bipolar disorder. Postgrad. Med. 122, 107−116.

Marangoni, C., Hernandez, M., Faedda, G.L., 2016. The role of environmental exposures as risk factors for bipolar disorder: a systematic review of longitudinal studies. J. Affect. Disord. 193, 165−174.

Melo, M.C.A., Daher, E.D.F., Albuquerque, S.G.C., De Bruin, V.M.S., 2016. Exercise in bipolar patients: a systematic review. J. Affect. Disord. 198, 32−38.

Merikangas, K.R., Jin, R., He, J.-P., Kessler, R.C., Lee, S., Sampson, N.A., Viana, M.C., Andrade, L.H., Hu, C., Karam, E.G., 2011. Prevalence and correlates of bipolar spectrum disorder in the world mental health survey initiative. Arch. Gen. Psychiatr. 68, 241−251.

Metcalfe, A., Macintosh, B., Scavone, A., Ou, X., Korczak, D., Goldstein, B., 2016. Effects of acute aerobic exercise on neural correlates of attention and inhibition in adolescents with bipolar disorder. Transl. Psychiatry 6, e814.

Mitchell, P.B., Goodwin, G.M., Johnson, G.F., Hirschfeld, R., 2008. Diagnostic guidelines for bipolar depression: a probabilistic approach. Bipolar Disord. 10, 144−152.

Naslund, J.A., Aschbrenner, K.A., Barre, L.K., Bartels, S.J., 2015. Feasibility of popular m-health technologies for activity tracking among individuals with serious mental illness. Telemed. e-Health 21, 213−216.

Pfennig, A., Bschor, T., Falkai, P., Bauer, M., 2013. The diagnosis and treatment of bipolar disorder: recommendations from the current s3 guideline. Deutsch. Ärzteb. Int. 110, 92.

Probst, M., 2012. The International Organization of Physical Therapists Working in Mental Health (IOPTMH). Ment. Health Phys. Act.Act. 5, 20−21.

Rosenbaum, S., Tiedemann, A., Sherrington, C., Curtis, J., Ward, P.B., 2014. Physical activity interventions for people with mental illness: a systematic review and meta-analysis. J. Clin. Psychiatr. 75, 964−974.

Smith, D.J., Martin, D., Mclean, G., Langan, J., Guthrie, B., Mercer, S.W., 2013. Multimorbidity in bipolar disorder and undertreatment of cardiovascular disease: a cross sectional study. BMC Med. 11, 1.

Song, J., Bergen, S.E., Kuja-Halkola, R., Larsson, H., Landén, M., Lichtenstein, P., 2015. Bipolar disorder and its relation to major psychiatric disorders: a family-based study in the Swedish population. Bipolar Disord. 17, 184−193.

Souza De Sa Filho, A., Marcos De Souza Moura, A., Khede Lamego, M., Barbosa Ferreira Rocha, N., Paes, F., Cristina Oliveira, A., Lattari, E., Rimes, R., Manochio, J., Budde, H., 2015. Potential therapeutic effects of physical exercise for bipolar disorder. CNS Neurol. Disord. - Drug Targets 14, 1255−1259.

Stubbs, B., Probst, M., Soundy, A., Parker, A., De Herdt, A., De Hert, M., Mitchell, A.J., Vancampfort, D., Health T.I.O.O.P.T.I.M., 2014. Physiotherapists can help implement physical activity programmes in clinical practice. Br. J. Psychiatr. 204, 164.

Subramaniapillai, M., Goldstein, B.I., Macintosh, B.J., Korczak, D.J., Ou, X., Scavone, A., Arbour-Nicitopoulos, K., Faulkner, G., 2016. Characterizing exercise-induced feelings after one bout of exercise among adolescents with and without bipolar disorder. J. Affect. Disord. 190, 467−473.

Swartz, H.A., Fagiolini, A., 2012. Cardiovascular disease and bipolar disorder: risk and clinical implications. J. Clin. Psychiatr. 73, 1563−1565.

Sylvia, L.G., Ametrano, R.M., Nierenberg, A.A., 2010. Exercise treatment for bipolar disorder: potential mechanisms of action mediated through increased neurogenesis and decreased allostatic load. Psychother. Psychosom. 79, 87−96.

Thomson, D., Turner, A., Lauder, S., Gigler, M.E., Berk, L., Singh, A.B., Pasco, J., Berk, M., Sylvia, L., 2015. A brief review of exercise, bipolar disorder and mechanistic pathways. Front. Psychol. 6, 147.

Vancampfort, D., Firth, J., Schuch, F., Rosenbaum, S., De Hert, M., Mugisha, J., Probst, M., Stubbs, B., 2016a. Physical activity and sedentary behavior in people with bipolar disorder: a systematic review and meta-analysis. J. Affect. Disord. 201, 145−152.

Vancampfort, D., Sienaert, P., Wyckaert, S., De Hert, M., Stubbs, B., Probst, M., 2016b. Sitting time, physical fitness impairments and metabolic abnormalities in people with bipolar disorder: an exploratory study. Psychiatr. Res. 242, 7−12.

Waxmonsky, J.A., Thomas, M.R., Miklowitz, D.J., Allen, M.H., Wisniewski, S.R., Zhang, H., Ostacher, M.J., Fossey, M.D., 2005. Prevalence and correlates of tobacco use in bipolar disorder: data from the first 2000 participants in the Systematic Treatment Enhancement Program. Gen. Hosp. Psychiatr. 27, 321−328.

Whiteford, H.A., Degenhardt, L., Rehm, J., Baxter, A.J., Ferrari, A.J., Erskine, H.E., Charlson, F.J., Norman, R.E., Flaxman, A.D., Johns, N., 2013. Global burden of disease attributable to mental and substance use disorders: findings from the Global Burden of Disease Study 2010. Lancet 382, 1575−1586.

# Schizophrenia and Exercise

*Shuichi Suetani[1,2,5], Davy Vancampfort[3,4]*

[1] Queensland Centre for Mental Health Research, The Park Centre for
Mental Health, Wacol, QLD, Australia; [2] Queensland Brain Institute, The
University of Queensland, St Lucia, QLD, Australia; [3] KU Leuven,
Department of Rehabilitation Sciences, Leuven, Belgium; [4] KU Leuven,
University Psychiatric Center KU Leuven, Leuven-Kortenberg, Belgium;
[5] Metro South Addiction and Mental Health Service, Queensland Health,
Brisbane, QLD, Australia

## OUTLINE

65

## INTRODUCTION

Often thought of as a stereotypical symbol of madness, schizophrenia remains to be one of the most misunderstood and least understood illnesses in the modern world. Schizophrenia affects approximately 1% of the population, with most people experiencing initial onset of symptoms early in adolescence and young adulthood. People with schizophrenia continue to suffer from significantly high burden of disease and low quality of life (Whiteford et al., 2013), as well as persisting differential mortality and morbidity gaps (Saha et al., 2007).

## CLINICAL FEATURES

Schizophrenia is a complex brain disorder that can lead to a range of deficits in physical, mental, and social functioning. While no signs or symptoms are specific to schizophrenia, its main symptoms can broadly be divided into positive, negative, and cognitive symptom domains (Howes and Murray, 2014; Kahn et al., 2015; Malaspina et al., 2014; van Os and Kapur, 2009).

### Positive Symptoms

Positive symptoms encompass psychotic symptoms such as delusions and hallucinations. Delusions are fixed, false beliefs that are not consistent with one's culture. Hallucinations are perceptual disturbances in the absence of external stimuli. An example of a delusion may be if you believe that the government is monitoring your every action through a microchip inserted in your brain, despite all objective evidence being contrary to this belief. Likewise, a hallucination may present as an experience of hearing a derogatory voice describing your every action, even when there is nobody around you. These are called positive symptoms because they are added to one's usual experiences. It is important to recognize that even though the positive symptoms or psychosis are intimately associated with schizophrenia and also with the concept of "madness," they are not the same thing. A wide range of mental disorders from anxiety spectrum disorders to bipolar disorder can have psychotic symptoms as part of their clinical presentation (van Os and Kapur, 2009; Kelleher and Cannon, 2016). In fact, psychotic experiences are reasonably common, albeit infrequent, even in the general population (i.e., people with no mental disorders; McGrath et al., 2015).

## Negative Symptoms

On the other hand, negative symptoms represent loss of one's usual experiences. They include social withdrawal, a reduced ability to feel pleasure in life, and diminished motivation or emotional expressiveness (Howes and Murray, 2014; Kahn et al., 2015; Malaspina et al., 2014). While perhaps not as clinically obvious, negative symptoms may have an even greater burden on the psychosocial functioning of people with schizophrenia than positive symptoms (Rabinowitz et al., 2012), and we currently have few treatment options aimed at specifically reducing negative symptoms (Arango et al., 2013).

## Cognitive Impairment

Finally, there is now an accumulating body of evidence to suggest that people with schizophrenia have impairments in a wide range of cognitive functions, including attention, working memory, executive function, and social cognition (van Os and Kapur, 2009; Kahn et al., 2015). This has led to a strong research focus on the cognitive symptom domain in people with schizophrenia in recent times, both for the enhanced understanding of the illness onset and progression and for the development of potential new treatment options targeting this symptom domain (Kahn and Keefe, 2013; Zipursky et al., 2013).

# EPIDEMIOLOGY AND RISK FACTORS

Analyses from the Global Burden of Disease Study 2015 (Disease et al., 2016) ranked schizophrenia on the 12th place on the list of leading causes of global years lived with disability. In one systematic review (McGrath et al., 2008) the median incidence (the number of new cases that occur in a population in a given period of time) of schizophrenia was estimated to be around 15.2 per 100,000 person-years. In other words, there were approximately 15 new cases of schizophrenia per 100,000 persons in the given population over 1 year. There were, however, a wide range of variations in reported incidence rates in different sub-populations. Higher incident rates were seen in (1) males compared with females, (2) urban areas compared with nonurban areas, and (3) migrant populations compared with native-born individuals (McGrath et al., 2004). In terms of prevalence (the number of existing cases in a population), another systematic review (Saha et al., 2005) estimated it to be between 3.3 and 7.2 per 1000 persons. Unlike the incidence rates, there were no significant differences between males and females or urban and nonurban sites. However, the prevalence rates were higher in migrant populations over native-born individuals and in more developed countries over less developed (Saha et al., 2005).

Even though we are still uncertain of the exact pathogenic mechanisms of schizophrenia, it is likely that schizophrenia occurs as a result of interplay between genetic vulnerabilities and environmental factors (Kahn et al., 2015; van Os and Kapur, 2009; van Os et al., 2017). In terms of genetic vulnerabilities, it is well established that schizophrenia "runs in the family." For example, a Danish national register-based cohort study (Gottesman et al., 2010) found that the risks of developing schizophrenia for offspring were (1) 27.4% if both parents had been hospitalized for schizophrenia, (2) 7.0% if one parent had been hospitalized for schizophrenia, and (3) 0.9% if neither parent had been hospitalized for schizophrenia. Likewise, twin studies estimate the rates of developing schizophrenia to be 42.2%—50.0% in identical twin pairs as opposed to 3.9%—4.1% for nonidentical twin pairs (Cardno and Gottesman, 2000). More recently, advancements in statistical genetics have identified distinct genetic regions that are more commonly shared between people with schizophrenia than people without the disorder. By comparing the DNA of over 35,000 people with schizophrenia to 100,000 unaffected individuals, researchers found over 100 schizophrenia-related genetic regions (Schizophrenia Working Group of the Psychiatric Genomics, 2014). This study has allowed us to understand more about the biological basis of schizophrenia and will potentially identify new therapeutic targets.

On the other hand, numerous potential environmental risk factors for schizophrenia have been identified over the years. These include (1) pregnancy-related factors such as older paternal age (Malaspina et al., 2001), neonatal vitamin D status (McGrath et al., 2010), and obstetric complications (Cannon et al., 2002), (2) social factors such as childhood trauma (Varese et al., 2012), social isolation, and stressful life events (Beards et al., 2013; Stilo et al., 2016), as well as (3) substance use, in particular cannabis (Di Forti et al., 2009). Therefore the current evidence suggests that even though schizophrenia affects less than 1% of the population, there are some distinct subgroups within the population with genetic and environmental vulnerabilities who have higher risk of developing and/or having schizophrenia (Kahn et al., 2015; McGrath et al., 2008; Stilo and Murray, 2010).

In terms of the onset of illness the Aetiology and Ethnicity of Schizophrenia and Other Psychoses study found that the age at first clinical contact for psychoses was significantly earlier in males (29.6 years) compared with females (32.6 years; Kirkbride et al., 2006). It is sobering to note, however, that the decline in cognitive function can already be seen in childhood in individuals who were later diagnosed with schizophrenia, sometimes as early as the age of 7 years (Reichenberg et al., 2010). Given that both the help-seeking behavior and the clinical diagnosis of schizophrenia rely heavily on the presence of positive symptoms, it is likely that the actual onset of schizophrenia per se generally occurs in early adolescence. This usually happens years before the person or the family members seek health services or the diagnosis of schizophrenia is made by a doctor (Kahn and Keefe, 2013). This period after the onset but before the diagnosis is sometimes called the prodromal phase, consisting mainly of subtle cognitive and social decline that often precede the emergence of positive symptoms. This is a particularly important point as this very early onset of the illness may affect social skills and educational attainment in childhood/adolescence, which may in turn lead to a life-long disrupted occupational and social trajectory with associated socioeconomic disadvantage in adulthood (Galletly et al., 2016). In clinical practice, it is often difficult to judge if a young person is experiencing the prodromal phase that will lead to schizophrenia or merely a normal developmental phase into adulthood. In recognition of this, combined with the finding that a shorter duration of untreated psychosis is associated with a better prognosis in schizophrenia (Penttila et al., 2014), there has been an increased clinical emphasis toward management of individuals at high risk of developing psychosis (sometimes called ultrahigh risk (Yung et al., 2004)) and to those in the early stages of psychotic illness—for example, early psychosis or first episode psychosis (McGorry, 2015; Stafford et al., 2013).

Although our understanding of schizophrenia is far from complete, these new insights from genetic and epidemiological studies represent an exciting opportunity for a better understanding of the gene and environment interplay and provide clues for both etiology of and potential treatment targets for schizophrenia (McGrath, 2015; van Os et al., 2017).

# CURRENT TREATMENT STRATEGIES FOR SCHIZOPHRENIA

Medication, in particular, antipsychotic medication, remains the cornerstone of treatment for people with schizophrenia (Leucht et al., 2013). For example, a systematic review consisting of 6493 participants (Leucht et al., 2012) demonstrated that antipsychotic medications significantly reduced relapse rates at 1 year compared with the placebo group (27% relapse rates in the group that continued maintenance medication compared with 64% relapse rate in the group that discontinued). Moreover, a Finnish national cohort study consisting of 66,881 individuals with schizophrenia showed that long-term treatment with antipsychotic medication was associated with approximately 20% lower mortality risk compared with those who were on no antipsychotic medication (Tiihonen et al., 2009). Similar benefit in mortality risk was also demonstrated in a Swedish national cohort more recently (Tiihonen et al., 2016).

There is also an accumulating evidence base to support the use of psychosocial treatment strategies such as psychotherapy/talking therapy such as cognitive behavior therapy, and vocational rehabilitation for people with schizophrenia (Galletly et al., 2016). Furthermore, as we explore further in the next section, there is an increased acknowledgment and awareness among psychiatry professionals of the importance of physical health and lifestyle modifications to target cardiometabolic risk factors for people with schizophrenia (Suetani et al., 2017).

## PHYSICAL HEALTH OF PEOPLE WITH SCHIZOPHRENIA

People with schizophrenia have approximately 10–20 years reduced life expectancy compared with the general population (Walker et al., 2015; Laursen, 2011). There is now an established body of evidence indicating that the majority of this reduced life expectancy is due to preventable physical illnesses such as cardiovascular diseases and diabetes mellitus (Olfson et al., 2015; Lawrence et al., 2013; Moore et al., 2015). There are many factors that contribute to these mortality and morbidity gaps. First, most antipsychotic medications contribute significantly to the deterioration of the cardiometabolic risk profile. This deterioration happens mainly through these their tendency to cause significant weight gain (Correll et al., 2015a,b), and this occurs at the very early stages of antipsychotic treatment (Correll et al., 2014; Foley and Morley, 2011). Despite this, monitoring of the cardiometabolic risk profile is often done poorly in mental health services (Mitchell et al., 2012). Furthermore, the research evidence suggests that even when people with schizophrenia do present to health services for physical illnesses, they are less likely to receive optimal health care (Mitchell et al., 2009; Kisely et al., 2009). These issues, however, need to be considered within the clinical features of schizophrenia itself. There are many psychiatric symptoms that may compromise the physical health status of people with schizophrenia. For example, positive symptoms such as paranoid ideation may lead to reluctance toward medical interventions, negative symptoms such as reduced motivation may lead to missed appointments, and cognitive symptoms such as memory impairment may lead to difficulty complying with treatment regimens. Thus all these factors are likely to contribute to the persisting differential morbidity and mortality gaps.

Cardiometabolic risk status for people with schizophrenia has been well described in the Survey of High Impact Psychosis (SHIP) study (Morgan et al., 2012). With data from over 1800 people living with psychosis in Australia, the SHIP study found that (1) three-quarters of participants were either overweight or obese with more than 80% having central abdominal obesity, (2) two-thirds of participants were current cigarette smokers, and (3) more than half the people in the study met the criteria for metabolic syndrome (Galletly et al., 2012). Similar findings were also seen in a recent UK study with a smaller sample number (Gardner-Sood et al., 2015). Moreover, a meta-analysis consisting of 136 studies and over 180,000 individuals found that people with schizophrenia were four times more likely to have abdominal obesity, 2.4 times more likely to have metabolic syndrome, and twice more likely to have diabetes mellitus compared with the general population (Vancampfort et al., 2013).

## PHYSICAL ACTIVITY AND SCHIZOPHRENIA

There has been much focus on improving the physical health of people with schizophrenia by reducing the cardiometabolic risk profile (Docherty et al., 2016; Suetani et al., 2015). In particular, increasing physical activity (PA) and reducing sedentary behavior of people with schizophrenia is rapidly gaining both research and clinical attention as an important, feasible and effective behavior modification target in this population (Vancampfort et al., 2010; Suetani et al., 2016a; Rosenbaum et al., 2016; Stubbs et al., 2017a).

To illustrate the magnitude of the problem, the following data may be helpful. Data from the SHIP study estimated that using the International Physical Activity Questionnaire (Craig et al., 2003), nearly 50% of people with psychosis were engaged in a low level of PA (Suetani et al., 2016b). In a cohort of 450 community patients with psychosis using a similar PA assessment as in the SHIP study, 44% were engaged in a low level of PA (Gardner-Sood et al., 2015). Even within a first episode psychosis sample, 34% of participants were classified as physically inactive (Lee et al., 2013). A recent meta-analysis consisting of 35 studies with 3453 people with schizophrenia estimated that they engaged in 80.4 min of light intensity PA, 16.2 min of moderate intensity PA, and only 1.1 min of vigorous intensity PA per day. When compared with the control sample, people with schizophrenia engaged in significantly less moderate intensity PA (14.2 min less per day) and vigorous intensity PA (3.4 min less per day), but there was no difference in the amount of light intensity PA per day. This review also estimated that 56.6% of people with schizophrenia met the recommended 150 min of moderate intensity PA per week (Stubbs et al., 2016a). Another systematic review (Stubbs et al., 2016b) estimated that people with schizophrenia over 12 h per day being sedentary, nearly 3 h more than the control group. Furthermore, there have been studies to suggest that people with schizophrenia have significantly reduced cardiorespiratory fitness (CRF; i.e., the ability of the circulatory, respiratory, and muscular systems to supply oxygen during sustained PA) compared with the general population, which in turn may be associated with the increased cardiovascular mortality rate (Vancampfort et al., 2015a,b).

## Factors Influencing Physical Activity Participation

In order to improve PA engagement, it is important to understand the factors that influence PA participation in people with schizophrenia. A landmark systematic review (Vancampfort et al., 2012) found that low PA engagement in people with schizophrenia was most consistently associated with the presence of negative symptoms and cardiometabolic comorbidities such as metabolic syndrome and obesity. In addition, there were less consistent associations between reduced PA and a number of factors including medication side effect, lack of knowledge in cardiometabolic risk factors, low self-efficacy and physical self-perception, unhealthy eating habits, and social isolation.

More recently, using the data from over 2000 people with schizophrenia from 47 low- and middle-income countries, Stubbs et al. (2018) found that low PA engagement was associated with factors including male sex, increasing age, unemployment, living in urban areas, inadequate fruit consumption, and mobility limitations.

In addition, many people with schizophrenia identify goals such as weight loss, improved mood, and reduced stress as motivating factors to engage in PA (Firth et al., 2016c). At the same time, it is interesting to note that related factors such as low mood and high level of stress, as well as lack of social support, were seen as major barriers to PA engagement.

## Benefits of Physical Activity for People with Schizophrenia

There are an increasing number of studies that suggest benefits of PA for both the physical and psychological well-being of people with schizophrenia (Rosenbaum et al., 2016). For example, one systematic review consisting of 20 studies with 695 participants found that even though PA interventions had no significant effect on body mass index, they led to improvement in measures of physical fitness, as well as in reducing both positive and negative symptoms of schizophrenia (Firth et al., 2015). Of particular note, the authors found the dose of PA to be a critical factor, as the benefits were seen in those who were engaged in around 90 min or more per week of moderate/vigorous PA. Furthermore, using data from 385 individuals from 10 studies, Firth et al. (2017) found that PA is effective in improving global cognition with greater amounts of PA associated with larger improvement. They also found that PA interventions that were supervised by PA professionals were more effective.

Another meta-analysis found that promoting PA may improve CRF of people with schizophrenia (Vancampfort et al., 2015c). This is a particularly important finding, given that CRF is an important independent modifiable risk factor for cardiometabolic diseases, and people with schizophrenia have a significantly lower level of CRF compared with the general population. A more recent study by Vancampfort et al. (2017) demonstrated that, like the benefits seen in cognitive symptoms, PA interventions with higher intensity or higher frequency were associated with more improvement in CRF, as well as being supervised by qualified professionals such as physiotherapists and exercise physiologists (EPs). The importance of PA supervision by qualified professionals was again highlighted in a systematic review that explored the predictors for dropouts from PA intervention studies in people with schizophrenia (Vancampfort et al., 2016). This review, consisting of 19 studies and 594 participants with schizophrenia assigned to PA interventions, found that PA provision by qualified professionals and continuous supervision of PA were associated with reduced rate of dropouts.

In summarizing the current evidence, PA is beneficial for people with schizophrenia in reducing symptoms in all three clinical domains (positive, negative, and cognitive symptoms), as well as improving CRF. Furthermore, the current evidence also indicates that the benefit of PA is much enhanced if PA interventions are delivered by qualified professionals such as physiotherapists and EPs.

## EXAMPLES OF PA INTERVENTION STUDIES

There have been several large notable clinical trials in this field. In this section, we will briefly outline some of these.

The Achieving Healthy Lifestyles in Psychiatric Rehabilitation (ACHIEVE) trial was an 18-month tailored intervention compromising of 291 overweight or obese participants with serious mental disorder (SMD) with 58% having a diagnosis of schizophrenia (Daumit et al., 2013). The intervention arm of ACHIEVE consisted of individual and group PA, nutritional counseling, and onsite PA sessions. This program was developed around social cognition and behavioral self-management theories, with a particular focus on skills building and environmental support. Group exercise started at a level appropriate for sedentary individuals, with gradual increases in duration and intensity. Trained members of the study staff led exercise classes for the first 6 months. Subsequently, exercise sessions were offered using a video specifically prepared for this trial. After 18 months the mean weight loss for the intervention group was 3.4 kg, compared with 0.3 kg in the control group. Likewise, 37.8% of people in the intervention group lost 5% or more of their initial weight, compared with 22.7% in the control group ($P = .009$).

More recently, the STRIDE trial (Green et al., 2015) consisted of 200 individuals with SMD and an initial BMI of over $27 \, kg/m^2$, with the majority (98%) of participants having a clinical diagnosis of either schizophrenia or affective psychosis/bipolar disorder. The intervention consisted of two phases of 6-month duration. The first 6 months of the intervention consisted of two 1-h group meetings covering topics such as nutrition, PA, and lifestyle changes. Each meeting also included a 20-min PA session. After the initial 6 months, the participants moved on to the maintenance phase for another 6 months. The maintenance phase consisted of monthly group participation and individual monthly contacts from intervention group facilitators. After 12 months, participants in the intervention group lost an average of 2.6 kg ($P = .004$). The intervention group also had a significant decline in the fasting glucose level, while those in the control group did not. Most of the weight loss in the intervention group occurred in the first 6 months (i.e., the active phase), and there was no statistically significant difference between the groups in the maintenance phase.

The In SHAPE study focused more strongly on the effect of PA in reducing weight over other lifestyle interventions (Bartels et al., 2013). This study compared the 12-month In SHAPE fitness program with a control condition which involved free fitness club membership and education. Participants in the intervention group received weekly supervised training session at a gym with a qualified fitness trainer who had received training for providing instructions on the principles of healthy eating and PA, as well as tailoring individual wellness plans to the needs of those with SMD. Among 133 participants with SMD and a BMI of more than $25 \, kg/m^2$, just over 40% of the participants had a diagnosis of schizophrenia. After 12 months, 40% of the intervention group achieved a clinically meaningful improvement in fitness (as defined by an improvement of more than 50 m in the 6-min walk test), compared with 20% in the control group. However, there was no significant difference between the groups in terms of clinically meaningful weight loss (defined as weight loss of more than 5% of the initial weight).

When the same research group later replicated the study at a larger scale ($n = 200$; Bartels et al., 2015), 51% of the participants in the intervention group achieved either clinically meaningful improvement in fitness or weight loss compared with only 38% in the control group. Moreover, the benefit appeared to be sustained 6 months after the completion of study, with 48% of people in intervention group still maintaining the improvement. This study was particularly notable for its pragmatic design which allowed for a more ethnically diverse (46% non-White) and older (mean age 44 years) study sample compared with most other trials.

Outside of the United States, a recent exploratory study with 31 participants in the United Kingdom showed the feasibility of a 10-week individualized PA training program aiming to achieve more than 90 min of moderate-to-vigorous intensity PA each week (Firth et al., 2018). This study had a retention rate of over 80%, and participants were able to engage in on average 107 min of moderate to vigorous intensity PA per week. In addition, significant improvements in both positive and negative symptoms were seen compared with the control group.

## Keeping the Body in Mind

The Keeping the Body in Mind (KBIM) Program run in Australia provides a pragmatic example of how lifestyle interventions with a strong focus on PA can be integrated within a mental health service setting. Beginning with the implementation of routine metabolic screening in a first-episode psychosis service, KBIM evolved over a number of years to incorporate a range of interventions (Curtis et al., 2011). An in-house gym was developed in the community center, with an EP working one-on-one with patients to prescribe and supervise individualized exercise programs. The multidisciplinary KBIM team includes a senior nurse, a dietician, an EP, and a peer-support worker, with medical input from psychiatrists and an endocrinologist. The 12-week program includes individual sessions with members of the KBIM team and the opportunity to participate in weekly sports groups, in addition to access an onsite gym supervised by the EP. The KBIM intervention group ($n = 16$) experienced significantly less weight gain of 1.8 kg compared with the standard care group ($n = 12$) who gained an average of 7.8 kg (Curtis et al., 2016). Furthermore, the KBIM program has been extended to other vulnerable groups such as people with a long history of schizophrenia and is now embedded as routine care within the service for over 550 patients across the KBIM catchment area. The success and continued adoption of the KBIM program indicate the feasibility of incorporating physical health services, including PA intervention, within mental health care. In fact, the weight of the accumulating evidence recently led to one prominent psychiatrist and a leading figure in this field to proclaim that "The greatest current barrier to increasing the life expectancy of persons with serious mental illness is no longer a knowledge gap—it is an implementation gap" (Bartels, 2015).

## FUTURE DIRECTION—SUSTAINABLE IMPLEMENTATION

In spite of the promising results outlined previously, the wider implementation of PA interventions with proven efficacy in research settings may not readily translate to clinical settings (Suetani et al., 2017; Lederman et al., 2017). A recent comprehensive review of the literature identified that most PA intervention studies have shown that benefits demonstrated during the intervention period disappear once the intervention is withdrawn (Gates et al., 2015). Therefore the main challenge for the field is to establish and evaluate programs that are embedded in routine clinical practice that benefit people with schizophrenia in the long term. In other words, we need to find ways for the benefits seen in these 12- or 18-month long clinical trials to be sustained over 12, 18, or more years, for people living with schizophrenia. To achieve this, novel approaches are needed to overcome issues related to cost-effectiveness, accessibility, and time or budget constraints. The use of m-health technologies provides a unique opportunity for continuing motivational support (Firth et al., 2016b). One of the next steps in the development of PA interventions therefore involves examining the potential of telephone, mobile technology, and social media to augment face-to-face interventions and enhance treatment effects beyond the end of the intervention.

Despite the challenges, we are optimistic that the rapidly increasing awareness and evidence base in this field will soon lead to a sustainable clinical change where PA interventions are incorporated into routine management of people with schizophrenia. In turn, we believe that such change will be essential in reducing the differential mortality and morbidity gaps suffered by our patients.

## CONCLUSION

PA interventions have the potential to help reduce the mortality and morbidity gaps suffered by people with schizophrenia. The evidence base for the efficiency of such intervention is accumulating. We believe that it is time to translate the research evidence into effective and sustainable clinical practice.

# References

Arango, C., Garibaldi, G., Marder, S.R., 2013. Pharmacological approaches to treating negative symptoms: a review of clinical trials. Schizophr. Res. 150, 346–352.

Bartels, S.J., Pratt, S.I., Aschbrenner, K.A., Barre, L.K., Jue, K., Wolfe, R.S., Xie, H., Mchugo, G., Santos, M., Williams, G.E., Naslund, J.A., Mueser, K.T., 2013. Clinically significant improved fitness and weight loss among overweight persons with serious mental illness. Psychiatr. Serv. 64, 729–736.

Bartels, S.J., Pratt, S.I., Aschbrenner, K.A., Barre, L.K., Naslund, J.A., Wolfe, R., Xie, H., Mchugo, G.J., Jimenez, D.E., Jue, K., Feldman, J., Bird, B.L., 2015. Pragmatic replication trial of health promotion coaching for obesity in serious mental illness and maintenance of outcomes. Am J Psychiatry 172, 344–352.

Bartels, S.J., 2015. Can behavioral health organizations change health behaviors? The STRIDE study and lifestyle interventions for obesity in serious mental illness. Am J Psychiatry 172, 9–11.

Beards, S., Gayer-Anderson, C., Borges, S., Dewey, M.E., Fisher, H.L., Morgan, C., 2013. Life events and psychosis: a review and meta-analysis. Schizophr. Bull. 39, 740–747.

Cannon, M., Jones, P.B., Murray, R.M., 2002. Obstetric complications and schizophrenia: historical and meta-analytic review. Am J Psychiatry 159, 1080–1092.

Cardno, A.G., Gottesman, I., 2000. Twin studies of schizophrenia: from bow-and-arrow concordances to star wars Mx and functional genomics. Am. J. Med. Genet. 97, 12–17.

Correll, C.U., Robinson, D.G., Schooler, N.R., Brunette, M.F., Mueser, K.T., Rosenheck, R.A., Marcy, P., Addington, J., Estroff, S.E., Robinson, J., Penn, D.L., Azrin, S., Goldstein, A., Severe, J., Heinssen, R., Kane, J.M., 2014. Cardiometabolic risk in patients with first-episode schizophrenia spectrum disorders: baseline results from the RAISE-ETP study. JAMA Psychiatry 71, 1350–1363.

Correll, C.U., Detraux, J., DE Lepeleire, J., DE Hert, M., 2015a. Effects of antipsychotics, antidepressants and mood stabilizers on risk for physical diseases in people with schizophrenia, depression and bipolar disorder. World Psychiatry 14, 119–136.

Correll, C.U., Joffe, B.I., Rosen, L.M., Sullivan, T.B., Joffe, R.T., 2015b. Cardiovascular and cerebrovascular risk factors and events associated with second-generation antipsychotic compared to antidepressant use in a non-elderly adult sample: results from a claims-based inception cohort study. World Psychiatry 14, 56–63.

Craig, C.L., Marshall, A.L., Sjostrom, M., Bauman, A.E., Booth, M.L., Ainsworth, B.E., Pratt, M., Ekelund, U., Yngve, A., Sallis, J.F., Oja, P., 2003. International physical activity questionnaire: 12-country reliability and validity. Med. Sci. Sports Exerc. 35, 1381–1395.

Curtis, J., Henry, C., Watkins, A., Newall, H., Samaras, K., Ward, P.B., 2011. Metabolic abnormalities in an early psychosis service: a retrospective, naturalistic cross-sectional study. Early Interv. Psychiatry 5, 108–114.

Curtis, J., Watkins, A., Rosenbaum, S., Teasdale, S., Kalucy, M., Samaras, K., Ward, P.B., 2016. Evaluating an individualized lifestyle and life skills intervention to prevent antipsychotic-induced weight gain in first-episode psychosis. Early Interv. Psychiatry 10, 267–276.

Daumit, G.L., Dickerson, F.B., Wang, N.Y., Dalcin, A., Jerome, G.J., Anderson, C.A., Young, D.R., Frick, K.D., Yu, A., Gennusa 3rd, J.V., Oefinger, M., Crum, R.M., Charleston, J., Casagrande, S.S., Guallar, E., Goldberg, R.W., Campbell, L.M., Appel, L.J., 2013. A behavioral weight-loss intervention in persons with serious mental illness. N. Engl. J. Med. 368, 1594–1602.

Di Forti, M., Morgan, C., Dazzan, P., Pariante, C., Mondelli, V., Marques, T.R., Handley, R., Luzi, S., Russo, M., Paparelli, A., Butt, A., Stilo, S.A., Wiffen, B., Powell, J., Murray, R.M., 2009. High-potency cannabis and the risk of psychosis. Br. J. Psychiatry 195, 488–491.

Disease, G.B.D., Injury, I., Prevalence, C., 2016. Global, regional, and national incidence, prevalence, and years lived with disability for 310 diseases and injuries, 1990-2015: a systematic analysis for the Global Burden of Disease Study 2015. Lancet 388, 1545–1602.

Docherty, M., Stubbs, B., Gaughran, F., 2016. Strategies to deal with comorbid physical illness in psychosis. Epidemiol. Psychiatr. Sci. 25, 197–204.

Firth, J., Cotter, J., Elliott, R., French, P., Yung, A.R., 2015. A systematic review and meta-analysis of exercise interventions in schizophrenia patients. Psychol. Med. 1–19.

Firth, J., Carney, R., Elliott, R., French, P., Parker, S., Mcintyre, R., Mcphee, J.S., Yung, A.R., 2018. Exercise as an intervention for first-episode psychosis: a feasibility study. Early Interv. Psychiatry 12, 307–315.

Firth, J., Cotter, J., Torous, J., Bucci, S., Firth, J.A., Yung, A.R., 2016b. Mobile phone ownership and endorsement of "mHealth" among people with psychosis: a meta-analysis of cross-sectional studies. Schizophr. Bull. 42, 448–455.

Firth, J., Rosenbaum, S., Stubbs, B., Gorczynski, P., Yung, A.R., Vancampfort, D., 2016c. Motivating factors and barriers towards exercise in severe mental illness: a systematic review and meta-analysis. Psychol. Med. 46, 2869–2881.

Firth, J., Stubbs, B., Rosenbaum, S., Vancampfort, D., Malchow, B., Schuch, F., Elliott, R., Nuechterlein, K.H., Yung, A.R., 2017. Aerobic exercise improves cognitive functioning in people with schizophrenia: a systematic review and meta-analysis. Schizophr. Bull. 43, 546–556.

Foley, D.L., Morley, K.I., 2011. Systematic review of early cardiometabolic outcomes of the first treated episode of psychosis. Arch. Gen. Psychiatry 68, 609–616.

Galletly, C.A., Foley, D.L., Waterreus, A., Watts, G.F., Castle, D.J., Mcgrath, J.J., Mackinnon, A., Morgan, V.A., 2012. Cardiometabolic risk factors in people with psychotic disorders: the second Australian national survey of psychosis. Aust. N.Z. J. Psychiatry 46, 753–761.

Galletly, C., Castle, D., Dark, F., Humberstone, V., Jablensky, A., Killackey, E., Kulkarni, J., Mcgorry, P., Nielssen, O., Tran, N., 2016. Royal Australian and New Zealand College of Psychiatrists clinical practice guidelines for the management of schizophrenia and related disorders. Aust. N.Z. J. Psychiatry 50, 410–472.

Gardner-Sood, P., Lally, J., Smith, S., Atakan, Z., Ismail, K., Greenwood, K.E., Keen, A., O'brien, C., Onagbesan, O., Fung, C., Papanastasiou, E., Eberherd, J., Patel, A., Ohlsen, R., Stahl, D., David, A., Hopkins, D., Murray, R.M., Gaughran, F., Team, I.M., 2015. Cardiovascular risk factors and metabolic syndrome in people with established psychotic illnesses: baseline data from the IMPaCT randomized controlled trial. Psychol. Med. 1–11.

Gates, J., Killackey, E., Phillips, L., Alvarez-Jimenez, M., 2015. Mental health starts with physical health: current status and future directions of non-pharmacological interventions to improve physical health in first-episode psychosis. Lancet Psychiatry 2, 726–742.

Gottesman, I., Laursen, T.M., Bertelsen, A., Mortensen, P.B., 2010. Severe mental disorders in offspring with 2 psychiatrically ill parents. Arch. Gen. Psychiatry. 67, 252–257.

Green, C.A., Yarborough, B.J., Leo, M.C., Yarborough, M.T., Stumbo, S.P., Janoff, S.L., Perrin, N.A., Nichols, G.A., Stevens, V.J., 2015. The STRIDE weight loss and lifestyle intervention for individuals taking antipsychotic medications: a randomized trial. Am. J. Psychiatry. 172, 71–81.

Howes, O.D., Murray, R.M., 2014. Schizophrenia: an integrated sociodevelopmental-cognitive model. Lancet 383, 1677–1687.

Kahn, R.S., Keefe, R.S., 2013. Schizophrenia is a cognitive illness: time for a change in focus. JAMA Psychiatry 70, 1107–1112.

Kahn, R.S., Sommer, I.E., Murray, R.M., Meyer-Lindenberg, A., Weinberger, D.R., Cannon, T.D., O'donovan, M., Correll, C.U., Kane, J.M., Van Os, J., Insel, T.R., 2015. Schizophrenia. Nat. Rev. Dis. Primers 1, 15067.

Kelleher, I., Cannon, M., 2016. Putting psychosis in its place. Am. J. Psychiatry 173, 951–952.

Kirkbride, J.B., Fearon, P., Morgan, C., Dazzan, P., Morgan, K., Tarrant, J., Lloyd, T., Holloway, J., Hutchinson, G., Leff, J.P., Mallett, R.M., Harrison, G.L., Murray, R.M., Jones, P.B., 2006. Heterogeneity in incidence rates of schizophrenia and other psychotic syndromes: findings from the 3-center AeSOP study. Arch. Gen. Psychiatry 63, 250–258.

Kisely, S., Campbell, L.A., Wang, Y., 2009. Treatment of ischaemic heart disease and stroke in individuals with psychosis under universal healthcare. Br. J. Psychiatry 195, 545–550.

Laursen, T.M., 2011. Life expectancy among persons with schizophrenia or bipolar affective disorder. Schizophr. Res. 131, 101–104.

Lawrence, D., Hancock, K.J., Kisely, S., 2013. The gap in life expectancy from preventable physical illness in psychiatric patients in Western Australia: retrospective analysis of population based registers. BMJ 346, f2539.

Lederman, O., Suetani, S., Stanton, R., Chapman, J., Korman, N., Rosenbaum, S., Ward, P.B., Siskind, D., 2017. Embedding exercise interventions as routine mental health care: implementation strategies in residential, inpatient and community settings. Australas. Psychiatry. https://doi.org/10.1177/1039856217711054.

Lee, E.H., Hui, C.L., Chang, W.C., Chan, S.K., Li, Y.K., Lee, J.T., Lin, J.J., Chen, E.Y., 2013. Impact of physical activity on functioning of patients with first-episode psychosis—a 6 months prospective longitudinal study. Schizophr. Res. 150, 538–541.

Leucht, S., Tardy, M., Komossa, K., Heres, S., Kissling, W., Salanti, G., Davis, J.M., 2012. Antipsychotic drugs versus placebo for relapse prevention in schizophrenia: a systematic review and meta-analysis. Lancet 379, 2063–2071.

Leucht, S., Cipriani, A., Spineli, L., Mavridis, D., Orey, D., Richter, F., Samara, M., Barbui, C., Engel, R.R., Geddes, J.R., Kissling, W., Stapf, M.P., Lassig, B., Salanti, G., Davis, J.M., 2013. Comparative efficacy and tolerability of 15 antipsychotic drugs in schizophrenia: a multiple-treatments meta-analysis. Lancet 382, 951–962.

Malaspina, D., Harlap, S., Fennig, S., Heiman, D., Nahon, D., Feldman, D., Susser, E.S., 2001. Advancing paternal age and the risk of schizophrenia. Arch. Gen. Psychiatry 58, 361–367.

Malaspina, D., Walsh-Messinger, J., Gaebel, W., Smith, L.M., Gorun, A., Prudent, V., Antonius, D., Tremeau, F., 2014. Negative symptoms, past and present: a historical perspective and moving to DSM-5. Eur. Neuropsychopharmacol. 24, 710–724.

Mcgorry, P.D., 2015. Early intervention in psychosis: obvious, effective, overdue. J. Nerv. Ment. Dis. 203, 310–318.

Mcgrath, J., Saha, S., Welham, J., EL Saadi, O., Maccauley, C., Chant, D., 2004. A systematic review of the incidence of schizophrenia: the distribution of rates and the influence of sex, urbanicity, migrant status and methodology. BMC Med. 2, 13.

Mcgrath, J., Saha, S., Chant, D., Welham, J., 2008. Schizophrenia: a concise overview of incidence, prevalence, and mortality. Epidemiol. Rev. 30, 67–76.

Mcgrath, J.J., Eyles, D.W., Pedersen, C.B., Anderson, C., Ko, P., Burne, T.H., Norgaard-Pedersen, B., Hougaard, D.M., Mortensen, P.B., 2010. Neonatal vitamin D status and risk of schizophrenia: a population-based case-control study. Arch. Gen. Psychiatry 67, 889–894.

Mcgrath, J.J., Saha, S., AL-Hamzawi, A., Alonso, J., Bromet, E.J., Bruffaerts, R., Caldas-de-Almeida, J.M., Chiu, W.T., De Jonge, P., Fayyad, J., Florescu, S., Gureje, O., Haro, J.M., Hu, C., Kovess-Masfety, V., Lepine, J.P., Lim, C.C., Mora, M.E., Navarro-Mateu, F., Ochoa, S., Sampson, N., Scott, K., Viana, M.C., Kessler, R.C., 2015. Psychotic experiences in the general population: a cross-national analysis based on 31,261 respondents from 18 countries. JAMA Psychiatry 72, 697–705.

Mcgrath, J.J., 2015. A Rosetta stone for epidemiology: genomic risk profile scores contain clues related to modifiable risk factors. Epidemiol. Psychiatr. Sci. 24, 1–5.

Mitchell, A.J., Malone, D., Doebbeling, C.C., 2009. Quality of medical care for people with and without comorbid mental illness and substance misuse: systematic review of comparative studies. Br. J. Psychiatry 194, 491−499.

Mitchell, A.J., Delaffon, V., Vancampfort, D., Correll, C.U., De Hert, M., 2012. Guideline concordant monitoring of metabolic risk in people treated with antipsychotic medication: systematic review and meta-analysis of screening practices. Psychol. Med. 42, 125−147.

Moore, S., Shiers, D., Daly, B., Mitchell, A.J., Gaughran, F., 2015. Promoting physical health for people with schizophrenia by reducing disparities in medical and dental care. Acta Psychiatr. Scand. 132, 109−121.

Morgan, V.A., Waterreus, A., Jablensky, A., Mackinnon, A., Mcgrath, J.J., Carr, V., Bush, R., Castle, D., Cohen, M., Harvey, C., Galletly, C., Stain, H.J., Neil, A.L., Mcgorry, P., Hocking, B., Shah, S., Saw, S., 2012. People living with psychotic illness in 2010: the second Australian national survey of psychosis. Aust. N.Z. J. Psychiatry 46, 735−752.

Olfson, M., Gerhard, T., Huang, C., Crystal, S., Stroup, T.S., 2015. Premature mortality among adults with schizophrenia in the United States. JAMA Psychiatry 1−10.

Penttila, M., Jaaskelainen, E., Hirvonen, N., Isohanni, M., Miettunen, J., 2014. Duration of untreated psychosis as predictor of long-term outcome in schizophrenia: systematic review and meta-analysis. Br. J. Psychiatry 205, 88−94.

Rabinowitz, J., Levine, S.Z., Garibaldi, G., Bugarski-Kirola, D., Berardo, C.G., Kapur, S., 2012. Negative symptoms have greater impact on functioning than positive symptoms in schizophrenia: analysis of CATIE data. Schizophr. Res. 137, 147−150.

Reichenberg, A., Caspi, A., Harrington, H., Houts, R., Keefe, R.S., Murray, R.M., Poulton, R., Moffitt, T.E., 2010. Static and dynamic cognitive deficits in childhood preceding adult schizophrenia: a 30-year study. Am. J. Psychiatry 167, 160−169.

Rosenbaum, S., Tiedemann, A., Stanton, R., Parker, A., Waterreus, A., Curtis, J., Ward, P.B., 2016. Implementing evidence-based physical activity interventions for people with mental illness: an Australian perspective. Australas. Psychiatry 24, 49−54.

Saha, S., Chant, D., Welham, J., Mcgrath, J., 2005. A systematic review of the prevalence of schizophrenia. PLoS Med. 2, e141.

Saha, S., Chant, D., Mcgrath, J., 2007. A systematic review of mortality in schizophrenia: is the differential mortality gap worsening over time? Arch. Gen. Psychiatry 64, 1123−1131.

Schizophrenia Working Group of The Psychiatric Genomics Consortium, 2014. Biological insights from 108 schizophrenia-associated genetic loci. Nature 511, 421−427.

Stafford, M.R., Jackson, H., Mazyo-Wilson, E., Morrison, A.P., Kendall, T., 2013. Early interventions to prevent psychosis: systematic review and meta-analysis. BMJ 346, f185.

Stilo, S.A., Murray, R.M., 2010. The epidemiology of schizophrenia: replacing dogma with knowledge. Dialogues Clin. Neurosci. 12, 305−315.

Stilo, S.A., Gayer-Anderson, C., Beards, S., Hubbard, K., Onyejiaka, A., Keraite, A., Borges, S., Mondelli, V., Dazzan, P., Pariante, C., DI Forti, M., Murray, R.M., Morgan, C., 2016. Further evidence of a cumulative effect of social disadvantage on risk of psychosis. Psychol. Med. 1−12.

Stubbs, B., Firth, J., Berry, A., Schuch, F.B., Rosenbaum, S., Gaughran, F., Veronesse, N., Williams, J., Craig, T., Yung, A.R., Vancampfort, D., 2016a. How much physical activity do people with schizophrenia engage in? A systematic review, comparative meta-analysis and meta-regression. Schizophr. Res. 176, 431−440.

Stubbs, B., Williams, J., Gaughran, F., Craig, T., 2016b. How sedentary are people with psychosis? A systematic review and meta-analysis. Schizophr. Res. 171, 103−109.

Stubbs, B., Chen, L.J., Chung, M.S., Ku, P.W., 2017a. Physical activity ameliorates the association between sedentary behavior and cardiometabolic risk among inpatients with schizophrenia: a comparison versus controls using accelerometry. Compr. Psychiatry 74, 144−150.

Stubbs, B., Vancampfort, D., Firth, J., Hallgren, M., Schuch, F., Veronese, N., Solmi, M., Gaughran, F., Kahl, K.G., Rosenbaum, S., Ward, P.B., Carvalho, A.F., Koyanagi, A., 2018. Physical activity correlates among people with psychosis: data from 47 low- and middle-income countries. Schizophr. Res. 193, 412–417.

Suetani, S., Whiteford, H.A., Mcgrath, J.J., 2015. An urgent Call to address the deadly consequences of serious mental disorders. JAMA Psychiatry 72, 1166–1167.

Suetani, S., Rosenbaum, S., Scott, J.G., Curtis, J., Ward, P.B., 2016a. Bridging the gap: what have we done and what more can we do to reduce the burden of avoidable death in people with psychotic illness? Epidemiol. Psychiatr. Sci. 25, 205–210.

Suetani, S., Waterreus, A., Morgan, V., Foley, D.L., Galletly, C., Badcock, J.C., Watts, G., Mckinnon, A., Castle, D., Saha, S., Scott, J.G., Mcgrath, J.J., 2016b. Correlates of physical activity in people living with psychotic illness. Acta Psychiatr. Scand. 134, 129–137.

Suetani, S., Scott, J.G., Mcgrath, J.J., 2017. The importance of the physical health needs of people with psychotic disorders. Aust. N.Z. J. Psychiatry 94–95.

Tiihonen, J., Lonnqvist, J., Wahlbeck, K., Klaukka, T., Niskanen, L., Tanskanen, A., Haukka, J., 2009. 11-year follow-up of mortality in patients with schizophrenia: a population-based cohort study (FIN11 study). Lancet 374, 620–627.

Tiihonen, J., Mittendorfer-Rutz, E., Torniainen, M., Alexanderson, K., Tanskanen, A., 2016. Mortality and cumulative exposure to antipsychotics, antidepressants, and benzodiazepines in patients with schizophrenia: an observational follow-up study. Am. J. Psychiatry 173, 600–606.

Van Os, J., Kapur, S., 2009. Schizophrenia. Lancet 374, 635–645.

Van Os, J., Reininghaus, U., Meyer-Lindenberg, A., 2017. The search for environmental mechanisms underlying the expression of psychosis: introduction. Schizophr. Bull. 283–286.

Vancampfort, D., Knapen, J., Probst, M., Van Winkel, R., Deckx, S., Maurissen, K., Peuskens, J., DE Hert, M., 2010. Considering a frame of reference for physical activity research related to the cardiometabolic risk profile in schizophrenia. Psychiatry Res. 177, 271–279.

Vancampfort, D., Knapen, J., Probst, M., Scheewe, T., Remans, S., De Hert, M., 2012. A systematic review of correlates of physical activity in patients with schizophrenia. Acta Psychiatr. Scand. 125, 352–362.

Vancampfort, D., Wampers, M., Mitchell, A.J., Correll, C.U., De Herdt, A., Probst, M., De Hert, M., 2013. A meta-analysis of cardio-metabolic abnormalities in drug naive, first-episode and multi-episode patients with schizophrenia versus general population controls. World Psychiatry 12, 240–250.

Vancampfort, D., Guelinkcx, H., Probst, M., Stubbs, B., Rosenbaum, S., Ward, P.B., De Hert, M., 2015a. Associations between metabolic and aerobic fitness parameters in patients with schizophrenia. J. Nerv. Ment. Dis. 203, 23–27.

Vancampfort, D., Rosenbaum, S., Probst, M., Soundy, A., Mitchell, A.J., DE Hert, M., Stubbs, B., 2015b. Promotion of cardiorespiratory fitness in schizophrenia: a clinical overview and meta-analysis. Acta Psychiatr. Scand. 132, 131–143.

Vancampfort, D., Rosenbaum, S., Ward, P.B., Stubbs, B., 2015c. Exercise improves cardiorespiratory fitness in people with schizophrenia: a systematic review and meta-analysis. Schizophr. Res. 169, 453–457.

Vancampfort, D., Rosenbaum, S., Schuch, F.B., Ward, P.B., Probst, M., Stubbs, B., 2016. Prevalence and predictors of treatment dropout from physical activity interventions in schizophrenia: a meta-analysis. Gen. Hosp. Psychiatry 39, 15–23.

Vancampfort, D., Rosenbaum, S., Schuch, F., Ward, P.B., Richards, J., Mugisha, J., Probst, M., Stubbs, B., 2017. Cardiorespiratory fitness in severe mental illness: a systematic review and meta-analysis. Sports Med. 47, 343–352.

Varese, F., Smeets, F., Drukker, M., Lieverse, R., Lataster, T., Viechtbauer, W., Read, J., Van Os, J., Bentall, R.P., 2012. Childhood adversities increase the risk of psychosis: a meta-analysis of patient-control, prospective- and cross-sectional cohort studies. Schizophr. Bull. 38, 661—671.

Walker, E.R., Mcgee, R.E., Druss, B.G., 2015. Mortality in mental disorders and global disease burden implications: a systematic review and meta-analysis. JAMA Psychiatry 72, 334—341.

Whiteford, H.A., Degenhardt, L., Rehm, J., Baxter, A.J., Ferrari, A.J., Erskine, H.E., Charlson, F.J., Norman, R.E., Flaxman, A.D., Johns, N., Burstein, R., Murray, C.J., Vos, T., 2013. Global burden of disease attributable to mental and substance use disorders: findings from the Global Burden of Disease Study 2010. Lancet 382, 1575—1586.

Yung, A.R., Phillips, L.J., Yuen, H.P., Mcgorry, P.D., 2004. Risk factors for psychosis in an ultra high-risk group: psychopathology and clinical features. Schizophr. Res. 67, 131—142.

Zipursky, R.B., Reilly, T.J., Murray, R.M., 2013. The myth of schizophrenia as a progressive brain disease. Schizophr. Bull. 39, 1363—1372.

# Exercise for Alcohol Use Disorders

## Mats Hallgren

Department of Public Health Sciences, Karolinska Institute, Stockholm, Sweden

*Exercise-Based Interventions for Mental Illness*
https://doi.org/10.1016/B978-0-12-812605-9.00005-8

83

# ALCOHOL USE DISORDERS: DEFINITION, PREVALENCE, AND SOCIETAL IMPACT

Problem drinking that becomes severe is often given the medical diagnosis of alcohol use disorder, or AUD. Key features of the disorder include an inability to control the amount of alcohol consumed, consumption that results in social or work-related problems, and tolerance or the need to drink increasing amounts of alcohol to obtain a desired effect (NIAAA, 2017). Both environmental and psychosocial factors play a role in the complex etiology of alcohol dependence. Genetic influences have been shown to play a major role in determining the risk of alcohol dependence, where heritability is estimated between 50% and 80% (Knopik et al., 2004). This means that at least half of the risk for developing an AUD is attributable to potentially modifiable environmental factors, including lifestyle habits. This is also relevant because available evidence suggests that many people with an AUD are insufficiently active (Smothers and Bertolucci, 2001) and have an impaired cardiorespiratory fitness (Herbsleb et al., 2013).

In 2013, the American Psychiatric Association issued the fifth edition of the *Diagnostic and Statistical Manual of Mental Disorders* (DSM-5), which sets out the criteria for diagnosing an AUD. Although there is considerable overlap between DSM-5 and its predecessor (DSM-IV), there are also notable differences. For alcohol problems, the DSM-IV described two distinct disorders—alcohol abuse and alcohol dependence, with specific criteria for each. The DSM-5 now integrates these into a single disorder (AUD). A previous criterion concerning legal problems (an abuse symptom) was removed and another criterion—craving—was added (the terms craving and "urge" to drink are often used interchangeably in the alcohol literature but have the same meaning). The diagnostic threshold was set to two or more symptoms out of 11, and a severity scale was introduced, where $0-1 =$ no disorder, $2-3 =$ mild, $4-5 =$ moderate, and $6+ =$ severe disorder. Emerging studies suggest that these diagnostic changes have resulted in a slightly higher estimated prevalence of AUDs in some countries (Lundin et al., 2015; Grant et al., 2015).

Public perceptions of "alcoholism" have fostered a general belief that AUDs are rare and linked to homelessness or poverty. However, this perception is not accurate—AUDs are actually among the most common of all psychiatric disorders. Data from the 2012−13 National Epidemiologic Survey on Alcohol and Related Conditions in the United States show that the 12-month and lifetime prevalence of AUD were 13.9% and 29.1%, respectively (Grant et al., 2015), making it comparable with other major health problems such as depression and diabetes (WHO, 2004). The 12-month prevalence was highest for men (17.6%) and younger adults aged 18–29 years (26.7%). Also relevant is that around 75% of those diagnosed with an AUD experience a mild-to-moderate level of the disorder, with a much smaller proportion having severe problems (Grant et al., 2015; Andreasson et al., 2013a). A Swedish study found that the majority of people who met the DSM-IV criteria for alcohol dependence did not drink at the highest consumption levels, were not living alone, and were not unemployed (Andreasson et al., 2013a). Most of those surveyed had few diagnostic criteria fulfilled (3 or 4) and few social problems. Thus rather than living in poverty, a more accurate profile of a "typical" alcohol-dependent person is someone who is employed and living in stable accommodation, but who drinks to excess and is to some extent adversely affected by their drinking behavior. This larger majority with "moderate" alcohol dependence is also an undertreated group that is less inclined to seek professional help. The individuals ultimately treated in specialist clinics tend to have more severe drinking problems and reach out for help as a last resort.

This description should not diminish the very substantial impact that AUDs have on the individual affected and those around them. The societal consequences of hazardous drinking include accidents, violence, and antisocial behaviors, and the estimated annual cost of excessive alcohol consumption in the United States is around US$223 billion (CDCP, 2016). The harm to others caused by AUDs is substantial (Navarro et al., 2011). A New Zealand study found that the prevalence of self-reported harm from others' drinking was around 18% in the past year and was higher in women and young people (Connor and Casswell, 2012). The most common sources of harm were aggression and crime and unintentional injury due to traffic accidents. Police records indicate that up to 50% of criminal offenses involve someone who has been drinking, and alcohol involvement increases with the seriousness of an offense (Connor and Casswell, 2012). These societal harms accrue from the drinking behavior of people with *and without* diagnosed AUDs. Indeed, on a population basis, the greatest overall harm caused by alcohol arises not from the minority of people who drink to excess but rather from the larger majority who drink at light to moderate levels—a situation referred to as the alcohol prevention paradox (Danielsson et al., 2012). Consequently, greater societal gain will be achieved by reducing consumption within a far larger group of "risky" drinkers with less serious problems than by trying to reduce consumption among a smaller number of severely dependent drinkers. In the present context, the alcohol prevention paradox is a reminder of the need to direct resources not only toward reducing severe alcohol dependence but also to those with milder forms of the disorder or with emerging alcohol dependency.

# HELP-SEEKING IS POOR AND TREATMENT RESPONSE LIMITED

The personal and societal impact of AUDs are immense, yet most people with the disorder never seek or receive treatment (Cunningham and Breslin, 2004; Kuramoto et al., 2011). A 2010 survey conducted in the United Kingdom found that only 1 of 18 people who met the criteria for alcohol dependence had received formal treatment (NHS, 2010). Similarly a Swedish study found that only 20% of recovered alcohol-dependent patients had received treatment (Blomqvist et al., 2007). This apparent reluctance to seek professional help is problematic as treatment greatly increases the rate of recovery from AUDs (Cohen et al., 2007).

One possible explanation for poor help-seeking is the stigma attached to alcohol and other substance use disorders. Compared with other mental illnesses, AUDs are particularly stigmatized, and this reduces the likelihood of seeking treatment because people fear being labeled "alcoholics," thereby losing status and facing discrimination (Andreasson et al., 2013b). Another issue concerns the range of treatment options available. Current treatments for AUDs include cognitive behavioral therapy (CBT) interventions, motivational interviewing, 12-step facilitation treatment, and pharmacological therapy (Berglund et al., 2003). While these interventions are effective for many people (Vasilaki et al., 2006), they may not appeal to—or be suitable for—all treatment seekers, especially those presenting with milder forms of alcohol dependence. Premature termination of treatment and nonadherence are factors consistently associated with worse outcomes, yet both are common problems in alcohol treatment regimes. A meta-analysis of alcohol treatment outcome studies found that average short-term abstinence rates were 21% for untreated individuals, compared with 43% for treated individuals, suggesting that current therapies are more effective than no treatment, but there is considerable opportunity for improvement (Monahan and Finney, 1996; Moyer and Finney, 2002). An Australian study involving 618 participants in a 12-step residential treatment program for alcohol and drugs reported a 57% dropout rate at 3 months (Deane et al., 2012). These statistics suggest that alternative treatment options are currently needed.

For the majority of people presenting with "mild to moderate" AUDs (i.e., between 2 and 5 DSM-V criteria fulfilled), lifestyle-oriented interventions such as physical activity may be viewed as less stigmatizing and more appealing than conventional treatments. Recent studies show that people with AUDs are interested and willing to engage in physical activity interventions (Giesen et al., 2015). In a large study based on case vignettes, the general public was found to be reluctant to endorse biologically focused treatments for substance abuse more than nonmedical treatment (Kuppin and Carpiano, 2008), which speaks to the acceptability of physical activity interventions. Similarly, in a US survey, respondents indicated a preference for informal help for milder substance use problems. The authors concluded that consumer dissatisfaction with existing treatment alternatives, rather than lack of availability per se, impedes service utilization. We suggest that broadening the array of effective, nonstigmatizing treatment options for AUDs could increase help-seeking and potentially reduce treatment nonadherence and drop out. When used as adjunct treatment, physical activity interventions might also facilitate engagement in traditional AUD interventions.

## COMORBID HEALTH PROBLEMS ARE COMMON IN AUDs

People with AUDs experience an excess mortality rate two times higher than those without AUDs (Roerecke and Rehm, 2013). Compared with the general population, those with AUDs in treatment have a more than 10-fold risk of mortality from liver cirrhosis, a sevenfold risk for injury fatalities and a twofold risk for cardiovascular and cancer deaths (Roerecke and Rehm, 2014). A 2016 meta-analysis found that the pooled prevalence for diabetes mellitus type 2 among 3998 people with AUDs was 12.4% (Vancampfort et al., 2016b). This compares to a projected (increasing) worldwide prevalence in 2030 of 7.7% among adults aged 20–79 years (Chen et al., 2012). A trend for higher prevalence was found in inpatient settings and with studies including patients with a higher percentage of physical comorbidity. Putting these figures in context, the pooled prevalence is similar to that observed in people with severe mental illness (psychosis) who are considered a "high-risk" group (Vancampfort et al., 2016b). Type II diabetes mellitus is a major risk factor for cardiovascular diseases; it confers about a twofold excess risk for coronary heart disease, major stroke subtypes, and deaths attributed to other vascular causes (Collaboration et al., 2010).

Also relevant is the finding that AUDs are associated with a high prevalence of the metabolic syndrome (MetS)—a cluster of risk factors including central obesity, high blood pressure, low high-density lipoprotein cholesterol, elevated triglycerides, and hyperglycemia. In the general population, these clustered risk factors have been associated with the development of cardiovascular disease and excess mortality (Mottillo et al., 2010). A 2016 systematic review and meta-analysis found that the pooled prevalence of MetS in AUDs after adjusting for publication bias was 21.8% (Vancampfort et al., 2016a). In the same study, abdominal obesity was observed in 38.3% of survey participants, hyperglycemia in

14.3%, and hypertension in 46.5%, highlighting the poor health status of many people with AUDs. Although the authors did not compare these rates with age- and gender-matched control participants, related studies suggest that the prevalence of MetS in AUDs is substantially higher than in healthy controls (Aneja et al., 2013; Kahl et al., 2010). Furthermore, a higher frequency of MetS was moderated by a higher percentage of psychiatric comorbidity (Vancampfort et al., 2016a), highlighting the connection between physical and mental health—a theme that appears throughout this book. Indeed, chronic health problems such as diabetes and MetS are associated with a higher prevalence of depression and anxiety, which in turn have been shown to increase the risk of relapse in people recovering from alcohol dependence (Brown et al., 1995). Of importance, regular exercise has been shown to significantly reduce the risk of developing cardiovascular disease and diabetes and is frequently prescribed for the management of these disorders (Voulgari et al., 2013). Treatments for substance abuse that are "wholistic" and benefit-related health problems are generally more effective than those targeting only one symptom. Physical activity is known to benefit mental and physical health synergistically (Penedo and Dahn, 2005) and maybe especially effective in the treatment of AUDs where multimorbidity—the presence of two or more health problems—is common.

## Psychiatric Comorbidity and Cognitive Deficits

In addition to physical health problems, mood disorders frequently coexist with AUDs. This is relevant because depression has been linked to the etiology of alcohol dependence (Boden and Fergusson, 2011). A 2015 epidemiological survey reported that the lifetime odds of having any mood disorder was 1.5 times higher in people with an AUD compared with the general population (Grant et al., 2015). Other US data show that in major depression, the lifetime prevalence rate is 40.3% for any AUD, and 21% for alcohol dependence (Kessler and Walters, 1998; Hasin et al., 2005). The "stress-vulnerability" model offers insights into the circular pathway between mood disorders and alcohol dependence (Brown et al., 1995). In essence, the model posits that exposure to stressful life events leads to lowered mood states and/or anxiety, which in turn increases the likelihood of drinking behavior as a coping mechanism in those vulnerable to alcohol problems (Keyes et al., 2011). Stressful events such as divorce and job loss have been shown to increase the risk of alcohol disorders in the general population, but epidemiologic consensus on the specificity of these associations across gender has not been reached.

It has also been suggested that alcohol exposure may cause metabolic changes which act to increase the risk of mood disorders. For example, McEachin et al. (2008) found that exposure to ethanol led to reductions in the production of methylenetetrahydrofolate reductase (MTHFR), an enzyme related to folate metabolism. Reduced folate levels have, in turn, been linked to increased risks of major depression, suggesting a possible causal link between alcohol dependence and major depression via reduced MTHFR production. Other researchers found that individuals with a particular genotype related to circadian rhythms were at greater risk of co-occurring alcohol and mood disorders (Sjoholm et al., 2010). The authors suggested that alcohol use alters circadian rhythms and metabolic patterns in individuals with this particular genotype, leading to an increased risk of depression.

AUDs are also associated with a range of cognitive deficits. Given acutely, alcohol is known to impair memory and attention and may increase disinhibition (Kallmen and Gustafson, 1998). In alcohol dependence, many cognitive functions are impaired including working memory, speed of processing, visuospatial abilities, executive functions, learning, and verbal fluency (Pitel et al., 2009). In the most severe cases, alcohol dependence may also produce dementia-like symptoms. Indeed, the influence of alcohol on the development of dementia is substantiated by evidence showing that up to 29% of dementia cases are alcohol related (Saxton et al., 2000). A recent meta-analysis examining cognition in alcohol abuse/dependence ($n = 62$ studies) found significant impairments across multiple cognitive functions, and these remained stable during the first year of abstinence from alcohol (Stavro et al., 2013). The mechanisms linking alcohol use with cognitive impairment are not fully understood. One hypothesis suggests that the prefrontal cortex is particularly vulnerable to the effect of alcohol—an idea supported by neuroimaging studies showing decreased metabolic rates in prefrontal regions in correlation with executive function deficits (Dao-Castellana et al., 1998). Another model suggests that long-term heavy drinking leads to a mild generalized dysfunction of the brain, resulting in a variable pattern of impairment (Parsons, 1994). Later in this chapter (see Mechanisms of Action: Mood States, Inflammation, and Cognition), evidence is presented showing that regular exercise can help maintain cognitive functioning and may also play a role in reducing the cognitive deficits and attentional biases that are often found in AUDs.

# CURRENT TREATMENT OPTIONS FOR AUDs

Treatments for AUDs have expanded greatly over the last 30 years and now include supportive counseling for individuals, groups and couples, psychosocial and behavioral therapy, and pharmacotherapy. A comprehensive review of all the available treatment options is beyond the scope of this chapter; however, it is important to outline the main treatments used today and briefly comment on their effectiveness. Interested readers can find detailed information in the article by Friedmann (2013), Alcohol Use in Adults, published in *The New England Journal of Medicine* (Friedmann, 2013), or through the National Institute for Alcoholism and Alcohol Abuse Website: www.niaaa.nih.gov.

*Motivational enhancement therapy* (MET) aims to generate rapid, internally motivated change in people with alcohol problems and is based on the principles of motivational interviewing. MET is goal oriented and attempts to directly influence behavior change. Treatment is generally divided into three phases: (1) building up motivation for change (in alcohol use), (2) strengthening the determination to change, and (3) strategies for the implementation of change. Studies suggest that MET is an effective treatment for mild to moderate AUD and may increase the number of days spent abstinent from alcohol (Sellman et al., 2001; Dieperink et al., 2014). MET is sometimes used in conjunction with CBT, which is an effective treatment for anxiety and depression in people with substance use disorders (Pasupuleti et al., 2017).

The *community reinforcement approach* (CRA)—also used in conjunction with family training (CRAFT) —is a behavioral therapy approach for treating addiction. Operant conditioning is used to help those with AUDs learn how to reduce the influence of alcohol on their behavior. CRAFT also aims to equip family members and friends with supportive techniques that encourage the alcohol-dependent person to begin and continue treatment and provides support to relatives and carers. A review of CRA studies found that it was more effective than usual care in reducing the number of drinking days, but there was conflicting evidence for its effect on continuous abstinence (Roozen et al., 2004).

*Twelve-step facilitation treatment* (TSF) is a set of guiding principles for recovery from addictive behaviors, including AUDs. Treatment is based on the notion that dependence is a disease and behavior change is facilitated through mutual help groups. One review involving eight trials and 3417 unique participants concluded that no experimental studies unequivocally demonstrate the effectiveness of TSF approaches for reducing alcohol dependence or problems (Ferri et al., 2006). However, other studies show that patients who receive TSF have higher rates of continuous abstinence than those receiving other behavioral therapies (Tonigan et al., 2003). Despite developments in behavioral therapies, mutual help groups that incorporate TSF, such as Alcoholics Anonymous, remain the most commonly sought after treatment for AUDs in the United States.

*Pharmacotherapy* for AUDs includes the prescription medicines disulfiram, naltrexone, and acamprosate, which aim to reduce alcohol craving and use. Medications marketed for other illnesses have also shown efficacy in treating AUDs, such as topiramate for epilepsy and migraines. Researchers are also studying medicines approved for smoking cessation for their impact on heavy drinking (Chatterjee et al., 2010). Positive results are generally found when medications are combined with behavioral treatment (NIAAA, 2017). Maintaining contact with patients and emphasizing adherence are key to successful treatment with medications.

## Brief Interventions and Internet-Based Support

Evidence suggests that brief psychological and behavioral interventions for people with risky drinking habits can be administered effectively via primary health care settings (Kaner et al., 2009) and through the Internet (Gupta et al., 2016). The latter mode of treatment may be especially suitable for people living in remote areas where access to conventional treatment is impractical or for those who prefer the anonymity of Internet-based support.

In sum, effective treatments for AUDs do exist. However, across all interventions, *maintenance* of treatment response remains limited with many individuals returning to the dependence syndrome following a period of abstinence. Estimated rates of relapse vary widely based on length of follow-up and the definition of relapse used (i.e., complete abstinence vs. reduction in heavy drinking), but typically fall between 40% and 60% within the first few months of treatment and are reportedly as high as 70%–80% by the end of the first year (McKay et al., 2006; Walitzer and Dearing, 2006). As noted previously, another significant issue is that help-seeking for AUDs is particularly low (around 20%), suggesting that current treatment options are not appealing to many people. What is now required are novel treatment strategies that are effective, nonstigmatizing, easily accessible, and which appeal to a broad spectrum of people with established and emerging alcohol use problems. In particular, treatments that are effective in ameliorating the physical and psychiatric comorbidities associated with AUDs are highly desirable, and physical activity is a key ingredient in this strategy. Regular exercise has extensive beneficial effects on physical health and psychological well-being. Meta-analytic reviews have supported the antidepressant effects of exercise among otherwise healthy adults (Conn, 2010), chronically ill patients (Herring et al., 2012), and patients with depressive disorders (Cooney et al., 2013a). Three recent Cochrane reviews have each concluded that exercise is moderately more effective than a control intervention for reducing depression symptoms (Cooney et al., 2013b; Mead et al., 2008; Rimer et al., 2012) and updated reviews suggest even stronger treatment effects after adjusting for publication bias (Schuch et al., 2016a). High levels of cardiovascular and metabolic disease contribute to multimorbidity and premature mortality in people with AUDs, especially among those with severe, long-term drinking problems. Of importance, it has been shown that people who are physically active and maintain their cardiorespiratory fitness across the lifespan have a reduced risk of experiencing a depressive episode, in addition to other detrimental health outcomes, such as cardiovascular disease and diabetes (Warburton et al., 2006). These benefits are unlikely to be achieved through pharmacological or psychological interventions alone.

## EVIDENCE OF THE BENEFITS OF EXERCISE FROM INTERVENTION STUDIES

Evidence supporting the use of exercise to treat substance use disorders is growing (Linke and Ussher, 2015). To date, most research has focused on smoking cessation (Ussher et al., 2014). Acute bouts of exercise can reduce the desire to smoke and lower tobacco withdrawal symptoms, while also improving mood and lowering anxiety, both of which are potential triggers for smoking relapse (Van Rensburg et al., 2009; Taylor et al., 2007; Ussher et al., 2001). A review of 17 randomized controlled trials (RCTs) exploring the effects of long-term exercise interventions found that regular exercise generally improved one or more smoking-related outcomes, and abstinence rates were comparable to CBT and/or nicotine replacement therapy (Zschucke et al., 2012). However, a subsequent review of 20 trials ($n = 5870$ participants) found that only two studies presented sufficient evidence for exercise aiding smoking cessation in the long term (Ussher et al., 2014). One explanation for this discrepancy is the criteria used to assess the evidence, where the latter Cochrane review adopted a narrower (stricter) inclusion criteria. For example, studies measuring a reduction in smoking, rather than abstinence, were summarizes but not formally included. The conclusion to be drawn is that exercise appears to benefit smoking cessation in the short-term, but evidence of long-term effectiveness is still lacking. The absence of such evidence may partly be attributable to the fact that very few trials have measured long-term outcomes.

Despite these limitations, evidence from smoking studies provides theoretical support for using exercise to treat AUDs. Both nicotine and alcohol are addictive substances with related underlying etiologies. It is also known that smoking and heavy drinking frequently co-exist. However, in the case of AUDs empirical evidence is currently limited to a small number of trials, none of which have assessed the long-term effects of exercise on alcohol consumption. In the first study to examine the acute effects of exercise on alcohol urges, Ussher et al. (2004) randomized 20 recently "detoxified" alcohol-dependent patients (mean age = 40 years) to 10 min of very light aerobic exercise (control), and 10 min of moderately intense (40%–60% of heart rate reserve) aerobic exercise (experimental condition). Changes in the urge to drink were assessed before, during, and after exercise. Relative to baseline, there was a significant decline in alcohol urges for the experimental condition during but not after the exercise session (Ussher et al., 2004), suggesting that moderate-to-vigorous physical activity may be needed to lower the urge to drink alcohol. Another study repeatedly examined the acute effects of moderate exercise on mood, anxiety, and alcohol cravings over a 12-week period in sedentary alcohol-dependent adults ($n = 26$; Brown et al., 2016). Improvements in mood and reductions in anxiety and craving were observed at every pre- to post-exercise session. The authors concluded that acute bouts of moderate-intensity exercise may help individuals with alcohol dependence manage mood and craving, thereby reducing relapse risk (Brown et al., 2016). These short-term studies build on an extensive literature demonstrating the mood enhancing effects of acute exercise in nonclinical populations (Ekkekakis et al., 2008). While these investigations are important, controlled trials provide additional information about long-term treatment effects and are needed to inform clinical decision-making.

The idea of using exercise to treat alcohol misuse is certainly not new. A 2017 meta-analysis described 21 studies published between 1971 and 2016 (Hallgren et al., 2017). In one of the first published studies, Gary and Guthrie (1972) randomized 20 residential inpatients with AUD to either usual treatment, consisting of group therapy and medication, or a 4-week aerobic (running) exercise program 5 days per week. Compared with standard care, the exercise group had larger improvements in fitness indicators (e.g., basal heart rate), self-concept, and sleep disturbance, but no differences in alcohol consumption between groups we found (Gary and Guthrie, 1972). In another early investigation, Sinyor et al. (1982b) explored the effect of a 6-week exercise regime on alcohol use among 58 inpatients receiving treatment at an inpatient rehabilitation center. The intervention included a choice of running, calisthenics, strength training, or cross-country skiing performed for 1 h five times/week at a moderate intensity. A control group received "standard care for alcohol dependence." At 3-month follow-up, the exercise group had significantly higher alcohol abstinence rates compared with the control group and measurable fitness gains. However, participants were not randomized to these treatments, so the positive outcomes could be attributable to factors unrelated to exercise (Sinyor et al., 1982a).

More recently, Brown et al. (2016) randomized 49 alcohol-dependent, sedentary patients to a 12-week moderate-intensity group aerobic exercise intervention or a "brief advice to exercise" intervention. Patients in the active exercise condition reported significantly fewer drinking and heavy drinking days compared with the advice condition. Moreover, adherence to exercise strengthened the beneficial effect of the intervention on alcohol use outcomes. This preliminary study indicated that group aerobic exercise can be an efficacious treatment for alcohol dependence. Some limitations were noted, including the absence of a usual care group, and there was no long-term follow-up. In another 2016 study, Giesen et al. (2016) examined the feasibility of a 1-year moderate to vigorous aerobic exercise program for patients with severe alcohol dependence ($n = 44$) in a long-term residential care setting. The program consisted of three components: (1) aerobic exercise (indoor and aqua cycling), (2) functional training (strengthening, coordination, and flexibility exercises), and (3) experience-orientated group events (e.g., bicycle tours, canoeing, or other day trips). All participants were encouraged to exercise at least twice per week. Changes in drinking behavior were not reported, but this long-term study showed that exercise is a safe and feasible intervention for people with severe alcohol dependence. Compared with baseline, participants reported improvements in life quality and engaged in significantly higher physical activity levels (Giesen et al., 2016).

The optimal dose and type of exercise needed to treat AUDs are currently unclear. Most studies have reported the effects of aerobic exercise on substance misuse; however, at least two studies have examined yoga as an adjunct treatment for alcohol dependence. Hallgren et al. (2014) randomized 18 alcohol-dependent outpatients to receive either treatment as usual (counseling and/or medication) or treatment as usual plus yoga once per week for 10 weeks, with additional home-based yoga exercises. Yoga was found to be a feasible and well-accepted adjunct treatment. Consumption reduced more in the usual care plus yoga group compared with usual care only, but the differences were not statistically significant. In another study, researchers tested the antidepressant efficacy and hormonal effects of yoga in 60 alcohol-dependent patients (Vedamurthachar et al., 2006). They found significant reductions in depression and cortisol levels in the yoga treatment group compared with a control intervention. These studies suggest that light exercises such as yoga may also have important benefits for those with AUDs, a finding consistent with studies showing that yoga-based exercise is effective in the treatment of depression (Helgadottir et al., 2016). Studies evaluating the exercise preferences of people with AUDs or comparing the effects of different types of exercise within a single study are currently lacking. Based on current evidence, exercise recommendations are presented at the end of this chapter (see Conclusions and Clinical Implications).

# REVIEWS OF THE EVIDENCE—POSITIVE EFFECTS ON HEALTH, DEPRESSION, AND PHYSICAL FITNESS

Two narrative reviews have summarized the current evidence base from studies of exercise for AUDs. A systematic review by Giesen et al.

(2015), including 14 RCTs, concluded that exercise may have beneficial effects on key domains of physical functioning, including fitness, basal heart rate, physical activity level, and strength (Giesen et al., 2015). Inconsistent effects with a trend toward a positive effect were observed for anxiety, mood management, alcohol craving, and drinking behavior. Exercise interventions were considered safe with no adverse events reported. Another narrative review examined studies reporting the use of exercise to treat AUDs published between 1970 and 2015, including the underlying mechanisms (Manthou et al., 2018). Eleven studies were identified, of which six concluded that exercise may have a positive impact on consumption, abstinence rates, or the urge to drink (Manthou et al., 2018).

To date, only one review has reported the pooled treatment effects of exercise in AUDs across multiple health outcomes (Hallgren et al., 2017). In this review, 21 studies and 1204 unique persons with AUDs (mean age 37.8 years, mean illness duration 4.4 years) were included. Across all studies with usable data, long-term exercise was not associated with significant reductions in alcohol consumption, measured by the number of standard drinks consumed per day, per week, and by the Alcohol Use Disorders Identification Test. Although the standard mean difference in alcohol consumption was not statistically significant after adjustment for publication bias (exercise vs. control), the direction of change favored the exercise participants, with mean reductions in consumption seen on all three measures. A similar nonsignificant trend was observed for changes in anxiety and self-efficacy (Hallgren et al., 2017). One should note, however, that across the multiple alcohol outcomes measured in this review, that all analyses were limited to three trials. However, the authors reported other important positive effects of exercise. Compared with control conditions, exercisers were found to have improved physical fitness and lower depression severity. These findings are noteworthy, as previous research has shown associations between cardiovascular health and depression (Penninx, 2017), which has in turn been linked to an increased risk of relapse in alcohol dependence (Hasin et al., 2002).

The recent meta-analysis by Hallgren et al. corroborates narrative reviews reporting a trend toward a positive effect of exercise on drinking behavior in people with AUDs (Manthou et al., 2018; Giesen et al., 2015). Taken together, current evidence suggests that exercise is a safe and feasible adjunct treatment option for people with AUDs. Exercise is likely to reduce depression and improve cardiometabolic health and physical fitness, but it remains unclear if participation in exercise significantly reduces alcohol consumption; additional trials are required to strengthen the evidence base.

## Dropout and Treatment Adherence

While most physical activity interventions have been shown to improve the health of people with psychiatric disorders, including substance abuse (Zschucke et al., 2012), treatment dropout poses an important challenge to the effectiveness of exercise interventions. Poor treatment adherence is of concern because it is associated with higher risk of relapse and greater resource utilization (Osterberg and Blaschke, 2005). In the meta-analysis by Hallgren et al. a pooled dropout of 40.3% across the included studies ($n = 10$) was found, with low-to-moderate heterogeneity. This result should be considered in the context of other exercise studies. A meta-analysis of dropouts from physical activity interventions in schizophrenia ($n = 19$ studies, 594 participants), indicated a pooled dropout rate of 26.7% (Vancampfort et al., 2016c). Another meta-analysis exploring dropouts from exercise RCTs among people with depression ($n = 40$ studies, 1720 participants) reported an adjusted dropout prevalence of 18.1% (Stubbs et al., 2016). Of relevance, both reviews found that supervision of exercise by a degree-qualified professional such as a physical therapist or exercise physiologist was associated with a significantly lower drop-out rate. In the recent AUD meta-analysis (Hallgren et al., 2017), dropout rates were notably higher than those reported in the previously mentioned reviews, indicating the need to consider treatment adherence strategies during the planning of these interventions. Male gender was the only factor found to moderate participant dropout. Participant age, illness duration, study duration (weeks), and length of exercise session (minutes) had no effect on the pooled dropout rate, which was also equivalent between intervention and control groups (Hallgren et al., 2017).

## Safety and Adverse Effects

While adverse health outcomes are rare in exercise studies for AUDs (Giesen et al., 2015), heavy drinking is associated with numerous health risks. In addition to an increased risk of cardiovascular disease, stroke, and some forms of cancer (NIH, 2016), regular heavy alcohol consumption can cause nerve damage (alcoholic neuropathy), which can produce pain, numbness, and muscle weakness in the extremities (Chopra and Tiwari, 2012), effects that could limit the type and/or intensity of exercise performed. In some instances, heavy drinking can also cause the number of red blood cells to be abnormally low, triggering symptoms such as fatigue, shortness of breath, and lightheadedness (NIH, 2016). Although most individuals with an AUD do not experience these symptoms, alcohol's negative health effects underscore the importance of a thorough preexercise medical assessment and the prescription of individually tailored exercise programs. Heavily dependent individuals undergoing withdrawal symptoms (e.g., delirium tremens) may require a period of specialized inpatient care lasting days or weeks before commencing a light exercise regime under close supervision.

## MECHANISMS OF ACTION: MOOD STATES, INFLAMMATION, AND COGNITION

Several psychobiological mechanisms have been proposed to explain the positive effects of exercise on mental health and the links with AUDs. From a psychological perspective, regular exercise can improve self-efficacy, body image, and may act as a distraction from stressful life events (Biddle et al., 2000). Exercise has well-established anxiolytic and mood enhancing effects, which have been linked to the monoaminergic system, specifically 5-HT (serotonin) release and metabolism (Chaouloff, 1997). These anxiolytic effects may inhibit the urge to drink alcohol (Ussher et al., 2004), and better mood states are understood to reduce the risk of alcohol use and relapse in dependent individuals (Davidson and Ritson, 1993). Related to these effects, exercise has also been shown to mediate stress reactivity (Hamer et al., 2012), and acute stress frequently precipitates alcohol consumption and relapse (Sinha, 2012). As major depression is often comorbid with AUDs, and alcohol itself modulates the immune system, another plausible mechanism concerns inflammation. Animal studies have shown that proinflammatory cytokines play a causal role in the development of depressive-like behavior (Ji et al., 2014). Results from a meta-analysis show that people suffering from major depression have an elevated level of inflammatory cytokines, specifically interleukin-6 (IL-6) and tumor necrosis factor $\alpha$ (TNF-$\alpha$) compared with healthy subjects (Valkanova et al., 2013). In an intervention study of exercise for depression, researchers found a relationship between high levels of TNF-$\alpha$ at baseline and a greater reduction in depressive symptoms at the end of the study. They also found that changes in IL-1$\beta$ were positively correlated with changes in depressive symptoms following the exercise treatment (Rethorst et al., 2013). As heavy alcohol use is generally associated with elevated proinflammatory markers (Morris et al., 2015), regular exercise could reduce systemic inflammation in alcohol dependent (AD) patients, leading to improved mood states, lower anxiety, and stress reactivity. An emerging literature based on functional magnetic resonance imaging and positron emission tomography studies demonstrates that exercise and commonly misused substances activate similar reward pathways in the brain (Weicker and Struder, 2001; Yau et al., 2011; Boecker et al., 2008). Exercise increases the concentration of certain neurotransmitters ($\beta$-endorphins, epinephrine, norepinephrine, serotonin, and dopamine), which contribute to the experience of exercise-induced reward. Exercise also evokes hippocampal neurogenesis, a process that may impact positively on stress-related disorders, and possibly alcohol dependence.

Research into the effects of exercise on cognition is growing rapidly. Convergent evidence from both human and animal studies suggests that physical activity facilitates neuroplasticity of certain brain structures and as a result cognitive functions (Hotting and Roder, 2013). While "moderate" alcohol consumption has been linked in some studies to improvements in cognition, primarily in older adults (Neafsey and Collins, 2011), heavy drinking can have profound negative effects on different aspects of cognition, including attention, memory, and executive function (Fillmore, 2007). Such deficits are postulated to elevate the risk of hazardous drinking by increasing attentional biases toward alcohol (or the salience of alcohol-related cues; Field and Cox, 2008). Recent studies have shown that acute bouts of exercise can reduce cigarette cravings and attenuate smoking-related attentional biases (Janse Van Rensburg et al., 2009, 2013); processes that could also apply to alcohol consumption. While previous studies have demonstrated positive associations between exercise and cognitive function in adult populations of varying age and health status (Hotting and Roder, 2013), and among cigarette smokers (Janse Van Rensburg et al., 2013), these effects have not been explored in the context of alcohol dependence.

## ALCOHOL CONSUMPTION AND PHYSICAL ACTIVITY IN THE GENERAL POPULATION

Although not the main focus of this chapter, it is important to recognize that the association between physical activity and alcohol consumption in the general population is complex. Many studies indicate a dose-response relationship between self-reported consumption and physical activity level (Piazza-Gardner and Barry, 2012), indicating that those who are physically active are more likely to drink alcohol and vice versa. This relationship is somewhat at odds with research showing that positive health-related behaviors, such as healthy eating, regular exercise, and avoiding tobacco use tend to cluster together (Fine et al., 2004). Several mechanisms have been suggested to explain the positive association between physical activity and drinking in the general population, including the "work hard-play hard" philosophy, motivations that are believed to overlap for drinking and exercise behaviors, and heavy drinking cultures that surround organized sport (Leasure et al., 2015). Biological explanations have also been suggested. Alcohol and exercise both have extensive effects on brain chemicals and circuitry, and some of these effects are overlapping. It is therefore conceivable that people who are not dependent on either alcohol or exercise may engage in both regularly to experience positive rewards (Leasure et al., 2015). Unlike the general population, however, the relationship between physical activity and alcohol use appears to be different in those with an AUD. Studies examining physical activity habits in alcohol dependence remain scarce, but available evidence suggests that many people with an AUD are insufficiently active (Smothers and Bertolucci, 2001) and have an impaired cardiorespiratory fitness (Herbsleb et al., 2013). Experience from clinical practice suggests that inactivity increases with the severity of dependence (though exceptions to this can also be found). For these reasons, prescribed exercise is a viable treatment option for many people with a diagnosed AU.

## CONCLUSIONS AND CLINICAL IMPLICATIONS

This chapter has presented a rationale for considering exercise as a treatment option for AUDs and summarized the scientific evidence to support this approach. Alcohol use disorders are highly prevalent, highly comorbid, and often go untreated. Current treatment options are effective for some but not all patients, and relapse is common. Physical exercise is a safe and feasible treatment alternative that is likely to improve comorbid health problems and may reduce heavy drinking. We preface this conclusion with a caveat; the evidence base is currently limited to a small number of studies of varying methodological quality (Hallgren et al., 2017). In particular, little is known about the optimal exercise type or "dose" required. Currently, studies shows that regular exercise can reduce the heightened cardiometabolic risks associated with AUDs, lower depression, and improve physical fitness. However, additional trials are needed to strengthen the case for prescribing exercise to reduce alcohol consumption per se.

The high prevalence of multimorbidity in AUDs is sufficient reason to recommend that physical activity habits should be routinely screened in clinical practice. Based on recent evidence reviews of exercise for depression studies (Schuch et al., 2016b), and public health guidelines for physical activity (Garber et al., 2011), we further recommend that (1) light to moderate exercise is initially prescribed for AUDs following a complete physical examination to rule out contraindications for exercise; (2) patients should be able to select their preferred type of physical training; (3) exercise should be performed at least three times per week; (4) patients are encouraged to increase their total daily physical activity—particularly those who find structured exercise regimes difficult or impractical; and (5) prescriptions should be monitored to identify nonadherence and obstacles to exercise participation. Where possible, exercise regimes should be prescribed by physiotherapists, exercise physiologists, or medical practitioners with training in exercise prescription. Finally, we encourage clinicians and patients alike to view exercise as part of an overall lifestyle change oriented toward healthier living, which also emphasizes proper nutrition and avoiding tobacco use.

# References

Andreasson, S., Danielsson, A.K., Hallgren, M., 2013a. Severity of alcohol dependence in the Swedish adult population: association with consumption and social factors. Alcohol 47, 21–25.

Andreasson, S., Danielsson, A.K., Wallhed-Finn, S., 2013b. Preferences regarding treatment for alcohol problems. Alcohol Alcohol. 48, 694–699.

Aneja, J., Basu, D., Mattoo, S.K., Kohli, K.K., 2013. Metabolic syndrome in alcohol-dependent men: a cross-sectional study. Indian J. Psychol. Med. 35, 190–196.

Berglund, M., Thelander, S., Jonsson, E. (Eds.), 2003. Treating Alcohol and Drug Abuse: An Evidence Based Review. Wiley-VCH, Weinheim, Germany.

Biddle, S.J.H., Fox, K.R., Boutcher, S.H., 2000. Physical Activity and Psychological Well-being. Routledge, London, Uk.

Blomqvist, J., Cunningham, J., Wallander, L., Collin, I., 2007. Att Förbättra Sina Dryckesvanoe - Om Olika Mönster För Förändring Och Om Vaå Vården Betyder. En Rapport Från Projektet 'Läsningar På Alkoholproblem' (Improving Drinking Habits - Different Patterns of Change and the Importance of Treatment). Stockholm University.

Boden, J.M., Fergusson, D.M., 2011. Alcohol and depression. Addiction 106, 906–914.

Boecker, H., Sprenger, T., Spilker, M.E., Henriksen, G., Koppenhoefer, M., Wagner, K.J., Valet, M., Berthele, A., Tolle, T.R., 2008. The runner's high: opioidergic mechanisms in the human brain. Cereb. Cortex 18, 2523–2531.

Brown, S.A., Vik, P.W., Patterson, T.L., Grant, I., Schuckit, M.A., 1995. Stress, vulnerability and adult alcohol relapse. J. Stud. Alcohol 56, 538–545.

Brown, R.A., Prince, M.A., Minami, H., Abrantes, A.M., 2016. An exploratory analysis of changes in mood, anxiety and craving from pre- to post-single sessions of exercise, over 12 weeks, among patients with alcohol dependence. Ment. Health Phys. Act. 11, 1–6.

CDCP, 2016. Excessive Drinking Costs U.S. $223.5 Billion. Online. Centers for Disease Control and Prevention. Available: http://www.cdc.gov/features/alcoholconsumption/.

Chaouloff, F., 1997. Effects of acute physical exercise on central serotonergic systems. Med. Sci. Sports Exerc. 29, 58–62.

Chatterjee, S., Steensland, P., Simms, J.A., Holgate, J., Bartlett, S.E., 2010. Neuronal nicotinic acetylcholine receptors as pharmacotherapeutic targets for the treatment of alcohol use disorders. Alcohol Clin. Exp. Res. 34, 18a.

Chen, L., Magliano, D.J., Zimmet, P.Z., 2012. The worldwide epidemiology of type 2 diabetes mellitus-present and future perspectives. Nat. Rev. Endocrinol. 8, 228–236.

Chopra, K., Tiwari, V., 2012. Alcoholic neuropathy: possible mechanisms and future treatment possibilities. Br. J. Clin. Pharmacol. 73, 348–362.

Cohen, E., Feinn, R., Arias, A., Kranzler, H.R., 2007. Alcohol treatment utilization: findings from the national epidemiologic survey on alcohol and related conditions. Drug Alcohol Depend. 86, 214–221.

Collaboration, Sarwar, N., Gao, P., Seshasai, S.R., Gobin, R., Kaptoge, S., DI Angelantonio, E., Ingelsson, E., Lawlor, D.A., Selvin, E., Stampfer, M., Stehouwer, C.D., Lewington, S., Pennells, L., Thompson, A., Sattar, N., White, I.R., Ray, K.K., Danesh, J., 2010. Diabetes mellitus, fasting blood glucose concentration, and risk of vascular disease: a collaborative meta-analysis of 102 prospective studies. Lancet 375, 2215–2222.

Conn, V.S., 2010. Depressive symptom outcomes of physical activity interventions: meta-analysis findings. Ann. Behav. Med. 39, 128–138.

Connor, J., Casswell, S., 2012. Alcohol-related harm to others in New Zealand: evidence of the burden and gaps in knowledge. N.Z. Med. J. 125, 11–27.

Cooney, G.M., Dwan, K., Greig, C.A., Lawlor, D.A., Rimer, J., Waugh, F.R., Mcmurdo, M., Mead, G.E., 2013a. Exercise for depression. Cochrane Database Syst. Rev. 9.

Cooney, G.M., Dwan, K., Greig, C.A., Lawlor, D.A., Rimer, J., Waugh, F.R., Mcmurdo, M., Mead, G.E., 2013b. Exercise for depression. Cochrane Database Syst. Rev. 9, CD004366.

Cunningham, J.A., Breslin, F.C., 2004. Only one in three people with alcohol abuse or dependence ever seek treatment. Addict. Behav. 29, 221–223.

Danielsson, A.K., Wennberg, P., Hibell, B., Romelsjo, A., 2012. Alcohol use, heavy episodic drinking and subsequent problems among adolescents in 23 European countries: does the prevention paradox apply? Addiction 107, 71–80.

Dao-Castellana, M.H., Samson, Y., Legault, F., Martinot, J.L., Aubin, H.J., Crouzel, C., Feldman, L., Barrucand, D., Rancurel, G., Feline, A., Syrota, A., 1998. Frontal dysfunction in neurologically normal chronic alcoholic subjects: metabolic and neuropsychological findings. Psychol. Med. 28, 1039–1048.

Davidson, K.M., Ritson, E.B., 1993. The relationship between alcohol dependence and depression. Alcohol Alcohol. 28, 147–155.

Deane, F.P., Wootton, D.J., Hsu, C.I., Kelly, P.J., 2012. Predicting dropout in the first 3 months of 12-step residential drug and alcohol treatment in an Australian sample. J. Stud. Alcohol Drugs 73, 216–225.

Dieperink, E., Fuller, B., Isenhart, C., Mcmaken, K., Lenox, R., Pocha, C., Thuras, P., Hauser, P., 2014. Efficacy of motivational enhancement therapy on alcohol use disorders in patients with chronic hepatitis C: a randomized controlled trial. Addiction 109, 1869–1877.

Ekkekakis, P., Hall, E.E., Petruzzello, S.J., 2008. The relationship between exercise intensity and affective responses demystified: to crack the 40-year-old nut, replace the 40-year-old nutcracker! Ann. Behav. Med. 35, 136–149.

Ferri, M., Amato, L., Davoli, M., 2006. Alcoholics Anonymous and other 12-step programmes for alcohol dependence. Cochrane Database Syst. Rev.

Field, M., Cox, W.M., 2008. Attentional bias in addictive behaviors: a review of its development, causes, and consequences. Drug Alcohol Depend. 97, 1–20.

Fillmore, M.T., 2007. Acute alcohol-induced impairment of cognitive functions: past and present findings. Int. J. Disabil. Hum. Dev. 6, 115–125.

Fine, L.J., Philogene, G.S., Gramling, R., Coups, E.J., Sinha, S., 2004. Prevalence of multiple chronic disease risk factors. 2001 National Health Interview Survey. Am. J. Prev. Med. 27, 18–24.

Friedmann, P.D., 2013. Alcohol use in adults. N. Engl. J. Med. 368, 365–373.

Garber, C.E., Blissmer, B., Deschenes, M.R., Franklin, B.A., Lamonte, M.J., Lee, I.M., Nieman, D.C., Swain, D.P., American College of Sports Medicine, 2011. American College of Sports Medicine position stand. Quantity and quality of exercise for developing and maintaining cardiorespiratory, musculoskeletal, and neuromotor fitness in apparently healthy adults: guidance for prescribing exercise. Med. Sci. Sports Exerc. 43, 1334–1359.

Gary, V., Guthrie, D., 1972. The effect of jogging on physical fitness and self-concept in hospitalized alcoholics. Q. J. Stud. Alcohol 33, 1073–1078.

Giesen, E.S., Deimel, H., Bloch, W., 2015. Clinical exercise interventions in alcohol use disorders: a systematic review. J. Subst. Abuse Treat. 52, 1–9.

Giesen, E.S., Zimmer, P., Bloch, W., 2016. Effects of an exercise program on physical activity level and quality of life in patients with severe alcohol dependence. Alcohol Treat. Q. 34, 63–78.

Grant, B.F., Goldstein, R.B., Saha, T.D., Chou, S.P., Jung, J., Zhang, H.T., Pickering, R.P., Ruan, W.J., Smith, S.M., Huang, B.J., Hasin, D.S., 2015. Epidemiology of DSM-5 alcohol Use disorder results from the national epidemiologic survey on alcohol and related conditions III. Jama Psychiatry 72, 757−766.

Gupta, H., Pettigrew, S., Lam, T., Tait, R.J., 2016. A systematic review of the impact of exposure to internet-based alcohol-related content on young People's alcohol use behaviours. Alcohol Alcohol. 51, 763−771.

Hallgren, M., Romberg, K., Bakshi, A.S., Andreasson, S., 2014. Yoga as an adjunct treatment for alcohol dependence: a pilot study. Complement. Ther. Med. 22, 441−445.

Hallgren, M., Vancampfort, D., Giesen, E.S., Lundin, A., Stubbs, B., 2017. Exercise as treatment for alcohol use disorders: systematic review and meta-analysis. Br. J. Sports Med.

Hamer, M., Endrighi, R., Poole, L., 2012. Physical activity, stress reduction, and mood: insight into immunological mechanisms. Methods Mol. Biol. 934, 89−102.

Hasin, D., Liu, X., Nunes, E., Mccloud, S., Samet, S., Endicott, J., 2002. Effects of major depression on remission and relapse of substance dependence. Arch. Gen. Psychiatry 59, 375−380.

Hasin, D.S., Goodwin, R.D., Stinson, F.S., Grant, B.F., 2005. Epidemiology of major depressive disorder: results from the national epidemiologic survey on alcoholism and related conditions. Arch. Gen. Psychiatry 62, 1097−1106.

Helgadottir, B., Hallgren, M., Ekblom, O., Forsell, Y., 2016. Training fast or slow? Exercise for depression: a randomized controlled trial. Prev. Med. 91, 123−131.

Herbsleb, M., Schulz, S., Ostermann, S., Donath, L., Eisentrager, D., Puta, C., Voss, A., Gabriel, H.W., Bar, K.J., 2013. The relation of autonomic function to physical fitness in patients suffering from alcohol dependence. Drug Alcohol Depend. 132, 505−512.

Herring, M.P., Puetz, T.W., O'connor, P.J., Dishman, R.K., 2012. Effect of exercise training on depressive symptoms among patients with a chronic illness: a systematic review and meta-analysis of randomized controlled trials. Arch. Intern. Med. 172, 101−111.

Hotting, K., Roder, B., 2013. Beneficial effects of physical exercise on neuroplasticity and cognition. Neurosci. Biobehav. Rev. 37, 2243−2257.

Janse Van Rensburg, K., Taylor, A., Hodgson, T., Benattayallah, A., 2009. Acute exercise modulates cigarette cravings and brain activation in response to smoking-related images: an fMRI study. Psychopharmacol. (Berl.) 203, 589−598.

Janse Van Rensburg, K., Elibero, A., Kilpatrick, M., Drobes, D.J., 2013. Impact of aerobic exercise intensity on craving and reactivity to smoking cues. Exp. Clin. Psychopharmacol. 21, 196−203.

Ji, W.W., Wang, S.Y., Ma, Z.Q., Li, R.P., Li, S.S., Xue, J.S., Li, W., Niu, X.X., Yan, L., Zhang, X., Fu, Q., Qu, R., Ma, S.P., 2014. Effects of perillaldehyde on alternations in serum cytokines and depressive-like behavior in mice after lipopolysaccharide administration. Pharmacol. Biochem. Behav. 116, 1−8.

Kahl, K.G., Greggersen, W., Schweiger, U., Cordes, J., Correll, C.U., Ristow, J., Burow, J., Findel, C., Stoll, A., Balijepalli, C., Gores, L., Losch, C., Hillemacher, T., Bleich, S., Moebus, S., 2010. Prevalence of the metabolic syndrome in men and women with alcohol dependence: results from a cross-sectional study during behavioural treatment in a controlled environment. Addiction 105, 1921−1927.

Kallmen, H., Gustafson, R., 1998. Alcohol and disinhibition. Eur. Addict. Res. 4, 150−162.

Kaner, E.F.S., Dickinson, H.O., Beyer, F., Pienaar, E., Schlesinger, C., Campbell, F., Saunders, J.B., Burnand, B., Heather, N., 2009. The effectiveness of brief alcohol interventions in primary care settings: a systematic review. Drug Alcohol Rev. 28, 301−323.

Kessler, R.C., Walters, E.E., 1998. Epidemiology of DSM-III-R major depression and minor depression among adolescents and young adults in the National Comorbidity Survey. Depress. Anxiety 7, 3−14.

Keyes, K.M., Hatzenbuehler, M.L., Hasin, D.S., 2011. Stressful life experiences, alcohol consumption, and alcohol use disorders: the epidemiologic evidence for four main types of stressors. Psychopharmacology 218, 1—17.

Knopik, V.S., Heath, A.C., Madden, P.A., Bucholz, K.K., Slutske, W.S., Nelson, E.C., Statham, D., Whitfield, J.B., Martin, N.G., 2004. Genetic effects on alcohol dependence risk: re-evaluating the importance of psychiatric and other heritable risk factors. Psychol. Med. 34, 1519—1530.

Kuppin, S., Carpiano, R.M., 2008. Public conceptions of serious mental illness and substance abuse, their causes and treatments: findings from the 1996 general social survey. Reprinted from Am J. Public Health 96, 1766—1771, 2006 Am. J. Public Health 98, S120—S125.

Kuramoto, S.J., Martins, S.S., Ko, J.Y., Chilcoat, H.D., 2011. Past year treatment status and alcohol abuse symptoms among US adults with alcohol dependence. Addict. Behav. 36, 648—653.

Leasure, J.L., Neighbors, C., Henderson, C.E., Young, C.M., 2015. Exercise and alcohol consumption: what we know, what we need to know, and why it is important. Front. Psychiatry 6, 156.

Linke, S.E., Ussher, M., 2015. Exercise-based treatments for substance use disorders: evidence, theory, and practicality. Am. J. Drug Alcohol Abuse 41, 7—15.

Lundin, A., Hallgren, M., Forsman, M., Forsell, Y., 2015. Comparison of DSM-5 classifications of alcohol use disorders with those of DSM-Iv, Dsm-III-R, and ICD-10 in a general population sample in Sweden. J. Stud. Alcohol Drugs 76, 773—780.

Manthou, E., Georgakouli, K., Fatouros, I.G., Gianoulakis, C., Theodorakis, Y., Jamurtas, A.Z., 2016. Role of exercise in the treatment of alcohol use disorders (Review). Biomed Rep. 4 (5), 535—545.

Mceachin, R.C., Keller, B.J., Saunders, E.F., Mcinnis, M.G., 2008. Modeling gene-by-environment interaction in comorbid depression with alcohol use disorders via an integrated bioinformatics approach. BioData Min. 1, 2.

Mckay, J.R., Franklin, T.R., Patapis, N., Lynch, K.G., 2006. Conceptual, methodological, and analytical issues in the study of relapse. Clin. Psychol. Rev. 26, 109—127.

Mead, G.E., Morley, W., Campbell, P., Greig, C.A., Mcmurdo, M., Lawlor, D.A., 2008. Exercise for depression. Cochrane Database Syst. Rev. CD004366.

Monahan, S.C., Finney, J.W., 1996. Explaining abstinence rates following treatment for alcohol abuse: a quantitative synthesis of patient, research design and treatment effects. Addiction 91, 787—805.

Morris, N.L., Ippolito, J.A., Curtis, B.J., Chen, M.M., Friedman, S.L., Hines, I.N., Haddad, G.E., Chang, S.L., Brown, L.A., Waldschmidt, T.J., Mandrekar, P., Kovacs, E.J., Choudhry, M.A., 2015. Alcohol and inflammatory responses: summary of the 2013 alcohol and immunology research interest group (AIRIG) meeting. Alcohol 49, 1—6.

Mottillo, S., Filion, K.B., Genest, J., Joseph, L., Pilote, L., Poirier, P., Rinfret, S., Schiffrin, E.L., Eisenberg, M.J., 2010. The metabolic syndrome and cardiovascular risk a systematic review and meta-analysis. J. Am. Coll. Cardiol. 56, 1113—1132.

Moyer, A., Finney, J.W., 2002. Outcomes for untreated individuals involved in randomized trials of alcohol treatment. J. Subst. Abuse Treat. 23, 247—252.

Navarro, H.J., Doran, C.M., Shakeshaft, A.P., 2011. Measuring costs of alcohol harm to others: a review of the literature. Drug Alcohol Depend. 114, 87—99.

Neafsey, E.J., Collins, M.A., 2011. Moderate alcohol consumption and cognitive risk. Neuropsychiatr. Dis. Treat. 7, 465—484.

NHS, 2010. Too Much of the Hard Stuff: What Alcohol Costs the NHS. National Health Service Confederation, United Kingdom.

NIAAA, 2017. Exploring Treatment Options for Alcohol Use Disorders. Online. National Institute for Alcohol Abuse and Alcoholism (NIAAA). Available: https://www.niaaa. nih.gov/alcohol-health/overview-alcohol-consumption/alcohol-use-disorders.

NIH, 2016. Alcohol's Effects on the Body. Online. National Institute of Health; National Institute for Alcohol Abuse and Alcoholism, Washington, USA. Available: https://www. niaaa.nih.gov/alcohol-health/alcohols-effects-body.

Osterberg, L., Blaschke, T., 2005. Adherence to medication. N. Engl. J. Med. 353, 487–497.

Parsons, O.A., 1994. Neuropsychological measures and event-related potentials in alcoholics - interrelationships, long-term reliabilities, and prediction of resumption of drinking. J. Clin. Psychol. 50, 37–46.

Pasupuleti, S., Escobar, R., Lopez, M., 2017. Substance use: review of cognitive behavioral therapy (Cbt) effectiveness studies and clinician perspective. Alcohol Clin. Exp. Res. 41, 362a.

Penedo, F.J., Dahn, J.R., 2005. Exercise and well-being: a review of mental and physical health benefits associated with physical activity. Curr. Opin. Psychiatry 18, 189–193.

Penninx, B.W.J.H., 2017. Depression and cardiovascular disease: epidemiological evidence on their linking mechanisms. Neurosci. Biobehav. Rev. 74, 277–286.

Piazza-Gardner, A.K., Barry, A.E., 2012. Examining physical activity levels and alcohol consumption: are people who drink more active? Am. J. Health Promot. 26, e95–104.

Pitel, A.L., Rivier, J., Beaunieux, H., Vabret, F., Desgranges, B., Eustache, F., 2009. Changes in the episodic memory and executive functions of abstinent and relapsed alcoholics over a 6-month period. Alcohol Clin. Exp. Res. 33, 490–498.

Rethorst, C.D., Toups, M.S., Greer, T.L., Nakonezny, P.A., Carmody, T.J., Grannemann, B.D., Huebinger, R.M., Barber, R.C., Trivedi, M.H., 2013. Pro-inflammatory cytokines as predictors of antidepressant effects of exercise in major depressive disorder. Mol. Psychiatry 18, 1119–1124.

Rimer, J., Dwan, K., Lawlor, D.A., Greig, C.A., Mcmurdo, M., Morley, W., Mead, G.E., 2012. Exercise for depression. Cochrane Database Syst. Rev. 7, CD004366.

Roerecke, M., Rehm, J., 2013. Alcohol use disorders and mortality: a systematic review and meta-analysis. Addiction 108, 1562–1578.

Roerecke, M., Rehm, J., 2014. Cause-specific mortality risk in alcohol use disorder treatment patients: a systematic review and meta-analysis. Int. J. Epidemiol. 43, 906–919.

Roozen, H.G., Boulogne, J.J., Van Tulder, M.W., Van Den Brink, W., De Jong, C.A.J., Kerkhof, A.J.F.M., 2004. A systematic review of the effectiveness of the community reinforcement approach in alcohol, cocaine and opioid addiction. Drug Alcohol Depend. 74, 1–13.

Saxton, J., Munro, C.A., Butters, M.A., Schramke, C., Mcneil, M.A., 2000. Alcohol, dementia, and Alzheimer's disease: comparison of neuropsychological profiles. J. Geriatr. Psychiatry Neurol. 13, 141–149.

Schuch, F.B., Vancampfort, D., Richards, J., Rosenbaum, S., Ward, P.B., Stubbs, B., 2016a. Exercise as a treatment for depression: a meta-analysis adjusting for publication bias. J. Psychiatr. Res. 77, 42–51.

Schuch, F.B., Vancampfort, D., Rosenbaum, S., Richards, J., Ward, P.B., Veronese, N., Solmi, M., Cadore, E.L., Stubbs, B., 2016b. Exercise for depression in older adults: a meta-analysis of randomized controlled trials adjusting for publication bias. Rev. Bras. Psiquiatr. 0 (0).

Sellman, J.D., Sullivan, P.F., Dore, G.M., Adamson, S.J., Macewan, I., 2001. A randomized controlled trial of motivational enhancement therapy (MET) for mild to moderate alcohol dependence. J. Stud. Alcohol 62, 389–396.

Sinha, R., 2012. How does stress lead to risk of alcohol relapse? Alcohol Res. 34, 432–440.

Sinyor, D., Brown, T., Rostant, L., Seraganian, P., 1982a. The role of a physical-fitness program in the treatment of alcoholism. J. Stud. Alcohol 43, 380–386.

Sinyor, D., Brown, T., Rostant, L., Seraganian, P., 1982b. The role of a physical fitness program in the treatment of alcoholism. J. Stud. Alcohol 35 (1272), 1278.

Sjoholm, L.K., Kovanen, L., Saarikoski, S.T., Schalling, M., Lavebratt, C., Partonen, T., 2010. CLOCK is suggested to associate with comorbid alcohol use and depressive disorders. J. Circadian Rhythms 8, 1.

Smothers, B., Bertolucci, D., 2001. Alcohol consumption and health-promoting behavior in a US household sample: leisure-time physical activity. J. Stud. Alcohol 62, 467–476.

Stavro, K., Pelletier, J., Potvin, S., 2013. Widespread and sustained cognitive deficits in alcoholism: a meta-analysis. Addict. Biol. 18, 203–213.

Stubbs, B., Vancampfort, D., Rosenbaum, S., Ward, P.B., Richards, J., Soundy, A., Veronese, N., Solmi, M., Schuch, F.B., 2016. Dropout from exercise randomized controlled trials among people with depression: a meta-analysis and meta regression. J. Affect. Disord. 190, 457–466.

Taylor, A.H., Ussher, M.H., Faulkner, G., 2007. The acute effects of exercise on cigarette cravings, withdrawal symptoms, affect and smoking behaviour: a systematic review. Addiction 102, 534–543.

Tonigan, L.S., Connors, G.J., Miller, W.R., 2003. Participation and involvement in alcoholics anonymous. In: Babor, T.F., Del Boca, F.K. (Eds.), Treatment Matching in Alcoholism. Cambridge University Press, New York, pp. 184–204.

Ussher, M., Nunziata, P., Cropley, M., West, R., 2001. Effect of a short bout of exercise on tobacco withdrawal symptoms and desire to smoke. Psychopharmacology 158, 66–72.

Ussher, M., Sampuran, A.K., Doshi, R., West, R., Drummond, D.C., 2004. Acute effect of a brief bout of exercise on alcohol urges. Addiction 99, 1542–1547.

Ussher, M.H., Taylor, A.H., Faulkner, G.E., 2014. Exercise interventions for smoking cessation. Cochrane Database Syst. Rev. CD002295.

Valkanova, V., Ebmeier, K.P., Allan, C.L., 2013. Crp, Il-6 and depression: a systematic review and meta-analysis of longitudinal studies. J. Affect. Disord. 150, 736–744.

Van Rensburg, K.J., Taylor, A., Hodgson, T., Benattayallah, A., 2009. Acute exercise modulates cigarette cravings and brain activation in response to smoking-related images: an fMRI study. Psychopharmacology 203, 589–598.

Vancampfort, D., Hallgren, M., Mugisha, J., DE Hert, M., Probst, M., Monsieur, D., Stubbs, B., 2016a. The prevalence of metabolic syndrome in alcohol use disorders: a systematic review and meta-analysis. Alcohol Alcohol. 51, 515–521.

Vancampfort, D., Mugisha, J., Hallgren, M., De Hert, M., Probst, M., Monsieur, D., Stubbs, B., 2016b. The prevalence of diabetes mellitus type 2 in people with alcohol use disorders: a systematic review and large scale meta-analysis. Psychiatr. Res. 246, 394–400.

Vancampfort, D., Rosenbaum, S., Schuch, F.B., Ward, P.B., Probst, M., Stubbs, B., 2016c. Prevalence and predictors of treatment dropout from physical activity interventions in schizophrenia: a meta-analysis. Gen. Hosp. Psychiatry 39, 15–23.

Vasilaki, E.I., Hosier, S.G., Cox, W.M., 2006. The efficacy of motivational interviewing as a brief intervention for excessive drinking: a meta-analytic review. Alcohol Alcohol. 41, 328–335.

Vedamurthachar, A., Janakiramaiah, N., Hegde, J.M., Shetty, T.K., Subbakrishna, D.K., Sureshbabu, S.V., Gangadhar, B.N., 2006. Antidepressant efficacy and hormonal effects of Sudarshana Kriya Yoga (SKY) in alcohol dependent individuals. J. Affect. Disord. 94, 249–253.

Voulgari, C., Pagoni, S., Vinik, A., Poirier, P., 2013. Exercise improves cardiac autonomic function in obesity and diabetes. Metabolism 62, 609–621.

Walitzer, K.S., Dearing, R.L., 2006. Gender differences in alcohol and substance use relapse. Clin. Psychol. Rev. 26, 128–148.

Warburton, D.E., Nicol, C.W., Bredin, S.S., 2006. Health benefits of physical activity: the evidence. Can. Med. Assoc. J. 174, 801–809.

Weicker, H., Struder, H.K., 2001. Influence of exercise on serotonergic neuromodulation in the brain. Amino Acids 20, 35–47.

WHO, 2004. Global Status Report on Alcohol. Geneva.

Yau, S.Y., Lau, B.W., So, K.F., 2011. Adult hippocampal neurogenesis: a possible way how physical exercise counteracts stress. Cell Transplant. 20, 99–111.

Zschucke, E., Heinz, A., Strohle, A., 2012. Exercise and physical activity in the therapy of substance use disorders. Sci. World J. 2012, 901741.

# Sedentary Behavior and Mental Health

*Lee Smith[1], Mark Hamer[2], Benjamin Gardner[3]*

[1] Cambridge Centre for Sport and Exercise Sciences Anglia Ruskin University, Cambridge, United Kingdom; [2] School of Sport, Exercise, and Health Sciences, National Centre for Sport & Exercise Medicine—East Midlands, Loughborough University, Loughborough, United Kingdom; [3] Department of Psychology, Institute of Psychiatry, Psychology and Neuroscience, King's College London, London, United Kingdom

## SEDENTARY BEHAVIOR

Sedentary behavior may be defined as any waking behavior characterized by an energy expenditure $\leq 1.5$ metabolic equivalents, while in a sitting, reclining, or lying posture (Tremblay et al., 2017). Common examples of sedentary behavior include TV viewing, desk-based occupations, computer use, sitting in the classroom, passive commuting (car, taxi), reading, and playing board games. Existing data have demonstrated a predominance of sedentary lifestyles in Western society. For example, objective data from general adult population studies in the United States and Great Britain have shown that, on average, adults spend approximately 60%–70% of their waking hours in sedentary activities, 25%–35% in light-intensity activity, and in a small proportion of people, the remainder is spent in moderate-to-vigorous physical activity (MVPA; e.g., brisk walking; Stamatakis et al., 2012). Recent data from London-based office workers demonstrated that on average, they sit for 10.6 h a day (Smith et al., 2015). The prevalence of sedentary behavior has also been shown to be high in young people (e.g., see Matthews et al., 2008). Literature suggests that prolonged bouts of sedentary behavior are associated with higher risk of cardiovascular disease and mortality, even after statistical adjustment for MVPA (Healy et al., 2008, 2011). Some data also suggest that interruptions in periods of sedentary time are beneficially associated with metabolic health (Healy et al., 2008; Dunstan et al., 2012). In light of this knowledge, national physical activity guidelines recommend to either place a limit on the time children and adults should spend engaged in specific sedentary behaviors (e.g., Australia and Canada recommend less than 2 h of screen time per day) or recommend minimizing time spent sedentary (e.g., UK guidelines recommend minimizing the time spent sedentary for extended periods).

There is an emerging and significant body of literature to suggest that excessive sitting time (i.e., sedentary behavior) is associated with mental health in children, adolescents, and adults, which will be the focus of this chapter.

## SEDENTARY BEHAVIOR AND MENTAL HEALTH IN ADULTS

### Depression and Anxiety

Depression is a mental disorder that causes a persistent feeling of sadness and loss of interest. The World Health Organization (WHO) has ranked depression as the fourth leading cause of disability worldwide and projects that by 2020, it will be the second leading cause. In systematic reviews and meta-analyses, depression has been shown to be associated with multiple noncommunicable diseases (e.g., see Van der Kooy et al., 2007). Prevention and treatment of depression is a key public health challenge. In adults a large body of work has focused on the association between sedentary behavior and depression. There is mounting evidence, predominantly from observational studies, to suggest sedentary behavior is a likely risk factor for depression and importantly a risk factor that is independent of physical activity (note: that a large body of literature shows that regular physical activity has antidepressive effects in patients and is associated with lower risk of developing depression in initially healthy individuals). A 2015 meta-analysis carried out by Zhai et al. aimed to quantitatively summarize the evidence from observational studies investigating the association between sedentary behavior and risk of depression. A total of 13 cross-sectional and 11 longitudinal studies were identified. The review found a 25% higher risk of depression among those with the highest levels of sedentary behavior. The review concluded that sedentary behavior is associated with increased risk of depression, despite effect estimates being somewhat attenuated when only longitudinal studies were included.

Data from longitudinal studies have been inconsistent. For example, several have demonstrated an association of self-reported TV/computer time (Sanchez-Villegas et al., 2010) and TV time alone (Lucas et al., 2011) with higher risk of depression at follow-up. In another prospective study the association between sedentary behavior and depressive symptoms was only apparent among individuals who did not meet the current physical activity guidelines (Sui et al., 2015). Other longitudinal studies have produced conflicting findings. In one of the most robust studies to date that included four assessments at different time points over 10-years follow-up, total sitting time was not prospectively associated with depressive symptoms using lagged mixed-effect modeling (van Uffelen et al., 2013). Instead, physical activity was the main factor in predicting depression over follow-up. Data in over 6000 men and women from the English Longitudinal Study of Ageing demonstrated cross-sectional associations between higher TV viewing and greater depressive symptoms, although TV viewing did not predict changes in symptoms over follow-up, suggesting that the difference in depressive scores persisted but did not increase over time (Hamer and Stamatakis, 2014). Interestingly, in that study, TV viewing time, but not computer use, was associated with higher depressive symptoms. Thus it is difficult to tease apart if the effects are being driven by physiological processes linked to excessive sitting or the contrasting environmental and social contexts in which they occur. For example, passive activities such as TV viewing may encourage a greater volume of prolonged sitting; conversely, Internet use may encourage social interaction. Another issue to consider is reverse causation in that depression may, in part, drive increases in sedentary habits. Several studies have provided evidence to support this notion (Brunet et al., 2014; Gardner et al., 2014). Thus associations between sedentary time and depression are likely to be bidirectional.

Anxiety is characterized by excessive and persistent worry which can inhibit one's ability to carry out daily activities. The WHO (2017) states that the proportion of the global population with anxiety disorders in 2015 was estimated to be 3.6%. Teychenne et al. (2015) reviewed the literature on the relationship between sedentary behavior and anxiety. A total of nine studies were identified of which seven were carried out in adult populations of which four were cross-sectional, and three were longitudinal. The review found moderate evidence for a positive relationship between total sedentary behavior and anxiety risk. However, when considering sedentary behavior domains, there was inconsistent evidence for the relationship between screen time, television viewing time, computer use, and anxiety risk.

It is not uncommon for someone with an anxiety disorder to also suffer from depression or vice versa. Nearly one-half of those diagnosed with depression are also diagnosed with an anxiety disorder. It is therefore difficult to disentangle whether sedentary behavior is associated with anxiety, depression, or both mental disorders. Future experimental work using gold standard experimental design is required. Such research may involve the implementation of sedentary behavior reduction strategies (see section *Strategies to Reduce Sedentary Behavior*) in all groups (anxiety/depression/anxiety and depression) and comparing changes in mental health outcomes to control conditions (receive no intervention).

There is a growing body of evidence to suggest that there is a relationship between inflammatory risk markers and depressive symptoms, as well as mood (e.g., see Carney et al., 2002). Interestingly, sedentary behavior has also been linked with inflammatory markers. A recent systematic review of 25 interventions found consistent, moderate quality evidence that uninterrupted sedentary behavior results in moderate and deleterious changes in insulin sensitivity, glucose tolerance, and plasma triglyceride levels (Saunders et al., 2012). In addition, we previously demonstrated longitudinal associations between sedentary behavior and increases in various acute phase reactants and coagulation markers in older adults over 4-year follow-up (Hamer et al., 2015). Screen time has been linked to an increase in the arousal of the central nervous system which could potentially lead to increased levels of anxiety (Wang et al., 2006). Moreover, screen time has been associated with disruptive sleep patterns which could also cause elevated levels of anxiety and potentially depression (Dworak et al., 2007).

# BIPOLAR DISORDER

The National Institute of Mental Health (2017) defines bipolar disorder as a brain disorder that causes unusual shifts in mood, energy, activity levels, and the ability to carry out day-to-day tasks. Aggregate estimates of the prevalence of bipolar disorder indicate that approximately 1.0% of the general population meet lifetime criteria for BD-I. Estimates of the lifetime prevalence of BD-II have been provided by only one investigation that reported a median lifetime prevalence of 1.2% (see Merikangas et al., 2011). A recent meta-analysis (Walker et al., 2015) demonstrated that mortality rates in those with bipolar are approximately two to three times higher than those of the general population. The higher premature mortality rates are in part attributable to cardiovascular disease (Goldstein et al., 2015; Vancampfort et al., 2013), which has been linked to excessive sedentary time. There is limited but important literature investigating sedentary behavior and bipolar. Vancampfort et al. (2016a) reviewed the literature on physical activity and sedentary behavior levels and its predictors in bipolar disorder. The review identified just three studies investigating sedentary behavior in people ($n = 149$) with bipolar disorder and found that, on average, this population spent a high proportion of their waking day in sedentary behavior; on average 613.3 min (95% CI $= 389.9–836.6$ min) during waking hours, which is comparable to general population statistics (e.g., see Smith et al., 2015). However, in another study, Vancampfort et al. (2016b) found that people with BD are more sedentary than general population controls ($812 \pm 168$ min/day vs. $539 \pm 129$ min/day ($P < 001$). Inconsistencies between findings are likely owing to the plethora of sedentary measurement techniques.

To date, there is no literature that investigates whether sedentary behavior is a risk factor for bipolar and whether a change in sedentary behavior results in a change in bipolar outcomes. Longitudinal and experimental works to investigate these questions are warranted. Nevertheless, prevalence of sedentary behavior is relatively high in those with BD, and reducing sedentary behavior in this population to, at a minimum, reduce its negative impact on other health parameters (e.g., cardiovascular disease, adiposity, cancer) is warranted.

# SCHIZOPHRENIA

The Mayo Clinic (2017) defines schizophrenia as a chronic and severe mental disorder in which people interpret reality abnormally and often results in some combination of hallucinations, delusions, and extremely disordered thinking and behavior that impairs daily functioning.

Like those with other mental health conditions, those with schizophrenia have been found to have a higher risk of comorbidities than the general population (Smith et al., 2013). Vancampfort et al. (2012) studied sedentary behavior in patients with schizophrenia. Participants were asked to report their overall sitting behavior. On average, patients with schizophrenia spent 8.5 h/day sitting (vs. 6.21 h in healthy controls). Importantly, the study found that overall sitting time was associated with a significantly greater likelihood of metabolic syndrome. Janney et al. (2015) objectively measured sedentary behavior (accelerometers) in 46 adults with schizophrenia or schizoaffective disorders. On average, 81% of the participant's monitoring time (or 13 h/day) was classified as sedentary behavior.

Soundy et al. (2013) carried out a systematic review on physical activity and sedentary behavior in outpatients with schizophrenia. Just three papers were identified that investigated sedentary behavior (Lindamer et al., 2008; Scheewe, 2009; Roick et al., 2007). Lindamer et al. (2008) and Scheewe (2009) were included in a meta-analyses (note: Roick et al. (2007) was not as the study used a subjective and not objective measure of sedentary behavior), and results showed that these participants spent 2191.4 min/week (on average approximately 313 min/day) undertaking sedentary activities and that patients spent significantly more time sedentary in comparison to healthy controls. Stubbs et al. (2016) carried out a review and meta-analysis to investigate sedentary behavior levels and predictors in people with psychosis, including schizophrenia spectrum and BDs. Thirteen studies were eligible including 2033 people with psychosis. People with psychosis spent 660.8 min/day being sedentary and engaged in significantly more sedentary behavior than controls. In subgroup analyses the pooled time of sedentary behavior among 733 people with schizophrenia spectrum was 673.9 min/day (528.4–819.3). Interventions need to be developed to reduce the high levels of sedentary behavior in this at-risk group.

## Sedentary Behavior and Mental Health in Children and Adolescents

A large body of literature exists on the relationship between sedentary behavior and mental health in children and adolescents. Suchert et al. (2015) reviewed the literature with the aim to identify studies assessing the relationship between sedentary behavior and indicators of mental health in school-aged children and adolescents. A total of 91 studies were identified. The review found strong evidence between high levels of sedentary behavior and more hyperactivity/inattention problems and internalizing problems as well as with less psychological well-being and perceived quality of life. However, for depressive symptoms, self-esteem, eating disorder symptoms, and anxiety symptoms, no clear conclusion could be drawn. Another review (Hoare et al., 2016) investigated the magnitude of associations between different types of sedentary behavior and mental health among adolescents and identified 32 studies, 24 of which were cross-sectional, six were longitudinal, and just one was an intervention study. Strong consistent evidence was found for the relationship between both depressive symptomatology and psychological distress and time spent using screens for leisure. Moderate evidence supported the relationship between low self-esteem and screen use (Liu et al., 2016). Poorer mental health status was found among adolescents using screen time more than 2—3 h/day. Existing literature suggests that screen time is associated with poor mental health in young people, although the majority of evidence has been of poor quality. In particular, there is a lack of prospective data and little objective assessment of sedentary time.

Existing data on objective sedentary time and depressive symptoms have produced mixed results. One study reported a somewhat paradoxical inverse association between objective sedentary time and psychological difficulties (Page et al., 2010), while others have reported null associations (Zahl et al., 2017). Greater total objective sedentary time in children has been previously related to higher social status in a representative sample of the English population (Coombs et al., 2013), possibly reflective of more time spent on homework and reading (sedentary behaviors) that are likely to benefit mental health.

## General Limitations of Current Research

There are two key methodological weaknesses relating to the previously mentioned literature in young people and adults: (1) most studies are observational and of a cross-sectional design; thus causality and/or direction of the relationship between mental health and sedentary behavior are challenging to tease apart. It is not clear whether poor mental health leads to higher levels of sedentary behavior or whether high levels of sedentary behavior leads to poor mental health, but it is likely the relationship is bidirectional. Moreover, with a lack of randomized controlled trials in this area, we cannot and must not infer causation between sedentary behavior and mental health. The limited but important literature in this area provides a rationale for further investigation using experimental designs. (2) Most studies used subjective measures of sedentary behavior. It is possible that when people report sedentary behavior, they underestimate levels owing to the fear of being judged and/or cannot accurately recall their sedentary behavior. More precise measures of sedentary behavior should be used in future research such as accelerometers/inclinometers.

## Strategies to Reduce Sedentary Behavior in Those With Mental Health Disorders

A paucity of relevant literature precludes evidence-based recommendations for sedentary behavior reduction specific to people with mental illness. To our knowledge, no interventions specifically targeting sedentary behavior reduction—as opposed to increased physical activity — have yet been trialed in people with mental illness. Standing is considered a form of light physical activity (Smith et al., 2015), and so reducing sedentary behavior, by definition, involves displacing waking time spent sitting or lying down with physical activity of at least light intensity. In principle, sedentary behavior reduction advice might therefore be formulated on the basis of empirical findings from trials of physical activity interventions for people with mental illness. In practice, however, key limitations of this literature hamper such efforts. First, few such interventions have been trialed, and these have typically been of low quality (NICE, 2014). Second, while studies have linked increases in physical activity with improved clinical outcomes among people with mental illness (e.g., see Rethorst et al., 2009), little has been documented about the mechanisms by which such interventions may increase activity. Recent advances in behavioral science have yielded a comprehensive taxonomy of 93 discrete techniques that may be used in behavioral interventions (e.g., providing information on health consequences, monitoring behavior, practical social support, using prompts and cues; Michie et al., 2013), and a list of nine discrete mechanisms by which these techniques may change behavior (e.g., by educating or training recipients, by making environmental modifications; Michie et al., 2011). No physical activity intervention for people with mental illness has yet been fully described in these specific terms, making it difficult to isolate the "active ingredients" of previous interventions. Lastly, a review of relevant interventions in nonclinical adult populations concluded that people are most likely to reduce sitting time in response to interventions that explicitly target sedentary behavior reduction, rather than the promotion of physical activity (Gardner et al., 2016).

Sedentary behavior is instrumental; people sit, for example, to watch television, for occupational purposes, to travel by car or bus, or to read, rather than for the purpose of sitting per se (Rhodes et al., 2012). Reducing sedentary behavior may therefore depend on understanding and targeting the behaviors that people undertake while sitting or promoting changes in the postures in which they perform them, rather than targeting sitting per se, which is likely to hold little personal meaning. Additionally, reducing sedentary behavior may be of minimal priority to people with mental illness. For example, people with first episode psychosis often experience problems with housing, employment, or education and prioritize resolving or coping with these issues over engaging in health-promoting behaviors (Gardner-Sood, 2015).

It would thus seem prudent to seek minor and minimally disruptive modifications to everyday activities and routines to displace sedentary behavior with standing and light activity. Previous reviews, albeit in nonclinical populations, suggest that environmental restructuring—that is, modifying physical environments to make standing more accessible—offers the most promising method for reducing sitting time (e.g., Gardner et al., 2016; Shrestha et al., 2016). In workplace contexts, this typically involves using height-adjustable sit-stand workstations (Shrestha et al., 2015), which allow users to carry out desk-based work in a standing or seated position. In home-based settings, this may involve making modifications such as placing the TV remote control away from a chair (e.g., White et al., 2017) or storing regularly used items on high shelves (Clemson et al., 2012), so requiring users to incorporate light physical activity—walking, stretching—into normally seated everyday tasks such as watching TV. Such home-based strategies are likely to apply to an inpatient setting.

While environmental modification operates by creating greater opportunity to be physically active (instead of sitting), behavior may also be changed by increasing motivation or perceptions of capability to displace sitting with nonseated activity (Michie et al., 2011). Educating people of the health risks of sitting can reduce sitting time (Gardner et al., 2016), presumably by enhancing motivation. Self-monitoring—keeping records of time spent sedentary, or in physical activity, so as to track progress—has also consistently been found to be conducive to increases in physical activity (Michie et al., 2009) and may aid sedentary behavior reduction (Gardner et al., 2016).

## SUMMARY

The literature discussed in this chapter suggests that sedentary behavior is associated with poor mental health in young people. Moreover, the evidence shows that sedentary behavior is a cause of concern for adults with depression, anxiety, bipolar, and schizophrenia. However, studies are predominantly observational and have overwhelmingly used subjective measures of sedentary behavior. Randomized controlled trials in all areas of sedentary behavior and mental health and across all age groups using objective methods (accelerometers/inclinometers) to monitor sedentary behavior are needed. Reducing sedentary behavior involves displacing sitting with physical activity of at least light intensity (e.g., standing). Sedentary behavior may best be reduced in those with mental health complications through minor and minimally disruptive modification to everyday activities and routine. This may be achieved through environmental restructuring (e.g., storing regularly used items away from seats and on shelves) or by increasing motivation to displace sitting with activity (e.g., by education).

# References

Brunet, J., Sabiston, C.M., O'Loughlin, E., Chaiton, M., Low, N.C., O'Loughlin, J.L., 2014. Symptoms of depression are longitudinally associated with sedentary behaviors among young men but not among young women. Prev. Med. 60, 16—20.

Carney, R.M., Freedland, K.E., Miller, G.E., Jaffe, A.S., 2002. Depression as a risk factor for cardiac mortality and morbidity. J. Psychosom. Res. 53 (4), 897—902.

Clemson, L., Fiatarone Singh, M.A., Bundy, A., Cumming, R.G., Manollaras, K., O'Loughlin, P., Black, D., 2012. Integration of balance and strength training into daily life activity to reduce rate of falls in older people (the LiFE study): randomised parallel trial. BMJ 345, 1—15.

Coombs, N., Shelton, N., Rowlands, A., Stamatakis, E., 2013. Children's and adolescents' sedentary behaviour in relation to socioeconomic position. J. Epidemiol. Community Health 67 (10), 868—874.

Dunstan, D.W., Kingwell, B.A., Larsen, R., Healy, G.N., Cerin, E., Hamilton, M.T., Shaw, J.E., Bertovic, D.A., Zimmet, P.Z., Salmon, J., Owen, N., 2012. Breaking up prolonged sitting reduces postprandial glucose and insulin responses. Diabetes Care 35, 976—983.

Dworak, M., Schierl, T., Bruns, T., Struder, H.K., 2007. Impact of singular excessive computer game and television exposure on sleep patterns and memory performance of school-aged children. Pediatrics 120 (5), 978—985.

Gardner, B., Iliffe, S., Fox, K.R., Jefferis, B.J., Hamer, M., 2014. Sociodemographic, behavioural and health factors associated with changes in older adults' TV viewing over 2 years. Int. J. Behav. Nutr. Phys. Act. 11, 102.

Gardner, B., Smith, L., Lorencatto, F., Hamer, M., Biddle, S., 2016. How to reduce sitting time? A review of behaviour change strategies used in sedentary behaviour reduction interventions among adults. Health Psychol. Rev. 10 (1), 89—112.

Gardner-Sood, P., 2015. Health Risk Perceptions in Psychosis (Doctoral thesis). King's College London, London.

Goldstein, B.I., Carnethon, M.R., Matthews, K.A., McIntyre, R.S., Miller, G.E., Raghuveer, G., Stoney, C.M., Wasiak, H., McCrindle, B.W., 2015. Major depressive disorder and bipolar disorder predispose youth to accelerated atherosclerosis and early cardiovascular disease: a scientific statement from the American Heart Association. Circulation 132, 965.

Hamer, M., Stamatakis, E., 2014. Prospective study of sedentary behavior, risk of depression, and cognitive impairment. Med. Sci. Sports Exerc. 46 (4), 718—723.

Hamer, M., Smith, L., Stamatakis, E., 2015. Prospective association of TV viewing with acute phase reactants and coagulation markers: English Longitudinal Study of Ageing. Atherosclerosis 239 (2), 322—327.

Healy, G.N., Dunstan, D.W., Salmon, J., Cerin, C., Shaw, J., Zimmet, P., Owen, N., 2008. Breaks in sedentary time: beneficial association with metabolic risk. Diabetes Care 31, 661—666.

Healy, G.N., Matthews, C.E., Dunstan, D.W., Winkler, E.A., Owen, N., 2011. Sedentary time and cardio-metabolic biomarkers in US adults: NHANES 2003-06. Eur. Heart J. 32, 590—597.

Hoare, E., Milton, K., Foster, C., Allender, S., 2016. The associations between sedentary behaviour and mental health among adolescents: a systematic review. Int. J. Behav. Nutr. Phys. Act. 13, 108.

Janney, C.A., Ganguli, R., Tang, G., Cauley, J.A., Holleman, R.G., Richardson, C.R., Kriska, A.M., 2015. Physical activity and sedentary behavior measured objectively and subjectively in overweight and obese adults with schizophrenia or schizoaffective disorders. J. Clin. Psychiatry 76 (10), 1277—1284.

Lindamer, L.A., McKibbin, C., Norman, G.J., Jordan, L., Harrison, K., Abeyesinhe, S., Patrick, K., 2008. Assessment of physical activity in middle aged and older adults with schizophrenia. Schizophr. Res. 104 (1—3), 294—301.

Liu, M., Wu, L., Yao, S., 2016. Dose-response association of screen time-based sedentary behaviour in children and adolescents and depression: a meta-analysis of observational studies. Br. J. Sports Med. 50, 1252—1258.

Lucas, M., Mekary, R., Pan, A., Mirzaei, F., O'Reilly, E.J., Willett, W.C., Koenen, K., Okereke, O.I., Ascherio, A., 2011. Relation between clinical depression risk and physical activity and time spent watching television in older women: a 10-year prospective follow-up study. Am. J. Epidemiol. 174, 1017—1027.

Matthews, C.E., Chen, K.Y., Freedson, P.S., Buchowski, M.S., Beech, B.M., Pate, R.R., Troiano, R.P., 2008. Amount of time spent in sedentary behaviours in the United States, 2003—2004. Am. J. Epidemiol. 167 (7), 875—881.

Mayo Clinic. Schizophrenia. 2017. https://www.mayoclinic.org/diseases-conditions/schizophrenia/symptoms-causes/syc-20354443.

Merikangas, K.R., Jin, R., He, J.-P., Kessler, R., Lee, S., Sampson, N., Viana, M., Andrade, L., Hu, C., Karam, E., Ladea, M., Mora, M., Browne, M., Ono, Y., Posada-Villa, J., Sagar, R., Zarkov, Z., 2011. Prevalence and correlates of bipolar spectrum disorder in the world mental health survey initiative. Arch. Gen. Psychiatry 68 (3), 241—251.

Michie, S., Abraham, C., Whittington, C., McAteer, J., Gupta, S., 2009. Effective techniques in healthy eating and physical activity interventions: a meta-regression. Health Psychol. 28 (6), 690—701.

Michie, S., van Stralen, M., West, R., 2011. The behaviour change wheel: a new method for characterising and designing behaviour change interventions. Implement. Sci. 6, 42.

Michie, S., Richardson, M., Johnston, M., Abraham, C., Francis, J., Hardeman, W., Eccles, M.P., Cane, J., Wood, C.E., 2013. The behavior change technique taxonomy (v1) of 93 hierarchically clustered techniques: building an international consensus for the reporting of behavior change interventions. Ann. Behav. Med. 46 (1), 81—95.

National Institute of Mental Health. Bipolar Disorder. 2017. https://www.nimh.nih.gov/health/topics/bipolar-disorder/index.shtml.

NICE, 2014. Psychosis and Schizophrenia in Adults: The NICE Guidance on Treatment and Management.

Page, A.S., Cooper, A.R., Griew, P., Jago, R., 2010. Children's screen viewing is related to psychological difficulties irrespective of physical activity. Pediatrics 126 (5), 1011—1017.

Rethorst, C.D., Wipfli, B.M., Landers, D.M., 2009. The antidepressive effects of exercise: a meta-analysis of randomized trials. Sports Med. 39, 491—511.

Rhodes, R.E., Mark, R.S., Temmel, C.P., 2012. Adult sedentary behavior: a systematic review. Am. J. Prev. Med. 42, e3—e28.

Roick, C., Fritz-Wieacker, A., Matschinger, H., Heider, D., Schindler, J., Riedel-Heller, S., Angermeyer, M.C., 2007. Health habits of patients with schizophrenia. Soc. Psychiatry Psychiatr. Epidemiol. 42 (4), 268—276.

Sanchez-Villegas, A., Ara, I., Guillén-Grima, F., Bes-Rastrollo, M., Varo-Cenarruzabeitia, J.J., Martínez-González, M.A., 2010. Physical activity, sedentary index, and mental disorders in the SUN cohort study. Med. Sci. Sports Exerc. 40, 827—834.

Saunders, T., Larouche, R., Colley, R., Tremblay, M., 2012. Acute sedentary behaviour and markers of cardiometabolic risk: a systematic review of intervention studies. J. Nutr. Metab. 2012, 1—12.

T.W. Scheewe, Physical activity and cardiovascular fitness in patients with schizophrenia, in: The Fourth European Congress of Psychomotricity, The Netherlands, Amsterdam. Int. J. Theory Res. Pract., vol. 4(1), 2009, pp. 67–71.

Shrestha, N., Kukkonen-Harjula, K.T., Verbeek, J.H., Ijaz, S., Hermans, V., Bhaumik, S., 2016. Workplace interventions for reducing sitting at work. Cochrane Database Syst. Rev. 17, 3.

Smith, D.J., Langan, J., McLean, G., Guthrie, B., Mercer, S.W., 2013. Schizophrenia is associated with excess multiple physical-health comorbidities but low levels of recorded cardiovascular disease in primary care: cross-sectional study. BMJ Open 3.

Smith, L., Hamer, M., Ucci, M., Marmot, A., Gardner, B., Sawyer, A., Wardle, J., Fisher, A., 2015a. Weekday and weekend patterns of objectively measured sitting, standing, and stepping in a sample of office-based workers: the active buildings study. BMC Public Health 15 (9).

Smith, L., Ekelund, U., Hamer, M., 2015b. The potential yield of non-exercise physical activity energy expenditure in public health. Sports Med. 45 (4), 449–452.

Soundy, A., Wampers, M., Probst, M., De Hert, M., Stubbs, B., Vancampfort, D., Attux, C., Leutwyler, H., Strohle, A., 2013. Physical activity and sedentary behaviour in outpatients with schizophrenia: a systematic review and meta-analysis. Int. J. Ther. Rehabil. 20 (12), 588–595.

Stamatakis, E., Hamer, M., Tilling, K., Lawlor, D., 2012. Sedentary time in relation to cardiometabolic risk factors: differential associations for self-report vs accelerometry in working age adults. Int. J. Epidemiol. 41, 1328–1337.

Stubbs, B., Williams, J., Gaughran, F., Craig, T., 2016. How sedentary are people with psychosis? A systematic review and meta-analysis. Schizophr. Res. 171 (1–3), 103–109.

Suchert, V., Hanewinkel, R., Isensee, B., 2015. Sedentary behavior and indicators of mental health in school-aged children and adolescents: a systematic review. Prev. Med. 76, 48–57.

Sui, X., Brown, W.J., Lavie, C.J., West, D.S., Pate, R.R., Payne, J.P., Blair, S.N., 2015. Associations between television watching and car riding behaviors and development of depressive symptoms: a prospective study. Mayo Clin. Proc. 90 (2), 184–193.

Teychenne, M., Costigan, S., Parker, K., 2015. The association between sedentary behaviour and risk of anxiety: a systematic review. BMC Public Health 15, 513.

Tremblay, M.S., Aubert, S., Barnes, J.D., Saunders, T.J., Carson, V., Latimer-Cheung, A.E., Chastin, S.F.M., Altenburg, T.M., Chinapaw, M.J.M., SBRN Terminology Consensus Project Participants, 2017. Sedentary behavior research network (SBRN) – terminology consensus project process and outcome. Int. J. Behav. Nutr. Phys. Act. 14 (1), 75.

Van der Kooy, K., van Hout, H., Marwijk, H., Marten, H., Stehouwer, C., Beekman, A., 2007. Depression and the risk for cardiovascular diseases: systematic review and meta-analysis. Int. J. Geriatr. Psychiatry 22, 613–626.

van Uffelen, J.G., van Gellecum, Y.R., Burton, N.W., Peeters, G., Heesch, K.C., Brown, W.J., 2013. Sitting-time, physical activity, and depressive symptoms in mid-aged women. Am. J. Prev. Med. 45 (3), 276–281.

Vancampfort, D., Probst, M., Knapen, J., Carraro, A., De Hert, M., 2012. Associations between sedentary behaviour and metabolic parameters in patients with schizophrenia. Psychiatry Res. 200 (2–3), 73–78.

Vancampfort, D., Vansteelandt, K., Correll, C.U., Mitchell, A.J., De Herdt, A., Sienaert, P., Probst, M., De Hert, M., 2013. Metabolic syndrome and metabolic abnormalities in bipolar disorder: a meta-analysis of prevalence rates and moderators. Am. J. Psychiatry 170.

Vancampfort, D., Firth, J., Schuch, F., Rosenbaum, S., De Hert, M., Mugisha, J., Probst, M., Stubbs, B., 2016a. Physical activity and sedentary behaviour in people with bipolar disorder: a systematic review and meta-analysis. J. Affect. Disord. 201, 145–152.

Vancampfort, D., Rosenbaum, S., Probst, M., Connaughton, J., du Plessis, C., Yamamoto, T., Stubbs, B., 2016b. Top 10 research questions to promote physical activity in bipolar disorders: a consensus statement from the International Organization of Physical Therapists in Mental Health. J. Affect. Disord. 195, 82–87.

Walker, E.R., McGee, R.E., Druss, B.G., 2015. Mortality in mental disorders and global disease burden implications: a systematic review and meta-analysis. JAMA Psychiatry 72 (4), 334–341.

Wang, X., Perry, A.C., 2006. Metabolic and physiologic responses to video game play in 7- to 10-year-old boys. Arch. Pediatr. Adolesc. Med. 160 (4), 411–415.

World Health Organization. Depression and other common mental disorders. 2017.

White, I., Smith, L., Aggio, D., Shankar, S., Begum, S., Matei, R., Fox, K., Hamer, M., Iliffe, S., Jefferis, B., Tyley, N., Gardner, B., 2017. On Your Feet to Earn Your Seat: pilot RCT of a theory-based sedentary behaviour reduction intervention for older adults. Pilot Feasibility Stud. 3, 23.

Zahl, T., Steinsbekk, S., Wichstrøm, L., 2017. Physical activity, sedentary behavior, and symptoms of major depression in middle childhood. Pediatrics 139 (2), e20161711.

Zhai, L., Zhang, Y., Zhang, D., 2015. Sedentary behaviour and the risk of depression: a meta-analysis. Br. J. Sports Med. 49, 705–709.

# 7

# Exercise for Older People With Mental Illness

*Li-Jung Chen[1], Po-Wen Ku[2], Kenneth R. Fox[3]*

[1] Department of Exercise Health Science, National Taiwan University of Sport, Taichung, Taiwan; [2] Graduate Institute of Sports and Health, National Changhua University of Education, Changhua, Taiwan; [3] Centre for Exercise, Nutrition and Health Sciences, University of Bristol, Bristol, United Kingdom

*Exercise-Based Interventions for Mental Illness*
https://doi.org/10.1016/B978-0-12-812605-9.00007-1

121

## INTRODUCTION

According to the World Health Organization (WHO), mental disorders are defined as a combination of abnormal thoughts, emotions, behaviors, and relationships with others, such as depression, schizophrenia, and intellectual disabilities (World Health Organization, 2017). Mental and neurological disorders, especially depression, are among the major contributors to the global burden of disease as assessed by disability-adjusted life years (DALYs) (World Health Organization, 2001). They accounted for 11% of DALYs in 1999 and are expected to rise to 15% by the year 2020 (World Health Organization, 2001). Major depression is also predicted to be the second leading cause of DALYs by 2020 (Lopez and World Health Organization, 2001; Murray and Lopez, 1996). Moreover, serious mental illnesses such as major depression, schizophrenia, and bipolar disorder are associated with substantially decreased life expectancy (on average 12.9 life-years lost for men and 11.8 life-years lost for women) (Chang et al., 2011), increased mortality (Fekadu et al., 2015), and increased disability in social, emotional, and physical domains of life (Bijl and Ravelli, 2000).

Research from a review of 155 surveys across 59 countries showed that the prevalence of common mental disorders within the past 12 months was 17.6% between 16 and 65 years of age and 29.2% across the lifetime (Steel et al., 2014). Among older adults, approximately 15% of those aged 60 years and over suffer from a mental disorder (World Health Organization, 2016b). Older age is associated with increased disease burden (Niccoli and Partridge, 2012), the use of medical services (World Health Organization and US National Institute of Aging, 2011), and significant health care costs (Seshamani and Gray, 2003). Moreover, there is a dramatically increasing population of older people around the world (World Health Organization, 2015). Between 2015 and 2050, the number of older adults aged 60 years and older is expected to more than double, and life expectancy at birth is also projected to rise by 7 years (United Nations, 2015). Given the increase in life expectancy, the number of older people who experience a mental illness may greatly increase. Therefore there is a need to address strategies for improving health in older adults living with mental disorders. Although a decrease in the prevalence of mental disorders with advanced age has been found in some studies (Klap et al., 2003; Reynolds et al., 2015), mental disorders among older adults can lead to serious life consequences (Fiske et al., 2009). For example, depression in older adults is more closely associated with increased risks of suicide than in younger adults (Fiske et al., 2009) and dementia, which is mainly a disease of later life, is one of the major contributors to disability and dependency (World Health Organization, 2016a).

The WHO reported that the most common mental illness among older adults is depression, followed by dementia (World Health Organization, 2016b). Depression prevalence varies according to diagnostic criteria. The prevalence of depression in older adults has been reported between 0.3% and 13.8% using the International Statistical Classification of Diseases and Related Health Problems, 10th Revision (ICD-10) criteria and between 1.0% and 38.6% with the EURO-D depression scale (Guerra et al., 2016). The prevalence figures according to the Diagnostic and Statistical Manual of Mental Disorders (DSM-MD) or ICD-10 depressive episode criterion among older adults in various countries are shown in Fig. 7.1 (Djernes, 2006; Guerra et al., 2016). Additionally, estimates of dementia prevalence for those aged 60 years and over range between 4.7% and 8.7% with the highest standardized prevalence being found in North Africa/Middle East (8.7%) and the lowest in Central Europe (4.7%; Fig. 7.2) (Prince et al., 2015).

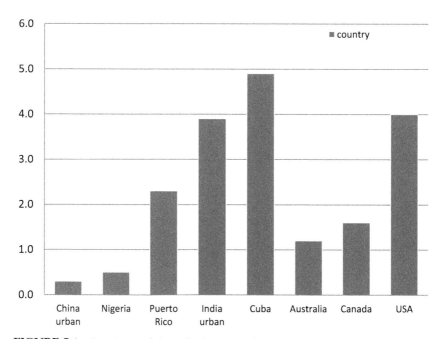

FIGURE 7.1 Prevalence of clinically diagnosed depression (%) in older adults. *Based on Guerra, M., Prina, A., Ferri, C., Acosta, D., Gallardo, S., Huang, Y., Jacob, K., Jimenez-Velazquez, I., Rodriguez, J.L., Liu, Z., 2016. A comparative cross-cultural study of the prevalence of late life depression in low and middle income countries. J. Affect. Disord. 190, 362—368. Djernes (2006).*

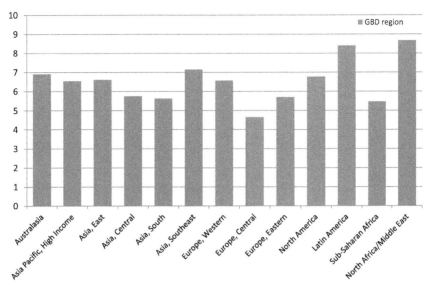

FIGURE 7.2    Estimates of dementia prevalence (percentage) for older adults by the global gurden of disease (GBD) regions. *Based on Prince et al. (2015).*

## Benefits of Physical Activity and Exercise

Exercise or physical activity has been identified as an effective method for health promotion (World Health Organization, 2010). Performing exercise or physical activity at moderate to vigorous intensity is associated with longevity (Arem et al., 2015; Wen et al., 2011), reduced hospitalization costs (Ku et al., 2016b), and reduced risk of cardiometabolic disease (Lin et al., 2015). Well-documented evidence has also demonstrated the benefits of exercise in terms of maintaining or improving various mental health conditions among older adults, such as reduced risks for cognitive impairment and dementia (Carvalho et al., 2014; Chu et al., 2015; Kirk-Sanchez and McGough, 2014; Ku et al., 2016a; Stubbs et al., 2017a), as well as reduced depressive symptoms (Ku et al., 2009).

Although physical activity patterns may vary across different countries, research has shown that older people are less likely than younger people to be regularly active and meet recommended physical activity guidelines, especially in Western countries (Fig. 7.3A) (Ku et al., 2006; McClain et al., 2014; Sun et al., 2013). A trend of decreased physical activity with increasing age has been documented in Canada, the United Kingdom, and the United States with on average around 20% difference between those aged 16–24 years and those aged 65 years and over. Although no similar trend was seen in Asian countries, the prevalence of

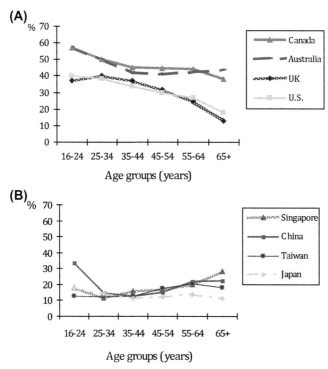

**FIGURE 7.3** Physical activity participation among different age groups in (A) Western and (B) Asian countries. *From Ku, P.W., Fox, K.R., Mckenna, J., Peng, T.L., 2006. Prevalence of leisure-time physical activity in Taiwanese adults: results of four national surveys, 2000–04. Prev. Med. 43, 454–457.*

engaging in physical activity remained low among older adults (Fig. 7.3B; Ku et al., 2006). Another study reviewed 53 articles showing that patterns of participation in physical activity decreased progressively with age from 50.8% in the 60- to 64-year age group to 15.4% in the 85+ years age group (Sun et al., 2013).

Among individuals with mental disorders, physical activity is consistently found to be much lower than otherwise healthy controls (Chen et al., 2016; Stubbs et al., 2016, 2017b). In this population, the negative symptoms of mental illness may affect exercise motivation, and the sedative effects of medication may also act as a barrier to exercise (Yung and Firth, 2016).

Older age, physical inactivity, and mental illness each contribute to an increased risk of poor physical health. Understanding the effects of exercise in older adults with mental disorders is of particular interest, especially given the world's population is rapidly aging. Several reviews have focused on the benefits of exercise for mitigating the symptoms of mental disorders among adults (Bridle et al., 2012; Pearsall et al., 2014; Rosenbaum et al., 2014; Vancampfort et al., 2015). This chapter provides a comprehensive review of the effects of exercise interventions on the two most common mental disorders (depression and dementia) facing older people and provides implications for clinical practice and future research.

# METHODS

## Search Strategy

An electronic database search of PubMed, PsycINFO, and Google Scholar was conducted with a combination of the keywords: (exercise or physical activity) and (older or elderly) and (mental illness or depression or depressed or dementia or Alzheimer's disease). The reference lists of related reviews were also hand-searched. The search was limited to the peer-reviewed journal articles written in English from January 2000 to March 2017.

## Selection Criteria

Studies of randomized controlled trials (RCT) examining the effects of exercise interventions on depression severity or cognitive function for older people with diagnosed depression or dementia (mean age equal or greater than 65 years old) were included. Only studies using psychiatric diagnoses such as the DSM-IV or ICD-10 were incorporated in this review. In order to mitigate the potential confounding effect on the association of exercise with mental illness, study samples based on other clinical populations (e.g., depressed older adults poststroke; Sims et al., 2009) or depressed individuals with Alzheimer's disease (Williams and Tappen, 2008) or those with more than one mental illness were excluded. Also, interventions incorporating strategies other than exercise were not included in analyses in order to clarify the independent effect of exercise (Christofoletti et al., 2008; Ciechanowski et al., 2004).

## Data Extraction and Appraisal

The first author undertook the initial screening and extracted the data from selected articles. These procedures were checked by the second author. If disagreements occurred about the inclusion and the extracted data, papers were reread, and discussions continued until agreement was reached.

# RESULTS

## Effects of Exercise on Severity of Depression

A total of eight eligible studies based on seven RCTs were identified and included in Table 7.1. The characteristics of these intervention studies are summarized in Table 7.2.

Six of seven trials, including various types of exercise, showed reductions in depression severity. The majority of studies had featured a 45- to 60-min, facility-based exercise regimen, 3 days per week for less than 16 weeks. The average duration of the interventions was 15 weeks (range: 8–24). Although the study by Brene et al. (2007) did not yield a significant effect for exercise, both an exercise group ($P = .09$) and a medication group (Sertraline; $P = .06$) produced a similar and borderline significant improvement when compared with the control group after adjusting for baseline depression status.

A high-intensity progressive resistance training program, but not an equivalent low-intensity regimen, showed a positive effect (Singh et al., 2005). In a study by Murri et al. (2015), the progressive aerobic group exercise combined with medical treatment (Sertraline) showed the greatest effect, followed by a nonprogressive mixed exercise group and a Sertraline only group. Similarly, a combination of Tai Chi and medication (Escitalopram) yielded a stronger effect than usual care (Lavretsky et al., 2011). Among the seven trials, the Hamilton Rating Scale of Depression and Geriatric Depression Scale were the most commonly used instruments for assessing depression.

## Effects of Exercise on the Cognitive Function of Older Adults With Dementia

After screening, 17 RCTs meeting the selection criteria were identified and are listed in Table 7.3. Table 7.4 summarizes the characteristics of these studies.

Most of the studies adopted aerobic exercise (n = 8) or combined exercise (e.g., aerobic, resistance, stretch, and balance activities; n = 6), followed by strength/resistance training (n = 2) and balance/stretch activity (n = 2). The majority of studies involved a 30- to 60-min home-based or facility-based exercise regimen for less than 16 weeks. Frequency of the interventions was diverse, including 1–2 sessions/week (n = 7), 3–4 sessions/week (n = 6), and 5–7 sessions/week (n = 5). The average duration of the interventions was $14.3 \pm 10.7$ weeks.

Cognitive outcome measures assessed in these studies were diverse. As a measure of global cognition, the Mini-Mental State Examination

TABLE 7.1 Summary of Exercise Interventions in Older Adults With Depression (Using Clinical Diagnosis)

| Author, Year (Country) | Participant, n (Mean Age ± SD) | Diagnostic Criteria | Intervention (I) | Control (C) | Outcome | Effect (Yes/No)[a] |
|---|---|---|---|---|---|---|
| Mather et al. (2002), UK | Primary care, psychiatric services, community I: n = 43 (63.7) C: n = 43 (66.2) | Mood (affective disorder), ICD-10 and GDS ≥ 10 | 10 weeks of 2 × 45-min weekly weight-bearing group exercise | Health education | HRSD and GDS | Yes (note: significant changes in all outcomes with no between-group difference) |
| Chou et al. (2004) and Chou (2008a), China | Outpatients (total n = 14, 72.6 ± 4.2) I: n = 7 C: n = 7 | Major depression/ dysthymia, DSM-IV, and CES-D ≥ 16 | 12 weeks of 3 × 45-min weekly Tai Chi training | Wait-list control | CES-D | Yes |
| Singh et al. (2005), USA | Community I: High, n = 20 (69 ± 5) I: Low, n = 20 (70 ± 7) C: GP care, n = 20 (69 ± 7) | Major/minor depression or dysthymia, DSM-IV, and GDS ≥ 14; | High intensity: 8 weeks of 3 × 60-min weekly PRT (80% of one repetition maximum), three sets of eight repetitions Low intensity: 8 weeks of 3 × 60-min weekly non-PRT (20% of one repetition maximum), three sets of eight repetitions | Standard GP care | GDS and HRSD | Yes (for both outcomes); high but not low intensity showed the reduction effect |

| Study | Sample | Diagnosis | Intervention | Control | Outcome | Result |
|---|---|---|---|---|---|---|
| Tsang et al. (2006), China | Care and attention homes I: n = 48 (82.1 ± 7.2) C: n = 34 (82.7 ± 6.8) | Diagnosed depression, GDS (cut-off NR) | 16 weeks of 3 × 30- to 45-min weekly Baduanjin (qigong). | Newspaper reading | GDS | Yes |
| Brenes et al. (2007), USA | Community I: Exercise, n = 14 (73.5 ± 7.8) I: Medication, n = 11 (76.4 ± 6.4) C: Usual care: n = 12 (73.9 ± 5.8) | Minor depression, DSM-IV | Exercise: 16 weeks of 3 × 60-min weekly aerobic and resistance training. Medication (Sertraline): 25 mg/day (week 1), 50 mg/day (week 2–3), 100 mg/day (week 4–7), 150 mg/day (week 8–16) | Usual care | HRSD and GDS | No (for both outcomes). Both exercise (vs. usual care, P = .09) and sertraline (vs. usual care, P = .06) showed nonsignificant effects on HRSD after adjusting for baseline dep. |
| Lavertsky et al. (2011), USA | Community I: EsCIT + TC, n = 36 (69.1 ± 7.0) C: EsCIT + HE: n = 37 (72.0 ± 7.4) | Major depression, DSM-IV, and HDRS ≥ 16 | EsCIT and 10 weeks of 1 × 120-min weekly Tai Chi class | EsCIT and health education | HDRS | Yes. EsCIT + TC showed greater reduction effect |

*Continued*

**TABLE 7.1** Summary of Exercise Interventions in Older Adults With Depression (Using Clinical Diagnosis)—cont'd

| Author, Year (Country) | Participant, n (Mean Age ± SD) | Diagnostic Criteria | Intervention (I) | Control (C) | Outcome | Effect (Yes/No)[a] |
|---|---|---|---|---|---|---|
| Murri et al. (2015), Italy | Outpatients<br>I: SERT + PAE, n = 42<br>(75.0 ± 6.2)<br>I: SERT + NPE, n = 37<br>(75.0 ± 6.3)<br>C: SERT, n = 42<br>(75.6 ± 5.6) | Diagnosed major depression and HDRS ≥ 18 | SERT + PAE:<br>Sertraline and 24 weeks of 3 × 60-min weekly progressive aerobic group exercise<br>SERT + NPE:<br>Sertraline and 24 weeks of 3 × 60-min weekly nonprogressive mixed exercise in a group | Standard care: sertraline by psychiatrists | HRSD | Yes.<br>SERT + PAE showed the greatest effect, followed by SERT + NPE and SERT. |

*AMS*, Alzheimer's Mood Scale; *C*, control group; *CSDD*, Cornell Scale for Depression; *DSM-IV*, Diagnostic and Statistical Manual of Mental Disorders; *GDS*, Geriatric Depression Scale; *EsCIT*, escitalopram; *GP*, general practitioner; *HE*, health education; *HRSD*, Hamilton Rating Scale of Depression; *I*, intervention group; *ICD-10*, The International Statistical Classification of Diseases and Related Health Problems 10th Revision; *MMSE*, Mini-Mental State Examination; *NR*, nor reported; *OAS*, Observed Affect Scale; *PHQ-9*, Patient Health Questionnaire; *PRT*, Progressive Resistance Training; *PSE*, Present State Examination; *TC*, Tai Chi; *SERT*, sertraline.
[a]*An effect was observed on at least one outcome measure.*

**TABLE 7.2** Descriptive Statistics for Studies Included in Table 7.1

| Variable | Number of Studies |
|---|---|
| *COUNTRY* | |
| USA | 3 |
| UK | 1 |
| Italy | 1 |
| China | 2 |
| Total sample size (n) (mean $\pm$ SD) | 14–121 (74.3 $\pm$ 37.4) |
| <50 | 2 |
| 50–99 | 4 |
| 100+ | 1 |
| *INTERVENTION CATEGORY[a]* | |
| Aerobic | 1 |
| Strength/resistance | 2 |
| Balance/stretch (e.g., Tai Chi, qigong) | 3 |
| Combined exercise | 2 |
| *INTERVENTION COMPONENTS[a]* | |
| Frequency (sessions per week) | |
| 1 | 1 |
| 2 | 1 |
| 3 | 5 |
| Time (minutes per session) | |
| 45 | 3 |
| 60 | 3 |
| >60 | 1 |
| Intensity | |
| Moderate-to-vigorous | 1 |
| Not reported | 6 |
| Duration (weeks) (mean $\pm$ SD) | 8–24 (15.0 $\pm$ 6.2) |
| <12 | 3 |
| 12–16 | 3 |
| >16 | 1 |

*Continued*

**TABLE 7.2**   Descriptive Statistics for Studies Included in Table 7.1—cont'd

| Variable | Number of Studies |
|---|---|
| *CONTROL PROGRAM[a]* | |
| Health education | 2 |
| Standard/usual care | 3 |
| Wait-list control | 1 |
| Others | 1 |
| *DEPRESSION MEASURE* | |
| HRSD | 5 |
| GDS | 4 |
| CES-D | 1 |
| *EFFECT* | |
| Yes[b] | 6 |
| No | 1 |

[a]*The number of studies may be over eight due to a multiple group intervention.*
[b]*An effect was observed on at least one outcome measure.*

(MMSE) was commonly utilized (n = 10). The Verbal Fluency Tests (n = 5) and the Clock Drawing Test (n = 4) were used for evaluating executive function. Other dimensions of cognition measured in these studies were memory, attention, hand—eye coordination, and language ability.

Among the 17 studies, 12 studies showed a positive effect of exercise on at least one measure of cognitive function, suggesting that exercise may be a promising treatment for dementia. In total, 16 studies assessed the effect of exercise on global cognition using the MMSE, Alzheimer's disease Assessment Scale cognitive subscale, or Clinical Dementia Rating Sum of Boxes. Among them, 10 studies revealed that the intervention had positive effects of exercise on global cognition. The remaining six studies did not show positive effects for exercise.

With regard to executive function, 4 of 13 studies showed significant effects for exercise. Studies examining the effects of the exercise on other dimensions are too few to allow us to reach a consistent finding. Overall, there was substantial heterogeneity in participants, type of intervention program, comparison groups, and outcome measures.

**TABLE 7.3** Summary of Exercise Interventions in Older Adults With Dementia

| Author, Year (Country) | Participant, n (Mean Age ± SD) | Diagnostic Criteria | Intervention (I) | Control (C) | Cognitive-Related Outcomes | Effect (Yes/No) |
|---|---|---|---|---|---|---|
| Van de Winckel et al. (2004), Belgium | Inpatients I: n = 15 (81.3 ± 4.2) C: n = 10 (81.9 ± 4.2) | Infarct dementia or NINCDS-ADRDA for AD | 12 weeks of 30-min daily group-based dance session | Conversation | MMSE  ADS6 | Yes. Significant effects after 6 and 12 weeks  Yes. A significant effect for subset (fluency) after 12 weeks |
| Stevens and Killeen (2006), Australia | Long-term care I: n = 24 (79.0) C1: n = 30 (81.0) C2: n = 21 (81.5) | Diagnosed dementia or MMSE (10–22) | 12 weeks of 3 × 30-min weekly joint and muscle group movement | C1: Usual care C2: Social visits | Clock-Drawing Test | Yes. Exercise group (vs. C1) had a significant lower rate of cognitive decline |
| Hokkanen et al. (2008), Finland | Dementia nursing home I: n = 19 (79.9 ± 7.7) C: n = 10 (84.5 ± 3.4) | Diagnosed vascular dementia, AD, and other types of dementia | 9 weeks of 1 × 30- to 45-min weekly dance and movement | Usual care | MMSE  Clock-Drawing Test  Word List Savings, The Picture Description Task | Yes: Slight improvement after 13 weeks (follow-up)  Yes: Significant effects after 9 weeks  No for these outcomes |

Continued

**TABLE 7.3** Summary of Exercise Interventions in Older Adults With Dementia—cont'd

| Author, Year (Country) | Participant, n (Mean Age ± SD) | Diagnostic Criteria | Intervention (I) | Control (C) | Cognitive-Related Outcomes | Effect (Yes/No) |
|---|---|---|---|---|---|---|
| Miu et al. (2008), China | Outpatients<br>I: n = 36 (75 ± 7)<br>C: n = 49 (785 ± 6) | Mild-to-moderate dementia and MMSE (10–26) | 12 months of 2 × 45- to 60-min weekly aerobic exercise training | Usual care | MMSE<br><br>ADAS-Cog | No<br><br>No |
| Kwak et al. (2008), South Korea | Community<br>I: n = 15 (79.7 ± 6.6)<br>C: n = 15 (82.3 ± 7.1) | Diagnosed AD or other dementia and MMSE (10–26) | 12 months of 2–3 × 30- to 60-min weekly chair exercise, resistance, and stretching training; $VO_{2max}$ (30%–60%) | Usual care | MMSE | Yes. Significant effects after 6 and 12 months. |
| Eggermont et al. (2009a), Netherlands | Nursing home<br>I: n = 30 (85.0 ± 5.0)<br>C: n = 31 (84.2 ± 4.6) | Diagnosed dementia and MMSE (10–24) | 6 weeks of 5 × 30-min weekly hand movements | Read aloud program | Executive function (Digital Span, Category Fluency, Stop Signal Test) Memory (RBMT, Eight Words Test) | No (for all outcomes) |
| Eggermont et al. (2009b), Netherlands | Nursing home (85.4)<br>I: n = 51<br>C: n = 46 | Diagnosed moderate dementia and MMSE (10–24) | 6 weeks of 5 × 30-min weekly self-paced walking | Social visits | Executive function (Digital Span, Category Fluency, Letter Fluency) Memory (Eight Words Test, Face Recognition, Picture Recognition) | No (for all outcomes) |

| Study | Participants | Diagnosis | Intervention | Control | Outcome measure | Effect |
|---|---|---|---|---|---|---|
| Steinberg et al. (2009), USA | Outpatients; I: n = 14 (76.5 ± 3.9) C: n = 13 (74.0 ± 8.1) | NINCDS-ADRDA and MMSE ≥ 10 | 12 weeks of daily aerobic brisk walking + strength + balance and flexibility training | Home safety training | Language disturbance (Boston Naming Test) <br> Verbal learning and memory (HVLT) | No <br><br> No |
| Kemoun et al. (2010), France | Nursing home; I: n = 16 (76.5 ± 3.9) C: n = 15 (74.0 ± 8.1) | DSM IV and MMSE < 23 | 15 weeks of 3 × 60-min weekly walking From light to moderate intensity | Usual care | French ERFC | Yes. Significant effects after 15 weeks |
| Venturelli et al. (2011), Italy | Nursing home; I: n = 12 (83 ± 6) C: n = 12 (85 ± 5) | MMSE (5–15) and CDR3–CDR4 | 24 weeks of 4 × 30-min weekly walking. Moderate intensity | Usual care | MMSE | Yes. Walking group had a significant lower rate of cognitive decline |
| Yágüez et al. (2011), UK | Outpatients; I: n = 15 (70.5 ± 8.0) C: n = 12 (75.7 ± 6.9) | ICD-10 (F00.0, F00.1, F00.2, F00.9) and MMSE (12–29) | 6 weeks of 2 h (30-min break) weekly movement training for improving balance and muscle (Brain Gym) | Usual care | CANTAB-Expedio: <br> • Matching to sample test (simultaneous and delayed), <br> • Pattern recognition memory, <br> • Rapid visual information processing, | Yes. Significant effects after 6 weeks on the simultaneous condition, but not on the delayed condition of matching to sample test. <br> Yes. Significant effects after 6 weeks on the pattern recognition memory. <br> Yes. Significant effects after 6 weeks on the |

Continued

**TABLE 7.3**  Summary of Exercise Interventions in Older Adults With Dementia—cont'd

| Author, Year (Country) | Participant, n (Mean Age ± SD) | Diagnostic Criteria | Intervention (I) | Control (C) | Cognitive-Related Outcomes | Effect (Yes/No) |
|---|---|---|---|---|---|---|
| | | | | | • Spatial working memory, • Paired Associate learning, • The motor screening | rapid visual information processing test. No significant effects on working memory and motor control. |
| Vreugdenhil et al. (2012), Australia | Outpatients I: n = 20 (73.5) C: n = 20 (74.7) | DSM IV and NINCDS-ADRDA | 16 weeks of 30-min daily brisk walking + body strength and balance training | Usual care | ADAS-Cog | Yes. Significant effects after 4 months |
| | | | | | MMSE | Yes. Significant effects after 4 months |
| Arcoverde et al. (2014), Brazil | Outpatients I: n = 10 (78.5) C: n = 10 (79.0) | NINCDS-ADRDA, NINCDS-AIREN, MMSE ≥ 15, and CDR 1 (moderate memory loss) | 16 weeks of 2 × 30-min weekly treadmill training; Moderate intensity of 60% $VO_{2max}$ | Usual care | MMSE | No |
| | | | | | CAMCOG | Yes. Significant effects after 16 weeks |
| | | | | | Clock-Drawing Test | No |
| | | | | | Executive function: Verbal Fluency Test RAVLT Digit Span Trail Making Test Stroop test | No significant effects for all outcome measures |

| | | | | | | |
|---|---|---|---|---|---|---|
| Cheng et al. (2014), China | Nursing home; I: mahjong, n = 36 (81.9 ± 6.2) I: tai chi, n = 39 (81.8 ± 7.4) C: n = 35 (80.9 ± 7.2) | MMSE (10–24) and CDR ≥ 0.5 | 12 weeks of 3 × 60-min weekly training 1. Mahjong 2. Tai Chi (sitting) | Handicrafts | CDR-Sum-of-box (SB): • Total • Cognition • Function | Mahjong: Yes. Significant effects on CDR-SB total compared with the control; Tai Chi: No |
| Bosser et al. (2015), Netherlands | Nursing home; I: combined, n = 41 (81.9 ± 6.2) I: aerobic, n = 41 (81.8 ± 7.4) C: social program, n = 41 (80.9 ± 7.2) | Diagnosed dementia and MMSE (9–23) | Combined exercise: 9 weeks of 4 × 30-min weekly aerobic and resistance training Aerobic exercise: 9 weeks of 4 × 30-min weekly moderate-to-high intensity walking | Social visits | Global cognition (MMSE) Visual memory (face recognition and picture recognition) Verbal memory Executive function | Combined exercise: Yes Combined exercise: Yes Combined exercise: Yes Combined exercise: Yes |
| Holthoff et al. (2015), Germany | Outpatients I: n = 15 (72.4 ± 4.3) C: n = 15 (70.7 ± 5.4) | NINCDS-ADRDA and mild to moderate AD | 12 weeks of 3 × 30-min weekly resistance leg training on a movement trainer | Clinical visits | MMSE Executive function and language ability (semantic word fluency) Reaction time and motor skills (FETZ-test, meter) | No Yes. Significant effects after 24 weeks (follow-up) Yes. Significant effects after 24 weeks (follow-up) |

Continued

**TABLE 7.3**   Summary of Exercise Interventions in Older Adults With Dementia—cont'd

| Author, Year (Country) | Participant, n (Mean Age ± SD) | Diagnostic Criteria | Intervention (I) | Control (C) | Cognitive-Related Outcomes | Effect (Yes/No) |
|---|---|---|---|---|---|---|
| Ohman et al. (2016), Finland | Community (dyads) I: home-based exercise, n = 70 (77.7 ± 5.4) I: group-based exercise, n = 70 (78.3 ± 5.1) C: usual care, n = 70 (78.1 ± 5.3) | Diagnosed dementia based on NINCDS-ADRDA | Home-based: 12 months of 2 × 60-min weekly mixed exercise Group-based: 12 months of 2 × 4-h weekly mixed exercise | Usual care | MMSE Clock-Drawing Test Verbal fluency | No Yes. Small effect for home-based group No |

ADAS-Cog; Alzheimer's Disease Assessment Scale-Cognitive Subscale; ADS6; Amsterdam Dementia Screening Test 6; CAMCOG, Cambridge Cognitive Examination; CANTAB-Expedio, Cambridge Neuropsychological Test Automated Battery-Expedio; CDR, Clinical Dementia Rating; DSM IV, Diagnostic and Statistical Manual of Mental Disorders, Fourth Edition; French ERFC, Rapid Evaluation of Cognitive Function (French version); HVLT, Hopkins Verbal Learning Test; ICD-10, International Statistical Classification of Diseases and Related Health Problems 10th Revision; MMSE, Mini-Mental State Examination; NINCDS-ADRDA; National Institute of Neurological and Communicative Disorders and Stroke and the Alzheimer's Disease and Related Disorders Association; NINCDS-AIREN, National Institute of Neurological Disorders and Stroke and Association Internationale pour la Recherché et l'Enseignement en Neurosciences; RAVLT; Rey Auditory Verbal Learning Test.

**TABLE 7.4** Descriptive Statistics for Studies Included in Table 7.3

| Variable | Number of Studies[a] |
|---|---|
| *REGION* | |
| America | 2 |
| Western Europe | 10 |
| East Asia | 3 |
| Australia | 2 |
| Total sample size (n) (mean ± SD) | 20–210 (61.4 ± 50.9) |
| <50 | 10 |
| 50–99 | 4 |
| 100+ | 3 |
| *INTERVENTION CATEGORY[a]* | |
| Aerobic | 8 |
| Strength/resistance | 2 |
| Balance/stretch (e.g., Tai Chi, qigong) | 2 |
| Combined exercise | 6 |
| *INTERVENTION COMPONENTS[a]* | |
| Frequency (sessions per week) | |
| 1–2 | 7 |
| 3–4 | 6 |
| 5–7 | 5 |
| Time (minutes per session) | |
| 30 | 9 |
| 31–60 | 6 |
| >60 | 2 |
| Not reported | 1 |
| Intensity | |
| Moderate-to-vigorous | 1 |
| Moderate | 2 |
| Low-to-moderate | 2 |
| Not reported | 12 |

*Continued*

**TABLE 7.4** Descriptive Statistics for Studies Included in Table 7.3—cont'd

| Variable | Number of Studies[a] |
|---|---|
| Duration (months) (mean ± SD) | 6—52 (14.3 ± 10.7) |
| <4 | 11 |
| 4—6 | 3 |
| >6 | 3 |
| **CONTROL PROGRAM[a]** | |
| Standard/usual care | 10 |
| Clinical visit/social visit/conversation | 5 |
| Others | 3 |
| **SELECTED COGNITION MEASURES[b]** | |
| Global cognitive function: MMSE | 10 (6) |
| Global cognitive function: ADAS-Cog | 2 (1) |
| Global cognitive function: CDR-(SB) | 1 (0) |
| Global cognitive function: ADS6 | 1 (1) |
| Global cognitive function: ERFC | 1 (1) |
| Global cognitive function: CAMCOG | 1 (1) |
| Executive function: Verbal Fluency Tests | 5 (1) |
| Executive function: Clock Drawing Test[c] | 4 (3) |
| Executive function: Digital Span | 3 (0) |
| Executive function: Stroop Test | 1 (0) |
| Memory: Eight Words Tests/Word List Savings | 3 (0) |
| Memory: Face Recognition | 2 (1) |
| Memory: Picture Recognition | 2 (1) |
| Memory: Verbal learning and memory | 1 (0) |
| Attention: Reaction Time | 1 (1) |
| Attention: Trail Making Test | 1 (0) |
| Hand—eye coordination: FETZ-test | 1 (1) |
| Language disturbance: Boston Naming Test | 1 (0) |
| Language disturbance: The Picture Description Task | 1 (0) |

**TABLE 7.4** Descriptive Statistics for Studies Included in Table 7.3—cont'd

| Variable | Number of Studies[a] |
|---|---|
| *EFFECT*[b] | |
| Total number of studies | 17 (12) |
| For AD patients only | 8 (7) |
| For patients with various types of dementia | 9 (5) |

[a]*The number of studies may be over 17 due to multiple groups in an intervention.*
[b]*The figure in brackets represents the total number of studies showing a significant effect on at least one outcome measure.*
[c]*The Clock Drawing Test in some studies were employed for assessing executive function instead of global cognition.*

# DISCUSSION

## Main Findings

This chapter reviewed studies assessing the effects of exercise interventions using RCTs on depression and dementia in older adults. Results from seven trials showed consistent and positive effects of exercise on depression severity for older adults, which are consistent with results of previous reviews (Bridle et al., 2012; Cooney et al., 2013; Schuch et al., 2016b).

In contrast, although some studies produced positive effects of exercise on global cognition in patients with dementia, the findings across 17 studies were mixed. Additionally, the effects of physical exercise on specific dimensions of cognition are inconsistent or too few to reach a robust conclusion. There is therefore insufficient evidence to confirm the benefits of exercise for improving cognitive performance, supporting two recent systematic reviews (Forbes et al., 2015; Ohman et al., 2014).

## Recommendations for Clinical Practice

Based on a few small trials, this review revealed that exercise programs, typically 45–60 min duration, performed three or more days per week for 12–16 weeks, maybe a safe and effective augmentation to antidepressant therapy in geriatric depression. Exercise may be not more effective than antidepressant medication for reducing symptoms of depression (Brenes et al., 2007). However, a combination of exercise and medication could provide greater reduction effect for alleviating depression severity than usual psychiatric care (Lavretsky et al., 2011; Murri et al., 2015).

The mechanisms by which exercise interventions might work for depression are not fully understood. Exercise may provide a sense of enjoyment and fulfillment, enhance self-efficacy and self-esteem by mastering new skills, and offer opportunity for social interaction, which may in turn contribute to the reduction in depression severity (Ku et al., 2012, 2017a,b). Biological mechanisms operating in exercise engagement may also include changes in endorphin and monoamine levels, reduction in the levels of the stress hormone cortisol, and also stimulate growth of new nerve cells relating the release of brain-derived growth neurotrophic factor (Cooney et al., 2013).

This review provides clinicians with a rationale for including exercise as a potential strategy in the medical treatment plan of late-life depression. Clinical professionals may consider utilizing exercise as an adjunct to the regimen of patients with geriatric depression, especially those who do not respond to antidepressant therapy.

As for the effects of exercise on cognitive function in patients with dementia, there remains insufficient evidence for firm conclusions to be drawn. However, there is increasing evidence suggesting that an exercise program including both patients with dementia and their caregivers may improve patients' physical limitations or independence (Forbes et al., 2015; Laver et al., 2016) and mitigate their caregiver's burden (Lamotte et al., 2016). Furthermore, no adverse events or side effects were reported in the identified trials (Forbes et al., 2015; Laver et al., 2016). Furthermore, the benefits of physical activity for physical health and key role in preventing further disease are equally applicable for older people with depression or dementia. This is particularly important as these conditions bring heightened risk of further disease development.

## Implications for Research

Depression and dementia are the most common mental disorders in older adults. However, they may have diverse symptomatology (sadness, diminished interest or pleasure, fatigue or loss of energy, disturbed sleep or appetite, feelings of worthlessness or inappropriate guilt, and poor concentration) or include different subtypes (e.g., Alzheimer's disease or vascular dementia; American Psychiatric Association, 2013). Hence, patients with similar scores on assessment of depression or cognitive dysfunction may have dissimilar symptoms or respond to exercise regimens differentially. The heterogeneity may reflect the range of potential underlying neurobiological processes (Schuch et al., 2016a) that may be operating and which also may be idiosyncratic to the individual. To reduce within-group variance and increase the effect size of exercise interventions, well-designed trials in the future are encouraged based on patients with more homogeneous depression severity and symptoms or a specific type of dementia.

Identifying the optimal type and dose of exercise and the setting in which it takes place are essential for the development of efficacious exercise programs for late-life mental illnesses. High intensity of progressive resistance training instead of low-intensity regimen was found to have benefits for geriatric depression (Singh et al., 2005). However, exercise intensity was not clearly reported in most of studies. It is possible that intensity was self-selected in these trials, which may make it easier for participants to adhere to the exercise protocols (Schuch et al., 2016a). This is critical if benefits are to be realized. There is some recent epidemiological evidence that light physical activity, independent of moderate-to-vigorous activity, is associated with a reduced risk of subsequent depressive symptoms or cognitive impairment in later life (Ku et al., 2017b; Stubbs et al., 2017a).

Comparison groups in the reviewed trials were diverse, such as health education, usual care, wait-list control, social visits, and social conversation. Social interaction may have a confounding impact on between-group comparisons and diminish internal validity. Chou (2008b) indicated that the effect of a Tai Chi intervention disappeared when changes of social support were further adjusted in analyses. It may be that the context and range of experience that an exercise program offers is as important as the process of exercise itself.

## CONCLUSIONS

Exercise as a nonpharmacological treatment is effective for reducing severity of late-life depression. However, this review found limited evidence that exercise consistently improves cognitive performance or delays cognitive decline in patients with dementia. This conclusion is based on a limited number of small trials with high heterogeneity.

## References

American Psychiatric Association, 2013. Diagnostic and Statistical Manual of Mental Disorders (Dsm-5®). American Psychiatric Association, Washington, DC.

Arcoverde, C., Deslandes, A., Moraes, H., Almeida, C., Araujo, N.B., Vasques, P.E., Silveira, H., Laks, J., 2014. Treadmill training as an augmentation treatment for alzheimer's disease: a pilot randomized controlled study. Arq. Neuropsiquiatr. 72, 190–196.

Arem, H., Moore, S.C., Patel, A., Hartge, P., Berrington De Gonzalez, A., Visvanathan, K., Campbell, P.T., Freedman, M., Weiderpass, E., Adami, H.O., Linet, M.S., Lee, I.M.,

Matthews, C.E., 2015. Leisure time physical activity and mortality: a detailed pooled analysis of the dose-response relationship. JAMA Intern. Med. 175, 959–967.

Bijl, R.V., Ravelli, A., 2000. Current and residual functional disability associated with psychopathology: findings from The Netherlands mental health survey and incidence study (nemesis). Psychol. Med. 30, 657–668.

Bossers, W.J., Van Der Woude, L.H., Boersma, F., Hortobágyi, T., Scherder, E.J., Van Heuvelen, M.J., 2015. A 9-week aerobic and strength training program improves cognitive and motor function in patients with dementia: a randomized, controlled trial. Am. J. Geriatr. Psychiatry 23, 1106–1116.

Brenes, G.A., Williamson, J.D., Messier, S.P., Rejeski, W.J., Pahor, M., Ip, E., Penninx, B.W., 2007. Treatment of minor depression in older adults: a pilot study comparing sertraline and exercise. Aging Ment. Health 11, 61–68.

Bridle, C., Spanjers, K., Patel, S., Atherton, N.M., Lamb, S.E., 2012. Effect of exercise on depression severity in older people: systematic review and meta-analysis of randomised controlled trials. Br. J. Psychiatry 201, 180–185.

Carvalho, A., Rea, I.M., Parimon, T., Cusack, B.J., 2014. Physical activity and cognitive function in individuals over 60 years of age: a systematic review. Clin. Interv. Aging 9, 661–682.

Chang, C.-K., Hayes, R.D., Perera, G., Broadbent, M.T.M., Fernandes, A.C., Lee, W.E., Hotopf, M., Stewart, R., 2011. Life expectancy at birth for people with serious mental illness and other major disorders from a secondary mental health care case register in london. PLoS One 6, e19590. https://doi.org/10.1371/journal.pone.0019590.

Chen, L.J., Steptoe, A., Chung, M.S., Ku, P.W., 2016. Association between actigraphy-derived physical activity and cognitive performance in patients with schizophrenia. Psychol. Med. 46, 2375–2384.

Cheng, S.-T., Chow, P.K., Song, Y.-Q., Yu, E.C.S., Lam, J.H.M., 2014. Can leisure activities slow dementia progression in nursing home residents? A cluster-randomized controlled trial. Int. Psychogeriatr. 26, 637–643.

Chou, K., 2008a. Effect of Tai Chi on Depressive Symptoms Amongst Chinese Older Patients with Major Depression: The Role of Social Support. Tai Chi Chuan. Karger Publishers.

Chou, K.L., 2008b. Effect of tai chi on depressive symptoms amongst Chinese older patients with major depression: the role of social support. Med. Sport Sci. 52, 146–154.

Chou, K.L., Lee, P.W., Yu, E., Macfarlane, D., Cheng, Y.H., Chan, S.S., Chi, I., 2004. Effect of tai chi on depressive symptoms amongst Chinese older patients with depressive disorders: a randomized clinical trial. Int. J. Geriatr. Psychiatry 19, 1105–1107.

Christofoletti, G., Oliani, M.M., Gobbi, S., Stella, F., Bucken Gobbi, L.T., Renato Canineu, P., 2008. A controlled clinical trial on the effects of motor intervention on balance and cognition in institutionalized elderly patients with dementia. Clin. Rehabil. 22, 618–626.

Chu, D.C., Fox, K.R., Chen, L.J., Ku, P.W., 2015. Components of late-life exercise and cognitive function: an 8-year longitudinal study. Prev. Sci. 16, 568–577.

Ciechanowski, P., Wagner, E., Schmaling, K., Schwartz, S., Williams, B., Diehr, P., Kulzer, J., Gray, S., Collier, C., Logerfo, J., 2004. Community-integrated home-based depression treatment in older adults: a randomized controlled trial. Jama 291, 1569–1577.

Cooney, G., Dwan, K., Greig, C., Lawlor, D., Rimer, J., Waugh, F., 2013. Exercise for depression (review). The cochrane collaboration. Cochrane Libr. 9, 1–125.

Djernes, J.K., 2006. Prevalence and predictors of depression in populations of elderly: a review. Acta Psychiatr. Scand. 113, 372–387.

Eggermont, L.H.P., Knol, D.L., Hol, E.M., Swaab, D.F., Scherder, E.J.A., 2009a. Hand motor activity, cognition, mood, and the rest-activity rhythm in dementia: a clustered rct. Behav. Brain Res. 196, 271–278.

Eggermont, L.H.P., Swaab, D.F., Hol, E.M., Scherder, E.J., 2009b. Walking the line: a randomised trial on the effects of a short term walking programme on cognition in dementia. J. Neurol. Neurosurg. Psychiatry 80, 802–804.

Fekadu, A., Medhin, G., Kebede, D., Alem, A., Cleare, A.J., Prince, M., Hanlon, C., Shibre, T., 2015. Excess mortality in severe mental illness: 10-year population-based cohort study in rural Ethiopia. Br. J. Psychiatry 206, 289–296.

Fiske, A., Wetherell, J.L., Gatz, M., 2009. Depression in older adults. Annu. Rev. Clin. Psychol. 5, 363–389.

Forbes, D., Thiessen, E.J., Blake, C.M., Forbes, S.C., Forbes, S., 2015. Exercise programs for people with dementia. Cochrane Database Syst. Rev.

Guerra, M., Prina, A., Ferri, C., Acosta, D., Gallardo, S., Huang, Y., Jacob, K., Jimenez-Velazquez, I., Rodriguez, J.L., Liu, Z., 2016. A comparative cross-cultural study of the prevalence of late life depression in low and middle income countries. J. Affect. Disord. 190, 362–368.

Hokkanen, L., Rantala, L., Remes, A.M., Härkönen, B., Viramo, P., Winblad, I., 2008. Dance and movement therapeutic methods in management of dementia: a randomized, controlled study. J. Am. Geriatr. Soc. 56, 771–772.

Holthoff, V.A., Marschner, K., Scharf, M., Steding, J., Meyer, S., Koch, R., Donix, M., 2015. Effects of physical activity training in patients with alzheimer's dementia: results of a pilot rct study. PLoS One 10, e0121478.

Kemoun, G., Thibaud, M., Roumagne, N., Carette, P., Albinet, C., Toussaint, L., Paccalin, M., Dugué, B., 2010. Effects of a physical training programme on cognitive function and walking efficiency in elderly persons with dementia. Dement. Geriatr. Cogn. Disord. 29, 109–114.

Kirk-Sanchez, N.J., Mcgough, E.L., 2014. Physical exercise and cognitive performance in the elderly: current perspectives. Clin. Interv. Aging 9, 51–62.

Klap, R., Unroe, K.T., Unützer, J., 2003. Caring for mental illness in the United States: a focus on older adults. Am. J. Geriatr. Psychiatry 11, 517–524.

Ku, P.W., Fox, K.R., Mckenna, J., Peng, T.L., 2006. Prevalence of leisure-time physical activity in taiwanese adults: results of four national surveys, 2000-2004. Prev. Med. 43, 454–457.

Ku, P.W., Fox, K.R., Chen, L.J., 2009. Physical activity and depressive symptoms in taiwanese older adults: a seven-year follow-up study. Prev. Med. 48, 250–255.

Ku, P.W., Fox, K.R., Chen, L.J., Chou, P., 2012. Physical activity and depressive symptoms in older adults: 11-year follow-up. Am. J. Prev. Med. 42, 355–362.

Ku, P.W., Chen, L.J., Xu, Z., 2016a. A review of late-life sedentary behaviors and cognitive aging. Phys. Educ. J. 49, 1–16.

Ku, P.W., Steptoe, A., Chen, Y.H., Chen, L.J., Lin, C.H., 2016b. Prospective association between late-life physical activity and hospital care utilization: a seven-year nationwide follow-up study. Age Ageing 46, 452–459.

Ku, P.-W., Steptoe, A., Chen, L.-J., 2017a. Prospective associations of exercise and depressive symptoms in older adults: the role of apolipoprotein e4. Qual. Life Res. 26, 1799–1808.

Ku, P.W., Steptoe, A., Liao, Y., Sun, W.J., Chen, L.J., 2017b. Prospective relationship between objectively measured light physical activity and depressive symptoms in later life. Int. J. Geriatr. Psychiatry. https://doi.org/10.1002/gps.4672.

Kwak, Y.-S., Um, S.-Y., Son, T.-G., Kim, D.-J., 2008. Effect of regular exercise on senile dementia patients. Int. J. Sports Med. 29, 471–474.

Lamotte, G., Shah, R.C., Lazarov, O., Corcos, D.M., 2016. Exercise training for persons with alzheimer's disease and caregivers: a review of dyadic exercise interventions. J. Mot. Behav. 1–13.

Laver, K., Dyer, S., Whitehead, C., Clemson, L., Crotty, M., 2016. Interventions to delay functional decline in people with dementia: a systematic review of systematic reviews. BMJ Open 6, e010767.

Lavretsky, H., Alstein, L.L., Olmstead, R.E., Ercoli, L.M., Riparetti-Brown, M., Cyr, N.S., Irwin, M.R., 2011. Complementary use of tai chi chih augments escitalopram treatment of geriatric depression: a randomized controlled trial. Am. J. Geriatr. Psychiatry 19, 839–850.

Lin, X., Zhang, X., Guo, J., Roberts, C.K., Mckenzie, S., Wu, W.C., Liu, S., Song, Y., 2015. Effects of exercise training on cardiorespiratory fitness and biomarkers of cardiometabolic health: a systematic review and meta-analysis of randomized controlled trials. J. Am. Heart. Assoc. 4, e002014. https://doi.org/10.1161/JAHA.115.002014.

Lopez, A.D., World Health Organization, 2001. The global burden of disease 1990–2020. In: Ragaini, R. (Ed.), International Seminar on Nuclear War and Planetary Emergencies: 25th Session. World Scientific Printers, Singapore.

Mather, A.S., Rodriguez, C., Guthrie, M.F., Mcharg, A.M., Reid, I.C., Mcmurdo, M.E., 2002. Effects of exercise on depressive symptoms in older adults with poorly responsive depressive disorder. Br. J. Psychiatry 180, 411–415.

Mcclain, J.J., Lewin, D.S., Laposky, A.D., Kahle, L., Berrigan, D., 2014. Associations between physical activity, sedentary time, sleep duration and daytime sleepiness in us adults. Prev. Med. 66, 68–73.

Miu, D.K.Y., Szeto, S.L., Mak, Y.F., 2008. A randomised controlled trial on the effect of exercise on physical, cognitive and affective function in dementia subjects. Asian J. Gerontol. Geriatr. 3, 8–16.

Murray, C.J.L., Lopez, A.D., 1996. The Global Burden of Disease: A Comprehensive Assessment of Mortality and Disability from Diseases, Injuries, and Risk Factors in I990 and Projected to 2020. Harvard University, Boston.

Murri, M.B., Amore, M., Menchetti, M., Toni, G., Neviani, F., Cerri, M., Rocchi, M., Zocchi, D., Bagnoli, L., Tam, E., 2015. Physical exercise for late-life major depression. Br. J. Psychiatry 207, 235–242.

Niccoli, T., Partridge, L., 2012. Ageing as a risk factor for disease. Curr. Biol. 22, R741–R752.

Ohman, H., Savikko, N., Strandberg, T.E., Pitkälä, K.H., 2014. Effect of physical exercise on cognitive performance in older adults with mild cognitive impairment or dementia: a systematic review. Dement. Geriatr. Cognit. Disord. 38, 347–365.

Ohman, H., Savikko, N., Strandberg, T.E., Kautiainen, H., Raivio, M.M., Laakkonen, M.L., Tilvis, R., Pitkälä, K.H., 2016. Effects of exercise on cognition: the Finnish alzheimer disease exercise trial: a randomized, controlled trial. J. Am. Geriatr. Soc. 64, 731–738.

Pearsall, R., Smith, D.J., Pelosi, A., Geddes, J., 2014. Exercise therapy in adults with serious mental illness: a systematic review and meta-analysis. BMC Psychiatry 14, 117. https://doi.org/10.1186/1471-244X-14-117.

Prince, M., Wimo, A., Guerchet, M., All, G., Wu, Y., Prina, M., 2015. World Alzheimer Report 2015: The global impact of dementia: an analysis of prevalence, incidence, cost and trends, 2015.

Reynolds, K., Pietrzak, R.H., El-Gabalawy, R.E., Mackenzie, C.S., Sareen, J., 2015. Prevalence of psychiatric disorders in u.S. Older adults: findings from a nationally representative survey. World Psychiatry 14, 74–81.

Rosenbaum, S., Tiedemann, A., Sherrington, C., Curtis, J., Ward, P.B., 2014. Physical activity interventions for people with mental illness: a systematic review and meta-analysis. J. Clin. Psychiatry 75, 964–974.

Schuch, F.B., Morres, I.D., Ekkekakis, P., Rosenbaum, S., Stubbs, B., 2016a. A critical review of exercise as a treatment for clinically depressed adults: time to get pragmatic. Acta Neuropsychiatr. 1–7.

Schuch, F.B., Vancampfort, D., Rosenbaum, S., Richards, J., Ward, P.B., Veronese, N., Solmi, M., Cadore, E.L., Stubbs, B., 2016b. Exercise for depression in older adults: a meta-analysis of randomized controlled trials adjusting for publication bias. Rev. Bras. Psiquiatr. 38, 247–254.

Seshamani, M., Gray, A., 2003. Health care expenditures and ageing: an international comparison. Appl. Health Econ. Health Policy 2, 9–16.

Sims, J., Galea, M., Taylor, N., Dodd, K., Jespersen, S., Joubert, L., Joubert, J., 2009. Regenerate: assessing the feasibility of a strength-training program to enhance the physical and mental health of chronic post stroke patients with depression. Int. J. Geriatr. Psychiatry 24, 76–83.

Singh, N.A., Stavrinos, T.M., Scarbek, Y., Galambos, G., Liber, C., Singh, M.A.F., 2005. A randomized controlled trial of high versus low intensity weight training versus general practitioner care for clinical depression in older adults. J. Gerontol. Ser. A Biol. Sci. Med. Sci. 60, 768–776.

Steel, Z., Marnane, C., Iranpour, C., Chey, T., Jackson, J.W., Patel, V., Silove, D., 2014. The global prevalence of common mental disorders: a systematic review and meta-analysis 1980–2013. Int. J. Epidemiol. 43, 476–493.

Steinberg, M., Leoutsakos, J.-M.S., Podewils, L.J., Lyketsos, C.G., 2009. Evaluation of a home-based exercise program in the treatment of alzheimer's disease: the maximizing independence in dementia (mind) study. Int. J. Geriatr. Psychiatry 24, 680–685.

Stevens, J., Killeen, M., 2006. A randomised controlled trial testing the impact of exercise on cognitive symptoms and disability of residents with dementia. Contemp. Nurse 21, 32–40.

Stubbs, B., Firth, J., Berry, A., Schuch, F.B., Rosenbaum, S., Gaughran, F., Veronesse, N., Williams, J., Craig, T., Yung, A.R., Vancampfort, D., 2016. How much physical activity do people with schizophrenia engage in? A systematic review, comparative meta-analysis and meta-regression. Schizophr. Res. https://doi.org/10.1016/j.schres.2016.05.017.

Stubbs, B., Chen, L.-J., Chang, C.-Y., Sun, W.-J., Ku, P.-W., 2017a. Accelerometer-assessed light physical activity is protective of future cognitive ability: a longitudinal study among community dwelling older adults. Exp. Gerontol. 91, 104–109.

Stubbs, B., Chen, L.J., Chung, M.S., Ku, P.W., 2017b. Physical activity ameliorates the association between sedentary behavior and cardiometabolic risk in people with schizophrenia: a comparison versus controls using accelerometry. Compr. Psychiatr. 74, 144–150.

Sun, F., Norman, I.J., While, A.E., May 6, 2013. Physical activity in older people: a systematic review. BMC Publ. Health 13 (449).

Tsang, H.W., Fung, K.M., Chan, A.S., Lee, G., Chan, F., 2006. Effect of a qigong exercise programme on elderly with depression. Int. J. Geriatr. Psychiatry 21, 890–897.

United Nations, 2015. World Population Prospects: The 2015 Revision. United Nations, New York.

Van De Winckel, A., Feys, H., De Weerdt, W., Dom, R., 2004. Cognitive and behavioural effects of music-based exercises in patients with dementia. Clin. Rehabil. 18, 253–260.

Vancampfort, D., Rosenbaum, S., Ward, P.B., Stubbs, B., 2015. Exercise improves cardiorespiratory fitness in people with schizophrenia: a systematic review and meta-analysis. Schizophr. Res. 169, 453–457.

Venturelli, M., Scarsini, R., Schena, F., 2011. Six-month walking program changes cognitive and adl performance in patients with alzheimer. Am. J. Alzheimers Dis. Other Demen. 26, 381–388.

Vreugdenhil, A., Cannell, J., Davies, A., Razay, G., 2012. A community-based exercise programme to improve functional ability in people with alzheimer's disease: a randomized controlled trial. Scand. J. Caring Sci. 26, 12–19.

Wen, C.P., Wai, J.P., Tsai, M.K., Yang, Y.C., Cheng, T.Y., Lee, M.C., Chan, H.T., Tsao, C.K., Tsai, S.P., Wu, X., 2011. Minimum amount of physical activity for reduced mortality and extended life expectancy: a prospective cohort study. Lancet 378, 1244–1253.

Williams, C., Tappen, R., 2008. Exercise training for depressed older adults with alzheimer's disease. Aging Ment. Health 12, 72–80.

World Health Organization, 2001. Mental Health: A Call for Action. World Health Organization, Geneva.

World Health Organization, 2010. Global Recommendations on Physical Activity for Health. World Health Organization, Geneva.

World Health Organization, 2015. World Report on Ageing and Health. Online. World Health Organization, Geneva. Available: http://apps.who.int/iris/bitstream/10665/186463/1/9789240694811_eng.pdf?ua=1 [.

World Health Organization, 2016a. Dementia. Online. World Health Organization, Geneva. Available: http://www.who.int/mediacentre/factsheets/fs362/en/.

World Health Organization, 2016b. Mental Health and Older Adults. Online. World Health Organization, Geneva. Available: http://www.who.int/mediacentre/factsheets/fs381/en/.

World Health Organization & Us National Institute of Aging, 2011. Global Health and Aging. World Health Organization, Geneva.

World Health Organization, 2017. Mental Disorders.

Yágüez, L., Shaw, K.N., Morris, R., Matthews, D., 2011. The effects on cognitive functions of a movement-based intervention in patients with alzheimer's type dementia: a pilot study. Int. J. Geriatr. Psychiatry 26, 173–181.

Yung, A.R., Firth, J., 2016. How should physical exercise be used in schizophrenia treatment? Expert Rev. Neurother. https://doi.org/10.1080/14737175.2017.1275571.

# Exercise for Adolescents and Young People With Mental Illness

*Alexandra G. Parker[1], Alan P. Bailey[2]*

[1] Institute for Health and Sport, Victoria University, Melbourne, Victoria, Australia; [2] Orygen, The National Centre of Excellence in Youth Mental Health and Centre for Youth Mental Health, University of Melbourne, Melbourne, VIC, Australia

## OUTLINE

*Exercise-Based Interventions for Mental Illness*
https://doi.org/10.1016/B978-0-12-812605-9.00008-3    149

# EXERCISE FOR ADOLESCENTS AND YOUNG PEOPLE WITH MENTAL ILLNESS

More than one-quarter of the world's population is aged between 10 and 24 years (WHO, 2009). This is the phase of life when most of the major mental disorders emerge, with three-quarters of all cases occurring by age 24 years (Kessler et al., 2005, 2007). Mental disorders cause the most disability than any other illness in young people worldwide (Gore et al., 2011) and are referred to as the "chronic diseases of the young" (Insel and Fenton, 2005). The high prevalence and age of onset mean that many young people will experience a mental disorder themselves or within their network of family and friends, as they make the transition from early adolescence to adulthood. There is a clear imperative to effectively treat these disorders in a timely manner to reduce symptomatology and prevent both functional disability (social, educational, and vocational abilities and opportunities), as well as relapse and the potential persistence of illness (McGorry et al., 2014). Additionally, many of the long-term health-related behaviors and patterns become established during the developmental phase of adolescence and early adulthood (Sawyer et al., 2012), further highlighting this critical timeframe for intervention.

At least one in four young people will experience a mental disorder in any given year (Patel et al., 2007), with anxiety, depressive, and substance use disorders having the highest prevalence (Australian Institute of Health and Welfare, 2011; Kessler et al., 2005). Data from Australia's youth mental health foundation, *Headspace*, indicate that young people who access these youth-specific mental health services (over 30,000 young people per annum) predominantly seek support for mental health concerns, with depression and anxiety as the main presenting issues (Rickwood et al., 2014). *Headspace* centers are enhanced primary care mental health services funded by the federal government, providing psychological assessment, mental health treatment, vocational and education assistance, primary health care, and substance use services to young people aged 12–25 years (Rickwood et al., 2014). As a reflection of the complicated phenomenology of mental disorders in young people, with comorbidity or mixed symptom patterns common

(Australian Institute of Health and Welfare, 2007), young people are also presenting with anger problems, suicidal thoughts or behavior, problems with relationships, physical health concerns, alcohol or other drug problems, and challenges with attaining or maintaining engagement in education and/or employment (Rickwood et al., 2014, 2015).

Many of the current evidence-based treatments for established mental disorders in young people, for example, psychotropic medications and specific psychotherapies, have modest effects (e.g., see Hetrick et al., 2012; Weisz et al., 2006) and treatment-induced side effects that can be intolerable and lead to further health complications (e.g., increased risk for metabolic syndrome; Curtis et al., 2012). It is because of these concerns that current approaches are favoring earlier, simpler, safer, and less complex interventions that aim to treat illness in earlier stages and prevent progression to more serious or complex disorders (McGorry et al., 2011, 2014). For these reasons, physical activity and exercise are interventions that are growing in interest and application in youth mental health. Additionally, of importance to help-seeking young people (Tylee et al., 2007), physical activity is a low-stigma intervention that has strong face validity as an intervention that can improve mental well-being (Jorm et al., 2008).

## YOUNG PEOPLE AND MENTAL ILL HEALTH

Adolescence and young adulthood is a time of significant biological, psychological, and psychosocial changes that increase susceptibility to developing mental disorders (e.g., onset of puberty, major structural and functional brain changes, individuation from parents and increased importance of peer/intimate relationships), with these changes occurring in the context of an increasingly longer and more complex transition into adulthood and adult roles (McGorry et al., 2014). This period of transition into adulthood is also marked by disengagement from regular physical activity and sporting clubs or associations (Baldursdottir et al., 2017; Zimmermann-Sloutskis et al., 2010). For example, data from a longitudinal study of over 3000 Swiss young people showed that physical inactivity, defined as less than 1 day per week of 30 min of physical activity and no participation in organized sports, increased by a factor of 2.6 in males and 1.9 in females from the ages of 14–16 to 20–22 years (Zimmermann-Sloutskis et al., 2010).

Whilst the effects of physical activity on mental health and well-being have been studied in adult populations (Cooney et al., 2013; Rosenbaum et al., 2016; Schuch, Vancampfort, et al., 2016; Stubbs et al., 2016), adolescents and young adults have received less attention, with most of the exercise and physical activity studies in youth mental health having a focus on depression symptoms as the intervention outcome (e.g., see de Silva et al., 2017 for an overview of the youth mental health evidence base). Although there is some evidence to support the role of physical activity in the prevention of mental disorders (Brown et al., 2013; Larun et al., 2006), this chapter will focus on exercise interventions for young people experiencing symptoms of or a diagnosable mental disorder. We only consider here controlled trials that better support conclusions regarding effectiveness and describe these studies in reverse chronological order, grouped by the mental health concern. Where possible, we comment on fidelity and feasibility (e.g., attendance rates, adherence to exercise protocols), longer term outcomes, and study quality. These factors are important in determining the strength of the evidence and clinical considerations of translating exercise interventions into practice.

## EXERCISE FOR DEPRESSION IN YOUNG PEOPLE: THE EVIDENCE

As of early 2018, 17 randomized controlled trials (RCTs) have been conducted investigating the effect of using exercise or physical activity to treat or reduce symptoms of depression in young people. Here we present a selection of these trials to provide an overview of the research activity. Trials have been comprehensively reviewed in two meta-analyses that included children and adolescents (Carter et al., 2016) and young people aged 12–25 years (Bailey et al., 2017) that overall show positive effects of exercise or physical activity as an intervention for depression symptoms or major depressive disorder. Effect sizes showed moderate (standardized mean difference [SMD] $= -0.48\%$, 95% confidence interval [CI] $= -0.87$ to $-0.10$, $P = 0.01$, $I^2 = 67\%$; Carter et al., 2016) to large (SMD $= -0.82$, 95% CI $= -1.02$ to $-0.61$, $P < .05$, $I^2 = 38\%$; Bailey et al., 2017) effects of physical activity on depressive symptoms. The effect sizes remained robust for trials that included only clinical samples (SMD $= -0.43$ and $-0.72$, respectively). The rationale for exercise interventions for depression includes biological and psychosocial components. The proposed biological processes include exercise modulating inflammatory and oxidative stress responses, neurogenesis, modulation of monoamines (e.g., serotonin), regulation of the hypothalamic pituitary adrenal (HPA) axis, and biorhythms (e.g., sleep), all of which may be disrupted or dysregulated in depression (Schuch et al., 2016). Proposed psychosocial processes include a behavioral activation effect that provides opportunity for achievement and improving self-efficacy, distraction from rumination or negative thoughts, and opportunities for social interaction (Salmon, 2001).

Balchin et al. (2016) used an RCT design to assign 30 non–help-seeking males (university students or staff; mean age 25.4 years) experiencing moderate depression to light-intensity, moderate-intensity, or vigorous-intensity exercise, lasting 1 h, three times per week, for 6 weeks. The light-intensity group walked or cycled, keeping their heart rate below 120 beats/min, and the moderate- or vigorous-intensity group jogged and/or ran at 45%–50% and 70%–75% of maximal heart rate, respectively. Sessions were supervised to ensure adherence to the exercise protocol. After the 6-week exercise intervention, depression symptoms measured by the Hamilton Rating Scale of Depression (HAM-D) showed a statistically and clinically significant reduction from baseline in both the moderate- and vigorous-intensity groups, with HAM-D scores changing from the moderate to normal range for both groups. No significant change was noted in the light-intensity group. When comparing final scores across the three groups, no significant differences were found; however, this trial was likely underpowered to detect a significant difference. Concerns with the trial design and quality include baseline imbalances (light-intensity group had higher body mass index at baseline), high dropouts (one in three participants did not complete the study), and a nonclinical/non–help-seeking sample was used.

An RCT by Sadeghi et al. (2016) assigned 46 help-seeking university students (22% female, mean age 21 years) diagnosed with depression and experiencing symptoms in the moderate range to either an exercise group, a group receiving cognitive behavioral therapy (CBT), or an unguided group meeting as a control group. The exercise group engaged in 45–60 min of vigorous-intensity aerobic exercise (60%–80% maximal heart rate), three times a week for 8 weeks. The CBT group received 12 sessions of group CBT over 8 weeks. The exercise group and the CBT group showed equivalent reductions in depression symptoms following the intervention period, and both performed better than the control group. This finding requires further exploration but suggests that exercise could be as effective as CBT ("gold standard" depression treatment). Another interpretation is that doing something structured that is guided by a qualified professional is beneficial, regardless of the treatment modality (CBT or exercise).

Using an RCT design, Carter et al. (2015) allocated 87 help-seeking adolescents (14–17 years, 78% female) with "severe" depression who were referred from the community to exercise adjunct to treatment as usual (TAU) or to TAU alone. Exercise consisted of circuit training (aerobic and strength exercises) performed at preferred intensities, twice a week for 6 weeks, supervised by an exercise physiologist, and designed to not go above 80% maximum heart rate. TAU was a range of different psychological therapies and medication where required. Both groups showed improvements in depression symptoms over the treatment period; however, there were no differences between the groups by the end of treatment. This is likely because TAU is a robust, effective intervention, leaving little room for exercise to exact any additional influence. Additionally, the exercise protocol may not have delivered an adequate "dosage" to produce an effect above TAU particularly as the intensity was set by the participant rather than prescribed and monitored for adherence. However, further testing would be needed to confirm/disprove this. An interesting finding of this study is that by 6-month follow-up, there was a significant group difference in depression symptoms, showing an advantage of the exercise over the TAU alone group. This is a difficult finding to explain. The authors suggest a delayed response; however, it may be due to factors not measured or controlled for in the study—for example, the amount of therapy received over the follow-up period and unbalanced dropout; those who did not improve may be less likely to re-engage for follow-up assessment (control group had slightly more lost to follow-up). Using exercise as an adjunct to traditional intervention such as psychotherapy and medication should be investigated further.

In one of the only high-quality RCTs conducted up to early 2018, Hughes et al. (2013) assigned 30 help-seeking adolescents (12—18 years, 58% female) diagnosed with moderate depression to an exercise condition or a control condition for 12 weeks. The exercise condition completed supervised moderate-intensity aerobic exercise on a treadmill or stationary bike for 30—40 min once a week, plus two to three additional sessions of preferred exercise in their own time (totaling >12 kg/kcal per week). The control group only engaged in stretching exercises over the same period (<4 kg/kcal per week). The exercise group expended twice as much energy each week as the stretching control group. Both groups showed improvements in blinded, clinician-rated depression symptoms after the intervention period. The exercise group showed greater reduction in depression symptoms at both 6 and 9 weeks compared with the control group, even though both were equivalent by the end of the treatment period (12 weeks). Adherence rates to number of sessions and weekly energy expenditure goals were 77% in the exercise group and 81% in the stretching group. In terms of clinician-rated remission status at the end of treatment, 86% of the exercise group was in remission versus 50% of the control group. At 6-month follow-up, remission rates were 100% versus 70%, and by 12 months, remission rates were 100% versus 88%. However, there were significant dropouts from both groups over the follow-up period. As these results were based on the reduced sample who completed the assessments, it is unclear how the dropouts fared thus making it difficult to interpret these follow-up findings, which highlight need for more studies looking at medium- and long-term effects of exercise.

Roshan et al. (2011) used an RCT design to assign 24 female high school students (mean age 16.9 years) diagnosed with severe depression to an exercise group or to a nonexercising, no-treatment control group. The exercise group walked laps of a 15-m swimming pool in water above waist height at a moderate intensity (60%—70% of maximal heart rate), three times a week for 6 weeks. The total number of laps increased from 34 in week 1 to 131 by week 6 for all participants. Aerobic fitness was improved after engaging in the exercise intervention. After the intervention period, the exercise group had experienced more than a 50% reduction in depression symptoms from baseline, which was significantly lower than the control group. However, findings are limited due to the use of a no-treatment control group, which fails to control for nonspecific intervention factors that may improve depression such as participant expectancy, contact with intervention personnel, and social interaction.

Chu et al. (2009) used an RCT design to assign 54 non—help-seeking female university students (mean age 25.8 years) experiencing moderate depression to a high-intensity exercise group, a moderate-intensity exercise group, or a stretching control group for 10 weeks. Each week, the high-intensity group did one supervised aerobic exercise session (65%—75% maximum $VO_2$ reserve) lasting 30—40 min, plus three to four extra sessions in their own time. The moderate-intensity group followed the same protocol except at a lower intensity (40%—55% maximum $VO_2$ reserve). The control group engaged in supervised stretching exercises only for the same period. Weekly energy expenditure did not differ between high- and moderate-intensity aerobic exercises but both were significantly higher than the control group. Attendance rates averaged 80%—100% and did not differ between groups; however, the high- and low-intensity groups engaged in more exercise sessions per week (3.7 and 4.9, respectively), compared with the control group (2.1 sessions). Depression symptoms were reduced in all three groups from baseline, but there were no significant differences in change scores between the groups after the study period. Post-hoc comparisons controlling for baseline depression symptoms suggest that high-intensity exercise may perform better than either the moderate-intensity group or the control group; however, further investigation is required to confirm these findings.

# EXERCISE FOR ANXIETY IN YOUNG PEOPLE: THE EVIDENCE

Compared with depression, exercise for anxiety has been relatively understudied in both adults and young people (de Silva et al., 2017; Stubbs et al., 2017). Three of our included studies were designed to reduce anxiety sensitivity, as an identified precursor to the experience of panic attacks and panic disorders. A component of the rationale for exercise interventions is to reduce intensity of anxiety through exposure to feared physiological sensations (Smits et al., 2007).

Herring et al. (2011, 2012) conducted an RCT to allocate 30 females (mean age 23.5 years) with a Diagnostic and Statistical Manual of Mental Disorders, Fourth Edition (DSM-IV) diagnosis of generalized anxiety disorder (GAD) to a resistance training group, aerobic exercise training group, or a waitlist control group. Both training groups engaged in twice-weekly supervised sessions for 6 weeks. The resistance training group engaged in leg press, leg curl, and leg extension exercises. The aerobic exercise training group (matched for time, work completed, progression in intensity, and body region exercised) participated in two sessions of 16 min of continuous cycling exercise per week. Those in the waitlist control condition completed assessments each week for 6 weeks, before commencing an exercise intervention that was not delivered under trial conditions; therefore no useable outcome data were collected for this group. Assessment time points were pre—post interventions, with additional variables collected on a weekly basis. Remission rates (measured by the Anxiety Disorders Interview Schedule for Diagnostic and Statistical Manual of Mental Disorders (DSM)-IV (ADIS-IV) rated by blinded clinicians) were 60% for the resistance group, 40% for the aerobic group, and 30% for the control group. Worry symptoms (measured by the Penn State Worry Questionnaire; Meyer et al., 1990) did not significantly differ between groups at endpoint, despite a significant condition-by-time interaction. This pilot study shows promising preliminary data of remission in GAD and likely reduction in worry symptoms; however, firmer conclusions would require replication in a larger sample. Of note was the acceptability data which demonstrated 100% attendance to both resistance and aerobic training sessions and 99%—100% compliance with the protocols. Participant ratings of perceived exertion (RPE) in exercise sessions indicated a significant difference between resistance and aerobic training (RPE of 14 "somewhat hard/hard" vs. 8 "very light"), which the authors suggest may account for the higher remission response in the resistance training group.

Smits et al. (2008) conducted an RCT, allocating 60 university students (75% female, mean age 20.7 years) who were screened for high anxiety sensitivity (>25 on the Anxiety Sensitivity Index [ASI]; Peterson and Reiss, 1992) to an exercise group, an exercise plus cognitive restructuring group, or a waitlist control group. Both exercise groups engaged in three weekly individual sessions over a 2-week period of supervised treadmill running at the prescribed intensity of 70% of maximal heart rate. The exercise group viewed a 15-min video explaining the rationale for the exercise intervention, and subjective units of distress were taken at 3-min intervals throughout the exercise session to focus attention on bodily sensations and anxiety. Participants in the exercise plus cognitive restructuring group followed a similar protocol, with two exceptions; additional content on cognitive restructuring was included in the introductory video and by the experimenter during exercise sessions. Assessment time points were pretreatment, mid-treatment, 1 week post-treatment, and 3-week follow-up. Anxiety sensitivity and clinical symptoms (depression and anxiety measured by the Beck Depression and Anxiety Inventories) were significantly reduced over time for both the active conditions compared with the waitlist control group; there was no group by time differences between the exercise and exercise plus cognitive restructuring groups. Given that attrition in the exercise plus cognitive restructuring group was almost twice that of the exercise alone group and that no group differences were found, the authors concluded that not only did the cognitive augmentation strategy not increase efficacy but also may be detrimental to treatment adherence. Despite some limitations with sample size and nonclinical levels of anxiety and depression, this study demonstrated promising effects of exercise at 70% maximal heart rate on reducing anxiety sensitivity, depression, and anxiety symptoms in those with high anxiety sensitivity.

Using an RCT design, Broman-Fulks et al. (2004) allocated 54 university students (76% female; mean age 21.2 years) who were screened for high anxiety sensitivity (>25 on ASI; Peterson and Reiss, 1992) to a supervised high-intensity aerobic exercise group or a low-intensity walking group. Approximately one-third of participants self-reported a history of panic symptoms. Participants in the high-intensity aerobic condition briskly walked/jogged on a treadmill to achieve predicted 60%–90% maximal heart rates for 20 min across two to four sessions per week, for a total of six exercise sessions within the 2-week intervention period, increasing treadmill speed and heart rates across subsequent sessions. The walking condition followed a similar protocol; however, treadmill speed was maintained at 1 mile (1.6 km) per hour to maintain a maximal heart rate below 60%. Assessment time points were pre–post intervention and 1-week follow-up. Anxiety sensitivity reduced in both groups, with the high-intensity group showing significant reductions in anxiety sensitivity between pre- and post-intervention and maintaining this reduction at 1-week follow-up; the low-intensity group showed significant reductions between preintervention and follow-up only. Attendance and adherence were only reported for the high-intensity group; the majority (87%) completed three sessions per week. There were some concerns with the quality of the study, including no reporting of how missing data were handled, and it is unclear if intervention adherence differed between groups.

In an attempt to replicate these preliminary positive findings, Broman-Fulks and Storey (2008) completed another RCT, allocating 35 university students (80% female; mean age 18.9 years) who were screened for high anxiety sensitivity (>26 on ASI-Revised; Taylor and Cox, 1998) to a high-intensity aerobic exercise group or no-treatment control group. Approximately 25% of participants self-reported a history of panic symptoms. The high-intensity aerobic condition followed the same protocol as Broman-Fulks et al. (2004); six 20-min treadmill jogging sessions aiming to reach 60%–90% of maximal heart rate over a 2-week period. Assessment time points were pre–post intervention and 1-week follow-up. Anxiety sensitivity reduced in the high-intensity aerobic exercise group only, showing a significant group by session interaction; however, there was no main effect of group, with the control and intervention groups not differing in anxiety sensitivity scores at postintervention or follow-up. The study was underpowered and combined with additional concerns over study quality (e.g., analysis of observed cases/completers only); firm conclusions of the effects of high-intensity aerobic exercise on anxiety sensitivity cannot be drawn.

## EXERCISE FOR BIPOLAR AFFECTIVE DISORDER IN YOUNG PEOPLE: THE EVIDENCE

As of early 2018, no trials examining the effects of exercise on bipolar disorder in young people have been completed, although examination of clinical trial registers indicates that some activity in this area is planned or underway.

## EXERCISE FOR EARLY PSYCHOSIS IN YOUNG PEOPLE: THE EVIDENCE

Only two trials that examine the effects of exercise on symptoms of psychosis in young people (<26 years) with a psychotic disorder are currently completed. In intervention trials in people with long-term schizophrenia, higher intensity exercise has been shown to reduce both positive and negative symptoms of the disorder and improve cognitive functioning (Firth et al., 2015).

In an RCT, Lin et al. (2015) assigned 140 females (mean age 24.6 years) from the Early Assessment Service for Young People with Psychosis program in Hong Kong to a yoga group, aerobic exercise group, or a waitlist control group. Participants were all experiencing early psychosis (diagnosed with a DSM-IV psychotic disorder within the preceding 5 years). The yoga group engaged in integrated yoga therapy (Hatha yoga) consisting of breathing control (5 min), body postures (40–45 min), and relaxation (5 min). The meditation component of Hatha yoga was excluded. Each session was done in small groups and conducted by a qualified instructor. The aerobic exercise group engaged in supervised small-group treadmill walking (15–25 min) and stationary cycling (25–30 min) which was maintained at a moderate intensity (50%–60% $VO_2$ max) by monitoring participant heart rate, followed by cool-down/ stretching. Each group did 60-min sessions, three times a week for 12 weeks, and all participants received protocol-based case management as standard care throughout the study period. Attendance rates were similar for both interventions (58% for yoga and 47% for exercise). Just over one in five participants dropped out of the study, and rates were similar across groups (24% yoga, 27% exercise, 18% control). Quality of life (both physical and mental components) was improved in both the exercise and yoga groups. Clinical symptoms of psychosis (Positive and Negative Symptoms Scale (PANSS) general and total) were reduced in both groups compared with control group after the intervention period, with negative symptoms improved in the yoga group only, whereas positive symptoms remained unchanged in both groups. Neither group showed significant improvements on aerobic fitness; however, there was a trend toward improvement in the exercise group. Analyses controlled for age, antipsychotic dose, and length of illness. This study provides preliminary evidence for using exercise or yoga in early psychosis but requires replication due to significant missing data across time points.

In a nonrandomized, comparative pilot study, Firth et al. (2016) recruited 31 young people (aged 18–35 years) with first episode psychosis from a community-based early intervention service in the United Kingdom. The exercise intervention group was compared with a separate group of seven young people attending the same service who received TAU. The exercise intervention was designed for participants to achieve 90 min of moderate-to-vigorous exercise per week. Two supervised gym sessions were offered each week for 10 weeks, with aerobic and resistance activities undertaken according to participant preference. Other sporting activities were offered either alternatively or additionally to help participants meet their weekly activity goal. Participants achieved on average 107 min of moderate-to-vigorous physical activity each week. After 10 weeks of exercise, reductions in participants' symptoms scores (PANSS total) significantly outperformed the TAU comparison group. Negative symptoms showed a 33% decrease in the exercise group, and general symptoms reduced by about 25%; both significant improvements over the TAU group. Positive symptoms also decreased; however, this did not differ significantly compared with the TAU group. Psychosocial functioning showed improvement with exercise, as were some domains of cognition (verbal short-term memory). This pilot study shows promising results for integrating an exercise intervention into usual treatment for early psychosis.

# EXERCISE FOR SUBSTANCE USE/ABUSE: THE EVIDENCE

There are no trials available that examine exercise in the treatment of diagnosed substance use disorders in young people. Here we review two studies that use exercise to intervene in hazardous alcohol use. Exercise is proposed to reduce excessive alcohol use by offering engagement in an alternative healthy activity, reducing mood and anxiety symptoms which may be motivators for substance use, potentially increasing self-efficacy and improving social connections that occur outside of unhealthy drinking contexts (Ham and Hope, 2003).

In a pilot RCT, Weinstock et al. (2014) assigned 31 university students (65% female, mean age 20.5 years), who were identified as "hazardous drinkers" (Alcohol Use Disorders Identification Test $\geq$ 8; four or more heavy drinking episodes in past 2 months), to either a single 50-min motivational enhancement therapy (MET) for exercise session plus weekly contingency management (CM) sessions for 8 weeks or to a one-off 50-min MET session as control group. The CM sessions involved setting exercise goals and receiving prizes if goals were met. The maximum monetary value of prizes if all exercise goals were met over 8 weeks was $230. After the intervention period, self-reported exercise frequency was higher in the MET + CM versus MET alone; however, energy expenditure as estimated from accelerometers did not differ between the groups. There were no significant group differences after the intervention period on number of drinking days, heavy drinking days, or total drinks per week. The intervention group had more drinking days at baseline, which needs to be considered in interpreting the results.

Murphy et al. (1986) used an RCT to allocate 60 male university students (mean age 25 years), who were "high-volume drinkers" (at least 45 drinks per month), to an exercise group, a meditation group, or a no-treatment control group for 8 weeks. The exercise group engaged in 20 min of warm-up, 30 min of running, and 20 min of cool down exercises, three times a week, plus an extra session of running in their own time each week. The meditation group completed 20 min of facilitated mediation, three times a week, and was asked to do mediation each morning and night, 7 days a week. The control group monitored their daily activities for the 8-week study period. Alcohol consumption reduced in all three groups; however, by the end of the intervention, alcohol consumption was significantly lower in the exercise group compared to the no intervention control group. No differences were shown between exercise and meditation groups. Additionally, those in the exercise group significantly improved their aerobic fitness. Six weeks after the intervention period, all groups had increased their alcohol consumption; however, only the exercise group remained lower than their baseline level of intake. Findings must be interpreted in the context of significant dropouts from the study—almost one in three by the end of treatment, and one in two by 6-week follow-up.

## SUMMARY OF THE EVIDENCE BASE FOR EXERCISE INTERVENTIONS IN YOUTH MENTAL HEALTH

Findings from the two meta-analyses (Bailey et al., 2017; Carter et al., 2016) and studies described in the previously mentioned depression section indicate the potential for exercise interventions in improving depression symptoms in young people. Acceptability of the intervention appears to be strong, as indicated by the high adherence and attendance rates; however, there remains the need for large, high-quality effectiveness trials to examine what types of activities and intensities lead to the best outcomes for young people with depression or depression symptoms and implementation studies within mental health care. Longer term follow-up beyond the immediate intervention period is also required. Similar conclusions can be drawn from the anxiety and early psychosis trials; exercise appears to be efficacious in reducing key clinical symptoms and can be delivered alongside usual treatment for early psychosis; however, knowledge of how to deliver exercise interventions for anxiety disorders in clinical settings remains limited. Overall, despite exercise having an advantage of being a transdiagnostic intervention, studies in adolescents and young people to date have, on the whole, selected participants based on a single primary presenting issue and, therefore, are unable to evaluate the potential of exercise improving multiple clinical concerns and domains.

## APPLICATION IN CLINICAL PRACTICE

As mentioned previously, much of the intervention studies have occurred in nonclinical settings and have often recruited young people with elevated symptoms of disorder to engage in stand-alone exercise interventions. A few exceptions to this offer us the opportunity to explore how exercise interventions may be integrated into usual mental health care for help-seeking young people. Carter et al.'s (2015) study demonstrated how preferred intensity supervised circuit training could be delivered alongside usual treatment within primary care or specialist youth mental health services. This model is an option where access to exercise specialists and exercise/gym equipment is possible within service delivery models and funding sources.

An alternative approach that demonstrated some promise was the study conducted by our research team in Melbourne, Australia (Parker et al., 2016), based in two headspace youth mental health services (integrated primary health, mental health, vocational/educational and substance use services). The intervention in this trial of 176 young help-seeking people was delivered by mental health clinicians and used a behavior change intervention to integrate weekly exercise planning, goal setting, and monitoring changes in mood and stress, to encourage young people with depression and anxiety symptoms to engage in more physical activity. Delivered in conjunction with psychological treatment, those who received the physical activity behavior change intervention reported a significantly greater reduction in depression scores compared with a psychoeducation control group, at the end of the 6-week intervention period. Although the intervention group did not engage in significantly greater amounts of self-reported physical activity at posttreatment assessment (perhaps due to low sensitivity of the physical activity measure or potentially a general behavioral activation effect), it is clear that including a physical activity behavior change intervention led to clinically significant improvements in depression symptoms over a short-time frame (Parker et al., 2016).

A final model with promise focuses on using lifestyle interventions of exercise and nutrition to prevent metabolic changes associated with antipsychotic medication use in young people experiencing a first episode of psychosis. A multidisciplinary intervention of supervised exercise, nutrition advice, and healthy cooking classes, delivered by exercise physiologists and dietitians, on a background of usual medical care and case management, has been shown to prevent weight gain and is important for maintaining healthy ranges of metabolic functioning (Curtis et al., 2016).

Exercise interventions may be more readily implemented within specialist mental health services that support a multidisciplinary clinical workforce and perhaps will be more challenging to integrate within primary care settings, where access to exercise specialists may be limited, especially if mental health concerns are the primary presenting issue of the young person. Certainly in Australia, there is a call to remove these barriers and ensure that young people with mental health concerns can access government-funded exercise physiologists and dietitians (Physical Health Policy Writing Group, 2016); however, this level of policy change takes time. Lederman et al. (2017) have proposed a series of recommendations for implementing exercise interventions into routine mental health care. For community settings, an abridged version of their advice is to ensure early intervention for psychosis to ensure prevention of rapid weight gain, routine metabolic monitoring of cardiometabolic indicators (see Curtis et al., 2012 for more information), multidisciplinary approach of mental health and allied health professionals, family, and carers, using a patient-centered approach, behavior change strategies to increase motivation, individualization to tailor intervention for specific needs (e.g., fitness levels, physical activity history, goals, motivation, available resources, and supports), and supervision by exercise specialists (e.g., accredited exercise physiologists and physiotherapists). Of particular importance is the need to deliver these interventions within multidisciplinary teams and tailoring interventions to match the individual's needs. Where exercise specialists are not available, the next best option is for mental health professionals to deliver behavior change strategies to assist young people with mental health problems to increase their engagement in physical activity.

Certainly, leaders in the exercise and mental health field are increasingly calling for a shift from efficacy studies to effectiveness trials (Schuch et al., 2017) and implementing a focus on movement within psychological treatments for mental disorders (Ekkekakis and Murri, 2017). Factors found to be associated with mental health clinicians providing exercise advice include beliefs regarding the acceptability of exercise, confidence to discuss exercise, and the clinician's own engagement in exercise (Burton et al., 2010). Perhaps, future implementation strategies in youth mental health could not only target the knowledge and capacity of the mental health workforce to deliver physical activity behavior change interventions but also behavior change interventions to increase their own levels of physical activity.

## CONCLUSIONS

The evidence base for using exercise interventions in youth mental health is growing, and early signs indicate the benefits across multiple mental disorders. Future directions need to consider how to gather sufficient efficacy and effectiveness evidence to support a personalized medicine approach (e.g., to enable the matching of exercise dose, type, frequency to a young person's presenting issues and preferences). Broader population health interventions are required to prevent disengagement from physical activity and reduce sedentary behaviors in young people generally, but particularly those at risk of developing mental health problems. Interventions should promote exercise as a pleasant and enjoyable activity to maximize adherence and sustained engagement (e.g., see Ekkekakis, 2017), and the tracking of long-term health and mental health outcomes is essential to demonstrate the longer-term effects of exercise in young people's lives. As a low-risk, low-stigma, and highly acceptable intervention, supporting young people to make a change in their levels of physical activity has an exciting contribution to make to youth mental health care.

# References

Australian Institute of Health and Welfare, 2007. Young Australians: Their Health and Well-being 2007 (Retrieved from Canberra).

Australian Institute of Health and Welfare, 2011. Young Australians: Their Health and Well-being 2011 Cat. No. PHE 140. AIHW, Canberra.

Bailey, A., Hetrick, S.E., Rosenbaum, S., Purcell, R., Parker, A.G., 2017. Treating depression with physical activity in adolescents and young adults: a systematic review and meta-analysis of randomised controlled trials. Psychol. Med. 10, 1−20. https://doi.org/10.1017/S0033291717002653 (ePub ahead of print).

Balchin, R., Linde, J., Blackhurst, D., Rauch, H.G.L., Schonbachler, G., 2016. Sweating away depression? The impact of intensive exercise on depression. J. Affect. Disord. 200, 218−221.

Baldursdottir, B., Valdimarsdottir, H.B., Krettek, A., Gylfason, H.F., Sigfusdottir, I.D., 2017. Age-related differences in physical activity and depressive symptoms among 10-19-year-old adolescents: a population based study. Psychol. Sport Exerc. 28, 91−99.

Broman-Fulks, J.J., Berman, M.E., Rabian, B.A., Webster, M.J., 2004. Effects of aerobic exercise on anxiety sensitivity. Behav. Res. Ther. 42, 126−136.

Broman-Fulks, J.J., Storey, K.M., 2008. Evaluation of a brief aerobic exercise intervention for high anxiety sensitivity. Anxiety Stress Coping 21 (2), 117−128.

Brown, H.E., Pearson, N., Braithwaite, R.E., Brown, W.J., Biddle, S.J.H., 2013. Physical activity interventions and depression in children and adolescents: a systematic review and meta-analysis. Sports Med. 43, 195−206.

Burton, N.W., Pakenham, K.I., Brown, W.J., 2010. Are psychologists willing and able to promote physical activity as part of psychological treatment? Int. J. Behav. Med. 17 (4), 287−297.

Carter, T., Guo, B., Turner, D., Morres, I., Khalil, E., Brighton, E., et al., 2015. Preferred intensity exercise for adolescents receiving treatment for depression: a pragmatic randomised controlled trial. BMC Psychiatry 15, 247.

Carter, T., Morres, I.D., Meade, O., Callaghan, P., 2016. The effect of exercise on depressive symptoms in adolescents: a systematic review and meta-analysis. J. Am. Acad. Child Adolesc. Psychiatry 55, 580−590.

Chu, I.H., Buckworth, J., Kirby, T.E., Emery, C.F., 2009. Effect of exercise intensity on depressive symptom in women. Ment. Health Phys. Act. 2, 37−43.

Cooney, G.M., Dwan, K., Greig, C.A., Lawlor, D.A., Rimer, J., Waugh, F.R., et al., 2013. Exercise for depression. Cochrane Database Syst. Rev. 9, (Art. No.: CD004366). https://doi.org/10.1002/14651858.CD004366.pub6.

Curtis, J., Newall, H.D., Samaras, K., 2012. The heart of the matter: cardiometablic care in youth with psychosis. Early Interv. Psychiatry 6, 347−353.

Curtis, J., Watkins, A., Rosenbaum, S., Teasdale, S., Kalucy, M., Samaras, K., Ward, P.B., 2016. Evaluating an individualized lifestyle and life skills intervention to prevent antipsychotic-induced weight gain in first-episode psychosis. Early Interv. Psychiatry 10 (3), 267−276.

de Silva, S., Bailey, A.P., Parker, A.G., Montague, A., Hetrick, S.E., 2017. An open-access evidence database of controlled trials and systematic reviews in youth mental health. Early Interv. Psychiatry. ePub ahead of print. https://doi.org/10.1111/eip.12423.

Ekkekakis, P., 2017. People have feelings! Exercise psychology in paradigmatic transition. Curr. Opin. Psychol. 16, 84–88.

Ekkekakis, P., Murri, M.B., 2017. Exercise as antidepressant treatment: time for the transition from trials to clinic? Gen. Hosp. Psychiatry 49, A1–A5.

Firth, J., Carney, R., Elliott, R., French, P., Parker, S., McIntyre, R., et al., 2016. Exercise as an intervention for first-episode psychosis: a feasibility study. Early Interv. Psychiatry. https://doi.org/10.1111/eip.12329.

Firth, J., Cotter, J., Elliott, R., French, P., Yung, A.R., 2015. A systematic review and meta-analysis of exercise interventions in schizophrenia patients. Psychol. Med. 45, 1343–1361.

Gore, F.M., Bloem, P.J.N., Patton, G.C., Ferguson, J., Joseph, V., Coffey, C., et al., 2011. Global burden of disease in young people aged 10-24 years: a systematic analysis. Lancet 377, 2093–2102.

Ham, L.S., Hope, D.A., 2003. College students and problematic drinking: a review of the literature. Clin. Psychol. Rev. 23 (5), 719–759.

Herring, M.P., Jacob, M.L., Suveg, C., Dishman, R.K., O'Connor, P.J., 2011. Feasibility of exercise training for the short-term treatment of generalized anxiety disorder: a randomized controlled trial. [GAD]. Psychother. Psychosom. 81 (1), 21–28. https://doi.org/10.1159/000327898.

Herring, M.P., Jacob, M.L., Suveg, C., Dishman, R.K., O'Connor, P.J., 2012. Feasibility of exercise training for the short-term treatment of Generalised Anxiety Disorder: a randomised controlled trial. Psychother. Psychosom. 81, 21–28.

Hetrick, S.E., McKenzie, J.E., Cox, G.R., Simmons, M.B., Merry, S.N., 2012. Newer generation antidepressants for depressive disorders in children and adolescents. Cochrane Database Syst. Rev. (11), Art. No.: CD004851. https://doi.org/10.1002/14651858.CD004851.pub3.

Hughes, C.W., Barnes, S., Barnes, C., Defina, L.F., Nakonezny, P., Emslie, G.J., 2013. Depressed adolescents treated with exercise (DATE): a pilot randomized controlled trial to test feasibility and establish preliminary effect sizes. [DD]. Ment. Health Phys. Act. 6 (2), 119–131.

Insel, T.R., Fenton, W.S., 2005. Psychiatric epidemiology: it's not just about counting anymore. Arch. Gen. Psychiatry 62 (6), 590–592.

Jorm, A.F., Morgan, A.J., Wright, A., 2008. Interventions that are helpful for depression and anxiety in young people: a comparison of clinicians' beliefs with those of youth and their parents. J. Affect. Disord. 111, 227–234.

Kessler, R.C., Amminger, G.P., Aguilar-Gaxiolac, S., Alonsod, J., Lee, S., Bedirhan Ustun, T., 2007. Age of onset of mental disorders: a review of recent literature. Curr. Opin. Psychiatry 20, 359–364.

Kessler, R.C., Berglund, P., Demler, O., Jin, R., Merikangas, K.R., Walters, E.E., 2005. Lifetime prevalence and age-of-onset distributions of DSM-IV disorders in the National Comorbidity Survey Replication. Arch. Gen. Psychiatry 62 (6), 593–602.

Larun, L., Nordheim, L.V., Ekeland, E., Hagen, K.B., Heian, F., 2006. Exercise in prevention and treatment of anxiety and depression among children and young people. Cochrane Database Syst. Rev. (3), Art. No.: CD004691. https://doi.org/10.1002/14651858.CD004691.pub2.

Lederman, O., Suetani, S., Stanton, R., Chapman, J., Korman, N., Rosenbaum, S., et al., 2017. Embedding exercise interventions as routine mental health care: implementation strategies in residential, inpatient and community settings. Australas. Psychiatry 25 (5), 451–455.

Lin, J., Chan, S.K.W., Lee, E.H.M., Chang, W.C., Tse, M., Weizhong Su, W., et al., 2015. Aerobic exercise and yoga improve neurocognitive function in women with early psychosis. NPJ Schizophr. 1, 15047.

McGorry, P.D., Goldstone, S., Parker, A.G., Rickwood, D., Hickie, I.M., 2014a. Cultures for mental health care of young people: an Australian blueprint for reform. Lancet Psychiatry 1 (7), 559−568.

McGorry, P.D., Keshavan, M., Goldstone, S., Amminger, G.P., Allott, K., Berk, M., et al., 2014b. Biomarkers and clinical staging in psychiatry. World Psychiatry 13, 211−223.

McGorry, P.D., Purcell, R., Goldstone, S., Amminger, G.P., 2011. Age of onset and timing of treatment for mental and substance use disorders: Implications for preventive intervention strategies and models of care. Curr. Opin. Psychiatry 24, 301−306.

Meyer, T.J., Miller, M.L., Metzger, R.L., Borkovec, T.D., 1990. Development and validation of the penn state worry questionnaire. Behav. Res. Ther. 28 (6), 487−495.

Murphy, T.J., Pagano, R.R., Marlatt, G.A., 1986. Lifestyle modification with heavy alcohol drinkers: effects of aerobic exercise and meditation. Addict. Behav. 11 (2), 175−186.

Parker, A.G., Hetrick, S.E., Jorm, A.F., MacKinnon, A.J., Yung, A.R., McGorry, P.D., et al., 2016. The effectiveness of simple psychological and physical activity interventions for high prevalence mental health problems in young people: a factorial randomised controlled trial. J. Affect. Disord. 196, 200−209.

Patel, V., Flisher, A.J., Hetrick, S., McGorry, P.D., 2007. Mental health of young people: a global public-health challenge. Lancet 369, 1302−1313.

Peterson, R.A., Reiss, S., 1992. Anxiety Sensitivity Index Manual Revised. International Diagnostic Systems, Worthington, Ohio.

Physical Health Policy Writing Group, 2016. Physical Challenge: Wider Health Impacts for Young People with a Mental Illness. Orygen, The National Centre of Excellence in Youth Mental Health, Melbourne.

Rickwood, D., Telford, N., Mazzer, K., Tanti, C., Parker, A.G., McGorry, P.D., 2015. Changes in psychological distress and psychosocial functioning for young people accessing headspace centres for mental health problems. Med. J. Aust. 202 (10), 537−542.

Rickwood, D., Telford, N., Parker, A.G., Tanti, C., McGorry, P.D., 2014. Headspace - Australian innovation in youth mental health care: who are the clients and why are they presenting to headspace centres? Med. J. Aust. 200 (2), 108−111.

Rosenbaum, S., Tiedemann, A., Stanton, R., Parker, A.G., Waterreus, A., Ward, P.B., 2016. Implementing evidence-based physical activity interventions for people with mental illness: an Australian perspective. Australas. Psychiatry 24 (1), 49−54. https://doi.org/10.1177/1039856215590252.

Roshan, V.D., Pourasghar, M., Mohammadian, Z., 2011. The efficacy of intermittent walking in water on the rate of MHPG sulfate and the severity of depression. Iran. J. Psychiatry Behav. Sci. 5 (2), 26−31.

Sadeghi, K., Ahmadi, S.M., Ahmadi, S.M., Rezaei, M., Miri, J., Abdi, A., et al., 2016. A comparative study of the efficacy of cognitive group therapy and aerobic exercise in the treatment of depression among the students. Global J. Health Sci. 8, 1−8.

Salmon, P., 2001. Effects of physical exercise on anxiety, depression, and sensitivity to stress: a unifying theory. Clin. Psychol. Rev. 21 (1), 33−61.

Sawyer, S.M., Afifi, R.A., Bearinger, L.H., Blakemore, S.J., Dick, B., Ezeh, A.C., Patton, G.C., 2012. Adolescence: a foundation for future health. Lancet 379, 1630−1640.

Schuch, F.B., Deslandes, A., Stubbs, B., Gosmann, N., da Silva, C., Fleck, M.P., 2016a. Neurobiological effects of exercise on major depressive disorder: a systematic review. Neurosci. Biobehav. Rev. 61, 1−11.

Schuch, F.B., Morres, I.D., Ekkekakis, P., Rosenbaum, S., Stubbs, B., 2017. A critical review of exercise as a treatment for clinically depressed adults: time to get pragmatic. Acta Neuropsychiatr. 29 (2), 65−71.

Schuch, F.B., Vancampfort, D., Richards, J., Rosenbaum, S., Ward, P.B., Stubbs, B., 2016b. Exercise as a treatment for depression: a meta-analysis adjusting for publication bias. J. Psychiatr. Res. 77, 42−51.

Smits, J.A.J., Berry, A.C., Rosenfield, D., Powers, M.B., Behar, E., Otto, M.W., 2008. Reducing anxiety sensitivity with exercise. Depress. Anxiety 25, 689–699.

Smits, J.A.J., Towers, M.B., Berry, A.C., Otto, M.W., 2007. Translating empirically supported strategies into accessible interventions. The potential utility of exercise for the treatment of panic disorder. Cognit. Behav. Pract. 14, 344–374.

Stubbs, B., Vancampfort, D., Rosenbaum, S., Firth, J., Cosco, T., Veronese, N., et al., 2017. An examination of the anxiolytic effects of exercise for people with anxiety and stress-related disorders: a meta-analysis. Psychiatry Res. 249, 102–108.

Stubbs, B., Vancampfort, D., Rosenbaum, S., Ward, P.B., Richards, J., Ussher, M., Schuch, F.B., 2016. Challenges establishing the efficacy of exercise as an antidepressant treatment: a systematic review and meta-analysis of group responses in exercise randomised controlled trials. Sports Med. 46, 699–713.

Taylor, S., Cox, B.J., 1998. An expanded Anxiety Sensitivity Index: evidence for a hierarchic structure in a clinical sample. J. Anxiety Disord. 12 (5), 463–483.

Tylee, A., Haller, D.M., Graham, T., Churchill, R., Sanci, L.A., 2007. Youth-friendly primary-care services: how are we doing and what more needs to be done? Lancet 369 (9572), 1565–1573.

Weinstock, J., Capizzi, J., Weber, S.M., Pescatello, L.S., Petry, N.M., 2014. Exercise as an intervention for sedentary hazardous drinking college students: a pilot study. Ment. Health Phys. Act. 7 (1), 55–62.

Weisz, J.R., McCarty, C.A., Valeri, S.M., 2006. Effects of psychotherapy for depression in children and adolescents: a meta-analysis. Psychol. Bull. 132 (1), 132–149.

WHO, 2009. Global Health Risks: Mortality and Burden of Disease Attributable to Selected Major Risks. World Health Organisation, Geneva.

Zimmermann-Sloutskis, D., Wanner, M., Zimmermann, E., Martin, B.W., 2010. Physical activity levels and determinants of change in young adults: a longitudinal panel study. Int. J. Behav. Nutr. Phys. Act. 7 (2), 1–13.

# Eating Disorders and Exercise—A Challenge

*Probst Michel*

Rehabilitation Sciences, KU Leuven, Leuven, Belgium

OUTLINE

# INTRODUCTION

"Exercise is good for all" and has well-established physical and psychological benefits. Is exercise also good for patients with eating disorders who struggle with weight and distorted eating behaviors? In the past, exercise was contraindicated for patients with anorexia nervosa (AN) in the treatment of eating disorders mainly because of ignorance and the fear of aggravating the disorder. Ziemer and Ross (1970) introduced an integration of isometric exercises within behavioral therapy. Isometric exercises under supervision were allowed as a type of reward when patients gained weight. Clinical experience subsequently indicated that restricting physical activity (i.e., bed rest) was not successful and led to covert exercise. Vandereycken et al. (1987) and Beumont et al. (1994) were the first to experiment with physical activity in a residential eating disorder treatment setting. To date, therapists are convinced that physical activity, in addition to improving physical health, has important positive psychosocial effects (i.e., improving feelings of well-being, quality of life, and preservation of autonomy) for patients with eating disorders (Bratland-Sanda et al., 2009). The challenge for clinicians is to identify a balance in the problematic exercise behavior of the patient. For clarity, the topic of eating disorders in sports is beyond the scope of this chapter (Dosil, 2008; Bratland-Sanda et al., 2013; Monthuy-Blanc and Bonansea, 2014).

# EATING DISORDERS: DIAGNOSTIC CHARACTERISTICS

The most clinically relevant diagnoses are AN, bulimia nervosa (BN), and binge eating disorder (BED).

AN is characterized by a refusal to maintain a minimally normal body weight and a distorted perception of one's body (weight, size, or shape), namely a negative experience of one's own appearance as too fat and an intense fear of gaining weight, even when severely underweight. The level of severity is expressed as the body mass index (BMI; APA, 2013).

BN is characterized by repeated episodes of binge eating, followed by inappropriate compensatory behaviors such as self-induced vomiting, misuse of laxatives, fasting, or excessive exercise. The frequency of binges indicates the severity level (APA, 2013).

BED is established as the third classical eating disorder. BED is characterized by recurrent episodes of binge eating and a sense of lack of control over eating; it is associated with psychiatric comorbidity and medical and psychosocial impairments (Javaras et al., 2008). Patients with AN often have a BMI less than $17.5 \, kg/m^2$, whereas patients with BN frequently have a normal BMI; individuals with BED predominately have a BMI greater than 25 kg/m². These diagnostic features may be accompanied by several somatic, psychiatric, behavioral, and social disturbances (APA, 2013). The most common somatic complaints (Becker et al., 2010; Mitchell and Crow, 2006; Mehler et al., 2010), as evaluated by medical doctors prior to a training program, includes cardiovascular disturbances, skeletal disturbances (osteoporosis), and metabolic disturbances (sensitivity to cold, sleep abnormalities, hypothermia, or hypercholesterolemia). Physical health problems in patients with BED are also strongly associated with obesity and physical inactivity (Vancampfort et al. 2014a,b). Exercise for individuals with BED is therefore more specific and treated in a separate section of this chapter.

## EXERCISE IN THE DIAGNOSTIC CRITERIA OF EATING DISORDERS

In the diagnostic criteria of AN, excessive exercise is related to performances in which weight loss is accomplished primarily through dieting, fasting, or excessive exercise (APA, 2013). Excessive exercise often precedes the onset of the disorder, and increased activity accelerates weight loss over the course of the disorder.

In BN, excessive activity is considered an inappropriate compensation to prevent weight gain.

In the literature concerning AN and BN the amount and/or drive of physical activity has figured prominently as a secondary diagnostic symptom. In BED a lack of physical activity and a sedentary lifestyle are present.

## THE MEANING OF EXERCISE AND EATING DISORDERS IN CLINICAL PRACTICE

Evaluating the level and understanding the meaning of physical activity in patients with eating disorders is an extremely difficult task. Every individual with an eating disorder has a different story, background, preferences, personality, and personal-related characteristics (e.g., gender, age, weight, eating behaviors, thoughts and feelings, figure, and activity). In some cases, exercise becomes the central activity in daily life. In addition, the definitions and terms are not always clear (Probst, 2013; Probst et al., 2014, Meyer and Taranis, 2011).

The urge to move may take many forms. Cultural and institutional differences make the interpretation more complex. Different bio—psycho—social mechanisms play a role. Periods of increased and reduced activity levels may alternate. Overt exercising refers to an open and deliberate involvement in exercise (strenuous high cardiovascular activity, such as swimming, cycling, or running) to burn off calories and as a consequence induce weight loss. These activities are performed individually and in a rigid and obsessive manner. Covert exercising refers to rigid strenuous activities in secret, such as sit-ups, extreme standing, adopting a sit position without touching the back of a chair or the floor, and going up and down the stairs. In this discussion, quantitative and qualitative dimensions must be considered (Probst et al., 2014; Rizk et al., 2015). The quantitative dimension refers to the levels of excessive activity, that is, the duration, frequency, and intensity, which exceed the required guidelines for good health and the risk of injury (Davis and Fox, 1993). According to the qualitative dimension, exercise becomes compulsive when it is characterized by the maintenance of a rigid exercise schedule. This rigid schedule increases in priority over other activities to maintain the pattern of exercise, detailed record keeping, and feelings of guilt and anxiety over missed exercise sessions (Johnston et al., 2011).

Excessive exercise is a voluntary increase in physical activities that is not motivated by pleasure or the desire to be healthy but out of concern with body weight (burning calories, ignoring hunger) and appearance (Probst, 2003, Van Steelandt et al., 2004, 2007). Physical activity is an effective method of caloric expenditure and appetite suppression, which fulfils the desire to lose weight. Food intake is carefully weighed against physical activity. These patients go through the day with an exceptional alertness during the day and deny feelings of tiredness (Probst, 2003). Where others sustaining the same effort may tire, they continue regardless of their poor physical condition without complaints. Is this a real sensibility for signs of fatigue, a dissociation of feelings of tiredness or denial? Another feature is the obsessive—compulsive characteristic of the need to exercise, which is common but not always present in eating disorders and becomes a ritualized, stereotype obsessive—compulsive behavior (Probst et al., 2003, Vansteelandt et al., 2004, 2007, Dalle et al., 2008, Meyer et al., 2011). The movement behaviors of these patients exhibit compulsive characteristics that resemble compulsory rituals. Compulsive exercising refers to predominately irrational, repeated, and, in some cases, aimless exercise without satisfaction and beyond the requirements of what is considered safe to alleviate feelings of anxiety and guilt from eating or binging. Here, patients handle tight schedules with repeated activities (e.g., cleaning) and exercise. They constantly feel an inner agitation and an involuntary or irresistible urge to do something constantly. They cannot obtain peace. Some patients may feel guilty if they are not sufficiently physically active (Mond et al., 2006). One of the greatest concerns with compulsive exercises is the high physical demand (e.g., heart problems, musculoskeletal problems, osteoporosis, severe dehydration, amenorrhea [loss of menstrual cycle], reproductive problems, and stress fractures) and a lack of rest and recuperation of the body. A third explanation is that hyperactivity may play an important role in affect regulation (Probst, 2003; Vansteelandt et al., 2004, 2007). Compulsion is also a way to escape the feelings of a vacuum or a manner to regulate emotions (e.g., reducing negative feelings). Physical activity reduces stress, bodily tension, and negative mood and increases tolerance.

## CASE 1. MRS. E

Mrs E. is a 25-year-old young woman with a diagnosis of AN of the restricting type and obsessive—compulsive personality disorder. Her disorder began 5 years earlier following a broken relationship. She worked part-time as a secretary in a private medical center. Prior to hospitalization, she followed a weekly outpatient psychotherapy program primarily for her low weight and problems with obsessive thinking. She reported feelings of overweight; she admitted that she was always concerned about her weight and shape, and she pursued "perfect health" by doing exercises. In the second week of hospitalization, the psychotherapist referred her to a physiotherapist who specialized in eating disorders to evaluate her level of exercise. She had a BMI of 13.8 kg/m$^2$. She weighed 40.6 kg for 171.5 cm. Her Global Assessment Functioning score was 45, which indicates the presence of serious symptoms (e.g., severe obsessional rituals) or serious impairments in social and occupational functioning (e.g., no friends; unable to maintain a job). Her score on the Body Attitude Test was 79. This score refers to the 90th percentile for AN (= extremely negative attitude toward an individual's body). In the first session, she provided an overview of her physical activities during the week: acrobatic gym (1 ½ h/week), cardio exercise (2 h/week), strength exercise (2 times for ½ h). In addition, she played 1 h of tennis per week, and she followed a body workout two times per week. Different team members had the impression that she was active after therapy hours. Thus the physiotherapist proposed that she wears an accelerometer for 7 days (SenseWear; Body-Media). The results based on a 91% duration on the body indicated an average of 18,850 steps per day and a mean total energy expenditure of 6727 kJ or approximately 1600 kilocalories (1 kJ = 0.239 kilocalories). Her daily average Metabolic Equivalent of Task (METs) during her 7 days was 1.6. These results were discussed with the patient and the team members.

### Reflections Related to Case 9.1

On the pretext of health, the patient used exercise to justify her behavior. She did not realize that with a BMI lower of 15 kg/m$^2$, she would agonize and torture her own body similar to self-harm behavior. With this physical activity program, she will not be able to increase her weight and settle down. Even a healthy individual with a BMI of 20 kg/m$^2$ would be completely exhausted. Her thoughts appeared rigid, and she did not appear to be open to reflection. She did not have insight regarding what is healthy and appropriate.

The results of the accelerometer indicated a high amount of mean steps; however, the daily mean total energy expenditure and average of the METs are relatively low. These findings illustrated that the perception of the physical activity level must be carefully evaluated. In general, there are indications that health care professionals estimate the activity level differently and mostly higher than objective measures and the real level of physical activity (Alexandridis et al., 2009). Moreover, the perceived high level of physical activity by the team members corresponds with light intensity activities (i.e., MET < 3).

## PREVALENCE OF HIGH LEVELS OF EXERCISE IN EATING DISORDERS

The prevalence rates of high-level physical activity in EDs ranges from 37% to 81% for patients with AN and 20%–57% for patients with BN (Hebebrand et al., 2003, Davis and Kaptein, 2006, Shroff et al., 2006, Rizk et al., 2015). The broad ranges may be explained by the substantial variations in terminology and the methodological heterogeneity in approaches to measuring physical activity, which have posed a substantial challenge in the research field of eating disorders. The question is why some patients with eating disorders develop a higher level of physical activity. Beumont et al. (1994) indicated that excessive exercise is more common in patients who are overwhelmed by anorexic preoccupations regarding weight and shape than individuals for whom the illness appears to relate to family problems and attempts to manipulate the environment. Soundy et al. (2018) determined that compared with healthy controls, individuals with AN are engaged in more light but not moderate or vigorous physical activity. Energy expenditure decreased with age and illness duration. Self-report questionnaires tend to indicate higher levels of physical activity versus objective measures in AN. This finding is in contradiction with Bratland-Sanda et al. (2010). The patients' self-reported moderate-to-vigorous physical activity (MVPA) was lower than the objectively assessed MVPA. Moreover, the MVPA was higher for an eating disorder group than controls. Probst (2003) determined that patients with eating disorders have a higher level of physical activity and unrest as measured by the physical activity and unrest questionnaire (Probst, 2003a; Ferri, 2008) than sportswomen and nonclinical nonphysically active women. No differences were identified between the subclasses of eating disorders. Patients with AN of the restricting type exhibited a high relation with body image (measured by the Body Attitude Test and Eating

Disorder Inventory (EDI) subscales) and perfectionism. No relation was identified for patients with BN. Female athletes and females not involved in sports exhibited a lower but similar relation for both groups.

## HOW SHOULD THE LEVEL OF ACTIVITY IN PATIENTS WITH EATING DISORDERS BE MEASURED?

To determine the level of physical activity in clinical practice, accelerometers or similar tools are used. Researchers have claimed that defining problematic exercise in eating disorders only quantitatively is not sufficient (Meyer and Taranis, 2011). To analyze the context of the levels of physical activity, questionnaires are used in combination with accelerometers. It is recommended to simultaneously assess other specific features (e.g., body image, perfectionism, and obsessive–compulsive features) related to eating disorder characteristics. Experience sampling methodology is a structured diary technique used to assess momentary mental state at random times during the day. This methodology, which partially solves the problems of self-report (Shiffman and Stone, 1998), may be useful in the investigation of hyperactivity in AN (Pieters et al., 2006).

### Different Questionnaires Assessing the Context of Physical Activity Are Available

The frequency–intensity time index of Kasari (1976) and Monotype (2002), Eating and Exercise Behavior Questionnaire (Brandon et al., 1988), Obligatory Exercise Questionnaire (Pasman and Thompson, 1988), Commitment to Exercise Scale (Davis et al., 1993), Reasons for Exercise Inventory (Cash et al., 1994), Exercise Dependence Questionnaire (Ogden et al., 1997), Exercise Orientation Questionnaire (Yates et al., 2001), The Physical Activity and Unrest Questionnaire (Probst, 2003; Ferri, 2008), the Exercise Dependence Scale-Revised (Downs et al., 2004), Exercise Addiction Inventory (Griffiths et al., 2005), Compulsive Exercise Test (Taranis et al., 2011), Exercise and Eating Disorder Questionnaire (Danielsen et al., 2015).

## HOW MUCH EXERCISE IS TOO MUCH AND WHEN DOES PHYSICAL ACTIVITY BECOME UNHEALTHY AND/OR HARMFUL IN PATIENTS WITH EATING DISORDERS?

The decision regarding whether the activity level is appropriate is extremely difficult. Questions regarding what is acceptable, what is objective, and what is excessive are difficult to objectify. In addition, some exercise is covert. In this section, arguments are provided to determine when physical activity becomes unhealthy or harmful in eating disorders, as well as strategies to curb problematic exercises or stimulate exercises. Fifty years of research has not provided a clear answer to these questions, which many clinicians struggle with. As a result of the unicity of the patient and the complexity of the problem, rigid answers do not work. In the past, exercise was not accepted in the treatment of eating disorders. However, clinical experiences have indicated that (1) exercise in the treatment of patients with AN does not have a detrimental impact on BMI or eating disorder symptoms and (2) forbidding exercise has an opposite effect; it appears better to allow activity to a certain degree than to forbid patients to be involved in activities, which leads to therapy resistance, a struggle with the therapist and hidden activities. In general, only minimal improvements in fitness and strength were noted, which may have been a result of insufficient training loads of short duration and small sample sizes. Clinicians struggle with controversial statements: exercise combined with disordered eating behavior has a negative influence on weight (restoration). Exercise is an unhealthy attempt to control weight and serves to alleviate anxiety. However, exercise results in physical and psychological improvements in health and well-being and may help patients in the weight restoration process. As a result of a loss of bone density and osteoporosis, exercise may be limited; however, exercise may also help reduce osteoporosis. To overcome these challenges, steps and recommendations may be made; however, it is ultimately the therapist in dialog with the patient (and the multidisciplinary team) who must agree on the best option for the patient. Rather than forbidding all activities, a dialog with the patient is needed. Listening to the detailed story of the patient (and the family) may help the therapist develop an impression regarding the function and quantity of the activity (the frequency, intensity, duration time, type, and volume). The therapist must investigate the physical and psychological needs and search for a balance between what is therapeutically acceptable and what is acceptable for the patient. Additional tools, such as questionnaires or accelerometers, may be used to provide additional information.

In addition to the refeeding program, movement and body-oriented therapy, which focuses on psychoeducation, exercise, and the body, is recommended. The aim of this therapy is to educate patients regarding their physical condition and help them accept the physical and psychological changes that result from increasing weight. Well-supervised and controlled progressive physical activity programs (fitness program, aerobics, dance and creative movement [rhythmic exercises, aerobics, and free movement expression], sports [swimming, volleyball, and gymnastics] and other physical activities) have been increasingly incorporated into our treatments programs (Alexandridis et al., 1995; Beumont et al., 1994;

Tokumura et al., 2003; Chantler et al., 2006; Del Valle et al., 2010; Sundgot-Borgen et al., 2002; Ziemer and Ross, 1970; Thiem et al., 2008; Probst and Diedens, 2017).

Overall, the incorporation of supervised physical activity or exercise training into the treatment for AN has occurred without significant negative side effects (Probst, 2013; Probst et al., 1995; Ng et al., 2013). The benefits of this type of training include increased strength and self-efficacy (Michielli et al., 1994), strength and cardiovascular fitness (Ng, 2013), and bone density (Rigotti et al., 1984). Individuals with AN have a reduced bone mineral density and an increased risk of osteoporosis and risk of fractures. Proactive monitoring and interventions are required to ameliorate bone loss in AN (Mehler and MacKenzie, 2009; Mehler et al., 2011; Solmi et al., 2016).

Psychoeducation refers to the process of providing education and information regarding a specific topic to patients with eating disorders (and their family members). To date, psychoeducation is considered an essential component of the therapy program of eating disorders. The goals are to clarify the positive and negative effects of physical activity and help patients better understand the effects of low body weight/fat on health, the effects of low weight on maturation, growth, and osteoporosis and the effects of exercise from physiological and psychological points of view including the risks (Probst, 2001). With this insightful information, patients are often better able to address the challenges, as well as experience more control and better well-being.

---

## CASE 2

A psychiatrist calls a specialized eating disorder center with a request for advice regarding a female patient with eating disorders. For some years, she began to run marathons without a history of fractures. Her training intensity was approximately 2 h, 5 days per week. The 23-year-old patient fulfils the criteria of a relative energy deficiency in sport (this term has replaced female triad): a low weight or low energy availability, a long period of amenorrhoea and serious decreased bone mineral density (osteoporosis and osteopenia). Her body mass index was 16.4 kg/m². Bone density is expressed in a T-score. This score compares the bone density with what is normally expected. A score of 2.5 or below indicates osteoporosis. Her osteoporosis T-scores were −3.3 (vertebral column), −2.9 (L neck femur), and −2.6 (total L of the hip). She had a body fat estimate conducted via dual-energy x-ray absorptiometry of 14.6%. The advice of the team was to reduce the length of training and inform her about the risks (psychoeducation). The patient accepted the advice and reduced her functioning; she reported that she currently runs 40 min/day at a slow rate. She indicates that this amount is half of the amount performed when training for marathons.

### Reflections Related to Case 2

In this case, refusing to allow the individual to run is not a solution; it is unrealistic and a risk for withdrawal from the therapy and the development of more secret physical activity behavior. Allowing exercise provides the opportunity for continuing the dialog and canalizing feelings of unrest in a more acceptable manner. In this situation, it is important to avoid discussions regarding the levels of exercise. Search for a common ground and an acceptable and balanced program that is in equilibrium between what is medically/therapeutically acceptable and what the patient desires. The goal will be to narrow, step by step, the gap between the two controversial opinions. Therefore, psychoeducation in which the patient is objectively informed about medical complications may be helpful. Her percentage body fat is acceptable; however, her osteoporosis scores indicated that the patient must be careful, particularly when she runs on a solid platform. It is important to reward her positive behavior and efforts to reduce the amount of exercise. In a subsequent phase the objective may be to decrease the quantity, for example, from 40 to 30 min and from 5 to 3 days. Therapists must always attempt to identify tools to objectify the physical activity of patients as a result of the different loadings of words or denial. What is slow for patients is perhaps not slow for the therapist. In addition, the 40 min may be questioned. Is it real time or the time she considers (subjective)?

---

To refine this issue, it appears reasonable to start from a more scientifically based existing recommendation. The guidelines of the American College of Sport Medicine (2013) are accepted worldwide as the minimum recommendations to remain healthy. These recommendations consist of moderate (cardiorespiratory) exercise of $\geq$30 min/day on $\geq$5 days/week for a total of $\geq$150 min/week or vigorous activity of $\geq$20 min/day on $\geq$3 day/week ($\geq$75 min/week). These recommendations are also appropriate for patients with eating disorders. There are no objective arguments or reasons to accept that the guidelines are not acceptable for eating disorders. The major issue is that the majority of patients with eating disorders are not satisfied with these guidelines. Some patients with AN will engage in substantially more exercise than prescribed, whereas most patients with BED do not reach these recommendations.

A fitness training program during refeeding supervised by a therapist who is familiar with the physical consequences of undernutrition may increase their fat-free mass and redirect the patients' hyperactivity in a healthy way, thereby reducing their fears of weight gain and improving their sense of self-control. The therapist may opt for strength training or aerobic fitness.

A supervised progressive power training program based on strength training (low intensity and high duration of stimuli) with the main goal of increasing muscle mass (physiological changes) may help eating disorder patients view strength as being helpful for mastering their body, developing self-confidence, self-sufficiency, and independence and decreasing hostility toward their body (psychological changes).

Aerobic or cardiovascular fitness is the most important component of physical fitness and is improved by activities such as walking, jogging, running, swimming, skating, cycling, stair climbing, and cross-country skiing. It has many physical health benefits (decreasing the risk of cardiovascular diseases, stroke, high blood pressure, and diabetes and increasing bone mass) as a result of increasing the capability of the cardiovascular system to supply oxygen and energy to the body; however, it does not come without risks. In addition to the physical benefits, aerobic fitness is an effective approach to combat anxiety, stress, and depression and may also lead to an increase in self-esteem. In most cases, hyperactivity is connected with a negative body experience. Thus attention must also focus on the body image (Probst et al., 2003).

Consistent with existing research findings (Hausenblas et al., 2008; Moola et al., 2013; Zunker et al., 2011), no adverse effects on weight gain in underweight patients were addressed.

Recommendations for clinical practice:

- Listen to the story of the patient and evaluate all aspects, including premorbid exercise behaviors and preferences, which is necessary to make a realistic individual program.
- Assess the activity levels, physical fitness, and health risks. If physical or psychological risks, for instance self-harm behavior, are present, refer to a medical doctor.
- Provide psychoeducation. A continuous dialog reduces the gap between a medical/treatment point of view and the patient's point of view. Keep in mind that what is clear for the therapist is not always clear for the patient. Psychoeducation will help overcome barriers.
- Based on clinical experience which demonstrates that restricting physical activity is not successful, it is better to allow than forbid patients to engage in controlled activities. The termination of physical activities is not an option unless there are medical or therapeutic reasons. In some cases the awareness of the absence of exercise is therapeutic.
- A healthy balance between (physical) activity and nutritional intake must be supported. Physical activity cannot compromise the weight restoration. Physical activity must be medically safe. At the risk of sounding arbitrary, the following rules may be taken into consideration.
  - BMI $< 12$ kg/m$^2$: limited light-intensity activities only after medical agreement
  - BMI $< 14$ kg/m$^2$: light housekeeping activities

- BMI $= 14-16 \text{ kg/m}^2$: physical activities that focus on strength training supervised by a specialized professional (e.g., physiotherapist or exercise physiologist)
- BMI $= 16-18 \text{ kg/m}^2$: patients receive more responsibility and autonomy. Strength and cardiovascular training is acceptable. The role of the specialized professional is coaching the patient.
- BMI $> 18 \text{ kg/m}^2$: patients receive complete autonomy; full sport participation is allowed.
- It is essential that patients are closely involved in the goals and planning of an individualized and tailored exercise program (the FITT principles: frequency, intensity, type, and time) based on the needs of individual patients but preferably in a group. The advantage of a group approach is the social contact, the support, and the interpersonal interactions. In some cases a written agreement may help.
- If compulsive features of physical activity are identified, the advice of an expert in obsessive—compulsive disorders is essential. In recent years, it has been indicated that it is even more important to address the compulsive element of this complex feature (Adkins and Keel, 2005; Meyer et al., 2011).
- Sport competition may compromise the psychological treatment. For moderate and severe AN, competition is not advisable during therapy. Training may be allowed once medically cleared and preferably under supervision.
- It is arbitrary and individual, but for nonathletes, more than 1 h of vigorous exercise more than five times per week may be dangerous and may be an indicator for developing an eating disorder.

This approach provides several therapeutic advantages: (1) the physical activity intensity and the heart rate are controlled; (2) the opportunity for the patient to engage in hidden or "secret" physical activities decreases; (3) the drive for physical activity is reduced; (4) the patients receive the message that "being fed" is not the sole focus of treatment; (5) it helps patients cope with shape and weight changes as a result of the recovery process; (6) the patients are given more responsibility, and compliance to treatment is enhanced; (7) it positively influences their physical and psychological well-being while maintaining good physical condition; and (8) it stimulates social contacts (Probst, 2014).

Sports are good! However, in some cases, sports are used for other reasons than health. Facing these issues is a challenge for all health care providers. The approach to dealing with this behavior depends on the context of the patient. Dealing with individuals who engage in this behavior is, in some cases, an exercise in powerlessness.

## CASE 3. A CASE OF A GIRL WITH ANORECTIC BEHAVIOR IN A COMMERCIAL GYM

For more than 1 year, a 21-year-old girl visited a commercial gym by herself five times per week. She runs for 1 h at a high intensity on the treadmill. She had no contact with other practitioners or fitness coaches. After a while, the fitness coaches became concerned because they observed significant weight loss. She appeared extremely lean. The coaches also received numerous concerned signals from other practitioners. Because of her intense level of exercise and her weight loss, the fitness coaches suspected eating disorder–related problems. The coaches were rightly concerned regarding the high risks and "how to deal with this behavior." An initial soft approach with the question "Do you follow a training program" resulted in a hostile response. She clearly did not appreciate that other people approached her.

### Reflections

What are potential guidelines in these extreme situations? Can these individuals be helped?

1. Do not believe that this behavior will disappear if one avoids the problem. Do not attempt to keep the problem hidden. Search for professional support that is the most appropriate.
2. Consult a professional who has experience with eating disorders. Be careful with providing well-intended comments. Well-intended messages may be incorrectly interpreted.
3. Invite the individual for a short meeting. The individual who has the best rapport with the client should arrange this private meeting. Express the concerns regarding the degree of intensity and weight. List the observations that have led you to be concerned as objectively as possible. Express support for the individual and concern for her best interests. Be empathic and caring. Provide a clear message that you believe that there is a problem, and that the manner in which she deals with her body is not safe in the long term. Be aware that it is not the job of the coach to refer to possible eating disorders.
4. If the center possesses devices for measuring body composition, one may ask her to submit to an examination of body composition. A BMI less than 16 $kg/m^2$ and a percent body fat below 15 are warning signs.
5. If she continues to deny the problem or is not open to a conversation, refer the individual to the general practitioner (GP) to request a medical certificate of permission. If the GP notes that there is a psychological problem, the GP will refer the individual to a psychiatrist.

**6.** If she continues to refuse, the individual in charge may ask her not to come to the gym because the company does not bear the responsibility for dangers. From that moment, it is her responsibility to seek help. The chance that she will visit another fitness center is substantial. It is clear that this step should not be taken lightly and preferably in consultation with a physician.

These directives may have no hold on the individual. However, the instructors cannot escape their responsibilities and have the task of expressing their concerns. To determine how an individual damaged himself or herself is not an option.

In the worst cases, this intervention will be a suggestion that may subsequently contribute to a request for help. Individuals who are not motivated cannot be helped. Denial is a typical feature for this group. This case is a good illustration that dealing with individuals who demonstrate these behaviors is an exercise in powerlessness.

# References

Adkins, E.C., Keel, P., 2005. Does "excessive" or "compulsive" best describe exercise as a symptom of bulimia nervosa? Int. J. Eat. Disord. 38 (1), 24—29. https://doi.org/10.1002/eat.20140.

Alexandridis, K., Probst, M., Van Coppenolle, H., 1995. Effects of a power training program on aspects of body experience and body composition in girls and women with anorexia nervosa. In: Van Coppenolle, H., Vanlandenwijck, Y., Simons, J., Van de Vliet, P., Neerinckx, E. (Eds.), First European Conference on Adapted Physical Activity and Sports: A White Paper on Research and Practice, pp. 237—240 (Leuven: Acco).

Alexandridis, K., Oberste-Frielinghaus, M., Diemel, H., 2009. Vergleich verschiedener diagnostische methoden zur Erfassung des Bewegungsverhalten von Patienten mit Anorexia nervosa und Bulimia nervosa. In: Paper Presented to the Kongress Essstörungen/Eating Disorders, at: Netzwerk Essstörungen, Alpbach, 22—24 October.

American College of Sports Medicine, 2013. ACSM's Guidelines for Exercise Testing and Prescription, ninth ed. American College of Sports Medicine. Lippincott Williams & Wilkins, Philadelphia.

American Psychiatric Association, 2013. Diagnostic and Statistical Manual of Mental Disorders DSM- V, fifth ed. APA Press, Washington, DC.

Becker, A., Thomas, J., Russell, K., Jacobowitz, E., 2010. Patients with eating disorder in Massachusetts general hospital handbook of general hospital psychiatry. In: Stern, T.A., Fricchione, G.L., Rosenbaum, J.F. (Eds.), Massachusetts General Hospital Handbook of General Hospital Psychiatry, sixth ed. Elsevier Health Sciences, London.

Beumont, P.J., Arthur, B., Russell, J.D., Touyz, S.W., 1994. Excessive physical activity in dieting disorder patients: proposals for a supervised exercise program. Int. J. Eat. Disord. 15, 21—36. https://doi.org/10.1002/1098-108X(199401)15:1<21::AID-EAT2260150104>3.0.CO;2-K.

Brandon, J.E., Loftin, J.M., Thompson, B., 1988. The eating and exercise behaviour questionnaire: a validity assessment. Health Educ. 19 (1), 6—10.

Bratland-Sanda, S., Sundgot-Borgen, J., 2013. Eating disorders in athletes: overview of prevalence, risk factors and recommendations for prevention and treatment. Eur. J. Sport Sci. 13 (5), 499−508. https://doi.org/10.1080/17461391.2012.740504.

Bratland-Sanda, J.H., Rosenvinge, J.H., Vrabel, K.A.R., Norring, C., Sundgot-Borgen, J., Rø, Ø., Martinsen, E.W., 2009. Physical activity in treatment units for eating disorders: clinical practice and attitudes. Eat. Weight Disord. 14 (2), e106−e112. https://doi.org/10.1007/bf03327807.

Bratland-Sanda, S., Sundgot-Borgen, J., Rø, Ø., Rosenvinge, J.H., Hoffart, A., Martinsen, E.W., 2010. "I'm not physically active - I only go for walks", Physical activity in patients with longstanding eating disorders. Int. J. Eat. Disord. 43 (1), 88−92. https://doi.org/10.1002/eat.20753.

Cash, T.F., Novy, P.L., Grant, J.R., 1994. Why do women exercise? Factor analysis and further validation of the reasons for exercise inventory. Percept. Mot. Skills 78 (2), 539−544.

Chantler, I., Szabo, C.P., Green, K., 2006. Muscular strength changes in hospitalized anorexic patients after an eight week resistance training program. Int. J. Sports Med. 27 (8), 660−665.

Dalle, Grave, R., Calugi, S., Marchesini, G., 2008. Compulsive exercise to control shape or weight in eating disorders: prevalence, associated features, and treatment outcome. Compr. Psychiatry 49, 346−352.

Danielsen, M., Bjørnelv, S., Rø, Ø., 2015. The exercise and eating disorder (EED) self-report questionnaire. Int. J. Eat. Disord. 48, 983−993.

Davis, C., Fox, J., 1993. Excessive exercise and weight preoccupations in women. Addict. Behav. 18, 201−2011.

Davis, C., Kaptein, S., 2006. Anorexia nervosa with excessive exercise: a phenotype with close links to obsessive-compulsive disorder. Psychiatry Res. 142, 209−2017.

Davis, C., Brewer, H., Ratusny, D., 1993. Behavioral frequency and psychological commitment: necessary concepts in the study of excessive exercising. J. Behav. Med. 16 (6), 611−628.

Del Valle, M.F., Pérez, M., Santana-Sosa, E., Fiuza-Luces, C., Bustamante-Ara, N., Gallardo, C., Villaseñor, A., Graell, M., Morandé, G., Romo, G., López-Mojares, L.M., Ruiz, J.R., Lucia, A., 2010. Does resistance training improve the functional capacity and well-being of very young anorexic patients? A randomized controlled trial. J. Adolesc. Health 46 (4), 352−358. https://doi.org/10.1016/j.jadohealth.2009.09.001.

Dosil, J., 2008. Eating Disorder in Athletes. Wiley & Sons, Chichester.

Downs, D.S., Hausenblas, H., Nigg, C.R., 2004. Factorial validity and psychometric examination of the exercise dependence scale revised. Meas. Phys. Educ. Exerc. Sci. 8 (4), 183−201.

Ferri, I., 2008. Hyperactivity in Eating Disorders Patients. Unpublished Master thesis. University of Padua, Italy.

Griffiths, M.D., Szabo, A., Terry, A., 2005. The exercise addiction inventory: a quick and easy screening tool for health practitioners. Br. J. Sports Med. 39 (6), e30.

Hausenblas, H.A., Cook, B.J., Chittester, N.I., 2008. Can exercise treat eating disorders? Exerc. Sport Sci. Rev. 36 (1), 43−47.

Hebebrand, J., Exner, C., Hebebrand, K., Holtkamp, C., Casper, R., REmschmidt, H., Herpertz-Dahlmann, B., Klingenspor, M., 2003. Hyperactivity in patients with anorexia nervosa and in semistarved rats: evidence for a pivotal role of hypoleptinemia. Physiol Behav. 79 (1), 25−37. https://doi.org/10.1016/S0031-9384(03)00102-1.

Javaras, K.N., Pope, H.G., Lalonde, J.K., Roberts, J.L., Nillni, Y.I., Laird, N.M., Bulik, C.M., Crow, S.J., McElroy, S.L., Walsh, B.T., Tsuang, M.T., Rosenthal, N.R., Hudson, J.I., 2008. Co-occurrence of binge eating disorder with psychiatric and medical disorders. J. Clin. Psychiatry 69 (2), 266−273.

Johnston, O., Reilly, J., Kremer, J., 2011. Excessive exercise from quantitative categorization to a qualitative continuum approach. Eur. Eat. Disord. Rev. 19, 237—248.

Kasari, D.S., 1976. The Effects of Exercise on Serum Lipid Levels in College Women. Unpublished master's thesis. University of Montana, Missoula.

Mehler, P.S., MacKenzie, T.D., 2009. Treatment of osteopenia and osteoporosis in anorexia nervosa: a systematic review of the literature. Int. J. Eat. Disord. 42 (3), 195—201. https://doi.org/10.1002/eat.20593.

Mehler, P.S., Birmingham, L.C., Crow, S., 2010. Medical complications of eating disorders. In: Grilo, L., Mitchell, J.E. (Eds.), The Treatment of Eating Disorders, a Clinical Handbook. Guilford, New York, pp. 66—82.

Mehler, P.S., Cleary, B.S., Gaudiani, J.L., 2011. Osteoporosis in anorexia nervosa. Eat. Disord. J. Treat. Prev. 19 (2), 194—202. https://doi.org/10.1080/10640266.2011.551636.

Meyer, C., Taranis, L., 2011. Exercise in the eating disorders: terms and definitions. Eur. Eat. Disord. Rev. 19 (3), 169—173. https://doi.org/10.1002/erv.1121.

Meyer, C., Taranis, L., Goodwin, H., Haycraft, E., 2011. Compulsive exercise and eating disorders. Eur. Eat. Disord. Rev. 19 (3), 174—189. https://doi.org/10.1002/erv.1122.

Michielli, D.W., Dunbar, C.C., Kalinski, M.I., 1994. Is exercise indicated for the patient diagnosed as anorectic. J. Psychosoc. Nurs. 32, 33—35.

Mitchell, J.E., Crow, S., 2006. Medical implications of anorexia and bulimia. Curr. Opin. Psychiatry 19, 438—443.

Mond, J.M., Hay, P.J., Rodgers, B., Owen, C., 2006. An update on the definition of "excessive exercise" in eating disorders research. Int. J. Eat. Disord. 39 (2), 147—153.

Monotype, H.J., 2002. Introduction: evaluation of some measurements of physical activity and energy expenditure. Med. Sci. Sports Exerc. 32, S439—S441.

Monthuy Blanc, J., Bonansea, M., 2014. Eating disorders in athletes. In: Probst, M., Carraro, A. (Eds.), Physical Activity and Mental Health. A Practice Oriented Approach. Edi-Ermes, Milan, pp. 115—122.

Moola, F.J., Gairdner, S.E., Amara, C., 2013. Exercise in the care of patients with anorexia nervosa: a systematic review of the literature. Men. Health Phys. Act. 6, 59—68.

Ng, L.W.C., Ng, D.P., Wong, W.P., 2013. Is supervised exercise training safe in patients with anorexia nervosa? A meta-analysis. Physiotherapy 99, 1—11.

Ogden, J., Veale, D., Summers, Z., 1997. The development and validation of the exercise dependence questionnaire. Addict. Res. 5, 343—356.

Pasman, L., Thompson, J.K., 1988. Body image and eating disturbances in obligatory runners, obligatory weightlifters, and sedentary individuals. Int. J. Eat. Disord. 7 (6), 759—769.

Pieters, G., Vansteelandt, K., Claes, L., Probst, M., Van Mechelen, I., Vandereycken, W., 2006. The usefulness of experience sampling in understanding the urge to move in anorexia nervosa. Acta Neuropsychiatr. 18, 30—37. https://doi.org/10.1111/j.0924-2708.2006. 00121.x.

Probst, M., Diedens, J., 2017. The body in movement: a clinical approach. In: Jáuregui Lobera, I. (Ed.), Eating Disorders - A Paradigm of the Biopsychosocial Model of Illness. Intech, Zagreb. Available from: http://www.intechopen.com/books/.

Probst, M., Van Coppenolle, H., Vandereycken, W., 1995. Body experience in anorexia nervosa patients: an overview of therapeutic approaches. Eat. Disord. J. Treat. Prev. 3, 186—198. https://doi.org/10.1080/10640269508249157.

Probst, M., Pieters, G., Vandereycken, W., 2003. Assessment of hyperactivity and excessive exercise in eating disorders. In: Presentation at the European Council on Eating Disorders, Budapest, 12 September.

Probst, M., Monthuy Blanc, J., Ademkova, M., 2014. Eating disorders and physical activity: a complex relationship. In: Probst, M., Carraro, A. (Eds.), Physical Activity and Mental Health. A Practice Oriented Approach. Edi-Ermes, Milan, pp. 101—114.

Probst, M., Majeweski, M.L., Albertsen, M.N., Catalan-Matamoros, D., Danielsen, M., De Herdt, A., Duskova Zakova, H., Fabricius, S., Joern, C., Kjölstad, G., Patovirta, M., Philip-Rafferty, S., Tyyskä, E., Vancampfort, D., 2013. Physiotherapy for patients with anorexia nervosa. Adv. Eat. Disord. 1 (3), 224–238.

Probst, M., 2003. Hyperactivity the unknown enemy in exercise therapy. In: Proceedings XIth European Congress of Sport Psychology. Fepsac-CR-Rom, Copenhagen, ISBN 87 89361 96 2 (PDF-file).

Probst, M., Goris, M., Vandereycken, W., VanCoppenolle, H., 2001. Body composition of anorexia nervosa patients assessed by underwater weighing and skinfold-thickness measurements before and after weight gain. Am. J. Clin. Nutr. 73, 190–197. https://doi.org/10.1093/ajcn/73.2.190.

Rigotti, N.A., Nussbaum, S.R., Herzog, D.B., Neer, R.M., 1984. Osteoporosis in women with anorexia nervosa. N. Engl. J. Med. 311 (25), 1601–1606.

Rizk, M., Lalanne, C., Berthoz, S., Kern, L., Godart, N., EVHAN Group, 2015. Problematic exercise in anorexia nervosa: testing potential risk factors against different definitions. PLoS One 10 (11), e0143352. https://doi.org/10.1371/journal.pone.0143352.

Shiffman, S., Stone, A.A., 1998. Introduction to the special section: ecological momentary assessment in health psychology. Health Psychol. 17 (1), 3–5. https://doi.org/10.1037/h0092706.

Shroff, H., Reba, L., Thornton, L.M., Tozzi, F., Klump, K.L., Berrettini, W.H., Brandt, H., Crwaford, S., Crow, S., Fichter, A.S., Goldman, D., Halmi, K.A., Johnson, C., Kaplan, A.S., Keel, P., LaVia, M., Michell, J., Rotondo, A., Strober, M., Treasure, J., Blake Woodside, D., Kaye, W., Bulik, C.M., 2006. Features associated with excessive exercise in women with eating disorders. Int. J. Eat. Disord. 39 (6), 454–461. https://doi.org/10.1002/eat.20247.

Solmi, M., Veronese, N., Correll, C.U., Favaro, A., Santonastaso, P., Cargaro, L., Vancampfort, D., Luchini, C., De Hert, M., Stubbs, B., 2016. Bone mineral density, osteoporosis, and fractures among people with eating disorders: a systematic review and meta-analysis. Acta Psychiatr. Scand. art.nr. ACP-2015-5386.

Soundy, A., Vancampfort, D., Veronese, N., Solmi, M., Luchini, C., Schuch, F., Probst, M., Stubbs, B., 2018. Do people with anorexia nervosa engage in more physical activity than healthy controls? Syst. Rev. Metaanal. Submitted.

Sundgot-Borgen, J., Rosenvinge, J.H., Bahr, R., Schneider, L.S., 2002. The effect of exercise, cognitive therapy, and nutritional counseling in treating bulimia nervosa. Med. Sci. Sports Exerc. 34 (2), 190–195.

Taranis, L., Touyz, S., Meyer, C., 2011. Disordered eating and exercise: development and preliminary validation of the compulsive exercise test (CET). Eur. Eat. Disord. Rev. 19 (3), 256–268. https://doi.org/10.1002/erv.110.

Thiem, V., Thomas, A., Markin, D., Birmingham, C.L., 2008. Pilot study of a graded exercise program for the treatment of anorexia nervosa. Int. J. Eat. Disord. 28 (1), 101–106.

Tokumura, M., Yoshiba, S., Tanaka, T., Nanri, S., Watanabe, H., 2003. Prescribed exercise training improves exercise capacity of convalescent children and adolescents with anorexia nervosa. Eur. J. Pediatr. 162, 430–431.

Vancampfort, D., De Herdt, A., Vanderlinden, J., Lannoo, M., Soundy, A., Pieters, G., Adriaens, A., De Hert, M., Probst, M., 2014a. Health related quality of life, physical fitness and physical activity participation in treatment-seeking obese persons with and without binge eating disorder. Psychiatry Res. 216 (1), 97–102.

Vancampfort, D., Probst, M., Adriaens, A., Pieters, G., De Hert, M., Stubbs, B., Soundy, A., Vanderlinden, J., 2014b. Changes in physical activity, physical fitness, self-perception and quality of life following a 6-month physical activity counseling and cognitive behavioral therapy program in outpatients with binge eating disorder. Psychiatry Res. 219 (2), 361–366.

Vandereycken, W., Depreitere, L., Probst, M., 1987. Body-oriented therapy for anorexia nervosa patients. Am. J. Psychother. 41, 252–259.

Vansteelandt, K., Pieters, G., Vandereycken, W., Claes, L., Probst, M., Van Mechelen, I., 2004. Hyperactivity in anorexia nervosa: a case study using experience sampling methodology. Eat. Behav. 5, 67–74.

Vansteelandt, K., Rijmen, F., Pieters, G., Probst, M., Vanderlinden, J., 2007. Drive for thinness, affect regulation and physical activity in eating disorders: a daily life study. Behav. Res. Ther. 45 (8), 1717–1734.

Yates, A., Edmand, J.D., Crago, M., Crowell, D., 2001. Using an exercise-based instrument to detect signs of an eating disorder. Psychiatry Res. 105 (3), 231–241.

Ziemer, R.R., Ross, J.L., 1970. Anorexia nervosa: a new approach. Am. Correct. Ther. J. 24, 34–42.

Zunker, C., Mitchell, J.E., Wonderlich, S.A., 2011. Exercise interventions for women with anorexia nervosa: a review of the literature. Int. J. Eat. Disord. 44 (7), 579–584. https://doi.org/10.1002/eat.20862.

# Behavioral and Psychological Approaches in Exercise-Based Interventions in Severe Mental Illness

*Ahmed Jerome Romain[1], Paquito Bernard[2, 3]*

[1] University of Montreal Hospital Research Centre, Montreal, QC, Canada;
[2] University of Quebec at Montreal, Montreal, QC, Canada; [3] Mental Health
University Institute at Montreal, Montreal, QC, Canada

O U T L I N E

Behavioral and psychological approaches applied to exercise can be defined as approaches whose objectives are, on the one hand, to study processes underlying the complexity of physical activity (PA) behavior and identify conditions that facilitate PA change. The major behavioral and psychological approaches include, but are not limited to, cognitive-behavioral therapy, behavioral economy, community psychology, ecological models, and socialcognitive theories. In that latter category, several observational and interventional investigations targeting PA change have been carried out (Gourlan et al., 2016). These theories provide evidence-based findings about the nature and complexity of PA behavior and its correlates, type of intervention to be adopted, and then specificity of intervention components (e.g., mode of delivery). Importantly, these approaches do not posit to be superior to atheoretical interventions; however, they "provide a basis for designing interventions to change behavior" (Michie et al., 2008), favor its reliability and overcome barriers to behavior modification.

In this chapter, we aim to address the different barriers and obstacles to PA among people with mental disorders, given the role they play in the initiation of PA. Then, we present the applicability of social-cognitive theories and also of behavior change techniques (BCTs) in the motivation to PA in people with mental disorders. Finally, we aim to provide a framework to apply the behavioral and psychological approaches in order to facilitate PA change in individuals with serious mental illness.

## BARRIERS AND OBSTACLES TO PA

If we had to tell a story about the necessity to write this chapter, the study by Archie et al. (2003) would constitute a starting point. In their pilot study, 10 participants with schizophrenia and schizoaffective disorders were offered 6-month free access to exercise facilities including various activities such as a pool, aerobic classes, treadmill, and tennis court. Then all participants received information about health behaviors (PA, healthy diet, health); and to improve access to exercise facilities, participants were offered parking vouchers and transportation tickets. When researchers examined the attendance to the exercise facilities at 6 months, 90% of participants dropped out of the intervention, and 60% of participants reported a lack of motivation as being the most common barrier to attendance, followed by lack of social support (20%) and low comfort level (20%). Despite some methodological concerns, this study highlights two points to consider; the first being that PA is hard to trigger behavior, and the second being that simply providing access to exercise facilities is not enough to increase motivation to achieve a more active lifestyle due to several barriers. From a more evidence-based perspective, systematic reviews based on randomized controlled trials (RCTs) showed that dropout rates in PA interventions are 18.1% (Stubbs et al., 2016) and 26.7% (Vancampfort et al., 2016a) among adults with depression or schizophrenia, respectively. Nevertheless, in clinical settings the dropout rates are expected to be higher notably because participants in research studies are typically healthier with less comorbidity. Therefore psychobehavioral approaches in PA interventions are necessary to initiate, increase, and maintain PA.

If PA is not an easy to modify behavior, it is mainly due to its specific characteristics that should be considered in PA interventions. Indeed, Rhodes and Nigg (2011) provided several points explaining why PA is a very specific behavior. They highlighted that (1) PA is an adoption behavior (as opposed to smoking cessation), where the absence of the behavior is the inverse of what is wanted; (2) PA is not a life-necessary behavior (compared with eating), so there are less opportunities to modify the behavior; (3) PA necessitates commitment in time, so people have to organize their time; (4) PA is a behavior whose physiological response is adaptive so it can be misinterpreted; (5) PA is a behavior that should be repeated frequently (compared with cancer screening that is a temporary one-time decision); (6) PA is a behavior that should be performed above the rest level. In combination, these six points contribute to show that people with mental illness may face several difficulties when trying to engage in a PA program.

Indeed, regarding the different barriers to PA among people with mental disorders, they had been reported by several systematic reviews that reached the same conclusions. The main identified PA barriers include a lack of motivation and (social) support; higher stress, depression and perceived fatigue levels; weight gain attributed to antipsychotic medication; no-remitted negative symptoms; and absence of previous PA experiences (Bernard et al., 2013; Firth et al., 2016c). It is interesting to note that, compared with the general population, time-related barriers, such as lack of time, were mostly unimportant for people with mental disorders, as was the access to fitness facilities (e.g., costs) which was also not perceived as an important barrier to PA (Firth et al., 2016c). Clearly, there is a need to realize PA interventions addressing these psychological barriers to further trigger motivation and increase adherence. One possibility is the use of sociocognitive theories of motivation to implement PA interventions and better handle the complexity of motivation.

## MOTIVATIONAL CORRELATES OF PA IN MENTAL DISORDERS

PA is a multicomponent behavior and is associated with several determinants such as demographics (e.g., age, sex), social (e.g., employment status), physiological (e.g., body mass index, physical fitness), clinical (e.g., mood disorders, negative affects), and motivational (e.g., intentions) factors. Understanding the modifiable correlates is crucial to better target interventions. Regarding motivational factors, this information is important since it provides understanding about the psychological mechanisms associated with PA initiation or maintenance (positive correlation) or with PA cessation (negative correlation). Recently, several reviews have gathered evidence about the different motivational correlates of PA among people with mental disorders.

These reviews indicate that physical self-perception, beliefs in benefits, higher PA intentions and self-efficacy, action planning, coping strategies, and autonomous motivation were found to be positively correlated with PA among people with schizophrenia, bipolar disorder, or alcohol use disorders (Vancampfort et al., 2012, 2013a, 2015b). As well, another motivational factor, the exercise schema (defined as cognitive generalizations about the self-being derived from past experiences; Markus, 1977) was also related to PA in people with mental disorders (Sørensen, 2006).

Inversely, factors such as fear and negative experiences related to PA, lack of knowledge regarding PA importance, and perception of situational barriers were found to be negatively related to PA. So these previous factors can be considered as behavioral predictors of relapse toward an inactive lifestyle (Vancampfort et al., 2015a, 2015b).

Interestingly, although the knowledge of these motivational factors helps to complete a missing piece in our understanding of some mechanisms involved in PA, most of these reviews were limited by the relative paucity of the literature available. Indeed, all these correlates are based on a small number of studies (e.g., maximum four for self-efficacy), so it is difficult to draw sound conclusions. Nevertheless, one important point is that most of the identified correlates are parts of several social-cognitive theories, which means that they can be targeted through appropriate intervention strategies.

## SOCIAL-COGNITIVE THEORIES AND PA

These social-cognitive theories such as the transtheoretical model (Prochaska and DiClemente, 1982), the self-determination theory (Deci and Ryan, 2000), the self-efficacy theory (Bandura, 1977), and the health action process approach (HAPA; Schwarzer and Renner, 2000) are theories or models known to be related to PA and have been extensively used over the last years. While these theories have been showed to effectively improve PA in various populations (Gourlan et al., 2016), their use remained sparse among people with severe mental illness. However, results from these studies are particularly informative.

As an example, we can consider the framework provided by the transtheoretical model (Prochaska and DiClemente, 1982). This model is comprised of several motivational constructs being the stages of change (where are people in terms of motivation), decisional balance (individual's evaluation of the pros and cons of a given behavior), self-efficacy (defined as the confidence in one's ability to realize an action; Bandura, 1977), and the experiential and behavioral processes of change (defined as the strategies that people used to modify their behavior). While this model has been extensively used in the general population (Romain et al., 2017; Romain et al., 2016) and in people with severe mental illness (SMI), few studies have addressed the relationships between its motivational components and PA behavior. Indeed, only two studies (Bezyak et al., 2011; Romain and Abdel-Baki, 2017) comprehensively assessed all constructs from the transtheoretical model and their association with PA among people with severe mental illness. These studies highlighted that constructs from the transtheoretical model were correlated to PA. More precisely, processes of change (mostly behavioral), stages of change, and self-efficacy were predictors of the PA level (Bezyak et al., 2011; Romain and Abdel-Baki, 2017) meaning that these motivational constructs may be key components to consider in PA interventions.

Interestingly, stages of change (the most descriptive and less explicative part of the transtheoretical model) were also associated with the different motivational regulations provided by the self-determination theory (SDT) framework. Indeed, as expected by the SDT, among people with schizophrenia, those in action and maintenance stages of change had higher levels of autonomous regulations compared with those in precontemplation and contemplation stages. Moreover, their level of amotivation was also lower than those in the initial stages of change (Vancampfort et al., 2014). This finding is particularly relevant because stages of change (Bezyak et al., 2011; Romain and Abdel-Baki, 2017) and autonomous regulation are related to various PA practice, such as walking and moderate and vigorous PA (Farholm et al., 2016; Vancampfort et al., 2013b), so they may constitute other components to consider regarding implementing PA interventions. A particularity of the SDT is that it is hypothesized that motivation is supported by the satisfaction of three psychological needs, namely competence, autonomy, and relatedness (see Deci and Ryan, 2000; Teixeira et al., 2012 for general reviews). Among these three psychological needs, the need for autonomy is the most important to consider in PA interventions (Radel et al., 2013), and the need-supportive environment can improve health-related quality of life. When these concepts were applied to people with severe mental illness, satisfaction of psychological needs negatively predicted amotivation and controlled motivation and also positively predicted autonomous motivation and mental health—related quality of life (Farholm et al., 2016).

In 2016, these rare studies on the sociocognitive constructs associated with PA have been investigated in a systematic review of cross-sectional studies, and only 21 studies were eligible for inclusion (Farholm and Sørensen, 2016a). This review highlights several key points to consider. The first point was that most motivational constructs considered were positively related to PA practice to various extents. Self-efficacy, autonomous motivation, outcome expectations, and stages of change were associated with PA behavior, confirming the importance of these psychological constructs in the PA motivational process. The second point was that the associations found between the different motivational constructs and PA were similar among people with mental disorders than among the general population. This finding is essential notably because it determines that the motivational mechanisms involved in PA are not altered by the presence of a severe mental illness, and this is true for all the psychological models considered (for more examples, see Arbour-Nicitopoulos et al., 2017 for HAPA; Bezyak et al., 2011 for the transtheoretical model; Farholm et al., 2016 for self-determination theory). In a practical and applied way, this finding means that these social-cognitive theories of motivation can be used to help implement PA interventions among people with severe mental illness.

However, although the previous systematic review constitutes the first step to appreciate the role of multidimensional factors in PA development, the inclusion of only cross-sectional studies limits its impact regarding the use of social-cognitive theories on PA and our understanding of how these theories are involved in the initiation, maintenance, or cessation of PA.

In the context of interventions studies, theory-based interventions remain limited. Research from Beebe et al. (2011) and Beebe and Smith (2010) among people with schizophrenia, and based on the self-efficacy theory, provide useful finding. These protocols included mixed sessions of supervised walking, and incentives for PA showed great potential to increase self-efficacy and outcome expectations but also to modify PA behavior. Indeed, in these studies, participants also accumulated more PA and maintained the behavior over several months after the intervention (Beebe et al., 2011). Recently, another systematic review (Farholm and Sørensen, 2016b) identified 11 theory-based interventions including six RCTs. Among the six RCTs, the different theories used were the transtheoretical model, the self-determination theory, social-cognitive theory, behavioral self-regulation theories, and the control theory. Excluding the very small number of studies, this systematic review highlights that theory-based interventions are feasible in the context of PA promotion among people with mental disorders. Nevertheless, most of the included studies did not necessarily detail how they implemented the theory in their PA interventions. So, although it was difficult to conclude on the real efficacy of these interventions, their use should be commended at least because several previous meta-analyses in the field of PA motivation determined that theory-based interventions are (1) effective in the promotion of PA, (2) that none of the theories were found to be superior, (3) the presence of a chronic disease was not considered as a significant moderator of the efficacy of these interventions, and (4) it is preferable to use only one theory in the intervention with all its components (Bernard et al., 2017; Gourlan et al., 2016; Romain et al., 2016).

# BCTS AS A PRACTICAL COMPONENT TO IMPLEMENT PA INTERVENTIONS

Even though we can say that "there is nothing more practical than a good theory" (Rothman, 2004), the main problem with theory-based interventions is the difficulty to implement the latter, given the absence of manuals explaining how targeting their specific psychological constructs in interventions.

To design PA interventions and optimize their efficacy, several reviews and RCTs have used taxonomies of BCTs. BCTs are "active ingredients" of effective interventions. A BCT is a "systematic procedure included as an active component of an intervention designed to change behavior" (Gellman, 2013). BCTs are observable, replicable, and irreducible components of an intervention and specify the content of "what" must be delivered. Two published taxonomies are very useful for care providers or exercise professionals: Behavior Change Technique Taxonomy (including 93 BCTs presented in 16 hierarchical clusters) and the CALO-RE taxonomy (dedicated to PA and healthy eating, 40 BCTs; Michie et al., 2011). Systematic reviews focusing on the associations between BCTs and health behavior change have identified a set of effective BCTs to modify smoking and alcohol habits (Michie et al., 2012), snacking, and PA. Findings suggest that a higher number of BCTs and specific BCTs are more effective (Hankonen et al., 2014). For PA, there is a set of BCTs identified as essential to the development of PA. Indeed, Michie et al. identified BCTs focusing on self-regulation (e.g., self-monitoring) as being most effective when coupled with BCTs targeting the self-control (e.g., prompt intention formation, prompt specific goal setting, provide feedback). These findings have been confirmed by Williams and French (2011). Through advanced meta-analytical techniques, it has also been found that the most effective combination of BCTs to increase PA includes (1) providing information about behavior health link with, (2) prompt intention formation, or (3) providing information on consequences of the lack of PA and (4) use of follow-up prompts (Dusseldorp et al., 2014). Another systematic review (Olander et al., 2013) examined BCTs associated with higher PA among people with obesity (a frequent condition in severe mental illness). The most effective were goal setting, barriers identification, set graded tasks, reinforcement of efforts (rewards), self-monitoring of PA, using prompts/cues, PA behavioral contract, and social comparison.

In mental health settings, although encouraged (Carney et al., 2016), the key BCTs are not known since this research field is in relative infancy. Nevertheless, we can mention that BCTs had been successfully applied among smokers with current depressive disorders to improve their exercise adherence, increase their PA level, and manage their smoking withdrawal symptoms (see details of CALO-RE BCTs use in Bernard et al. (2015)). Moreover, a systematic review (Farholm and Sørensen, 2016b) identified that the most commonly used BCTs in published interventions were goal setting, social and instrument support, coping strategies, self-monitoring, decisional balance, and rewards. However, this list was not associated with any indicator of efficacy, so we cannot deduce whether the presence (or absence) of these BCTs was related to higher efficacy. However, recent trials advocated the use of such techniques along with sociocognitive theories among people with severe mental illness with great benefits. In the ACHIEVE trial an 18-month lifestyle intervention combining group weight management, individual weight management, and group exercise session, Daumit et al. (2013) used several psycho-logical theories such as the self-efficacy theory, behavioral self-management, the relapse prevention model, and the transtheoretical model. Beyond the theories, the core BCTs of the intervention were self-monitoring, goal setting, feedback, problem-solving, social support, skills training, environmental supports, and environmental contin-gencies, reinforcement, and rewards (Casagrande et al., 2010). In the ACHIEVE trial, BCTs were delivered throughout the interview to facili-tate the initiation and maintenance of PA and healthy eating to further reduce weight over the long-term with success.

## PA PREFERENCES MAY BE THE NEXT STEP TO MAXIMIZE LONG-TERM ADHERENCE

In PA interventions among people with serious mental illness, there is a need to increase PA maintenance over the long-term, and patient-oriented approaches may be an opportunity. A 2008 review expressed that people with severe mental illness "who did not receive their preferred treatment may experience resentful demoralization, may be less motivated and may not comply with the proposed program" (preference collaboration review group 2008). Even though this review was not specifically focused on PA, the rationale also applies to this behavior. Indeed, a mismatch between patients' preferences and proposed programs may decrease adherence to PA interventions and ultimately results in reduced PA participation (Abrantes et al., 2011). Given the potential advantages of a more patient-centered approach even in PA, preferences may form an incentive to remind that PA is not a "one size fits all" intervention (Vancampfort et al., 2015c) but a behavior whose multiple aspects (see Fig. 10.1) should be considered as opportunities.

In fact, while the principles of autonomy and intrinsic motivation are not always easy to integrate into clinical practice, PA offers this possibility.

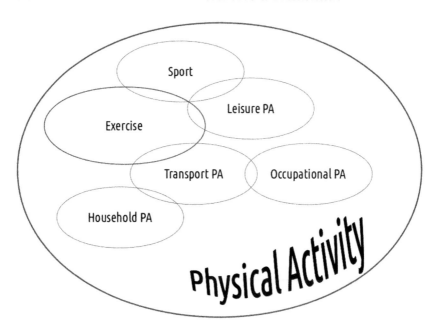

FIGURE 10.1     Domain of physical activity as part of daily living.

Targeting interventions on PA preferences are easier to develop, and recent studies provided evidence about the patients' preferences regarding PA and its components (nature, supervision, frequency, and location). Indeed, there is growing interest toward the PA preferences of people with mental disorders. In fact, across studies, there was a group of PA that was consistently identified by people experiencing mental illness. That latter were walking, running, cycling, weightlifting, yoga, dance, swimming, and fitness/cardio machine (Abrantes et al., 2011; Firth et al., 2016d; Romain et al., 2016; Subramaniapillai et al., 2016; Ussher et al., 2007). Nevertheless, despite similarities in PA modalities across diagnostic groups, some notable differences have been identified within the literature based on specific populations. For example, individuals with early psychosis were more likely to report a preference toward resistance-based activity (weightlifting), aerobic PA (e.g., running; Firth et al., 2016d; Romain et al., 2016; Subramaniapillai et al., 2016), and exercise of high intensity (Subramaniapillai et al., 2016). These preferences are in contrast with those from people with established and long-term psychosis, depression, or those with substance misuse disorders (e.g., alcohol dependence, drug dependence) whom reported a preference toward less physically demanding PA such as walking (Subramaniapillai et al., 2016) performed at moderate intensity (Abrantes et al., 2011). Interestingly, when people with mental disorders were asked to select an exercise modality, they reported a preference toward self-paced PA (Abrantes et al., 2011) but with professional guidance (meaning multiple contacts with a health/exercise professional) (Subramaniapillai et al., 2016) and including monitoring of PA with tools (e.g., accelerometers, log book). As a practical application of this framework, a preference-based protocol was utilized to inform a study conducted among young people with first-episode psychosis in the United Kingdom (Firth et al., 2016b). Following the intervention, an improvement in social functioning, negative symptoms, waist circumference, PA participation, and also cognitive functions was observed. In this program the most popular PA modality was gym sessions (79% of exercise sessions recorded), meaning that this program is easy to implement when a gym is readily available. In addition, it should be noted that the retention rate was 81%. In particular, this study demonstrates that preference-based PA protocols are not only feasible but also have efficacy in regards to increasing PA and health, even after 6 months (Firth et al., 2016a). In a very practical way, these previous studies provide tools that can be used to develop more patient-oriented programs.

# A FRAMEWORK FOR EXERCISE INTERVENTIONS FOR ADULTS WITH SEVERE MENTAL ILLNESS (SMI)

In general, interventions generally involve specific information about volume (frequency, duration, intensity) and type of exercise (e.g., aerobic, resistance, yoga), but it is equally important to consider the psychobehavioral approaches that should also be included. Indeed, there is a large body of evidence highlighting that the addition of behavioral components during an exercise intervention may increase initiation and adherence rates, limit dropout, and increase participant's autonomy.

Given that this book aims to provide practical advice to professionals, we developed a framework for PA interventions in people with serious mental illness in order to guide implementation.

Exercise professionals should bear in mind that PA behavior change is a medium-term process. There are milestones to take into account to adopt PA interventions targeting adults with SMI. Several sociocognitive theories highlight that steps involved in exercise initiation or maintenance are different (Nigg et al., 2008). Furthermore, previous qualitative investigations examining personal experiences of exercisers with SMI concluded that different phases characterized the process of initiating and maintaining exercise participation (Carless and Douglas, 2010; Hargreaves et al., 2017).

Obtaining a high rate of active participants after an exercise intervention is a shared aim for exercise professionals. In this sense, it could be emphasized that an active daily lifestyle can be achieved in different ways (Omorou et al., 2016). An examination of Fig. 10.1 suggests that the different PA domains may be considered as a set of opportunities for future interventions to favor a higher PA level. In other words, exercise or sports activities are not the unique postintervention solution. In recent years, gardening (Soga et al., 2017), dog walking (Christian et al., 2013), and active travel (cycling, walking; Rissel et al., 2012) were found to be related with higher PA.

A summary of the main evidence-based behavioral approaches is provided in the last section. This intervention framework (Fig. 10.2) is intended for care providers and exercise professionals to improve understanding related to the exercise benefits for adults with SMI. The authors deliberately do not include details about length of milestones. They are subject to clinical decisions, patients' profiles, and clinical settings (Carless and Douglas, 2010). For each milestone the framework describes the most effective procedures of exercise planning, BCTs, and examples of different modes of delivery. BCTs described are initially detailed in CALO-RE and Behavior Change Technique Taxonomy.

# INITIATION: TO FILL THE GYM

## Exercise

### Collective Endorsement of Exercise as Treatment by Care Providers

The promotion of exercise initiation by all care providers is a powerful action lever to increase PA initiation in mental health services. Previous studies have shown that mental health nurses play an important role in promoting PA initiation by, for example, accompanying participants to their first PA session and by further informing participants about the benefits of PA initiation (Leutwyler et al., 2013). We also advocate that

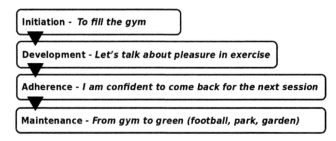

FIGURE 10.2   Framework of exercise intervention for adults with SMI.

psychiatrists or physicians should conduct systematic screening of PA as a vital sign, at least once per month among their patients, to provide reassurance about physical capacity, given an informative leaflet about PA and discuss about personalized interventions and referral pathways (Vancampfort et al., 2016b).

## Behavior Change Techniques

### Initial Interview

It is recommended to carry out an initial formal interview before commencing an exercise intervention in order to identify previous PA experiences, expectations, and PA behavior across all domains (see Fig. 10.1; Laitakari and Asikainen, 1998). A group format could facilitate exchanges between participants and allows for peer experience account to reinforce self-efficacy.

This initial interview could integrate the following BCTs.

Provide general information about exercise interventions and possible negative (e.g., muscle soreness) or positive (e.g., well-being) outcomes.

Provide specific information related to PA and its possible benefits for physical and mental health.

Provide information about what significant others might think of their PA (friend, family, care providers).

### Implementation Intentions

Patients list three positive outcomes they associate with attending the exercise sessions and three barriers. Then, they can identify what they perceive as being the most significant obstacle to them engaging in exercise and write it down. Together with their exercise specialist, patients define a specific solution for this barrier. Finally, they formulate if-then plans according to the following format: "If [obstacle], then I will [solution]" (Sailer et al., 2015).

## DEVELOPMENT: LET'S TALK ABOUT PLEASURE IN EXERCISE

## Exercise

### A Self-Paced Intensity During First Sessions

Exercise professionals should develop strategies along with exercise interventions to develop and maintain positive affect associated with PA. Increased positive affect during an initial exercise session is positively associated with adherence over both the short and medium term (Suterwala et al., 2016). In his work, Ekkekakis et al. suggest to "let them roam free" in terms of exercise intensity (Ekkekakis, 2009). He argues that offering the possibility to self-select an exercise intensity can positively influence affective response to exercise (compared with prescribed exercise intensity). Indeed, research has suggested that self-selected intensity is often closely related to intensity recommended by the American College of Sports Medicine. Several RCTs found a significant reduction of depressive symptoms following a self-selected intensity intervention in women diagnosed with mild depression (Callaghan et al., 2011), and out- and in-patients with MDD (Doose et al., 2015; Schuch et al., 2015).

## Behavior Change Techniques

Collective goal setting: collaboratively developing a collective behavior goal achievable in a timely fashion (Beebe et al., 2009; Beebe and Smith, 2010).
Provide instruction on how to perform PA: It is important to familiarize participants with different exercises or techniques.
Demonstration of physical exercise by professional or peer.
Graded tasks: patient could choose the increment of task difficulty at each session beginning. Exercise professionals should help them to self-assess their perceived effort (e.g., Borg rating scale).
Material reward: inform that valued objects (e.g., vouchers, coffee, cap) will be delivered if the first three sessions are completed. This strategy produces benefits at short-term in adults with SMI (Farholm and Sørensen, 2016b).

## ADHERENCE: I FEEL CONFIDENT IN MY ABILITY TO COME BACK TO THE NEXT SESSION

### Exercise

#### Delivery Style of Behavioral Support

Exercise professionals have to carefully deliver their intervention. Indeed, a style of delivery including task-involving climate, expression of empathy, providing choice (to bolster autonomy), and clear relevance of exercise results in higher adherence rate (Standage and Vallerand, 2014). The care providers can self-measure their delivery style with the Behavior Change Counselling Index (Lane et al., 2005). Task-involving climates refer to situations in which the patient's ability is evaluated and recognized in a self-referenced fashion (e.g., via improving one's skill level and putting forth effort to master tasks). Care providers can provide opportunities for choice within exercise sessions. For instance, providing patients with a number of options for warm-up activities (e.g., perform three tasks among five available). Relevance refers to explaining the rationale and importance of the activity to the patient's health. Exercise professionals should provide examples with relevant statements, including ways to help patients see the connection between a specific task (e.g., leg press task) and the possible real-life consequences (e.g., decrease leg pain during bike ride).

## Behavior Change Techniques

Teach to use prompts: present several environmental prompts which can be used to remind them to pursue their exercise participation. Prompts can include diary, text messages, or electronic alert.

Prompt social rewards contingent on effort or progress: adults with SMI can experience some difficulties to self-measure their progress. It can be interesting to develop a simplified visual tool illustrating attendance or performance. For instance, we can imagine a colored graph showing the improvement in the walking session lengths since the beginning of the intervention (Beebe et al., 2012).

Environmental reevaluation and restructuring: encourage the patients to consider the effects of not exercising on others, including friend, partner, and family. Help exercise participants to modify environmental variables (e.g., sports clothes, avoid escalator, and lift).

Goal setting about the behavior (e.g., bi-weekly exercise sessions): it can be necessary to combine goal setting with a written specification (e.g., behavioral contract) agreed to by the participant and witnessed by the exercise professional. This engagement strategy could be supported by significant others and other care providers.

## MAINTENANCE: FROM GYM TO GREEN (FOOTBALL, PARK, GARDEN)

### Exercise

#### *The Exercise Professional as a Counselor*

This milestone is the most important and maybe the most challenging to achieve. Indeed, the exercise professional should progressively target behavioral change. If a clinical objective is almost achieved (e.g., weight change, improved self-esteem), exercise professionals should prepare patients to adopt a more active lifestyle. Consequently, exercise professionals may help participants to identify and explore different PA opportunities (Fig. 10.1). Based on evidence, many strategies should be considered and combined such as bike-share schemes, participation in local sports teams, or sport organizations in mental health services (Pringle, 2009), active leisure activities (e.g., hiking group, country dance line; Fenton et al., 2017), and gardening (Währborg et al., 2014). It is important to note that a local network between the different mental health services is necessary to limit barriers and reduce stigma associated with SMI.

## Behavior Change Techniques

Review outcome goal(s) jointly with patient and consider personalized goal(s).

Action planning: encourage patient to plan the activities in terms of context, duration, frequency; e.g., if/then plan).

Barrier identification and problem-solving: help patients to analyze, identify factors influencing the PA behaviors (e.g., negative affect, cold weather, and budget) and several associated solutions. This BCT should be performed repeatedly to favor the trial-and-error learning in the different PA domains (Fig. 10.1).

Self-monitoring of PA behavior: a repeated use of PA self-monitoring strategies (pedometer, applications, and notebook) is very helpful to identify current habits and progress.

Self-incentive: encourage patient to plan reward self in future if progress has been achieved (e.g., first week with daily ride bike).

## References

Abrantes, A.M., Battle, C.L., Strong, D.R., Ing, E., Dubreuil, M.E., Gordon, A., Brown, R.A., 2011. Exercise preferences of patients in substance abuse treatment. Ment. Health Phys. Act. 4, 79–87. https://doi.org/10.1016/j.mhpa.2011.08.002.

Arbour-Nicitopoulos, K.P., Duncan, M.J., Remington, G., Cairney, J., Faulkner, G.E., 2017. The utility of the health action process approach model for predicting physical activity intentions and behavior in schizophrenia. Front. Psychiatry 8. https://doi.org/10.3389/fpsyt.2017.00135.

Archie, S., Wilson, J.H., Osborne, S., Hobbs, H., McNiven, J., 2003. Pilot study: access to fitness facility and exercise levels in olanzapine-treated patients. Can. J. Psychiatry 48, 628–632.

Bandura, A., 1977. Self-efficacy: toward a unifying theory of behavioral change. Psychol. Rev. 84, 191–215.

Beebe, L.H., Smith, K., 2010. Feasibility of the walk, address, learn and cue (WALC) intervention for schizophrenia spectrum disorders. Arch. Psychiatr. Nurs. 24, 54–62. https://doi.org/10.1016/j.apnu.2009.03.001.

Beebe, L.H., Burk, R., McIntyre, K., Smith, K., Velligan, D., Resnick, B., Tavakoli, A., Tennison, C., Dessieux, O., 2009. Motivating persons with schizophrenia spectrum disorders to exercise: rationale and design. Clin. Schizophr. Relat. Psychoses 3, 111–116. https://doi.org/10.3371/CSRP.3.2.6.

Beebe, L.H., Smith, K., Burk, R., McIntyre, K., Dessieux, O., Tavakoli, A., Tennison, C., Velligan, D., 2011. Effect of a motivational intervention on exercise behavior in persons with schizophrenia spectrum disorders. Community Ment. Health J. 47, 628–636. https://doi.org/10.1007/s10597-010-9363-8.

Beebe, L.H., Smith, K., Burk, R., McIntyre, K., Dessieux, O., Tavakoli, A., Velligan, D., 2012. Motivational intervention increases exercise in schizophrenia and co-occurring substance use disorders. Schizophr. Res. 135, 204–205. https://doi.org/10.1016/j.schres.2011.12.008.

Bernard, P., Romain, A.J., Esseul, E., Artigusse, M., Poy, Y., Baghdadli, A., Ninot, G., 2013. Barrières et motivation à l'activité physique chez l'adulte atteint de schizophrénie : revue de littérature systématique. Sci. Sports 28, 247–252. https://doi.org/10.1016/j.scispo.2013.02.005.

Bernard, P., Ninot, G., Cyprien, F., Courtet, P., Guillaume, S., Georgescu, V., Picot, M.-C., Taylor, A., Quantin, X., 2015. Exercise and counseling for smoking cessation in smokers with depressive symptoms: a randomized controlled pilot trial. J. Dual Diagn. 11, 205–216. https://doi.org/10.1080/15504263.2015.1113842.

Bernard, P., Carayol, M., Gourlan, M., Boiché, J., Romain, A.J., Bortolon, C., Lareyre, O., Ninot, G., 2017. Moderators of theory-based interventions to promote physical activity in 77 randomized controlled trials. Health Educ. Behav. 44, 227–235. https://doi.org/10.1177/1090198116648667.

Bezyak, J.L., Berven, N.L., Chan, F., 2011. Stages of change and physical activity among individuals with severe mental illness. Rehabil. Psychol. 56, 182–190. https://doi.org/10.1037/a0024207.

Callaghan, P., Khalil, E., Morres, I., Carter, T., 2011. Pragmatic randomised controlled trial of preferred intensity exercise in women living with depression. BMC Publ. Health 11, 465. https://doi.org/10.1186/1471-2458-11-465.

Carless, D., Douglas, K., 2010. Sport and Physical Activity for Mental Health (1 edition). Chichester, West Sussex, UK. Wiley-Blackwell, Ames, Iowa.

Carney, R., Bradshaw, T., Yung, A.R., 2016. Physical health promotion for young people at ultra-high risk for psychosis: an application of the COM-B model and behaviour-change wheel. Int. J. Ment. Health Nurs. 25, 536–545. https://doi.org/10.1111/inm.12243.

Casagrande, S.S., Jerome, G.J., Dalcin, A.T., Dickerson, F.B., Anderson, C.A., Appel, L.J., Charleston, J., Crum, R.M., Young, D.R., Guallar, E., Frick, K.D., Goldberg, R.W., Oefinger, M., Finkelstein, J., Gennusa, J.V., Fred-Omojole, O., Campbell, L.M., Wang, N.-Y., Daumit, G.L., 2010. Randomized trial of achieving healthy lifestyles in psychiatric rehabilitation: the ACHIEVE trial. BMC Psychiatry 10, 108. https://doi.org/10.1186/1471-244X-10-108.

Christian, H.E., Westgarth, C., Bauman, A., Richards, E.A., Rhodes, R.E., Evenson, K.R., Mayer, J.A., Thorpe, R.J., 2013. Dog ownership and physical activity: a review of the evidence. J. Phys. Act. Health 10, 750–759.

Daumit, G.L., Dickerson, F.B., Wang, N.-Y., Dalcin, A., Jerome, G.J., Anderson, C.A.M., Young, D.R., Frick, K.D., Yu, A., Gennusa, J.V., Oefinger, M., Crum, R.M., Charleston, J., Casagrande, S.S., Guallar, E., Goldberg, R.W., Campbell, L.M., Appel, L.J., 2013. A behavioral weight-loss intervention in persons with serious mental illness. N. Engl. J. Med. 368, 1594–1602. https://doi.org/10.1056/NEJMoa1214530.

Deci, E.L., Ryan, R.M., 2000. The "what" and "why" of goal pursuits: human needs and the self-determination of behavior. Psychol. Inq. 11, 227–268.

Doose, M., Ziegenbein, M., Hoos, O., Reim, D., Stengert, W., Hoffer, N., Vogel, C., Ziert, Y., Sieberer, M., 2015. Self-selected intensity exercise in the treatment of major depression: a pragmatic RCT. Int. J. Psychiatry Clin. Pract. 19, 266–275. https://doi.org/10.3109/13651501.2015.1082599.

Dusseldorp, E., van Genugten, L., van Buuren, S., Verheijden, M.W., van Empelen, P., 2014. Combinations of techniques that effectively change health behavior: evidence from Meta-CART analysis. Health Psychol. 33, 1530–1540. https://doi.org/10.1037/hea0000018.

Ekkekakis, P., 2009. Let them roam free? Physiological and psychological evidence for the potential of self-selected exercise intensity in public health. Sports Med. Auckl. N.Z. 39, 857–888. https://doi.org/10.2165/11315210-000000000-00000.

Farholm, A., Sørensen, M., 2016a. Motivation for physical activity and exercise in severe mental illness: a systematic review of cross-sectional studies: motivation, physical activity, and mental illness. Int. J. Ment. Health Nurs. 25, 116–126. https://doi.org/10.1111/inm.12217.

Farholm, A., Sørensen, M., 2016b. Motivation for physical activity and exercise in severe mental illness: a systematic review of intervention studies: motivation, exercise, and mental illness. Int. J. Ment. Health Nurs. 25, 194–205. https://doi.org/10.1111/inm.12214.

Farholm, A., Sørensen, M., Halvari, H., 2016. Motivational factors associated with physical activity and quality of life in people with severe mental illness. Scand. J. Caring Sci. https://doi.org/10.1111/scs.12413.

Fenton, L., White, C., Gallant, K.A., Gilbert, R., Hutchinson, S., Hamilton-Hinch, B., Lauckner, H., 2017. The benefits of recreation for the recovery and social inclusion of individuals with mental illness: an integrative review. Leis. Sci. 39, 1–19. https://doi.org/10.1080/01490400.2015.1120168.

Firth, J., Carney, R., French, P., Elliott, R., Cotter, J., Yung, A.R., 2016a. Long-term maintenance and effects of exercise in early psychosis: maintaining exercise in early psychosis. Early Interv. Psychiatry. https://doi.org/10.1111/eip.12365.

Firth, J., Carney, R., Jerome, L., Elliott, R., French, P., Yung, A.R., 2016b. The effects and determinants of exercise participation in first-episode psychosis: a qualitative study. BMC Psychiatry 16. https://doi.org/10.1186/s12888-016-0751-7.

Firth, J., Rosenbaum, S., Stubbs, B., Gorczynski, P., Yung, A.R., Vancampfort, D., 2016c. Motivating factors and barriers towards exercise in severe mental illness: a systematic review and meta-analysis. Psychol. Med. 1–13. https://doi.org/10.1017/S0033291716001732.

Firth, J., Rosenbaum, S., Stubbs, B., Vancampfort, D., Carney, R., Yung, A.R., 2016d. Preferences and motivations for exercise in early psychosis. Acta Psychiatr. Scand. 134, 83–84. https://doi.org/10.1111/acps.12562.

Gellman, M., 2013. Encyclopedia of Behavioral Medicine. Springer.

Gourlan, M., Bernard, P., Bortholon, C., Romain, A., Lareyre, O., Carayol, M., Ninot, G., Boiché, J., 2016. Efficacy of theory-based interventions to promote physical activity. A meta-analysis of randomised controlled trials. Health Psychol. Rev. 10, 50–66. https://doi.org/10.1080/17437199.2014.981777.

Hankonen, N., Sutton, S., Prevost, A.T., Simmons, R.K., Griffin, S.J., Kinmonth, A.L., Hardeman, W., 2014. Which behavior change techniques are associated with changes in physical activity, diet and body mass index in people with recently diagnosed diabetes? Ann. Behav. Med. 1–11. https://doi.org/10.1007/s12160-014-9624-9.

Hargreaves, J., Lucock, M., Rodriguez, A., 2017. From inactivity to becoming physically active: the experiences of behaviour change in people with serious mental illness. Ment. Health Phys. Act. 13, 83–93. https://doi.org/10.1016/j.mhpa.2017.09.006.

Laitakari, J., Asikainen, T.M., 1998. How to promote physical activity through individual counseling—a proposal for a practical model of counseling on health-related physical activity. Patient Educ. Couns. 33, S13–S24.

Lane, C., Huws-Thomas, M., Hood, K., Rollnick, S., Edwards, K., Robling, M., 2005. Measuring adaptations of motivational interviewing: the development and validation of the behavior change counseling index (BECCI). Patient Educ. Couns. 56, 166–173. https://doi.org/10.1016/j.pec.2004.01.003.

Leutwyler, H., Hubbard, E.M., Jeste, D.V., Vinogradov, S., 2013. "We're not just sitting on the periphery": a staff perspective of physical activity in older adults with schizophrenia. Gerontologist 53, 474–483. https://doi.org/10.1093/geront/gns092.

Markus, H., 1977. Self-schemata and processing information about the self. J. Pers. Soc. Psychol. 35, 63–78. https://doi.org/10.1037/0022-3514.35.2.63.

Michie, S., Johnston, M., Francis, J., Hardeman, W., Eccles, M., 2008. From theory to intervention: mapping theoretically derived behavioural determinants to behaviour change techniques. Appl. Psychol. 57, 660–680. https://doi.org/10.1111/j.1464-0597.2008.00341.x.

Michie, S., Ashford, S., Sniehotta, F.F., Dombrowski, S.U., Bishop, A., French, D.P., 2011. A refined taxonomy of behaviour change techniques to help people change their physical activity and healthy eating behaviours: the CALO-RE taxonomy. Psychol. Health 26, 1479–1498. https://doi.org/10.1080/08870446.2010.540664.

Michie, S., Whittington, C., Hamoudi, Z., Zarnani, F., Tober, G., West, R., 2012. Identification of behaviour change techniques to reduce excessive alcohol consumption. Addict. Abingt. Engl. 107, 1431–1440. https://doi.org/10.1111/j.1360-0443.2012.03845.x.

Nigg, C.R., Borrelli, B., Maddock, J., Dishman, R.K., 2008. A theory of physical activity maintenance. Applied Psychology 57 (4), 544–560. https://doi.org/10.1111/j.1464-0597.2008.00343.x.

Olander, E.K., Fletcher, H., Williams, S., Atkinson, L., Turner, A., French, D.P., 2013. What are the most effective techniques in changing obese individuals' physical activity self-efficacy and behaviour: a systematic review and meta-analysis. Int. J. Behav. Nutr. Phys. Act. 10, 29. https://doi.org/10.1186/1479-5868-10-29.

Omorou, A.Y., Coste, J., Escalon, H., Vuillemin, A., 2016. Patterns of physical activity and sedentary behaviour in the general population in France: cluster analysis with personal and socioeconomic correlates. J. Public Health (Oxf, Eng) 38 (3), 483–492. https://doi.org/10.1093/pubmed/fdv080.

Pringle, A., 2009. The growing role of football as a vehicle for interventions in mental health care. J. Psychiatr. Ment. Health Nurs. 16, 553–557. https://doi.org/10.1111/j.1365-2850.2009.01417.x.

Prochaska, J.O., DiClemente, C.C., 1982. Transtheoretical therapy: toward a more integrative model of change. Psychother. Theory Res. Pract. 19, 276. https://doi.org/10.1037/h0088437.

Radel, R., Pelletier, L., Sarrazin, P., 2013. Restoration processes after need thwarting: when autonomy depends on competence. Motiv. Emot. 37, 234–244. https://doi.org/10.1007/s11031-012-9308-3.

Rhodes, R.E., Nigg, C.R., 2011. Advancing physical activity theory: a review and future directions. Exerc. Sport Sci. Rev. 39, 113–119.

Rissel, C., Curac, N., Greenaway, M., Bauman, A., 2012. Physical activity associated with public transport use—a review and modelling of potential benefits. Int. J. Environ. Res. Public. Health 9, 2454–2478. https://doi.org/10.3390/ijerph9072454.

Romain, A.J., Abdel-Baki, A., 2017. Using the transtheoretical model to predict physical activity level of overweight adults with serious mental illness. Psychiatry Res. https://doi.org/10.1016/j.psychres.2017.08.093.

Romain, A.J., Bortolon, C., Gourlan, M., Carayol, M., Lareyre, O., Ninot, G., Boiché, J., Bernard, P., 2016a. Matched or nonmatched interventions based on the transtheoretical model to promote physical activity. A meta-analysis of randomized controlled trials. J. Sport Health Sci. https://doi.org/10.1016/j.jshs.2016.10.007.

Romain, A.J., Longpré-Poirier, C., Tannous, M., Abdel-Baki, A., 2016b. Preferences of physical activity and perception of health behaviour in early psychosis individuals. In: Presented at the Early Intervention in Psychiatry. Wiley-Blackwell, Milan, p. 193.

Romain, A.J., Horwath, C., Bernard, P., 2017. Prediction of physical activity level using processes of change from the transtheoretical model: experiential, behavioral, or an interaction effect? Am. J. Health Promot. https://doi.org/10.1177/0890117116686900.

Rothman, A.J., 2004. "Is there nothing more practical than a good theory?": Why innovations and advances in health behavior change will arise if interventions are used to test and refine theory. Int. J. Behav. Nutr. Phys. Act. 1, 11. https://doi.org/10.1186/1479-5868-1-11.

Sailer, P., Wieber, F., Pröpster, K., Stoewer, S., Nischk, D., Volk, F., Odenwald, M., 2015. A brief intervention to improve exercising in patients with schizophrenia: a controlled pilot study with mental contrasting and implementation intentions (MCII). BMC Psychiatry 15, 211. https://doi.org/10.1186/s12888-015-0513-y.

Schuch, F.B., Vasconcelos-Moreno, M.P., Borowsky, C., Zimmermann, A.B., Rocha, N.S., Fleck, M.P., 2015. Exercise and severe major depression: effect on symptom severity and quality of life at discharge in an inpatient cohort. J. Psychiatr. Res. 61, 25–32. https://doi.org/10.1016/j.jpsychires.2014.11.005.

Schwarzer, R., Renner, B., 2000. Social-cognitive predictors of health behavior: action self-efficacy and coping self-efficacy. Health Psychol. 19, 487–495.

Soga, M., Gaston, K.J., Yamaura, Y., 2017. Gardening is beneficial for health: a meta-analysis. Prev. Med. Rep. 5, 92–99. https://doi.org/10.1016/j.pmedr.2016.11.007.

Sørensen, M., 2006. Motivation for physical activity of psychiatric patients when physical activity was offered as part of treatment. Scand. J. Med. Sci. Sports 16, 391–398. https://doi.org/10.1111/j.1600-0838.2005.00514.x.

Standage, M., Vallerand, B., 2014. Group-based settings in sport and exercise. In: Group Dynamics in Exercise and Sport Psychology. Routledge.

Stubbs, B., Vancampfort, D., Rosenbaum, S., Ward, P.B., Richards, J., Soundy, A., Veronese, N., Solmi, M., Schuch, F.B., 2016. Dropout from exercise randomized controlled trials among people with depression: a meta-analysis and meta regression. J. Affect. Disord. 190, 457–466. https://doi.org/10.1016/j.jad.2015.10.019.

Subramaniapillai, M., Arbour-Nicitopoulos, K., Duncan, M., McIntyre, R.S., Mansur, R.B., Remington, G., Faulkner, G., 2016. Physical activity preferences of individuals diagnosed with schizophrenia or bipolar disorder. BMC Res. Notes 9. https://doi.org/10.1186/s13104-016-2151-y.

Suterwala, A.M., Rethorst, C.D., Carmody, T.J., Greer, T.L., Grannemann, B.D., Jha, M., Trivedi, M.H., 2016. Affect following first exercise session as a predictor of treatment response in depression. J. Clin. Psychiatry 77, 1036–1042. https://doi.org/10.4088/JCP.15m10104.

Teixeira, P., Carra\cca, E., Markland, D., Silva, M., Ryan, R., 2012. Exercise, physical activity, and self-determination theory: a systematic review. Int. J. Behav. Nutr. Phys. Act. 9, 78.

Ussher, M., Stanbury, L., Cheeseman, V., Faulkner, G., 2007. Physical activity preferences and perceived barriers to activity among persons with severe mental illness in the United Kingdom. Psychiatr. Serv. Wash. DC 58, 405–408. https://doi.org/10.1176/appi.ps.58.3.405.

Vancampfort, D., Knapen, J., Probst, M., Scheewe, T., Remans, S., De Hert, M., 2012. A systematic review of correlates of physical activity in patients with schizophrenia: physical activity correlates in schizophrenia. Acta Psychiatr. Scand. 125, 352–362. https://doi.org/10.1111/j.1600-0447.2011.01814.x.

Vancampfort, D., Correll, C.U., Probst, M., Sienaert, P., Wyckaert, S., De Herdt, A., Knapen, J., De Wachter, D., De Hert, M., 2013a. A review of physical activity correlates in patients with bipolar disorder. J. Affect. Disord. 145, 285−291. https://doi.org/10.1016/j.jad.2012.07.020.

Vancampfort, D., De Hert, M., Vansteenkiste, M., De Herdt, A., Scheewe, T.W., Soundy, A., Stubbs, B., Probst, M., 2013b. The importance of self-determined motivation towards physical activity in patients with schizophrenia. Psychiatry Res. 210, 812−818. https://doi.org/10.1016/j.psychres.2013.10.004.

Vancampfort, D., Vansteenkiste, M., De Hert, M., De Herdt, A., Soundy, A., Stubbs, B., Buys, R., Probst, M., 2014. Self-determination and stage of readiness to change physical activity behaviour in schizophrenia. Ment. Health Phys. Act. 7, 171−176. https://doi.org/10.1016/j.mhpa.2014.06.003.

Vancampfort, D., De Hert, M., Stubbs, B., Soundy, A., De Herdt, A., Detraux, J., Probst, M., 2015a. A systematic review of physical activity correlates in alcohol use disorders. Arch. Psychiatr. Nurs. 29, 196−201. https://doi.org/10.1016/j.apnu.2014.08.006.

Vancampfort, D., Stubbs, B., Sienaert, P., Wyckaert, S., De Hert, M., Rosenbaum, S., Probst, M., 2015b. What are the factors that influence physical activity participation in individuals with depression? A review of physical activity correlates from 59 studies. Psychiatr. Danub. 27, 210−224.

Vancampfort, D., Stubbs, B., Ward, P.B., Teasdale, S., Rosenbaum, S., 2015c. Why moving more should be promoted for severe mental illness. Lancet Psychiatry 2, 295. https://doi.org/10.1016/S2215-0366(15)00099-1.

Vancampfort, D., Rosenbaum, S., Schuch, F.B., Ward, P.B., Probst, M., Stubbs, B., 2016a. Prevalence and predictors of treatment dropout from physical activity interventions in schizophrenia: a meta-analysis. Gen. Hosp. Psychiatry 39, 15−23. https://doi.org/10.1016/j.genhosppsych.2015.11.008.

Vancampfort, D., Stubbs, B., Probst, M., De Hert, M., Schuch, F.B., Mugisha, J., Ward, P.B., Rosenbaum, S., 2016b. Physical activity as a vital sign in patients with schizophrenia: evidence and clinical recommendations. Schizophr. Res. 170, 336−340. https://doi.org/10.1016/j.schres.2016.01.001.

Währborg, P., Petersson, I.F., Grahn, P., 2014. Nature-assisted rehabilitation for reactions to severe stress and/or depression in a rehabilitation garden: long-term follow-up including comparisons with a matched population-based reference cohort. J. Rehabil. Med. 46, 271−276. https://doi.org/10.2340/16501977-1259.

Williams, S.L., French, D.P., 2011. What are the most effective intervention techniques for changing physical activity self-efficacy and physical activity behaviour—and are they the same? Health Educ. Res. 26, 308−322. https://doi.org/10.1093/her/cyr005.

# 11

# Exercise Interventions in Secure and Forensic Services

*Brendon Stubbs[1,2], Simon Rosenbaum[3,4]*

[1] Institute of Psychiatry, Psychology and Neuroscience, King's College London and Head of Physiotherapy, South London and Maudsley NHS Foundation Trust, London, United Kingdom; [2] Physiotherapy Department, South London and Maudsley NHS Foundation Trust, London, United Kingdom; [3] School of Psychiatry, Faculty of Medicine, University of New South Wales, Sydney, Australia; [4] The Black Dog Institute, Sydney, Australia

## SECURE AND FORENSIC SERVICES

Secure or forensic hospitals treat people with severe mental illness, which may include schizophrenia or personality disorders among others, who have typically engaged in a serious criminal offence and require mental health treatment as opposed to serving a prison sentence (Fazel et al., 2016a). In addition, people with serious mental illness who cannot be managed on general psychiatry wards may on occasion also be transferred to secure hospitals (Fazel et al., 2016b). Over the last 20 years, there has been a considerable increase in the provision and occupancy of secure psychiatric hospitals, most notably in high-income countries (Priebe et al., 2005, 2008). Secure forensic hospitals often have many rules and regulations, typically have locked doors and greatly reduced freedom (e.g., ability to freely leave the ward), in which the person is gradually rehabilitated, with a focus on recovery and freedom increased incrementally over time as they make progress under the careful watch of the multidisciplinary team. Providing care and rehabilitation for patients in forensic services is costly, with estimates of €340,000 per year at high-secure hospitals across Europe (Fazel et al., 2016a). To place this cost in context, in England and Wales, the budget for secure care in 2015 was in excess of €1.2 billion, equating to approximately one-fifth of the overall mental health budget, despite this population representing only around 1% of patients who use mental health services (Fazel et al., 2016a; Wilson et al., 2011).

## PHYSICAL HEALTH OF SECURE FORENSIC SERVICE USERS

It is well established that people with serious mental disorders (e.g., schizophrenia) have a greatly reduced life expectancy (equating to 15–20 years of shortened life) versus the general population (Walker et al., 2015; Chang et al., 2010). The largest portion of the early death is attributable to physical health conditions, primarily cardiovascular or metabolic (Correll et al., 2017) or respiratory disease (Das-Munshi et al., 2017). This mortality gap has been labeled a human rights disgrace (Thornicroft, 2011) since many of the physical health causes could be preventable and/or better managed. While it is established that, in general, people with severe mental disorders have greatly increased levels of cardiometabolic abnormalities and physical diseases at a much younger age (Vancampfort et al., 2015, 2016a; Stubbs et al., 2016a), considerably less is known about this pertinent issue in people residing in secure services. There are many reasons to hypothesize that such patients would be at the greatest risk of poorer physical health, including obesity and metabolic disease. First, the environment of secure care is by definition more restrictive, and it is not possible for patients to readily leave the ward freely to go outdoors and exercise or attend the gym. Not only does this reduce access to lifestyle services (e.g., a gym) but also has the potential to predispose this group to high levels of sedentary behavior, which has been independently associated with increased risk of diabetes, cardiometabolic disease, and premature mortality in the general population (Biswas et al., 2015). Second, this population often has the most pronounced mental health symptoms and consequently often takes multiple psychotropic medications and/or very high doses (Machin and McCarthy, 2017). Not only does the severity of mental health symptoms act as a potential barrier to engagement in healthy lifestyle behaviors (Firth et al., 2016a), psychotropic medication, and in particular antipsychotic medication, has been implicated in increasing the risk of cardiometabolic abnormalities, particularly at the highest doses (Vancampfort et al., 2015, 2016a). Third, patients tend to stay in secure care for prolonged periods, and staff in secure services often lack the confidence and training to efficiently promote good physical health and lifestyle behaviors (McCurdy and Croxford, 2015). Fourth, while it is acknowledged that people with mental illness are three times more likely to smoke than the general population, the levels, amounts of smoking, and dependency on tobacco have historically been highest in secure settings (Hehir et al., 2013), thus predisposing this population to poor physical health.

Despite these risk factors, remarkably less is known about the physical health and lifestyle behaviors of people in secure and forensic services. In a study conducted in Australia in a small—medium secure unit ($n = 15$), it was established that 80% of patients smoked, 80% had a body mass index (BMI) above the "normal" range, and 87% had an increased risk of experiencing a cardiovascular event in the next 10 years using a validated algorithm (Vasudev et al., 2012). In this study (Vasudev et al., 2012), despite implementing a program to improve physical health in the unit, there was no change in cardiovascular risk factors after 1 year. In a UK study the authors investigated diabetes prevalence in 500 patients in secure care and found that 17.6% of the sample had type II diabetes (Puzzo et al., 2017). This compares with approximately 10% in a recent global meta-analysis of the worldwide prevalence of diabetes in adults with serious mental disorders, not in secure care (Vancampfort et al., 2016a). Interestingly, the authors (Puzzo et al., 2017) noted that glucose levels were higher in the higher-secure setting compared with those in medium-secure wards.

In the general serious mental illness literature, there is robust evidence that lifestyle interventions, which contain physical activity, are associated with improvements in glucose and other diabetes markers (Taylor et al., 2017). There is, however, a paucity of evidence for nonpharmacological interventions in secure care. Nonetheless, there is evidence that staff-targeted interventions can improve secure forensic staff confidence in dealing with physical health and lifestyle. A recent staff training package demonstrated that it was possible to improve secure forensic staffs knowledge and confidence in physical health care (Haddad et al., 2016). While this suggested that confidence improved, it remains unclear if such confidence translates into actual improvements in outcomes for patients.

# THE POTENTIAL AND IMPORTANCE OF EXERCISE IN SECURE CARE

As many chapters in this book have elaborated, physical activity and structured exercise can have a pronounced improvement in the health and well-being of people with mental health diagnoses. Briefly, there is robust evidence from randomized control trials that physical activity can reduce symptoms of depression in those with major depression or subthreshold depression (Schuch et al., 2016) and also improve cardiorespiratory fitness (Stubbs et al., 2016b). Moreover, physical activity can reduce psychiatric symptoms in people with schizophrenia (Firth et al., 2015; Rosenbaum et al., 2014) and improve cognition (Firth et al., 2016b) with possible increases in hippocampal volume (Firth et al., 2018). Physical activity is also effective in reducing symptoms of posttraumatic stress disorder (Rosenbaum et al., 2015) and people with anxiety disorders (Stubbs et al., 2017). Generally, the evidence for exercise has shown that more favorable effect sizes are noted when the dose is higher, the intervention considers a motivational component and a qualified exercise professional (e.g., a physiotherapist or exercise physiologist) design and delivers the intervention (Vancampfort et al., 2017). Moreover, interventions containing a motivational component and delivered by recognized professionals have demonstrated to be indicators of reduced dropout in adults with depression and schizophrenia (Stubbs et al., 2016c; Vancampfort et al., 2016b).

Despite the promising and ever-expanding evidence of exercise for people with severe mental disorders generally, there is a paucity of robust evidence from secure and forensic services. In one of the earlier studies, an exercise intervention delivered three times per week (two indoor and one outdoor session) by fitness instructors for 8–12 weeks in a secure setting found promising results (Tetlie et al., 2008). The authors found that 87% (13/15) completed the exercise program, and while they did not note any changes in body weight, BMI, or blood chemistry, they noted statistical improvements in well-being. While the results show promise, the small sample size and lack of a control group preclude any definitive conclusions being made regarding the efficacy of the intervention. In a more recent study (Wynaden et al., 2012) which surveyed secure patients' experiences of participating in an exercise program, it was reported across 56 patients that exercise helped them to manage their psychiatric symptoms, as well as improving their level of fitness, confidence, and self-esteem. While these results are encouraging, the lack of details regarding the intervention, the reliance on self-report, and absence of validated outcome measures clearly precludes any definitive conclusions being made. To date, there are no robust, controlled trials that have compared the efficacy of exercise as an intervention for any outcomes in people with severe mental illnesses in secure settings, which is an incredible gap within the literature. Nonetheless, a previous narrative review suggested that in order to be successful, lifestyle interventions should include a program of motivational and reinforcement strategies, and facility-specific environmental restructuring to include maximizing the therapeutic use of green space (Long et al., 2015). This is an important point as there is growing evidence that engaging in physical activity is facilitated by having aesthetically pleasing environments and in particular natural green open spaces. While this may be difficult to manufacture in preexisting secure units, it does emphasize the benefits of (where possible) facilitating leave from the ward environment for physical activity and exercise purposes.

## DEVELOPING PHYSICAL ACTIVITY PROGRAMS FOR PEOPLE WITH MENTAL ILLNESS IN SECURE CARE

In the absence of robust controlled trials in the specific context of secure and forensic services, it is not possible to make specific recommendations for the optimal interventions. However, the expansive evidence given in the earlier chapters for each specific mental health disorder should serve as the guide for the clinician. Briefly, there is good evidence that following the American College of Sports Medicine recommendations can improve mental health symptoms in various mental illness populations (Firth et al., 2015, 2016b; Rosenbaum et al., 2014). Notably, interventions which are individualized and contain a motivational component and are supervised typically see better outcomes and less dropout in people with mental illness (Stubbs et al., 2016b,c; Stubbs et al., 2016; Vancampfort et al., 2016b). This could include aerobic exercise/ physical activity aiming to achieve 150 minutes of moderate-vigorous PA per week. Resistance training should also form a core component of the exercise interventions, with emerging evidence that 2-3 sessions per week can improve depressive (Gordon et al 2018) and anxiety symptoms (Gordon et al 2017).

Some additional nuances should be noted and taken into consideration though. First, lone working may not be permissible in forensic settings due to the potential risk involved, and clinicians should consider this aspect and the importance of working with other colleagues. Second, some gym/exercise equipment (e.g., free weights) may not be readily available and/or kept in securely locked cupboards due to the need for heightened risk management. Clinicians should consider that when setting exercise programs for patients in these settings, adopting and promoting body weight exercise programs for resistance training effects (e.g., pushups, triceps dips) can be highly valuable and popular. Early intervention is key to prevent potential weight gain from the likely start of psychotropic medication and also from the deterioration of mood upon admission to secure services. Previous research has shown that early interventions lifestyle programs work best when started early and at psychotropic medication inception (Firth et al., 2016c; Curtis et al., 2016). This provides an opportunity for clinicians to engage early with newly admitted patients and develop a rapport and intervene at this critical time. Given the background of the reasons why people have been admitted to secure care, risk assessment is of paramount importance and a high priority for the clinical team. Patients are initially kept on the ward on admission for a set period (which will vary depending on local policy) so that they can be observed and supported. As an example of a forward-thinking clinical team, at River House in the South London and Maudsley NHS Foundation Trust, one consultant Psychiatrist Dr Shubulade Smith, ensures that the first time a patient leaves the ward this is with staff to go to the gym. This helps to prioritize the importance of exercise in the clinical team and also serves the purpose of providing a meaningful supervise trip off the ward.

# CONCLUSION

People residing in secure and forensic services often have high levels of cardiometabolic disease, including obesity, and are anecdotally very sedentary due to the restrictions on their freedom. This is a population who can benefit greatly from the use of exercise to improve their physical and mental health. However, there is limited robust evidence to guide the delivery of exercise interventions in secure forensic services. Nonetheless, evidence on the use of exercise in severe mental illnesses in nonsecure care settings is robust and should form the basis to guide the clinical care of people residing in these populations. It is recommended that clinicians engage with new patients in secure settings early on admission and set a precedent for prioritizing physical activity during their rehabilitation stay. As with other areas of mental health, early intervention is key to prevent the onset of weight gain after the initiation of psychotropic medication. Also of importance, admission to a secure setting can be a time of profound deterioration in peoples' mental state, and promoting physical activity can help prevent the onset of a worsening of a person's mental health.

## References

Biswas, A., Oh, P.I., Faulkner, G.E., et al., 2015. Sedentary time and its association with risk for disease incidence, mortality, and hospitalization in adults: a systematic review and meta-analysis. Ann. Intern. Med. 162 (2), 123–132.

Chang, C.K., Hayes, R.D., Broadbent, M., et al., 2010. All-cause mortality among people with serious mental illness (SMI), substance use disorders, and depressive disorders in southeast London: a cohort study. BMC Psychiatry 10, 77.

Correll, C.U., Solmi, M., Veronese, N., et al., 2017. Prevalence, incidence and mortality from cardiovascular disease in patients with pooled and specific severe mental illness: a large-scale meta-analysis of 3,211,768 patients and 113,383,368 controls. World Psychiatry 16 (2), 163–180.

Curtis, J., Watkins, A., Rosenbaum, S., et al., 2016 Jun. Evaluating an individualized lifestyle and life skills intervention to prevent antipsychotic-induced weight gain in first-episode psychosis. Early Interv. Psychiatry 10 (3), 267–276.

Das-Munshi, J., Chang, C.K., Dutta, R., et al., 2017. Ethnicity and excess mortality in severe mental illness: a cohort study. Lancet Psychiatry 4 (5), 389–399.

Fazel, S., Wolf, A., Fiminska, Z., Larsson, H., 2016a. Mortality, rehospitalisation and violent crime in forensic psychiatric patients discharged from hospital: rates and risk factors. PLoS One 11 (5), e0155906.

Fazel, S., Hayes, A.J., Bartellas, K., Clerici, M., Trestman, R., 2016b. Mental health of prisoners: prevalence, adverse outcomes, and interventions. Lancet Psychiatry 3 (9), 871−881.

Firth, J., Cotter, J., Elliott, R., French, P., Yung, A.R., 2015. A systematic review and meta-analysis of exercise interventions in schizophrenia patients. Psychol. Med. 45 (7), 1343−1361.

Firth, J., Rosenbaum, S., Stubbs, B., Gorczynski, P., Yung, A.R., Vancampfort, D., 2016a. Motivating factors and barriers towards exercise in severe mental illness: a systematic review and meta-analysis. Psychol. Med. 46 (14), 2869−2881.

Firth, J., Stubbs, B., Rosenbaum, S., et al., 2016b. Aerobic exercise improves cognitive functioning in people with schizophrenia: a systematic review and meta-analysis. Schizophr. Bull. 43 (3), 546−556.

Firth, J., Carney, R., Elliott, R., et al., 2016c. Exercise as an intervention for first-episode psychosis: a feasibility study. Early Interv. Psychiatry 12 (3), 307−315.

Firth, J., Stubbs, B., Vancampfort, D., et al., 2018. Effect of aerobic exercise on hippocampal volume in humans: a systematic review and meta-analysis. Neuroimage 166, 230−238.

Gordon, B.R., McDowell, C.P., Lyons, M., Herring, M.P., 2017 Dec. The effects of **resistance** exercise training on anxiety: A meta-analysis and meta-regression analysis of randomized controlled trials. Sports Med. 47 (12), 2521−2532.

Gordon, BR, McDowell, CP, Hallgren, M, Meyer, JD, Lyons, M, Herring, MP, 2018 Jun 1. Association of efficacy of **resistance** exercise training with depressive symptoms: meta-analysis and meta-regression analysis of randomized clinical trials. JAMA Psychiatry 75 (6), 566−576. https://doi.org/10.1001/jamapsychiatry.2018.0572.

Haddad, M., Llewellyn-Jones, S., Yarnold, S., Simpson, A., 2016. Improving the physical health of people with severe mental illness in a low secure forensic unit: an uncontrolled evaluation study of staff training and physical health care plans. Int. J. Ment. Health Nurs. 25 (6), 554−565.

Hehir, A.M., Indig, D., Prosser, S., Archer, V.A., 2013. Implementation of a smoke-free policy in a high secure mental health inpatient facility: staff survey to describe experience and attitudes. BMC Publ. Health 13, 315.

Long, C., Rowell, A., Rigg, S., Livesey, F., McAllister, P., 2015. What is effective in promoting a healthy lifestyle in secure psychiatric settings? A review of the evidence for an integrated programme that targets modifiable health risk behaviours. J. Forensic Pract. 18 (3), 204−215.

Machin, A., McCarthy, L., 2017. Antipsychotic prescribing of consultant forensic psychiatrists working in different levels of secure care with patients with schizophrenia. BJPsych Bull. 41 (2), 103−108.

McCurdy, K., Croxford, A., 2015. Improving feedback from outpatient medical appointments attended by escorted psychiatric patients in the North London forensic service. BMJ Qual. Improv. Rep. 4 (1).

Priebe, S., Badesconyi, A., Fioritti, A., et al., 2005. Reinstitutionalisation in mental health care: comparison of data on service provision from six European countries. British Medical Journal 330 (7483), 123−126.

Priebe, S., Frottier, P., Gaddini, A., et al., 2008. Mental health care institutions in nine European countries, 2002 to 2006. Psychiatr. Serv. 59 (5), 570−573.

Puzzo, I., Gable, D., Cohen, A., 2017. Using the National Diabetes Audit to improve the care of diabetes in secure hospital in-patient settings in the UK. J. Forensic Psychiatr. Psychol. 28 (3), 100−105.

Rosenbaum, S., Tiedemann, A., Sherrington, C., Curtis, J., Ward, P.B., 2014 Sep. Physical activity interventions for people with mental illness: a systematic review and meta-analysis. J. Clin. Psychiatry 75 (9), 964−974.

Rosenbaum, S., Vancampfort, D., Steel, Z., Newby, J., Ward, P.B., Stubbs, B., 2015. Physical activity in the treatment of post-traumatic stress disorder: a systematic review and meta-analysis. Psychiatr. Res. 230 (2), 130–136.

Schuch, F.B., Vancampfort, D., Richards, J., Rosenbaum, S., Ward, P.B., Stubbs, B., 2016. Exercise as a treatment for depression: a meta-analysis adjusting for publication bias. J. Psychiatr. Res. 77, 42–51.

Stubbs, B., Koyanagi, A., Veronese, N., et al., 2016a. Physical multimorbidity and psychosis: comprehensive cross sectional analysis including 242,952 people across 48 low- and middle-income countries. BMC Med. 14 (1), 189.

Stubbs, B., Rosenbaum, S., Vancampfort, D., Ward, P.B., Schuch, F.B., 2016b. Exercise improves cardiorespiratory fitness in people with depression: a meta-analysis of randomized control trials. J. Affect. Disord. 190, 249–253.

Stubbs, B., Vancampfort, D., Rosenbaum, S., et al., 2016c. Dropout from exercise randomized controlled trials among people with depression: a meta-analysis and meta regression. J. Affect. Disord. 190, 457–466.

Stubbs, B., Vancampfort, D., Rosenbaum, S., et al., 2017. An examination of the anxiolytic effects of exercise for people with anxiety and stress-related disorders: a meta-analysis. Psychiatr. Res. 249, 102–108.

Taylor, J., Stubbs, B., Hewitt, C., et al., 2017. The effectiveness of pharmacological and non-pharmacological interventions for improving glycaemic control in adults with severe mental illness: a systematic review and meta-analysis. PLoS One 12 (1), e0168549.

Tetlie, T., Eik-Nes, N., Palmstierna, T., Callaghan, P., Nottestad, J.A., 2008. The effect of exercise on psychological & physical health outcomes: preliminary results from a Norwegian forensic hospital. J. Psychosoc. Nurs. Ment. Health Serv. 46 (7), 38–43.

Thornicroft, G., 2011. Physical health disparities and mental illness: the scandal of premature mortality. Br. J. Psychiatry 199 (6), 441–442.

Vancampfort, D., Stubbs, B., Mitchell, A.J., et al., 2015. Risk of metabolic syndrome and its components in people with schizophrenia and related psychotic disorders, bipolar disorder and major depressive disorder: a systematic review and meta-analysis. World Psychiatry 14 (3), 339–347.

Vancampfort, D., Correll, C.U., Galling, B., et al., 2016a. Diabetes mellitus in people with schizophrenia, bipolar disorder and major depressive disorder: a systematic review and large scale meta-analysis. World Psychiatry 15 (2), 166–174.

Vancampfort, D., Rosenbaum, S., Schuch, F.B., Ward, P.B., Probst, M., Stubbs, B., 2016b. Prevalence and predictors of treatment dropout from physical activity interventions in schizophrenia: a meta-analysis. Gen. Hosp. Psychiatry 39, 15–23.

Vancampfort, D., Rosenbaum, S., Schuch, F., et al., 2017 Feb. Cardiorespiratory fitness in severe mental illness: a systematic review and meta-analysis. Sports Med. 47 (2), 343–352.

Vasudev, K., Thakkar, P.B., Mitcheson, N., 2012. Physical health of patients with severe mental illness: an intervention on medium secure forensic unit. Int. J. Health Care Qual. Assur. 25 (4), 363–370.

Walker, E.R., McGee, R.E., Druss, B.G., Apr 2015. Mortality in mental disorders and global disease burden implications: a systematic review and meta-analysis. JAMA Psychiatry 72 (4), 334–341.

Wilson, S., James, D., Forrester, A., 2011. The medium-secure project and criminal justice mental health. Lancet 378 (9786), 110–111.

Wynaden, D., Barr, L., Omari, O., Fulton, A., 2012. Evaluation of service users' experiences of participating in an exercise programme at the Western Australian state forensic mental health services. Int. J. Ment. Health Nurs. 21 (3), 229–235.

# 12

# mHealth and Physical Activity Interventions Among People With Mental Illness

*Rebekah Carney[1], Joseph Firth[2]*

[1] Faculty of Biology, Medicine and Health, University of Manchester, Manchester, United Kingdom; [2] Division of Psychology and Mental Health, University of Manchester, Manchester, United Kingdom

# INTRODUCTION

This chapter will describe innovative developments in mobile health ("mHealth") and give specific examples of different technologies that are currently available. It will explain how mHealth interventions can be used to help people with serious mental health conditions, such as schizophrenia, bipolar disorder, and major depression. Additionally, the growing use of mHealth approaches for increasing physical activity will be discussed, with reference to novel research published in this area.

# WHAT IS mHEALTH?

Over the past decade, electronic health or "eHealth" technologies have been rapidly gathering momentum, particularly in the area of mental health (see Fig. 12.1, Firth et al., 2016). Use of the Internet and electronic resources has facilitated a transformation in health care, resulting in greater access, reach, and service provision (WHO, 2011). "mHealth" is one aspect of this which refers specifically to the use of mobile technologies such as smartphones, mobile devices, and wearable monitoring devices to support and advance health care (WHO, 2011). The growing prevalence of smartphone technology has resulted in increasing interest in using mHealth across all areas of medicine.

mHealth is a growing avenue of research, given that smartphone ownership is now approximately 70% in developed countries (Pew Research Center, 2016). This figure continues to rise as mobile technologies become more accessible, affordable, and widely available. The development of wireless Internet access and high-speed mobile coverage has facilitated the global use of portable technologies across many platforms and locations. According to the 2017 British White Paper (Cisco, 2017), in the year 2016 alone:

- Global mobile data traffic grew by 63%
- Mobile devices reached 8 billion worldwide (almost half a billion devices and connections were added in 2016)
- Average smartphone usage grew 38%
- There were a total of 325 million wearable devices worldwide
- Mobile network connection speeds increased more than threefold

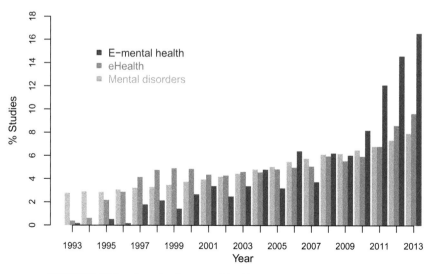

**FIGURE 12.1** Growth of e-mental health research (Firth et al., 2016).

## mHealth Technologies

A range of mHealth technologies are available which have the potential to revolutionize health care, including the following.

### Smartphone Devices

Smartphone devices have many different functions. Texts and instant messaging enable communication at any point in time or place. Prompts and reminders can facilitate medication adherence, inform patients of upcoming appointments, or act as cues to engage in specific behaviors. For example, motivational messages reminding people of the benefits of exercise could be used to regularly encourage individuals to engage in physical activity. Communicative functions also facilitate social and medical support, such as online forums, group chats with peers or other patients, and the ability to communicate directly with health care providers.

### Internet-Delivered Education

Health interventions can be delivered via Internet platforms, such as online interfaces to access educational programs. Internet-based interventions can differ in their content and mode of delivery (Webb et al., 2010). Some may adopt a more interactive approach, such as guided problem-solving, and access to an online advisor, whereas others may provide psychoeducation programs to increase patient's knowledge about conditions or specific behaviors (e.g., physical exercise). With the advent of high-speed mobile data coverage, interventions of this kind can be accessed via smartphones and tablets anywhere, at any time.

### Smartphone "Apps"

Smartphone software applications or "apps" have a variety of functions which can be used for both physical and mental health care. "Apps" are readily available to smartphone users and can be used on the go, in any location. A 2015 study found that over 165,000 health-focused apps were available for people to download on their own devices, most of which were focused on mental health (IMS Report, 2015).

### Wearable Technology

Wearable devices such as activity trackers (e.g., Fitbit, Garmin, Apple watch) have also become widely available. A plethora of research indicates that monitoring and tracking of exercise behaviors significantly increase physical activity levels (Bravata et al., 2007). Basic devices such as pedometers allow people to set goals and receive immediate feedback on the number of steps taken daily. However, more modern wearable technologies are a significant advancement over traditional step trackers. For

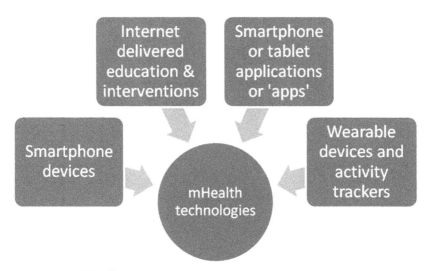

FIGURE 12.2    Different types of mHealth technologies.

example, Fitbit and other wearable fitness trackers enable multiple activities to be captured throughout the day, such as total activity, step count, distance travelled, heart rate, sleep duration, and flights of stairs climbed (Fig. 12.2).

Wearables are generally used in conjunction with smartphone apps and online platforms which display a range of data . This permits a vast amount of additional functions such as:

- Individualized goal setting
- Charting of progress over time
- Feedback on activity levels and other data
- Reminders and prompts
- Access to on-screen information, for example, workouts/diet plans
- Social connection through forums
- Rewards and achievements

## mHealth for Physical Health Care

The use of mobile technologies in medicine is becoming increasingly common. Smartphones enable clinicians to access medical reference databases and provide a valuable educational tool (Ozdalga et al., 2012). mHealth also has clinical utility and can facilitate adherence and self-management of chronic diseases such as cardiovascular disease and diabetes (Hamine et al., 2015). Prompts and reminders sent via text message or apps, the ability to track dietary intake and medication, and look up information and provide a secure mode of communication between clinician and patient are all examples of useful tools available via smartphones.

Clinicians also have the opportunity to collect and access real-time patient data. Physical health monitoring tools such as blood glucose meters, electrocardiograms, blood pressure monitors, and weighing machines can be connected to smartphones via Bluetooth or wireless interfaces (Worringham et al., 2011; Hamine et al., 2015). For instance, a randomized controlled trial (RCT) by Quinn et al. (2008) used innovative mHealth methods to assist with mobile diabetes management. WellDoc was a mobile-based software tool connected to a Bluetooth-adapted blood glucose monitor (One Touch Ultra). Patient data were transmitted automatically to a diabetes management app where they were given tailored feedback on medication and diet. Clinicians could also access data to identify whether any interventions were required. This approach demonstrated significant improvements in treatment adherence and patient outcomes. Similar benefits to patient care have been observed for the management of lung disease (Ryan et al., 2012), cardiovascular disease (Istepanian et al., 2009; Logan et al., 2012), and cardiac rehabilitation (Worringham et al., 2011).

## SUMMARY

### What Can mHealth Be Used for?

1. Deliver psychosocial interventions or extend the reach and scope of existing treatments
2. Providing real-time individualized user feedback and support
3. Providing access to information and resources for both patient and clinician
4. Promoting engagement and increase access to health care services

## mHEALTH FOR MENTAL HEALTH CARE

Use of mHealth technology is gaining popularity in mental health care settings. As mobile technologies become increasingly available and affordable, we can assume that the desire to adopt these methods will continue to increase. mHealth approaches may be particularly useful for people who may struggle with access and engagement with typical health care services, for example, people with severe mental illness (SMI).

Serious mental disorders, such as schizophrenia, schizoaffective disorder, and bipolar disorder, are associated with a high degree of functional and cognitive impairment which dramatically reduce quality of life compared with the general population (WHO, 2015). People with SMI are usually offered a combination of pharmacological and psychological treatments and are often required to engage with services long-term, regardless of symptomatic remission. However, this patient group also experience difficulties fully engaging with treatments and services (Kreyenbuhl et al., 2009). This is often associated with the stigma attached to having a mental health diagnosis (Brain et al., 2014). However, the remote and confidential nature of mHealth technologies may provide new and useful tools for overcoming these barriers and promoting engagement in this group.

## mHealth Uses for People With SMI

Mobile technologies have great potential within mental health care across a range of disciplines including:

- Promoting medication adherence
- Detecting relapse and early warning signs through self-report of mental state and well-being
- Identifying at-risk individuals
- Real-time monitoring of symptoms
- Relaying emergency information, such as suicidal ideation
- Self-management techniques for mental health symptoms
- Administering digitally tailored interventions
- Encouraging behavior change, for example, exercise
- The ability to send and receive clinically relevant messages
- Appointment and medication reminders

mHealth has already proven acceptable and useful for many of these factors. For example, an early study required outpatients at high-risk for relapse to fill in assessments on a smartphone when prompted by a text message (Španiel et al., 2012). This information was relayed back to clinicians who decided upon the necessary action to prevent relapse. Patients in the intervention arm had significantly lower levels of hospitalization, fewer inpatient days, and reduced costs, thus demonstrating the clinical utility of mHealth approaches (Španiel et al., 2012).

## Ownership and Endorsement of mHealth Technologies for People With SMI

Although mHealth for mental health care is becoming increasingly popular among users, the feasibility and acceptability of these approaches must be established before they are added to health care provision for people with SMI.

### Questions

- Do people with SMI have access to mobile technology to facilitate mHealth methods?
- Do people with SMI want to receive mental health support via mHealth technologies?
- What are the potential barriers to using mHealth to improve outcomes in people with mental illness?

### Ownership

A 2015 systematic review and meta-analysis of existing studies found mobile phone ownership among people with psychotic disorders is high. Data from 12 independent studies between 2007 and 2015 revealed mobile phone ownership has risen rapidly over time, with a current average of 81.4% of people with psychotic disorders reportedly owning a mobile phone (Firth et al., 2015). Additionally, 68% of young people with psychotic disorders report owning a smartphone. This figure continues to rise. A 2017 Australian survey found approximately three-quarters of people with SMI who use mental health services in Australia had regular access to the Internet, mostly accessed via smartphones (Thomas et al., 2017). There is also support for using multiple devices as platforms for mHealth technologies. A web-based survey of 457 people with schizophrenia revealed that indeed 90% had access to more than one device (e.g., computer, smartphone, tablet; Gay et al., 2016).

### Endorsement

Research indicates that the usage of mobile phones among people with psychosis is high and often comparable to the general population. Across five studies of mobile phone ownership in 890 people with psychosis, 56.5% used their devices on a daily basis (Firth et al., 2015), suggesting this population use their smartphones much the same as anybody else. Patient's opinions on using their phones for mHealth services are also favorable. Data across seven individual studies of people with psychosis found:

- 60.2% patients favored using mobile phones for tracking/monitoring of mental health symptoms (95% confidence interval [CI] = 42.6%–76.5%, $N = 3$, $n = 251$)
- 56.1% wanted to receive information about physical or mental health (95% CI = 33.4%–77.5%, $N = 4$, $n = 944$)
- 55.5% wanted text message appointment/medication reminders (95% CI = 35.8%–74.3%, $N = 5$, $n = 968$)
- 51.1% favored using mobile phones to facilitate patient contact with health professionals (95% CI = 36.4%–65.6%, $N = 5$, $n = 989$; data from Firth et al., 2016)

A favorable view for using mHealth technologies within mental health care is also held across wider patient populations. For example, a survey of 1592 patients with SMI found 72% owned a mobile device, and indeed 81% of mobile owners were interested in receiving mental health services via mobile technologies (Ben-Zeev et al., 2013). Therefore the penetrability of mHealth within mental health care has great potential. Younger patients in particular envisage technology as becoming a fundamental part of their mental health care and recovery (Gay et al., 2016). There is mixed evidence to suggest mHealth methods may be more appropriate for younger patients, and initial studies suggest that mobile phone ownership is higher in this group (Sanghara et al., 2010; Ben-Zeev et al., 2013; Torous et al., 2014). However, the benefits of mHealth have also been demonstrated in older samples of people with SMI (Depp et al., 2016).

### Barriers for People With SMI

Previous studies have found that health care providers question the acceptability of technology-enabled mental health services for people with SMI suggesting they may experience multiple barriers to mHealth implementation. Such barriers include:

- Cognitive impairment
- Positive symptoms such as paranoia
- Negative symptoms such as apathy, low motivation
- Socioeconomic factors including low income, unstable housing resulting in decreased access to Internet-enabled devices
- Social isolation resulting in decreased use of new technologies

Nonetheless, research published to date indicates that people with psychosis use mobile technologies much the same as the general population, despite experiencing a range of these barriers.

## mHealth Interventions in Mental Health Settings

Research assessing the penetrability of mHealth approaches within mental health care is growing. A wide range of evidence suggests smartphone technologies can provide a valuable adjunct to traditional care for people with depression, anxiety, psychosis, substance use disorders, and eating disorders (Donker et al., 2013). For example, a 2017 meta-analysis identified nine RCTs of psychological interventions delivered via smartphones to target symptoms of anxiety. Significant reductions in anxiety were found compared with control conditions, suggesting smartphone apps may be a viable mode of delivery for treatment of clinical and subclinical anxiety disorders (Firth et al., 2017). A further meta-analysis published in the same year also shows that smartphone-delivered interventions were a useful tool to improve depressive symptoms and are a promising self-management tool for depression (Firth et al., 2017). For example, there have been several RCTs of apps to assist with the delivery of cognitive-behavioural therapy and other therapies for depression (Watts et al., 2013; Kauer et al., 2012). This suggests smartphone technologies may be feasible for a wide range of conditions.

### Smartphone Apps for SMI

Identifying the clinical utility of mHealth for the care of schizophrenia is also a popular area of research. Smartphone apps are a useful tool for improving the mental health and well-being of people with schizophrenia (Firth et al., 2015). The two main uses of apps in schizophrenia research include real-time monitoring of symptoms and the delivery of therapeutic interventions (Table 12.1).

### Symptom Monitoring

The first study of smartphone apps for mental health symptom management was conducted by Palmier-Claus et al. (2012, 2014). The "Clin-Touch" app was used to administer psychological assessments including the Positive and Negative Syndrome Scale and Calgary Depression Scale. Patients with SMI were prompted to complete these assessments up to six times per day over a 1 week period. Positive and affective symptoms recorded on the app correlated highly with data collected through traditional methods, suggesting apps can be used to obtain clinically meaningful data from patients. Additionally, a further study found people with schizophrenia preferred to use an app to report their symptoms rather than text messaging and felt comfortable using their own phones for recording information about their mood and symptoms (Ainsworth et al., 2013).

### Intervention Delivery

The "FOCUS" app for self-management of schizophrenia was developed with extensive user involvement and feedback from the target population (Ben-Zeev et al., 2014). FOCUS used real-time interventions to target a range of mental health concerns, such as medication adherence, social functioning, mood problems, hallucinations, and poor sleep. Participants could access the intervention content at any time and were prompted to complete surveys three times daily. There was a high degree of engagement with the app, and 93.7% of participants were satisfied. Eighty-seven percent of participants also claimed FOCUS helped them to self-manage their symptoms.

**TABLE 12.1** Summary of Smartphone Apps for Mental Health Outcomes in Schizophrenia

| Reference | Description of Intervention | Sample | Acceptability | User Experience | Reported Benefits |
|---|---|---|---|---|---|
| Ainsworth et al. (2013) | "ClinTouch" app A randomized control trial comparing how patients reported their symptoms using an app to when they used text message services. The smartphone app and text messaging system were used for 6 days each, and participants received four surveys about their symptoms per day. | 24 people with SZ | Participants completed significantly more entries using the app (69%) than the text message service (59%). | The app was rated as pleasing overall, and not stressful, stigmatizing, or challenging. Participants valued using their own phones to complete surveys. | The app was perceived as useful and participants thought it could help them and other service users. |
| Ben Zeev et al. (2014) | "FOCUS" app Single-arm feasibility study of real-time illness management support for schizophrenia. The smartphone app provided constant | 33 people with SZ | FOCUS was used on 86.5% days during the study for an average of 5.2 times per day. One person dropped out due to losing the phone. | 97.3% were satisfied with the usability of the app. | 87% found the app helped them manage their symptoms. The majority of app usage was self-initiated and not in relation to prompts (62.5%). |

Continued

**TABLE 12.1**  Summary of Smartphone Apps for Mental Health Outcomes in Schizophrenia—cont'd

| Reference | Description of Intervention | Sample | Acceptability | User Experience | Reported Benefits |
|---|---|---|---|---|---|
| | access to real-time interventions to target medication adherence, social functioning, mood, hallucinations, and poor sleep. Participants completed surveys three times a day. | | | | |
| Palmier-Claus et al. (2012, 2014) | "ClinTouch" app Pilot and feasibility study of a smartphone app to deliver 12 items from the Positive and Negative Syndrome Scale (PANSS) and Calgary Depression Scale (CDS) up to six times a day over 1 week. | 36 people with a range of psychotic disorders | 72% all entries were completed, and the app was used 4.4 times on average per day. | Not reported. | The app provided clinically valid self-report measurements of mental health symptoms compared with pen and pencil methods. |

*SZ*, schizophrenia.

### *Other Uses*

People with schizophrenia report using Web-based technology to assist with self-management of mental health. This includes using online platforms to discover different coping strategies (such as using music to manage voices) and using smartphones to set alarms/reminders for medication management and keeping track of appointments (Gay et al., 2016). There is also evidence to suggest people with schizophrenia are as engaged with smartphone apps as other patient populations, such as people with diabetes (Ashurst et al., 2014).

## SUMMARY

### Mobile Technology for Mental Health

mHealth innovations can open up opportunities for mental health care. The exponential growth of smartphone technologies provides a novel platform to extend support out of the traditional settings and reach beyond the limits of a physical clinic or service. Clinicians can maintain long-term contact with patients over prolonged periods of time and check in on patients regularly. mHealth approaches can also be used to deliver mental health interventions and facilitate greater engagement with health care.

## HOW CAN mHEALTH INCREASE PHYSICAL ACTIVITY IN PEOPLE WITH SMI?

### Why Is It Important to Increase Physical Activity in People With SMI?

People with SMI experience poor physical health at an early age, and their life expectancy is up to 15 years lower than the general population (Hjorthoj et al., 2017). A leading cause of premature mortality in this group is cardiovascular disease and poor metabolic health (Mitchell et al., 2013). This often arises as a combination of factors including metabolic side effects of antipsychotic medication and high rates of unhealthy lifestyle habits.

People with schizophrenia are significantly less likely to engage in physical activity and are more likely to have more sedentary lifestyles than people without mental health problems (Stubbs et al., 2016a). A meta-analysis by Stubbs et al. (2016a,b) found that people with psychosis spent on average 11 h per day sedentary, and in fact, the true figure is likely to be even higher (12.5 h a day) when activity is measured using more objective methods (e.g., accelerometers). This inactivity is linked to various poor outcomes, including:

- Poor cardiovascular fitness (Vancampfort et al., 2015b)
- Long-term physical health conditions associated with weight gain and metabolic health (Vancampfort et al., 2015b)
- Functional impairment and poor quality of life (Strassnig et al., 2012)
- Increased severity of psychiatric symptoms (Vancampfort et al., 2012)
- Increased cognitive deficits (Kimhy et al., 2014)

Yet it is important to note that physical activity represents a potentially modifiable risk factor. Therefore there is a clear need to encourage people with SMI to increase their physical activity.

## Current Physical Activity Interventions in SMI

A growing number of lifestyle interventions have been developed to help increase physical activity in people with SMI (more details can be found in Chapter 4). A systematic review and meta-analysis were conducted by Firth et al. (2015) on 17 existing RCTs of physical activity interventions for people with schizophrenia. Interventions which encouraged participants to achieve at least 90 min of moderate-to-vigorous activity per week demonstrated significant improvements in cardiometabolic risk, functional disability, psychiatric symptoms, comorbid disorders, and cognition (Firth et al., 2015).

Multiple factors determine whether an exercise intervention is effective. Simply providing advice and access to leisure facilities is insufficient enough to encourage the general population to exercise (Greaney et al., 2016). People with SMI experience additional barriers to achieving the recommended levels of exercise, and indeed previous interventions have found that providing advice and access alone is not an effective approach to increase activity levels in people with SMI. For example, an intervention consisting of free gym memberships, introductory sessions, and exercise plans for people with schizophrenia encountered difficulties with adherence (Archie et al., 2003). Only 30% of people completed the intervention, and 90% of participants had stopped exercising entirely within 6 months. This is in contrast to interventions which place a higher emphasis on social support. For instance, studies which include supervised or guided sessions have significantly higher rates of engagement and adherence. This was highlighted in a 2015 review which found that across 10 trials, exercising in a group promoted greater adherence to an intervention than exercising alone (78.8% vs. 55%; Firth et al., 2015).

However, individualized lifestyle interventions can be costly and require resources often above and beyond what is typically available within services. Long-term support is usually required to ensure sustained changes in exercise practices, which limits the scope of existing interventions. There is a need to investigate and develop more cost-effective methods of intervention delivery. A systematic review of health and economic outcomes from a range of mHealth interventions found that in 74% of cases mHealth was cost-effective compared with other delivery methods (Iribarren et al., 2017). Therefore using mHealth to support traditional methods of physical health promotion may increase scalability, reach, and allow interventions to have a wider impact, while proving cost-effective.

## Using mHealth to Increase Physical Activity

Interventions delivered by the Internet and through smartphone apps have proliferated over the past decade. In both clinical and nonclinical populations, these interventions have been shown to be effective for targeting multiple behaviors, including physical activity, nutrition, alcohol, and tobacco use (Oosterveen et al., 2017; Fanning et al., 2012). For instance, in the general population, mobile devices have been found to be an effective platform to help people increase their physical activity (Fanning et al., 2012). This includes both mobile phone–delivered interventions, for example, via Short Message Service or Web-based (Stephens and Allen, 2013) and the use of smartphone apps (Coughlin et al., 2016). As previously discussed, there are many different ways technologies can be used to help increase physical activity. A 2015 review of 12 studies concluded that mobile phone apps were not only useful for increasing physical activity but were also associated with significant reductions in weight (Flores Mateo et al., 2015).

Indeed, mHealth can be used to administer interventions based on established psychological theories to increase physical activity. A review by Direito et al. (2016) discussed how mHealth interventions can be used to facilitate a range of theoretically derived behavior change techniques (Michie et al., 2011 see Table 12.2 for examples). The main techniques included:

## Previous Research Using mHealth to Increase Physical Activity in People With SMI

The application of mHealth technologies to increase physical activity in populations at risk for poor physical and mental health is gathering interest. Pervasive usage of mobile devices in both clinical and nonclinical populations provides a novel opportunity for health care providers. Here

**TABLE 12.2**    Examples of Behavior Change Techniques Delivered via mHealth

| Behavior Change Technique | mHealth Example |
| --- | --- |
| Goal setting | Setting a step goal with patients using a health app |
| Self-monitoring of behavior | Instruct patients to keep track of their steps or exercise per week manually using a health app or automatically using wearable activity trackers |
| Provision of social support | Patients can join social media groups with other people who are trying to improve their physical health |
| Feedback on behavior | Patients can check progress on charts, for example, reviewing steps taken over the past week |
| Instructions on how to perform a behavior | Patients can access workout plans or exercise videos on their phones or tablets |
| Adding objects to the environment | Wearable activity trackers can be used, for example, Fitbit to help people monitor behaviors |
| Information about health consequences | Educational materials can be accessed which inform patients about the risks of sedentary lifestyles and the benefits of engaging in exercise |
| Prompts and cues | Reminders and motivational messages can be sent which encourage patients to exercise and remind them to reach their targets |

we will discuss previous research that has drawn upon technological advances to increase physical activity in people with SMI using smartphone apps and wearable devices.

### *Smartphone Apps*

The number of commercially available smartphone apps for physical activity continues to rise. It is perhaps unsurprising that their use for psychiatric populations is becoming increasingly popular. Although there have been relatively few high-quality trials of apps for physical activity in schizophrenia, the studies to date have shown promising results.

For instance, Macias et al. (2015) conducted a pilot study of the "WellWave" app to promote walking in people with SMI. Users were given prompts and suggested daily activities to encourage them to become more active. A library of reading materials and videos was available, containing information on recovery and other motivational tools. Users could also speak directly to study staff via the app and were prompted to complete self-report questionnaires on well-being. Daily app usage was high (94%) and participants responded well to prompts (73%). After just 4 weeks, one-third of users reported significant improvements in their physical health.

As well as a range of psychoeducational and social functions, smartphone apps can be a source of information for clinicians. Ben-Zeev et al. (2016) found smartphone apps were feasible behavioral sensors for people with schizophrenia. Nine outpatients and 11 inpatients carried a smartphone with them for 1 or 2 weeks respectively. Participants' physical activity, location, speech, and use of the smartphone were recorded. In line with previous research, both groups of participants engaged in high levels of sedentary behavior. The apps were perceived as useful and acceptable by 95% of patients as a tool to monitor their behavior, despite clinicians being concerned about patients becoming more paranoid as a result. Behavioral sensing data are useful for clinicians as it enables inferences to be made regarding patients' functioning and can also serve to highlight changes in behavior that may be linked to relapse or poor mental health (such as staying in the one location, engaging in less activity).

### Wearable Devices

Wearable devices permit a range of additional functions. An innovative set of studies conducted by Naslund et al., (2016) and Aschbrenner et al. (2016) looked at the use of Fitbit activity trackers in conjunction with smartphone apps to encourage people with SMI to increase their physical activity. To assess the initial feasibility of using Fitbit, 11 obese people with SMI were enrolled in a 6-month lifestyle program based on the Diabetes Prevention Program, USA (Kramer et al., 2009; see Table 12.3 for a description of the intervention).

People were highly engaged with the intervention and used the Fitbit on average 84.7% days of the intervention. All participants found the Fitbit useful, easy to use, and were highly satisfied with the device as it helped motivate them to become more active. High levels of engagement were observed throughout the study. Seventy-two percent of participants lost weight, with 28% achieving clinically significant weight loss. Seventeen percent of participants also had demonstrable benefits to physical fitness (Aschbrenner et al., 2016).

When asked specifically about the mHealth component, participants reported a range of benefits to using the Fitbit and app including:
- Enjoyment and increased motivation
- Being able to set daily step goals
- Sense of accomplishment when goals were met
- Increased awareness of own physical activity
- Sense of empowerment when progress is made
- Useful prompts and encouraging messages

**TABLE 12.3**   Aschbrenner et al. (2016) 24-Week Peer-Group Lifestyle Intervention for People With SMI, Consisting of Three Components

|  | Peer Group Component | Guided Exercise Component | mHealth Component |
|---|---|---|---|
| Overview | This component was modelled on the Diabetes Prevention Program (Kramer et al., 2009) and consisted of 1-h weight management group per week. | Twice-weekly (optional) exercise sessions by a personal trainer. | Ongoing throughout the intervention, participants given "Fitbit" accelerometers. |
| Aim | To encourage peer-to-peer cooperation and create a supportive network for weight loss. | To give participants the opportunity to reach their weekly activity goal. | To facilitate and reinforce self-monitoring and allow people to connect with others to provide support. |
| Content | Groups were facilitated by lifestyle coaches. Attendees were taught about the principles of healthy eating and exercise. Group discussion, team building, problem-solving, and planning of healthy meals were all key components of the sessions. | Exercise sessions starting at sedentary level and gradually increasing in intensity. Sessions consisted of a mixture of strength and cardio training as well as brisk walking outdoors. | Participants given smartphones and "Fitbit" with access to a private Facebook group. They tracked steps per day, progress over time, and set daily goals. Participants received three reminders per week via text from the lifestyle coach reminding them of weight, exercise, and motivating them to engage in healthy behaviors. |

- Being able to see their data on the app
- Convenient way of keeping lots of data in one place

Participants also reported using the range of other functions of the smartphone app for other behaviors, despite not being told to by the researchers. For example, three people used the app to track diet, two recorded weight, and five logged how much water they consumed. Some technical difficulties were experienced, generally relating to use of the smartphone app. However, participants claimed this could be avoided by having an initial session or tutorial showing them how to use it, and it did not affect their positive experience.

## Other Technological Approaches to Increase Physical Activity in People With SMI

Another area of health technology which offers substantial promise is the use of "exergames" and Virtual Reality (VR) platforms. Physically active video games or exergames are a novel opportunity to help people with SMI engage in exercise. Exergames require the user to move their body in order to progress through a game or program, resulting in a physically interactive platform (Oh and Yang, 2010). Consoles such as the Nintendo Wii and Microsoft Kinect allow users to engage in a variety of exergames such as completing aerobic exercise routines (Kimhy et al., 2015) or following visual cues to complete dance games (Eggenberger et al., 2016). Previous research has demonstrated that exergames are effective in increasing physical activity and can also improve symptoms of depression (Li et al., 2016) and cognitive function (Firth et al., in press) in both clinical and nonclinical populations.

VR involves being placed in an immersive three-dimensional environment where the user can interact with computer-generated stimuli (Gregg and Tarrier, 2007). To date, two studies have explored the clinical utility of exergames and VR for people with schizophrenia (Table 12.4). Chan et al. (2010) had participants guide themselves through a VR game using specific body movements, such as squats. Kimhy et al. (2015) focused more on exercise and encouraged participants to achieve 150 min of moderate physical activity per week using a range of methods such as aerobic programs as part of the games used during the intervention. Indeed, both approaches were useful and showed significant benefits to cognitive functioning in people with schizophrenia. Therefore increasing patient's physical activity using exergames may even have wider neurocognitive benefits, outside of improved physical health.

## SUMMARY

### Increasing Physical Activity in People With SMI

mHealth represents a potentially efficacious mode of delivery for healthy lifestyle interventions for people with SMI. A range of options are available to encourage people with SMI to exercise, such as smartphone apps, the use of wearable devices, online peer support forums, and engaging with exergames. The studies to date, although relatively few, have provided promising results suggesting this approach is feasible within this group. Using innovative technologies to help people with SMI become more active can also have wider benefits, such as improved social and cognitive functioning.

**TABLE 12.4**  Exergames for SMI

| Study Name | Sample | Description of Intervention | Key Findings |
|---|---|---|---|
| Chan et al. (2010) | 27 people with schizophrenia; (mean age 66.1 years, 66% male) 12 people in VR condition; 15 in control condition | 30 min of exergame co-ordination training using a virtual reality environment. Sessions were conducted two times per week for 5 weeks. Example of the task: "Shark Bait" Users are presented with a video of themselves which looks like they are beneath the sea. They are able to navigate themselves by leaning side to side or squatting down. The aim is to chase a star and avoid obstacles such as sharks. Additional obstacles can be added to increase the difficulty of the game. | All participants in VR group completed all the activity sessions. There were significant improvements in overall cognitive functioning for the VR group and across two subdomains of cognition (repetition and memory). |
| Kimhy et al. (2015) | 33 people with schizophrenia; (mean age 36.9 years, 64% male) 16 people in exergame condition; 17 in control condition | 60 min of whole-body aerobic training using the "Your Shape Fitness Evolved" program on Microsoft Kinect, as well as a treadmill, exercise bike, and elliptical trainer. Sessions were conducted three times per week for 12 weeks and participants were supervised by a trainer. | 79% of participants completed the study. Participants in the exergame condition improved their aerobic fitness by 18% compared with a −0.5% decline in the treatment as usual (TAU) group and improved their neurocognition by 15.1% (vs −2.0% TAU). |

*SMI*, serious mental illness; *VR*, virtual reality.

# CONCLUSIONS AND FUTURE DIRECTIONS

Early results in mHealth are encouraging in SMI. The exponential growth of mHealth technologies is an exciting opportunity for health care providers, across both physical and mental health. Current research indicates that people with SMI are willing to use mHealth technologies for many aspects of physical and mental health care. Mobile devices are more accessible and affordable than ever before and open up important opportunities for health promotion. Future research should focus on identifying ways to implement mHealth within mental health services for people with SMI.

## Recommendations

With rapid technological developments, the propensity for mHealth to be integrated into all aspects of mental health care is becoming more likely. Despite the growing evidence for mHealth, some existing studies fail to account for many factors which permit their implementation within services. According to Torous et al. (2017), future developments should ensure mHealth technologies:

- are accessible
- support interoperability across multiple platforms
- report on costs
- discuss their scalability
- be replicable
- provide data security
- comply with national guidelines
- conduct usability testing

Therefore more rigorous, well-conducted studies are required evaluating the effectiveness of mHealth methods, prior to its implementation within health care. A specific focus should be given to mHealth interventions to increase the physical activity of people with SMI, given the high rates of comorbidity and premature mortality in this group.

## CONCLUSIONS

mHealth technologies provide a mechanism to deliver more accessible and effective health care. The broad clinical potential of these technologies is likely to expand, and future research should focus on identifying the most cost-effective, efficient, and feasible ways to implement mHealth within mental health care. Future research will enable the clinical potential of these new, innovative technologies to be established.

# References

Ainsworth, J., Palmier-Claus, J.E., Machin, M., Barrowclough, C., Dunn, G., Rogers, A., et al., 2013. A comparison of two delivery modalities of a mobile phone-based assessment for serious mental illness: native smartphone application vs text- messaging only implementations. J. Med. Internet Res. 15 (4), e60. https://doi.org/10.2196/jmir.2328.

Archie, S., Wilson, J.H., Osborne, S., Hobbs, H., McNiven, J., 2003. Pilot study: access to fitness facility and exercise levels in olanzapine-treated patients. Can. J. Psychiatry 48 (9), 628−632.

Aschbrenner, K.A., Naslund, J.A., Shevenell, M., Kinney, E., Bartels, S.J., 2016. A pilot study of a peer-group lifestyle intervention enhanced with mHealth technology and social media for adults with serious mental illness. J. Nerv. Ment. Dis. 204 (6), 483−486.

Ashurst, E.J., Jones, R.B., Abraham, C., Jenner, M., Boddy, K., Besser, R.E., et al., 2014. The diabetes app challenge: user-led development and piloting of internet applications enabling young people with diabetes to set the focus for their diabetes consultations. Med. 2.0. 3 (2), e5. https://doi.org/10.2196/med20.3032.

Ben-Zeev, D., Davis, K.E., Kaiser, S., Krzsos, I., Drake, R.E., 2013. Mobile technologies among people with serious mental illness: opportunities for future services. Adm. Policy Ment. Health 40 (4), 340−343.

Ben-Zeev, D., Brenner, C.J., Begale, M., Duffecy, J., Mohr, D.C., Mueser, K.T., 2014. Feasibility, acceptability, and preliminary efficacy of a smartphone intervention for schizophrenia. Schizophr. Bull. 40 (6), 1244−1253.

Ben-Zeev, D., Wang, R., Abdullah, S., Brian, R., Scherer, E.A., Mistler, L.A., et al., 2016. Mobile behavioral sensing for outpatients and inpatients with schizophrenia. Psychiatr. Serv. 67 (5), 558−561.

Brain, C., Sameby, B., Allerby, K., Quinlan, P., Joas, E., Lindstrom, E., et al., 2014. Stigma, discrimination and medication adherence in schizophrenia: results from the Swedish COAST study. Psychiatry Res. 220 (3), 811−817.

Bravata, D.M., Smith-Spangler, C., Sundaram, V., Gienger, A.L., Lin, N., Lewis, R., et al., 2007. Using pedometers to increase physical activity and improve health: a systematic review. JAMA 298 (19), 2296−2304.

Chan, C.L., Ngai, E.K., Leung, P.K., Wong, S., 2010. Effect of the adapted Virtual Reality cognitive training program among Chinese older adults with chronic schizophrenia: a pilot study. Int. J. Geriatr. Psychiatry 25 (6), 643−649.

Cisco, 2017. Cisco Visual Networking Index: Global Mobile Data Traffic Forecast Update, 2016-2021. White Paper. http://www.cisco.com/c/en/us/solutions/collateral/service-provider/visual-networking-index-vni/mobile-white-paper-c11-520862.html.

Coughlin, S.S., Whitehead, M., Sheats, J.Q., Mastromonico, J., Smith, S., 2016. A review of smartphone applications for promoting physical activity. Jacobs J Community Med 2 (1).

Depp, C.A., Harmell, A.L., Vahia, I.V., Mausbach, B.T., 2016. Neurocognitive and functional correlates of mobile phone use in middle-aged and older patients with schizophrenia. Aging Ment. Health 20 (1), 29−35.

Direito, A., Carraça, E., Rawstorn, J., Whittaker, R., Maddison, R., 2016. mHealth technologies to influence physical activity and sedentary behaviors: behavior change techniques, systematic review and meta-analysis of randomized controlled trials. Ann. Behav. Med. https://doi.org/10.1007/s12160-016-9846-0 [Epub ahead of print].

Donker, T., Petrie, K., Proudfoot, J., Clarke, J., Birch, M.R., Christensen, H., 2013. Smartphones for smarter delivery of mental health programs: a systematic review. J. Med. Internet Res. 15 (11), e247. https://doi.org/10.2196/jmir.2791.

Eggenberger, P., Wolf, M., Schumann, M., de Bruin, E.D., 2016. Exergame and balance training modulate prefrontal brain activity during walking and enhance executive function in older adults. Front. Aging Neurosci. 8, 66.

Fanning, J., Mullen, S.P., McAuley, E., 2012. Increasing physical activity with mobile devices: a meta-analysis. J. Med. Internet Res. 14 (6), e161.

Firth, J., Cotter, J., Torous, J., Bucci, S., Firth, J.A., Yung, A.R., 2015. Mobile phone ownership and endorsement of "mHealth" among people with psychosis: a meta- analysis of cross-sectional studies. Schizophr. Bull. 42 (2), 448—455.

Firth, J., Torous, J., Yung, A.R., 2016. Ecological momentary assessment and beyond: the rising interest in e-mental health research. J. Psychiatr. Res. 80, 3—4.

Firth, J., Torous, J., Nicolas, J., Carney, R., Rosenbaum, S., Sarris, J., 2017. Can smartphone mental health interventions reduce symptoms of anxiety? A meta-analysis of randomized controlled trials. J. Affect. Disord. 218, 15—22.

Firth, J., Torous, J., Nicholas, J., Carney, R., Pratap, A., Rosenbaum, S., Sarris, J., 2017. The efficacy of smartphone-based mental health interventions for depressive symptoms: a meta-analysis of randomized controlled trials. World Psychiatry 16 (3), 287—298.

Flores Mateo, G., Granado-Font, E., Ferré-Grau, C., Montaña-Carreras, X., 2015. Mobile phone apps to promote weight loss and increase physical activity: a systematic review and meta-analysis. J. Med. Internet Res. 17 (11), e253. https://doi.org/10.2196/jmir.4836.

Gay, K., Torous, J., Joseph, A., Pandya, A., Duckworth, K., 2016. Digital technology use among individuals with schizophrenia: results of an online survey. JMIR Ment. Health 3 (2), e15. https://doi.org/10.2196/mental.5379.

Greaney, M.L., Askew, S., Foley, P., Wallington, S.F., Bennett, G.G., 2016. Linking patients with community resources: use of a free YMCA membership among low-income black women. Transl. Behav. Med. 1—8.

Gregg, L., Tarrier, N., 2007. Virtual reality in mental health: a review of the literature. Soc. Psychiatry Psychiatr. Epidemiol. 42 (5), 343—354.

Hamine, S., Gerth-Guyette, E., Faulx, D., Green, B.B., Ginsburg, A.S., 2015. Impact of mHealth chronic disease management on treatment adherence and patient outcomes: a systematic review. J. Med. Internet Res. 17 (2), e52. https://doi.org/10.2196/jmir.3951.

Hjorthoj, C., Sturup, A.E., McGrath, J.J., Nordentoft, M., 2017. Years of potential life lost and life expectancy in schizophrenia: a systematic review and meta- analysis. Lancet Psychiatry 4 (4), 295—301.

IMS Institute Reports, 2015. Patient Adoption of mHealth. Available from: http://www.theimsinstitute.org/en/thought-leadership/ims-institute/reports/patientadoption-of-mhealth.

Iribarren, S.J., Cato, K., Falzon, L., Stone, P.W., 2017. What is the economic evidence for mHealth? A systematic review of economic evaluations of mHealth solutions. PLoS One 12 (2), e0170581. https://doi.org/10.1371/journal.pone.0170581.

Istepanian, R.S., Zitouni, K., Harry, D., Moutosammy, N., Sungoor, A., Tang, B., et al., 2009. Evaluation of a mobile phone telemonitoring system for glycaemic control in patients with diabetes. J. Telemed. Telecare 15 (3), 125—128.

Kauer, S.D., Reid, S.C., Crooke, A.H., Khor, A., Hearps, S.J., Jorm, A.F., et al., 2012. Self- monitoring using mobile phones in the early stages of adolescent depression: randomized controlled trial. J. Med. Internet Res. 14 (3), e67. https://doi.org/10.2196/jmir.1858.

Kimhy, D., Vakhrusheva, J., Bartels, M.N., Armstrong, H.F., Ballon, J.S., Khan, S., et al., 2014. Aerobic fitness and body mass index in individuals with schizophrenia: implications for neurocognition and daily functioning. Psychiatry Res. 220 (3), 784—791.

Kimhy, D., Vakhrusheva, J., Bartels, M.N., Armstrong, H.F., Ballon, J.S., Khan, S., et al., 2015. The impact of aerobic exercise on brain-derived neurotrophic factor and neurocognition in individuals with schizophrenia: a single-blind, randomized clinical trial. Schizophr. Bull. 41 (4), 859—868.

Kramer, M.K., Kriska, A.M., Venditti, E.M., Miller, R.G., Brooks, M.M., Burke, L.E., et al., 2009. Translating the Diabetes Prevention Program: a comprehensive model for prevention training and program delivery. Am. J. Prev. Med. 37 (6), 505—511.

Kreyenbuhl, J., Nossel, I.R., Dixon, L.B., 2009. Disengagement from mental health treatment among individuals with schizophrenia and strategies for facilitating connections to care: a review of the literature. Schizophr. Bull. 35 (4), 696–703.

Li, J., Theng, Y.L., Foo, S., 2016. Effect of exergames on depression: a systematic review and meta-analysis. Cyberpsychol. Behav. Soc. Netw. 19 (1), 34–42.

Logan, A.G., Irvine, M.J., McIsaac, W.J., Tisler, A., Rossos, P.G., Easty, A., et al., 2012. Effect of home blood pressure telemonitoring with self-care support on uncontrolled systolic hypertension in diabetics. Hypertension 60 (1), 51–57.

Macias, C., Panch, T., Hicks, Y.M., Scolnick, J.S., Weene, D.L., Öngür, D., et al., 2015. Using smartphone apps to promote psychiatric and physical well-being. Psychiatr. Q. 86 (4), 505–519.

Michie, S., Ashford, S., Sniehotta, F.F., Dombrowski, S.U., Bishop, A., French, D.P., 2011. A refined taxonomy of behavior change techniques to help people change their physical activity and healthy eating behaviors: the CALO-RE taxonomy. Psychol. Health 26, 1479–1498.

Mitchell, A.J., Vancampfort, D., Sweers, K., van Winkel, R., Yu, W., De Hert, M., 2013. Prevalence of metabolic syndrome and metabolic abnormalities in schizophrenia and related disorders—a systematic review and meta-analysis. Schizophr. Bull. 39 (2), 306–318.

Naslund, J.A., Aschbrenner, K.A., Bartels, S.J., 2016. Wearable devices and smartphones for activity tracking among people with serious mental illness. Ment. Health Phys. Act. 10, 10–17.

Oh, Y., Yang, S., 2010. Defining exergames and exergaming. Proc Meaningful Play 1–17.

Oosterveen, E., Tzelepis, F., Ashton, L., Hutchesson, M.J., 2017. A systematic review of eHealth behavioral interventions targeting smoking, nutrition, alcohol, physical activity and/or obesity for young adults. Prev. Med. 99, 197–206.

Ozdalga, E., Ozdalga, A., Ahuja, N., 2012. The smartphone in medicine: a review of current and potential use among physicians and students. J. Med. Internet Res. 14 (5), e128. https://doi.org/10.2196/jmir.1994.

Palmier-Claus, J.E., Ainsworth, J., Machin, M., Barrowclough, C., Dunn, G., Barkus, E., et al., 2012. The feasibility and validity of ambulatory self-report of psychotic symptoms using a smartphone software application. BMC Psychiatry 12, 172.

Palmier-Claus, J.E., Taylor, P.J., Ainsworth, J., Machin, M., Dunn, G., Lewis, S.W., 2014. The temporal association between self-injurious thoughts and psychotic symptoms: a mobile phone assessment study. Suicide Life Threat. Behav. 44 (1), 101–110.

Pew Research Center, 2016. Smartphone Ownership and Internet Usage Continues to Climb in Emerging Economies. Available from: http://www.pewglobal.org/2016/02/22/smartphone-ownership-and-internet-usage-continues-to-climb-in-emerging-economies/.

Quinn, C.C., Clough, S.S., Minor, J.M., Lender, D., Okafor, M.C., Gruber-Baldini, A., 2008. WellDoc™ mobile diabetes management randomized controlled trial: change in clinical and behavioral outcomes and patient and physician satisfaction. Diabetes Technol. Ther. 10 (3), 160–168.

Ryan, D., Price, D., Musgrave, S.D., Malhotra, S., Lee, A.J., Ayansina, D., et al., 2012. Clinical and cost effectiveness of mobile phone supported self-monitoring of asthma: multicentre randomised controlled trial. BMJ 344, e1756. https://doi.org/10.1136/bmj.e1756.

Sanghara, H., Kravariti, E., Jakobsen, H., Okocha, C.I., 2010. Using short message services in mental health services: assessing feasibility. Ment. Health Rev. 15, 28–33.

Španiel, F., Hrdlicka, J., Novák, T., KOŽENÝ, J., Hoeschl, C., Mohr, P., et al., 2012. Effectiveness of the information technology-aided program of relapse prevention in schizophrenia (ITAREPS): a randomized, controlled, double-blind study. J. Psychiatr. Pract. 18 (4), 269–280.

Stephens, J., Allen, J., 2013. Mobile phone interventions to increase physical activity and reduce weight: a systematic review. J. Cardiovasc. Nurs. 28 (4), 320–329.

Strassnig, M., Brar, J.S., Ganguli, R., 2012. Health-related quality of life, adiposity, and sedentary behavior in patients with early schizophrenia: preliminary study. Diabetes Metab. Syndr. Obes. 5, 389–394.

Stubbs, B., Firth, J., Berry, A., Schuch, F.B., Rosenbaum, S., Gaughran, F., et al., 2016a. How much physical activity do people with schizophrenia engage in? A systematic review, comparative meta-analysis and meta-regression. Schizophr. Res. 176 (2–3), 431–440.

Stubbs, B., Williams, J., Gaughran, F., Craig, T., 2016b. How sedentary are people with psychosis? A systematic review and meta-analysis. Schizophr. Res. 171 (1–3), 103–109.

Thomas, N., Foley, F., Lindblom, K., Lee, S., 2017. Are people with severe mental illness ready for online interventions? Access and use of the Internet in Australian mental health service users. Australas. Psychiatry. https://doi.org/10.1177/1039856217689913 [Epub ahead of print].

Torous, J., Chan, S.R., Tan, S.Y.M., Behrens, J., Mathew, I., Conrad, E.J., et al., 2014. Patient smartphone ownership and interest in mobile apps to monitor symptoms of mental health conditions: a survey in four geographically distinct psychiatric clinics. JMIR Ment. Health 1 (1), e5. https://doi.org/10.2916/mental.4004.

Torous, J., Firth, J., Mueller, N., Onnela, J.P., Baker, J.T., 2017. Methodology and reporting of mobile heath and smartphone application studies for schizophrenia. Harv. Rev. Psychiatry. https://doi.org/10.1097/HRP.0000000000000133 [Epub ahead of print].

Vancampfort, D., Knapen, J., Probst, M., Scheewe, T., Remans, S., De Hert, M., 2012. A systematic review of correlates of physical activity in patients with schizophrenia. Acta Psychiatr. Scand. 125 (5), 352–362.

Vancampfort, D., Rosenbaum, S., Probst, M., Soundy, A., Mitchell, A.J., De Hert, M., et al., 2015b. Promotion of cardiorespiratory fitness in schizophrenia: a clinical overview and meta-analysis. Acta Psychiatr. Scand. 132 (2), 131–143.

Watts, S., Mackenzie, A., Thomas, C., Griskaitis, A., Mewton, L., Williams, A., et al., 2013. CBT for depression: a pilot RCT comparing mobile phone vs. computer. BMC Psychiatry 13, 49. https://doi.org/10.1186/1471-244X-13-49.

Webb, T., Joseph, J., Yardley, L., Michie, S., 2010. Using the internet to promote health behavior change: a systematic review and meta-analysis of the impact of theoretical basis, use of behavior change techniques, and mode of delivery on efficacy. J. Med. Internet Res. 12 (1), e4. https://doi.org/10.2196/jmir.1376.

World Health Organization, 2011. mHealth: New Horizons for Health through Mobile Technologies: Second Global Survey on EHealth. WHO, Geneva, Switzerland.

World Health Organization, 2015. Burden of Disease: DALYs. World Health Organization, Geneva, Switzerland. Available from: http://www.who.int/healthinfo/global_burden_disease/GBD_report_2004update_part4.pdf?ua=1.

Worringham, C., Rojek, A., Stewart, I., 2011. Development and feasibility of a smartphone, ECG and GPS based system for remotely monitoring exercise in cardiac rehabilitation. PLoS One 6 (2), e14669. https://doi.org/10.1371/journal.pone.0014669.

## Further Reading

Bogart, K., Wong, S.K., Lewis, C., Akenzua, A., Hayes, D., Prountzos, A., et al., 2014. Mobile phone text message reminders of antipsychotic medication: is it time and who should receive them? A cross-sectional trust-wide survey of psychiatric inpatients. BMC Psychiatry 14 (15). https://doi.org/10.1186/1471-244X-14-15.

De Hert, M., Cohen, D., Bobes, J., Cetkovich-Bakmas, M., Leucht, S., Ndetei, D.M., et al., 2011. Physical illness in patients with severe mental disorders. II. Barriers to care, monitoring and treatment guidelines, plus recommendations at the system and individual level. World Psychiatry 10 (2), 138–151.

Firth, J., Torous, J., 2015. Smartphone apps for schizophrenia: a systematic review. JMIR mHealth uHealth 3 (4), e102. https://doi.org/10.2196/mhealth.4930.

Lederman, R., Wadley, G., Gleeson, J., Alvarez-Jimenez, M., Spiteri-Staines, A., 2011. Supporting young people with psychosis in the community: an ICT enabled relapse prevention tool. In: PACIS 2011 Proceedings. Paper 104. Available from: http://aisel.aisnet.org/pacis2011/104.

Miller, B.J., Stewart, A., Schrimsher, J., Peeples, D., Buckley, P.F., 2015. How connected are people with schizophrenia? Cell phone, computer, email, and social media use. Psychiatry Res. 225, 458–463.

Vancampfort, D., Stubbs, B., Mitchell, A.J., De Hert, M., Wampers, M., Ward, P.B., et al., 2015a. Risk of metabolic syndrome and its components in people with schizophrenia and related psychotic disorders, bipolar disorder and major depressive disorder: a systematic review and meta-analysis. World Psychiatry 14 (3), 339–347.

# Integration of the Exercise Professional Within the Mental Health Multidisciplinary Team

*Robert Stanton*

School of Health, Medical and Applied Sciences, Central Queensland University, Rockhampton, QLD, Australia

OUTLINE

# INTRODUCTION

It is well established that the physical health of people with mental illness is substantially worse than the remainder of the population, with high rates of cardiometabolic diseases common (Correll et al., 2014; McCloughen et al., 2012). As a result, people with mental illness experience a mortality gap of between 10 and 32 years (Colton and Manderscheid, 2006; O'Donoghue et al., 2014; Walker et al., 2015). A range of lifestyle factors, including sedentary behavior, low levels of physical activity and exercise, low cardiorespiratory fitness, poor diet and smoking, coupled with medication side effects have significant impacts on the development of cardiometabolic diseases (Suetani et al., 2016b; Galletly et al., 2012).

There is now overwhelming evidence supporting physical activity and exercise in minimizing cardiometabolic risk factors in people with mental illness (Vancampfort et al., 2016c; Knapen et al., 2014). Exercise is a safe, low-cost, and well-accepted strategy with the added benefits of reducing symptoms (Cooney et al., 2013; Firth et al., 2015), improving cognition (Firth et al., 2016), and enhancing quality of life (Greer et al., 2016). Yet despite evidence of efficacy, there remains a gap in the implementation of PA interventions as part of mental health care. There is therefore an urgent need to translate results from efficacy studies into routine care. However, there are many and varied challenges in implementing sustainable system-wide changes within routine mental health services (Suetani et al., 2016a).

## Meeting Needs and Role Delineation

Two of the important and overlapping challenges are "meeting needs," and "role delineation." To implement exercise and physical activity interventions into routine care for people with mental illness, one must carefully consider not just the health service constraints such as physical space, staff, and funding but increasingly the service users' needs such as access, cost, and appropriateness. These efforts are then dovetailed with "role delineation," which then answers the question of who has responsibility for the design and implementation of physical activity and exercise interventions.

The association between physical activity and mental illness is not a new concept. Even in Roman times the physician Claudius Galenus was documented to have prescribed exercise for a myriad of ailments, including for depression (Tipton, 2014). In recent times the role of implementing physical health interventions including physical activity and exercise programs has fallen to nursing staff or physiotherapists. In fact, the first physiotherapy mental health specialization began in the early 1960s (Probst, 2012). Traditionally, nursing staff have adopted this important role; however, even though nurses who work in mental health settings see physical health care including physical activity and exercise prescription as an important part of their role (Happell et al., 2012; Robson et al., 2013), they are often poorly trained and ill-equipped to deliver high-quality physical health care services. More recently, the role of the Physical Health Nurse Consultant has been proposed to overcome the systemic and cultural barriers to physical health care delivery in mental health settings (Happell et al., 2015). While this is largely a coordination role, linking consumers with physical health care services, there is significant potential to improve the physical health of people with mental illness. A logical solution to embed physical activity and exercise in mental health services, however, is to implement an exercise professional role.

## WHAT IS AN EXERCISE PROFESSIONAL?

Exercise professionals are health professionals trained in the assessment, prescription, and delivery of exercise and physical activity interventions for healthy and clinical populations. Oftentimes, exercise professionals have university qualifications in exercise science, exercise physiology, physiotherapy, or related fields. In many cases, exercise professionals are accredited by health professional bodies as having met the knowledge and practical skills commensurate with the title, in essence making them registered health professionals. Registration may include recognition under national health schemes. For example, in Australia, Accredited Exercise Physiologists (AEPs) hold a 4-year university degree specializing in exercise and movement for the prevention and management of chronic diseases and injuries. AEPs can be registered under the national health scheme, Medicare, allowing rebates to patients referred under defined conditions. Many of Australia's private health funds also recognize AEPs and provide capped rebates for some services. Typically, AEPs provide support for people with common chronic health conditions such as cardiovascular disease, diabetes, osteoporosis, and arthritis. However, increasingly, AEPs are engaging with the mental health care sector to provide specialized exercise assessment, prescription, and delivery of services across a range of mental health settings.

Similar specialist exercise services are embedded in mental health services elsewhere in the world. For example in the United Kingdom and some European countries, physiotherapists are the group of health professionals most widely utilized in the mental health care sector to provide exercise and physical activity interventions, particularly in inpatient mental health settings. A 2012 consensus statement from the International Organization of Physiotherapists in Mental Health (IOPTMH) regarding physical activity for people with schizophrenia highlighted the need for shared decision-making when considering physical activity interventions to ensure the needs and capabilities of the consumer are met (Vancampfort et al., 2012). Moreover, this consensus statement highlighted the need for additional training in physical and mental health symptom recognition to enable physiotherapists to better engage with mental health consumers.

A 2014 survey of IOPTMH members highlighted the status of physiotherapists in mental health care (Stubbs et al., 2014). Results revealed that physiotherapists believe they are best placed and well trained to lead physical activity and exercise interventions and initiate and manage healthy lifestyle interventions for people experiencing mental illness. Although there are calls to increase the role of physiotherapists in mental health settings internationally, and in routine practice physiotherapists often treat individuals with comorbid physical and mental health issues (Connaughton, 2014), at last count less than 0.2% (29/17,980) of physiotherapists reported working in mental health (Health Workforce Australia, 2014). The reasons for this are unclear but may reflect the historical perspective that physiotherapists are best suited to treat musculoskeletal or neurological conditions rather than behavior change—focused physical health interventions.

## Why the Need for an Exercise Professional?

In mental health settings, nurses are the group of health professionals with the strongest therapeutic relationships with consumers (Blythe and White, 2012). However, studies of nurses in mental health settings show that nurses lack specialized training in the design and delivery of exercise interventions (Stanton et al., 2015b). People with mental illness present unique challenges to exercise prescription not only because of their mental illness but also the high prevalence of comorbid physical illness. More often than not, comorbid physical illness is due to a combination of medication side-effects and unhealthy lifestyle behaviors such as smoking, poor nutrition, alcohol, and other substance misuse and low physical activity and high levels of sedentary behavior. Exercise and physical activity are well-established as strategies to combat the poor physical health of people with mental illness; however, the failure to see exercise as part of routine care is not a gap in knowledge of effectiveness per se rather an implementation gap (Bartels, 2015). That is, we know exercise works; we just aren't doing it effectively.

Embedding an exercise professional in the mental health setting will increase the effectiveness of intervention delivery through targeted health behavior change. It will resolve the issue of role delineation and at the same time reduce the workload on nursing staff, allowing them to direct their specialized training to mental health care. Well-planned integration of an exercise professional ensures the complex and sometimes conflicting needs of all stakeholders are met; that is, the service provider, consumer, staff, and carers and family. Exercise professionals are agents for change and a focus for stakeholders as they will know who to talk to regarding physical activity and exercise, particularly in the transition between phases of service use, for example, from inpatient to community, where therapeutic contact changes. They will also become agents for change in staff behavior. This is important since health professionals who engage in healthy behaviors are more likely to promote similar behaviors to those they care for, resulting in beneficial effects for patients (Hjorth et al., 2015).

### Clinicians Beliefs of Exercise in Mental Health

Clinicians tend to favor and support treatment options they specialize in and are familiar with. For example, compared with psychologists, psychiatrists are less likely to endorse lifestyle therapies and psychological interventions (Jorm et al., 1997). Over time however, psychiatrists, in particular, have changed their beliefs regarding the helpfulness of physical therapy interventions such as exercise or yoga to be more consistent with those from other disciplines such as general practice and psychology (Morgan et al., 2013). Exercise is well supported by general practitioners and mental health clinicians for people with mental illness (Morgan et al., 2013; Stanton et al., 2014). However, some gaps in knowledge and practice are evident. For example, psychologists report being confident when providing exercise advice and physical activity counselling to patients, and do so as part of routine care, but are less confident with individual tailoring to the patients' needs and preferences (Burton et al., 2010). Similarly, general practitioners are supportive of the role exercise may play in the treatment of mental illness; however, the limited knowledge of illness-specific exercise prescription guidelines and the continued reliance on pharmacotherapy are likely to impede the implementation of exercise as part of usual care in primary care settings (Stanton et al., 2014).

It is worth considering that the personal exercise behaviors of some health care specialists such as physicians, nurses, and pharmacists are predictive of exercise counselling to patients (Lobelo, 2009; Lobelo and de Quevedo, 2014; de Quevedo and Lobelo, 2013; Fie et al., 2012). However, in the mental health sector, this does not appear to be the case. One study of Australian nurses working in mental health care reported no association between physical activity participation and the frequency of exercise prescription to consumers (Stanton et al., 2015b). One strategy to address this discrepancy might be to target interventions for mental health clinicians. This is certainly the case for nurses since nurses have the strongest therapeutic relationship with consumers (Blythe and White, 2012; Bradshaw and Pedley, 2012).

## What Are Important Attributes of Exercise Professionals?

Qualitative studies which have examined consumer participation in physical activity and exercise interventions in the inpatient setting suggest that an inclusive, holistic program, delivered by someone with excellent leadership skills is highly valued (Thibeault et al., 2010). Although difficult to quantify, the therapeutic relationship is an important feature noted by consumers (McAndrew et al., 2014).

One of the challenges of interpreting the findings from studies which examine the effect of exercise on people with mental illness is the high dropout rate; that is, people who commence but do not complete the study. Although this can be controlled for in the final analysis using statistical procedures, it remains a concern nonetheless. To emphasize this point, a recent meta-analysis of studies examining exercise in people with schizophrenia reported dropout in the intervention arm to be more than double that of the nonexercise control arm (Vancampfort et al., 2016b). Interestingly, consumer characteristics such as age, gender, or illness duration or severity were not predictive of dropout. Rather, the most significant predictor of dropout was instructor qualifications, whereby lower dropout rates were observed in studies which employed qualified instructors. This finding is replicated in another meta-analysis of studies examining exercise interventions for people with depression (Stubbs et al., 2016). Clearly, this points to a need to have qualified exercise professionals who are well-versed in designing and delivering exercise interventions for people with mental illness and who can provide motivation which promotes exercise adherence in an environment which is nonjudgmental and supportive.

These findings support earlier calls for exercise professionals such as physiotherapists and AEPs as the clinician of choice for implementing exercise interventions for people with mental illness (Stanton, 2013). However, qualifications alone are unlikely to lead to effective exercise interventions. Exercise professionals should be knowledgeable on local and national health priorities and policies for the physical health care of people with mental illness. This is important to enable the exercise professional to undertake their role in a mental health setting without compromising personal or consumer safety and ensuring they comply with relevant mental health acts. A need for this type of education, along with other treatment practices such as sensory modulation and de-escalation techniques, has been recently identified and may help exercise professionals transition from nonmental health roles (Furness et al., 2017).

Exercise professionals should be aware of and be able to implement evidence-based exercise interventions which are grounded in behavior change theories such as self-determination theory or the transtheoretical model of behavior change. Self-determination theory in particular has been highlighted in recent years has having significant value in explaining participation in exercise and physical activity interventions for people with mental illness (Vancampfort et al., 2015). It considers motivation as a multidimensional construct and places one level of self-determination or autonomous motivation on a continuum from amotivation to high motivation. A feature of exercise professionals is their understanding of and ability to implement long-term sustainable behavior change. This is important to prepare consumers for the transition from inpatient to community settings or when reduced social support is available, such as when changing locations.

Exercise professionals must also be cognizant of the need to work as part of the multidisciplinary team which may comprise psychiatrists, mental health nurses, physicians, and carers. In particular, the exercise professional should consider the potential harms associated with exercise participation. This might include those associated with increased risk for cardiometabolic disease but may extend to risk associated with severe mania, where excessive exercise may result. There is a need for exercise professionals to communicate concerns regarding consumer behavior in the context of their treatment, stage of recovery, and personal circumstances to the multidisciplinary team members in order to most effectively use exercise as part of mental health care.

## EXAMPLES OF INTEGRATION

The purpose of this chapter, and particularly, this section, is not to reiterate the already-demonstrated benefits of exercise reported in the many randomized controlled trials, systematic reviews, and meta-analyses; rather to demonstrate how, and the benefits from, integrating physical activity and exercise programs led by exercise professionals. In this regard, there are far fewer accounts published in the peer-reviewed literature from which to draw models of integration. This section will outline examples in different settings, highlight the commonalities among the programs, then draw together a possible framework on how mental health settings may effectively integrate exercise professionals into multidisciplinary teams.

### The Keeping the Body in Mind Example

The Keeping the Body in Mind (KBIM) program was developed as a formal response to pragmatic approaches to address the cardiometabolic risk profiles of youth attending an early psychosis program (Rosenbaum et al., 2014). Now delivered as part of standard care, the program is based around onsite facilities including a gymnasium and cooking facilities.

The KBIM program is a 12-week individualized lifestyle intervention comprising exercise physiology and dietetic services, along with a clinical nurse consultant and youth peer worker, for youth (14–25 years) with first episode psychosis.

The program has undergone comprehensive evaluation (Curtis et al., 2015). Program participants experienced significantly less weight gain following commencement of antipsychotic medication compared with those accessing usual care. The proportion of participants experiencing clinically significant weight gain (>7% baseline body mass) was 13% in the intervention group compared with 75% in the usual care group. Importantly, participants in the intervention group did not experience a significant increase in waist circumference, while those in the usual care group saw an average of 7.1 cm increase in waist girth. These are clinically important outcomes since early weight gain and cardiometabolic abnormalities are indicative of poor physical health in the future (Correll et al., 2015; Tek et al., 2015). In addition to the positive cardiometabolic outcomes of the KBIM program, participants demonstrated improvements in cardiorespiratory fitness, and in self-reported physical activity, sleep quality, and reductions in energy intake.

## The Secure Extended Care Facility Example

In another Australian example of effective integration of an exercise professional in a mental health setting, Furness et al. (2017) describe how an AEP was embedded in a secure extended care unit. Secure extended care units present unique challenges in that they are designed to provide long-term treatment and care, often up to 24 months, to consumers who may be under involuntary treatment orders and with varying levels of legal and leave status. Facility staff who participated in interviews, including nurses, noted that they were not effective in providing concurrent physical and mental health care, often as a consequence of the complexities of secure facility services, and the potential risks. They expressed concerns regarding high levels of sedentary behavior, and facility expansion provided opportunities to develop new care models of care to better address physical health, in line with national mental health care priorities.

In this example, managers identified through the relevant literature that an AEP was the most appropriate allied health professional to address physical health care; however, comparative examples of embedded AEP roles on which to base a new position are lacking. A key driver for AEP implementation was to better manage cardiometabolic risk and exercise; a role for which AEPs are well suited. The AEPs role was built around assessing the consumers' suitability for exercise, cardiometabolic, and functional risk stratification, using a shared decision-making approach to activity selection based on activity suitability and preferences, access and leave restrictions, and comorbid conditions, maintaining engagement through program progression and providing feedback and routine monitoring of progress. Multidisciplinary team integration was achieved through regular case conferences and team meetings. This treatment pathway ensured staff were aware of the role of the AEP, the effect the AEPs had on treatment outcomes, and treatment was person-centered and holistic.

Despite positive views from staff regarding the benefits to consumers associated with having an AEP, staff also expressed concerns about employing nonnursing staff and the lack of AEPs awareness of risks associated with working in a mental health setting. Staff also highlighted a lack of understanding about the role of an AEP—a factor which likely leads to the low rates to referral to AEPs from mental health professionals (Happell et al., 2013; Stanton, 2013). Although more research is needed to examine the true impact of AEP integration on consumer behavior and health outcomes, in the view of staff and management the process of literature review, stakeholder consultations, and action has resulted in a new role aligned with the vision of improving the physical health of mental health consumers.

## The Forensic Secure Facility Example

Some studies, however, have considered consumers view of integrated exercise programs. For example, Wynaden et al. (2012) evaluated an established AEP-led exercise program based in a secure forensic mental health unit, under the West Australian "Plan-Do-Study-Act"—a quality improvement initiative that engages consumers to comment on standards of care and demonstrates that their views are valued and can effect change. The exercise program included gym and sport-based activities, education sessions on exercise and nutrition, and self-management strategies. In this exercise program, AEPs were responsible for providing a range of activities suited to the broad range of interests and capacities of consumers; however, physical health care in the broader sense was the responsibility of all members of staff.

In evaluating the exercise program, 56 consumers completed a survey to evaluate motives and perceived benefits of the exercise program, with responses overwhelmingly positive. Consumers provided a variety of reasons for attending the program including to improve health and fitness, to overcome boredom, and to improve symptoms. Consumers found exercise programs enjoyable that they provided much-needed structure and routine to their day, led to an improvement in mood and well-being, and improved social, cognitive, and physical skills. Consumers also noted that team-based activities were the highest rated in terms of benefits, suggesting social interaction and the development of trust may be important factors in developing exercise activities for mental health consumers. Indeed, consumers reported that new relationships based on mutual trust and respect were important features of the program. Consumers also reported developing a greater sense of autonomy in physical health care.

## The Inpatient Example

Programs centered in inpatient facilities are also effective and well received by consumers. Prior to the implementation of an exercise professional role, management of the inpatient mental health facility located within regionally based private hospital consulted with industry experts and consumers. Specifically, the attributes of the exercise professional necessary for success, the types of programs possible on the ward, the potential risks and benefits to consumers, staff, and the organization (reputational risk), and likelihood of consumer engagement. A university-trained exercise scientist was appointed in a casual role to provide exercise programs three times weekly. Interventions were developed through consultation with experts in exercise and mental illness, facility staff, and consumers, based on providing low resource-dependent, safe opportunities to undertake aerobic and resistance training programs. An important feature of this particular model of integration was that the exercise program was not "prescribed." Consumers were able to undertake activities that were perceived as enjoyable and at an intensity that was comfortable. This high degree of autonomy places control of the exercise in the hands of the consumer and is thought to be a major contributor to the benefits of the program.

Using discharge surveys, evaluation of the intervention with respect to consumer satisfaction showed a greater proportion of consumers rated the exercise program as "Excellent" compared with all other therapeutic activities (Stanton et al., 2015a). Exercise program participation also resulted in significant acute changes in affect, particularly in consumers with depressive disorders (Stanton et al., 2016b). Interestingly, sleep quality as measured by the Richards-Campbell Sleep Questionnaire was significantly and negatively correlated with exercise intensity (Stanton et al., 2016a). Although the mechanisms for this association were not evaluated, changes in arousal may be one possible explanation. This is a plausible explanation for the findings of this study since when consumers were stratified by diagnosis, the relationship remained significant only for those with anxiety disorders, but not for those with depressive or bipolar disorders.

## Community Linkage Example

An alternative approach to embedding an exercise professional within the multidisciplinary team is to engage with community partners such as commercial fitness centers or gymnasiums. There are a number of significant advantages of this approach including less capital investment to establish and staff a program, forging community linkages to reduce stigma, offering consumers a sense of community and belonging, and promoting effective self-management strategies following discharge. However, these advantages are offset by potential disadvantages including limited support to attend a community program including financial and transport, poor understanding among fitness instructors of mental illness in the broad sense, and a lack of "mental health friendly" facilities where consumers feel safe and valued.

An example of community-level integration is the InSHAPE program (Van Citters et al., 2010). InSHAPE is a long-term health promotion program based in a US-based community mental health facility. It was developed with consultation from consumers as a multidisciplinary and multifaceted lifestyle intervention based around social inclusion, with the exercise component using community-based facilities accessible by all community members. Fitness instructors mentored consumers through individually tailored exercise, goal setting, and dietary plans, following training in mental health, behavioral change through motivation and goal setting, and healthy eating. Fitness instructors provided support through regular contact, providing motivation, and addressing cognitive and social challenges which limit community engagement by people with mental illness.

A unique aspect to InSHAPE, is that consumers were provided with free access to community-based fitness facilities, funded through community partnerships and not-for-profit agencies. Although this may not replicate an ecologically valid scenario in all settings, it addresses one of the significant barriers to exercise participation experienced by people with mental illness. As with healthy lifestyle interventions conducted in commercial and other fitness center settings, the In SHAPE program offered group meetings, rewards and incentives, and education.

A 9-month follow-up of consumer showed a significant shift toward readiness to engage in exercise and dietary changes, coupled with a significant increase in actual exercise behavior and perceived satisfaction with fitness. Program participation led to significant reduction in central obesity and a moderate effect on systolic blood pressure in those with preexisting hypertension. Self-reported physical and mental health showed significant improvements, with greater contact with the fitness mentor associated with greater improvements in mental functioning (Van Citters et al., 2010). Although weight status did not change, this is likely to reflect the fitness instructors priorities on undertaking exercise rather than making dietary changes and the financial and logistical challenges associated with implementing long-term dietary change.

Extending the InSHAPE program to young adults (aged 21–30 years) with mental illness yielded important results with respect to cardiometabolic risk (Naslund et al., 2017). Around half of young, overweight, or obese adults with schizophrenia or mood disorder who participated in the InSHAPE program reported clinically significant reductions in body weight or improvements in cardiorespiratory fitness. Young adults are at significant risk of cardiometabolic abnormalities following commencement of pharmaceutical treatment, and therefore early lifestyle interventions to combat weight gain are particularly important. This degree of cardiometabolic risk reduction is comparable to that achieved in adult consumers (Naslund et al., 2017). InSHAPE demonstrates that successful outcomes may be achieved through engaging with existing community resources. Community programs are likely to increase accessibility to health improvement programs and ensure such programs are increasingly feasible for service providers and consumers alike.

## A Common Theme

A common conclusion from the previously mentioned examples of integrating exercise professionals into multidisciplinary mental health care teams is that the implementation of a program which is supervised and tailored to the consumers' needs leads to better outcomes for consumers, compared with simply providing opportunities for exercise. This argument is strongly supported by the findings from recent systematic reviews and meta-analyses, showing that exercise interventions which are developed and supervised by exercise professionals such as physiotherapists or AEPs result in greater adherence and better outcomes for consumers (Stubbs et al., 2016; Vancampfort et al., 2016a, Vancampfort et al., 2016b). While there are many well-conducted trials examining the effect of exercise on a broad range of mental health conditions, there are as yet, few well-documented examples demonstrating how to implement an exercise professional in mental health settings, and more translational work is required.

Integration of an exercise professional into the multidisciplinary mental health care team is a challenging process. There are a number of factors to consider including human and physical resource implications, risk management, and budget implications. Some considerations to develop and implement successful interventions are outlined in Table 13.1. These insights are gained from the personal experience of the author in recruiting exercise professionals for a variety of mental health settings and ongoing discussion with service providers, staff, and experts in exercise and mental illness. This list is neither complete nor detailed since all services will raise different issues regarding the implementation of an exercise professional, but it provides a starting point for discussion among management and team members.

**TABLE 13.1** Considerations for the Development and Implementation of an Exercise Program

| Point | Questions to be Considered | Possible Stakeholder Involvement | Responses |
|---|---|---|---|
| What is the need? | What is the consumer consensus of the need for exercise? Does exercise fit with our model of care and service priorities? | Management, consumers, staff, industry experts in exercise, and mental health. | Increasingly mental health services call for integration of mental and physical health, consistent with national priorities. Consumers find exercise beneficial and enjoyable. |
| What are the resources? | Are there existing staff and resources that can be utilized? Can staff be seconded from other service areas? Who can the service engage within the community? Can tertiary sector engagement be achieved to facilitate student placement or internships, undertake quality assurance, process, clinical, or consumer evaluations of existing services, or identify the need for service improvement? How much space is necessary for a range of activities? | Management, consumers, staff, industry experts in exercise and mental health. | Exercise programs can be implemented at low cost, using minimal resources. Walking programs, for example, requires few if any additional resources. Some exercise resources may be shared between departments, for example, occupational therapy or physiotherapy. Engaging with community resources or private providers will reduce space requirements. |
| Environment | Is the staff culture one of empowerment? Is the initiative supported by management? Are staff confident and knowledgeable in physical health care? What are staff attitudes toward physical health care? | Management, staff. | Educate staff on the benefits of exercise and the need for holistic approaches to care. In particular, exercise programs will reduce boredom, potentially reduce the need for seclusion or restraint and positively impact cardiometabolic and mental health. Ensure staff are consulted on and engaged in the implementation process |

*Continued*

**TABLE 13.1**  Considerations for the Development and Implementation of an Exercise Program—cont'd

| Point | Questions to be Considered | Possible Stakeholder Involvement | Responses |
|---|---|---|---|
| Are there risks? | Is exercise likely to increase risk for adverse cardiometabolic events? Are there reputational or other risks; for example, harm to self or others? | Management, staff, industry experts in exercise and mental health. | There are few adverse events reported in the literature. As part of routine care, an exercise professional should undertake a cardiometabolic risk assessment in association with other clinical staff, further reducing risk. Consultation with treating staff and education on mental health will improve detection of other potential risks. |
| What are the financial implications? | Is the program feasible in the current economic climate? | Management, staff. | What are the cost implications of failing to implement an exercise program, given knowledge of the cardiometabolic risk and mortality gap associated with mental illness? |
| How do we recruit an exercise specialist? | Are traditional avenues of promoting new positions appropriate for an emerging position in health care? What are the minimum qualifications? | Management, industry experts in exercise and mental health. | Increasingly, exercise professionals are using social media, in addition to other electronic services to source positions in health care. A broad range of targeted promotional strategies will be required to recruit and train the best applicant. Engagement with industry representatives is essential. |

| | | | |
|---|---|---|---|
| Staff retention | Is the position susceptible to high staff turnover thereby reducing therapeutic engagement and relationship building? | Management, consumers, staff, industry experts in exercise and mental health. | Provide a highly supportive environment with regular staff feedback and consultation. Provide an appropriate degree of autonomy in the multidisciplinary team. |
| Evaluation | How do I know if consumers or the organization are benefiting? What is the impact on team culture? Is the intervention cost-effective? What are the metrics for success; for example, program attendance, reduced cardiometabolic risk profile, symptom severity, or functional independence. Organizational metrics might include reduced use of restraint or seclusion, improved medication adherence, reduced length of stay or readmission. | Management, consumers, staff, industry experts in exercise and mental health, academics. | These are all components of evaluation that form a usual part of service evaluation. Quality assurance, file audits, staff and consumer interviews, and observations are all techniques to evaluate the benefits to consumers, staff, and the financial bottom line. Evaluations should be ongoing with results feeding the cycle of continuous improvement. Where possible, the process, outcomes, and future enhancement should be made public to improve the implementation and delivery of exercise for people with mental illness. |

**TABLE 13.2**   The 5A Model of Health Behavior Change

| Step | Action |
|------|--------|
| Assess | Assess consumers' current activity levels using a validated self-report tool such as IPAQ-SF or SIMPAQ. <br> Assess behavioral and cardiometabolic risk factors—e.g., family history. <br> Assess readiness to change and barriers/facilitators for change. <br> Assess confidence and importance of targeted behavior change. |
| Advise | Provide individualized guidance, informed by the best evidence on exercise and mental health, on the risks and benefits of exercise. <br> Provide tailored advice to the consumers priorities, capacity, interests. |
| Agree | Develop solution focussed, assessment-informed goals to increase physical activity. <br> Ensure agreed goals are SMART (specific, measurable, realistic, achievable, and time-bound), e.g., I will walk twice a week for 10 min after work, for the next 4 weeks. Vague goals such as, "I'll go and do more exercise" are not measurable and demonstrate a lack of commitment. |
| Assist | Aid the consumer to overcome identified goals. <br> Identify suitable community opportunities, peer-support, or other strategies to help consumers achieve their agreed goals |
| Arrange | Follow-up with consumers in a timely manner through face-to-face or other means. <br> Assess progress toward agreed goals and review as necessary. |

## Practice Considerations

In practice, however, due to high workload, consumer to clinician ratios, or fractional appointments of exercise professionals within mental health settings, the exercise professional may not be well positioned to undertake extensive assessment and behavioral counselling sessions in order to individually prescribe lifestyle interventions. In these cases, there is a strong argument for brief, targeted interventions for behavior change. For example, the 5A's model, adapted from smoking cessation interventions, appears to be an effective framework for behavior change interventions where therapeutic contact time is limited, such as in primary care settings. Table 13.2 summarizes the steps for the 5A's model. Each step involves consumer engagement, which is a priority for mental health reform and ensures the consumer is the focus of health behavior interventions. A detailed example of this is provided in Beaulac et al. (2011).

## FUTURE STEPS

It is now well recognized that exercise benefits both physical and mental health of people across a wide range of mental illnesses. What remains, however, is an implementation gap. Despite the well-understood benefits, exercise is not yet part of routine care for people with mental illness. In order to bridge this gap, there are a number of barriers to address.

First, there needs to be greater inclusion of exercise professionals in the multidisciplinary team. Positions need to be created with the support of health care managers, based on the understanding of what the exercise professional brings to the team and the measurable and deliverable key performance indicators. To achieve this requires systemic culture change across mental health including the disciplines of psychiatry, psychology, mental health nursing, and occupational therapy to acknowledge the contribution a "new" team member provides but also requires lobbying from the peak exercise professional bodies to raise awareness of the importance of the role. The IOPTMH, Exercise and Sports Science Australia (ESSA), British Association of Sport and Exercise Sciences (BASES), American College of Sports Medicine (ACSM), and Canadian Society for Exercise Physiology (CSEP), along with similar organization internationally, should actively seek to work with health care systems to embed exercise and physical activity interventions as part of usual care. Although there are policy steps toward this in Australia, the United Kingdom, and other countries, including joint consensus statements from ESSA, ACSM, BASES, and Sport and Exercise Science New Zealand (SESNZ) (Rosenbaum et al., 2017), practice implementation has some way to go, particularly in light of the funding models currently in place (Pratt et al., 2016).

There is also a need to actively promote the success of the many pilot trials presented by clinicians at conferences and meetings, which, unlike peer-reviewed published studies, often fail to capture the attention of researchers and policymakers. These unpublished works collectively hold a significant body of implementation knowledge and experience. Assimilation and wide dissemination of these projects will provide great insight into addressing the implementation gap of exercise professionals as part of the multidisciplinary mental health team.

Researchers need to work more collaboratively with key stakeholders including consumers and carers, and mental health care providers to answer the implementation questions at the core of integration. From the formers' perspective, these include cost and accessibility of services, level of care and support shown by exercise professionals, and venues where stigma and judgment are absent. In addition to the concerns consumers and carers may have, it is important to address those of the service providers. These include detailed economic analyses including human and physical resource allocation, service use data, key performance indicators, such as improved physical health, behavior change, and long-term sustainability of service provision. Consumer acceptability of exercise interventions is also a key factor.

# References

Bartels, S.J., 2015. Can behavioral health organizations change health behaviors? The STRIDE study and lifestyle interventions for obesity in serious mental illness. Am. J. Psychiatry 172 (1), 9–11.

Beaulac, J., Carlson, A., Boyd, R.J., 2011. Counseling on physical activity to promote mental health: practical guidelines for family physicians. Can. Fam. Physician 57 (4), 399–401.

Blythe, J., White, J., 2012. Role of the mental health nurse towards physical health care in serious mental illness: an integrative review of 10 years of UK literature. Int. J. Ment. Health Nurs. 21 (3), 193–201.

Bradshaw, T., Pedley, R., 2012. Evolving role of mental health nurses in the physical health care of people with serious mental health illness. Int. J. Ment. Health Nurs. 21 (3), 266–273.

Burton, N.W., Pakenham, K.I., Brown, W.J., 2010. Are psychologists willing and able to promote physical activity as part of psychological treatment? Int. J. Behav. Med. 17 (4), 287–297.

Colton, C., Manderscheid, R., 2006. Congruencies in increased mortality rates, years of potential life lost, and causes of death among public mental health clients in eight states. Prev. Chronic Dis. 3 (2), 1–14.

Connaughton, J., November 2014. Matters of the mind: physiotherapy's role in mental health. InMotion 28–31.

Cooney, G.M., Dwan, K., Greig, C.A., Lawlor, D.A., Rimer, J., Waugh, F.R., Mcmurdo, M., Mead, G.E., 2013. Exercise for depression. Cochrane Database Syst. Rev. 9, CD004366.

Correll, C.U., Robinson, D.G., Schooler, N.R., et al., 2014. Cardiometabolic risk in patients with first-episode schizophrenia spectrum disorders: baseline results from the RAISE-ETP study. JAMA Psychiatry 71 (12), 1350–1363.

Correll, C.U., Detraux, J., DE Lepeleire, J., De Hert, M., 2015. Effects of antipsychotics, antidepressants and mood stabilizers on risk for physical diseases in people with schizophrenia, depression and bipolar disorder. World Psychiatry 14 (2), 119–136.

Curtis, J., Watkins, A., Rosenbaum, S., Teasdale, S.B., Kalucy, M., Samaras, K., Ward, P.B., 2015. Evaluating an individualised lifestyle and life-skills intervention to prevent antipsychotic-induced weight gain in first episode psychosis. Early Interv. Psychiatry. https://doi.org/10.1111/eip.12230.

De Quevedo, G., Lobelo, F., 2013. Healthcare providers as role models for physical activity. Circulation 127 (AP420), AP420.

Fie, S., Norman, I.J., While, A.E., 2012. The relationship between physicians' and nurses' personal physical activity habits and their health-promotion practice: a systematic review. Health Educ. J. 72 (1), 102–119.

Firth, J., Cotter, J., Elliott, R., French, P., Yung, A.R., 2015. A systematic review and meta-analysis of exercise interventions in schizophrenia patients. Psychol. Med. 1–19.

Firth, J., Stubbs, B., Rosenbaum, S., Vancampfort, D., Malchow, B., Schuch, F., Elliott, R., Nuechterlein, K.H., Yung, A.R., 2017. Aerobic exercise improves cognitive functioning in people with schizophrenia: a systematic review and meta-analysis. Schizophr. Bull. 43 (3), 546–556.

Furness, T., Hewavasam, J., Barnfield, J., Mckenna, B., Joseph, C., 2017. Adding an accredited exercise physiologist role to a new model of care at a secure extended care mental health service: a qualitative study. J. Ment. Health 1–7.

Galletly, C., Foley, D., Waterreus, A., Watts, G., Castle, D., Mcgrath, J., Mackinnon, A., Morgan, V., 2012. Cardiometabolic risk factors in people with psychotic disorders: the second Australian national survey of psychosis. Aust. N.Z. J. Psychiatry 46 (8), 753–761.

Greer, T.L., Trombello, J.M., Rethorst, C.D., Carmody, T.J., Jha, M.K., Liao, A., Grannemann, B.D., Chambliss, H.O., Church, T.S., Trivedi, M.H., 2016. Improvements in psychosocial functioning and health-related quality of life following exercise augmentation in patients with treatment response but nonremitted major depressive disorder: results from the tread study. Depress. Anxiety 33 (9), 870–881.

Happell, B., Scott, D., Platania-Phung, C., Nankivell, J., 2012. Nurses' views on physical activity for people with serious mental illness. Ment. Health Phys. Act. 5 (1), 4–12.

Happell, B., Platania-Phung, C., Scott, D., Nankivell, J., 2013. Communication with colleagues: frequency of collaboration regarding physical health of consumers with mental illness. Psychiatr. Care 50 (1), 33–43.

Happell, B., Gaskin, C.J., Stanton, R., 2015. Addressing the physical health of people with serious mental illness: a potential solution for an enduring problem. Int. J. Soc. Psychiatry 62 (2), 201–202.

Health Workforce Australia, 2014. Australia's Health Workforce Series – Physiotherapists in Focus. Health Workforce Australia, Adelaide, Australia.

Hjorth, P., Davidsen, A.S., Kilian, R., Jensen, S.O.W., Munk-Jørgensen, P., 2015. Intervention to promote physical health in staff within mental health facilities and the impact on patients' physical health. Nord. J. Psychiatry 1–10.

Jorm, A.F., Korten, A.E., Jacomb, P.A., Rodgers, B., Pollitt, P., Christensen, H., Henderson, S., 1997. Helpfulness of interventions for mental disorders: beliefs of health professionals compared with the general public. Br. J. Psychiatry 171 (3), 233–237.

Knapen, J., Vancampfort, D., Moriën, Y., Marchal, Y., 2015. Exercise therapy improves both mental and physical health in patients with major depression. Disabil. Rehabil. 37 (16), 1490–1495.

Lobelo, F., DE Quevedo, I.G., 2014. The evidence in support of physicians and health care providers as physical activity role models. Am. J. Lifestyle Med. https://doi.org/10.1177/1559827613520120.

Lobelo, F., 2009. Physical activity habits of doctors and medical students influence their counselling practices. Br. J. Sports Med. 43 (2), 89–92.

Mcandrew, S., Chambers, M., Nolan, F., Thomas, B., Watts, P., 2014. Measuring the evidence: reviewing the literature of the measurement of therapeutic engagement in acute mental health inpatient wards. Int. J. Ment. Health Nurs. 23 (3), 212–220.

Mccloughen, A., Foster, K., HUWS-Thomas, M., Delgado, C., 2012. Physical health and wellbeing of emerging and young adults with mental illness: an integrative review of international literature. Int. J. Ment. Health Nurs. 21 (3), 274–288.

Morgan, A.J., Jorm, A.F., Reavley, N.J., 2013. Beliefs of Australian health professionals about the helpfulness of interventions for mental disorders: dfferences between professions and change over time. Aust. N.Z. J. Psychiatr. 47 (9), 840–848.

Naslund, J.A., Aschbrenner, K.A., Scherer, E.A., Pratt, S.I., Bartels, S.J., 2017. Health promotion for young adults with serious mental illness. Psychiatr. Serv. 68 (2), 137–143.

O'donoghue, B., Schäfer, M.R., Becker, J., Papageorgiou, K., Amminger, G.P., 2014. Metabolic changes in first-episode early-onset schizophrenia with second-generation antipsychotics. Early Interv. Psychiatry 8 (3), 276–280.

Pratt, S.I., Jerome, G.J., Schneider, K.L., Craft, L.L., Buman, M.P., Stoutenberg, M., Daumit, G.L., Bartels, S.J., Goodrich, D.E., 2016. Increasing US health plan coverage for exercise programming in community health settings for people with serious mental illness: a position statement from the Society of Behavior Medicine and the American College of Sports Medicine. Transl. Behav. Med. 6 (3), 478–481.

Probst, M., 2012. The international organization of physical therapists working in mental health (IOPTMH). Men. Health Phys. Act. 5, 20−21.

Robson, D., Haddad, M., Gray, R., Gournay, K., 2013. Mental health nursing and physical health care: a cross-sectional study of nurses' attitudes, practice, and perceived training needs for the physical health care of people with severe mental illness. Int. J. Ment. Health Nurs. 22 (5), 409−417.

Rosenbaum, S., Lim, L.X., Newall, H., Curtis, J., Watkins, A., Samaras, K., Ward, P.B., 2014. Observation to action: progressive implementation of lifestyle interventions to improve physical health outcomes in a community-based early psychosis treatment program. Aust. N.Z. J. Psychiatry 48 (11), 1063−1064.

Rosenbaum, S., HOBSON-Powell, A., Davison, K., Elliot, C., Ward, P.B., 2017. Role of physical activity in closing the life expectancy gap of people with mental illness. Med. Sci. Sports Exerc. 49 (S5), 842−843.

Stanton, R., Frank, C., Reaburn, P., Happell, B., 2014. A pilot study of the views of general practitioners regarding exercise for the treatment of depression. Perspect. Psychiatr. Care 51 (4), 253−259.

Stanton, R., Donohue, P., Garnon, M., Happell, B., 2015a. Participation in and satisfaction with an exercise program for inpatient mental health consumers. Perspect. Psychiatr. Care 52 (1), 62−67.

Stanton, R., Happell, B., Reaburn, P., 2015b. Investigating the exercise prescription practices of nurses working in inpatient mental health settings. Int. J. Ment. Health Nurs. 24 (2), 112−120.

Stanton, R., Garnon, M., Donohue, P., Happell, B., 2016a. The relationship between exercise intensity and sleep quality in people hospitalised due to affective disorders: a pilot study. Issues Ment. Health Nurs. 37 (2), 70−74.

Stanton, R., Reaburn, P., Happell, B., 2016b. The effect of acute exercise on affect and arousal in inpatient mental health consumers. J. Nerv. Ment. Dis. 204 (9), 658−664.

Stanton, R., 2013. Accredited exercise physiologists and the treatment of people with mental illnesses. Clin. Pract. 2 (2), 5−9.

Stubbs, B., Soundy, A., Probst, M., De Hert, M., De Herdt, A., Vancampfort, D., 2014. Understanding the role of physiotherapists in schizophrenia: an international perspective from members of the international organisation of physical therapists in mental health (IOPTMH). J. Ment. Health 23 (3), 125−129.

Stubbs, B., Vancampfort, D., Rosenbaum, S., Ward, P.B., Richards, J., Soundy, A., Veronese, N., Solmi, M., Schuch, F.B., 2016. Dropout from exercise randomized controlled trials among people with depression: a meta-analysis and meta regression. J. Affect. Disord. 190, 457−466.

Suetani, S., Rosenbaum, S., Scott, J.G., Curtis, J., Ward, P.B., 2016a. Bridging the gap: what have we done and what more can we do to reduce the burden of avoidable death in people with psychotic illness? Epidemiol. Psychiatr. Sci. 1−6.

Suetani, S., Waterreus, A., Morgan, V., Foley, D.L., Galletly, C., Badcock, J.C., Watts, G., Mckinnon, A., Castle, D., Saha, S., Scott, J.G., Mcgrath, J.J., 2016b. Correlates of physical activity in people living with psychotic illness. Acta Psychiatr. Scand. n/a.

Tek, C., Kucukgoncu, S., Guloksuz, S., Woods, S.W., Srihari, V.H., Annamalai, A., 2015. Antipsychotic-induced weight gain in first-episode psychosis patients: a meta-analysis of differential effects of antipsychotic medications. Early Interv. Psychiatry. https://doi.org/10.1111/eip.12251.

Thibeault, C.A., Trudeau, K., D'entremont, M., Brown, T., 2010. Understanding the milieu experiences of patients on an acute inpatient psychiatric unit. Arch. Psychiatr. Nurs. 24 (4), 216−226.

Tipton, C.M., 2014. The history of "Exercise Is Medicine" in ancient civilizations. Adv. Physiol. Educ. 38 (2), 109.

Van Citters, A.D., Pratt, S.I., Jue, K., Williams, G., Miller, P.T., Xie, H., Bartels, S.J., 2010. A pilot evaluation of the in shape individualized health promotion intervention for adults with mental illness. Community Ment. Health J. 46 (6), 540–552.

Vancampfort, D., DE Hert, M., Skjerven, L.H., Gyllensten, A.L., Parker, A., Mulders, N., Nyboe, L., Spencer, F., Probst, M., 2012. International organization of physical therapy in mental health consensus on physical activity within multidisciplinary rehabilitation programmes for minimising cardio-metabolic risk in patients with schizophrenia. Disabil. Rehabil. 34 (1), 1–12.

Vancampfort, D., Stubbs, B., Venigalla, S.K., Probst, M., 2015. Adopting and maintaining physical activity behaviours in people with severe mental illness: the importance of autonomous motivation. Prev. Med. 81, 216–220.

Vancampfort, D., Rosenbaum, S., Schuch, F., Ward, P.B., Richards, J., Mugisha, J., Probst, M., Stubbs, B., 2016a. Cardiorespiratory fitness in severe mental illness: a systematic review and meta-analysis. Sports Med. 47 (2), 343–352.

Vancampfort, D., Rosenbaum, S., Schuch, F.B., Ward, P.B., Probst, M., Stubbs, B., 2016b. Prevalence and predictors of treatment dropout from physical activity interventions in schizophrenia: a meta-analysis. Gen. Hosp. Psychiatr. 39, 15–23.

Vancampfort, D., Stubbs, B., Probst, M., DE Hert, M., Schuch, F.B., Mugisha, J., Ward, P.B., Rosenbaum, S., 2016c. Physical activity as a vital sign in patients with schizophrenia: evidence and clinical recommendations. Schizophr. Res. 170 (2), 336–340.

Walker, E., Mcgee, R.E., Druss, B.G., 2015. Mortality in mental disorders and global disease burden implications: a systematic review and meta-analysis. JAMA Psychiatry 72 (4), 334–341.

Wynaden, D., Barr, L., Omari, O., Fulton, A., 2012. Evaluation of service users' experiences of participating in an exercise programme at the western australian state forensic mental health services. Int. J. Ment. Health Nurs. 21 (3), 229–235.

# Integrating Physical Activity Into Routine Medical Care: The Physician's Perspective

*Martha Ward[1], Aniyizhai Annamalai[2],*
*Lydia Chwastiak[3]*

[1] Departments of Psychiatry and Behavioral Sciences and Medicine, Emory University, Atlanta, GA, United States; [2] Departments of Medicine and Psychiatry, Yale University, New Haven, CT, United States; [3] Department of Psychiatry and Behavioral Sciences, University of Washington School of Medicine, Seattle, WA, United States

## OUTLINE

*Exercise-Based Interventions for Mental Illness*
https://doi.org/10.1016/B978-0-12-812605-9.00014-9

# INTRODUCTION

Exercise is a very powerful tool for both the treatment and prevention of chronic disease, for mitigating the harmful effects of obesity, and for lowering mortality rates (Klein et al., 2004). In fact, there is a linear relationship between activity level and health status. People who maintain an active way of life live longer, healthier lives. In contrast, physical *inactivity* has an astonishing array of harmful health effects. People who live sedentary lives begin to suffer prematurely from chronic disease and die at a younger age. Patients with mental illness—in particular, those with serious mental illnesses (SMI) such as schizophrenia—are much more likely than the general population to live a sedentary lifestyle, placing them at risk for chronic medical conditions and poorer outcomes (Druss et al., 2011). Regular physical activity as a component of a healthy lifestyle may be especially critical for persons with SMIs, who have a life expectancy that is more than decade shorter than that of the general population (Druss et al., 2011). Research on this "mortality gap" has found that 67% of deaths among people with mental illness were due to chronic medical conditions: persons with SMI experience higher standardized mortality ratios compared with the general population for cardiovascular, respiratory, and infectious diseases. Cardiovascular disease and its associated metabolic risk factors are the largest contributors to this early mortality (Compton et al., 2006; Osborn et al., 2007).

The relationship between mental illness, medical comorbidity, and premature mortality is complex and multifactorial. Adverse social determinants of health, metabolic side effects of psychotropic medication, and lack of access to quality medical care are partly to blame (Druss and

Walker, 2011; Druss et al., 2016; Newcomer, 2005). Modifiable risk behaviors—in particular, poor health behaviors such as lack of physical activity—are the cause of much of the morbidity and early mortality related to chronic diseases (www.cdc.gov/chronicdisease/overview/index.htm).

Physicians in both primary care and mental health specialty settings are a trusted source of health information and should therefore play a central role in delivering effective physical activity interventions for patients with SMI. The role of the physician should include (1) routine screening and assessment of patients' level of physical activity; (2) counseling patients about recommended levels of physical activity, including "prescribing" physical activity; and (3) providing referrals to evidence-based physical activity programs and supporting engagement with these interventions.

## RESEARCH EVIDENCE

### Physician Counselling

Physicians can provide a "prescription" (or brief advice) for physical activity to help support a patient in making changes in current levels or type of physical activity (Grandes et al., 2009). Guidelines from around the globe recommend that health care providers counsel their patients to engage in physical activity in order to improve health (EU Physical Activity Guidelines, 2008; Global recommendations on physical activity for health, 2010) based on research supporting the effectiveness of primary care clinician counseling to increase physical activity (Elley et al., 2003). Despite these expert recommendations and guidelines, routine physical activity screening is rare in actual primary care practice (Joy et al., 2013; Lobelo et al., 2014). And, despite the clear health benefits and the evidence supporting physician counseling, rates of physician counseling for physical activity remain low. Data from the 2010 US National Health Interview Survey revealed that less than one-third of all adults who visited a physician in the last year were advised by their physician to start or continue exercising (Barnes and Schoenborn, 2012).

Primary care providers (PCPs) have been identified as ideal candidates for counseling their patients on physical activity, given their contact with a large percentage of the population and the trusted relationships they have with patients (AuYoung et al., 2016). However, many individuals with mental illness (particularly those with SMI) underuse primary care services (Position Statement 16, 2012). Because persons with SMI are more likely to receive care through outpatient mental health centers than primary care, psychiatrists may be the only health care providers that these individuals engage with (Alakeson and Frank, 2010). Increasingly, both professional organizations and patient advocacy groups have acknowledged the need for psychiatrists to address physical health, including physical activity (Position Statement on the Role of Psychiatrists, 2015).

## Evidence-Based Lifestyle Interventions

The 2014 National Institute for Health and Care Excellence Guidelines for the treatment of adults with schizophrenia recommend that mental health care providers should offer a combined healthy eating and physical activity program to patients with schizophrenia or other psychotic disorders, especially those taking antipsychotic medications (www.nice.org.uk/guidance/cg178/evidence/full-guideline-490503565). Lifestyle interventions, which include regular physical activity and dietary changes, are a key strategy for the prevention and treatment of cardiovascular disease (CVD) and related comorbidities. Data show that 5% or greater weight loss is clinically significant, as it can result in decreased risk of cardiovascular disease. Moreover, improved fitness (independent of weight loss) decreases CVD-associated mortality (Klein et al., 2004). More than 18 clinical trials have been published on lifestyle modification interventions that are effective among persons with SMI (McGinty et al., 2016). These studies indicate that lifestyle programs which are of longer duration (three or more months) consist of a manualized, combined education- and activity-based approach, and incorporate both nutrition and physical exercise are likely to be the most effective in reducing weight, improving physical fitness, and improving overall health (Bartels and Desilets, 2012). Large-scale randomized controlled trials (Daumit et al., 2013a) suggest that up to 40% of patients can achieve clinically significant weight loss. This may be particularly important among young adults experiencing a first episode of psychosis, given that this population presents an opportunity for primary prevention (Phutane et al., 2011), and the observation that weight gain and adverse metabolic effects appear to begin within the first 2 months of treatment (Kane et al., 2016).

People with SMI have limited access to evidence-based lifestyle programs despite substantial research support for their effectiveness. Such programs are not typically available at community mental health centers, where most persons with SMI seek care (Gierisch et al., 2014 #1689). Locating lifestyle modification groups at community mental health centers represents an opportunity to deliver evidence-based health promotion interventions in a setting that is more convenient and comfortable for many individuals with SMI and facilitates the integration of physical activity goals into mental health treatment, capitalizing on frequent clinical contacts with case managers, peers, nurses, and psychiatrists to reinforce patient goals and progress. Lifestyle modification group facilitators can interact directly with clinical providers to evaluate the risk of adverse metabolic effects of the client's pharmacologic regimen. Clinical providers can support attendance at groups and assist clients in practical ways to attain their goals.

## "EXERCISE IS MEDICINE"

Given the research evidence that even brief counseling and simple behavior changes such as pedometer programs can significantly increase levels of physical activity among patients (Bravata et al., 2007; Reid and Morgan, 1979), the "Exercise is Medicine" (EIM) initiative was established in 2007 by American College of Sports Medicine and the American Medical Association (Sallis, 2009). The stated goal of the EIM initiative is "to make physical activity assessment and exercise prescription a standard part of the disease prevention and treatment paradigm for all patients." One of the basic tenets of EIM is that clinicians should regard physical activity as a vital sign. They should assess exercise habits of all patients and administer a physical activity or exercise prescription when appropriate. The exercise vital sign is a simple way to introduce the topic of exercise into the exam room with every patient (Sallis, 2011). It is important for physicians to counsel patients and help remove barriers to physical activity and make physical activity a habit, not an option.

### Barriers: Patient Factors

Psychiatric symptoms can present barriers to effective counseling on the benefits of physical activity. Amotivation is common in both psychotic and depressive disorders and can contribute to a lack of engagement with the provider and poor adherence to recommendations. Among patients with psychosis, positive symptoms, including paranoia and hallucinations, may impair attention and have been shown to impact the development of a therapeutic alliance with providers (Kilbourne et al., 2006; Lester et al., 2003). Patients with schizophrenia can experience cognitive impairment, including deficits in memory, processing speed, and executive function (Reichenberg et al., 2009). Such deficits may impair patients' ability to process and retain information regarding exercise recommendations and to plan and enact exercise goals. Many medications used to treat psychiatric disorders (particularly antipsychotics and mood stabilizers) can cause sedation, which can impair attention during physician visits. Extrapyramidal side effects of antipsychotic medications, such as tremor, bradykinesia, and rigidity, can make exercise challenging and uncomfortable.

Individuals with mental illness also disproportionately face many of the same barriers to physical activity as the general population. These barriers include low-income status, pre-existing poor health, overweight or obesity, and the perception that great effort is needed to exercise (Reichert et al., 2007; Trost et al., 2002; Wilcox et al., 2000). Overweight and obesity are also highly prevalent in persons with mental illness. Those with SMI are twice as likely as individuals without mental illness to be overweight or obese, and these conditions can present challenges to physical activity (Consensus development conference, 2004; Weil et al., 2002).

Socioeconomic disadvantage is associated with mental illness, particularly more SMI (Muntaner et al., 2004). This disadvantage may create barriers to affording gym memberships and appropriate clothing and shoes for exercise. Exercising outdoors may not be a viable option for individuals with low-income status, as they often live in areas where the environment is unsafe due to traffic and violent crime (Estabrooks et al., 2003; Powell et al., 2006). Social isolation is common in persons with mental illness, and this can lead to lack of social contacts to accompany patients during physical activity. Moreover, many individuals with SMI live in group homes, where sedentary lifestyle is the norm, and community examples of physical activity are rare.

## OVERCOMING BARRIERS

What can busy physicians do during an office visit to encourage physical activity in a patient? Research suggests that the most effective strategy to support routine physician screening and counseling about physical activity is a multilevel approach to overcome patient, physician, and systems-level barriers. The "5As" model is a promising approach, given its efficacy in counseling for other health behavior change, such as tobacco cessation (Quinn et al., 2009). This model focuses on the steps that a provider may take in guiding patients toward realistic, proximal goals for behavior change (assess, advise, agree, assist, and arrange).

| | | |
|---|---|---|
| **Assess** | Physical activity level<br>Physical abilities<br>Beliefs and knowledge | Individual<br><br>"How much exercise do you currently get each day?"<br><br>"What kinds of things make it hard to exercise?" |
| **Advise** | Health risks<br>Benefits of change<br>Appropriate "dose" of physical activity | Health Policy<br><br>"The national guidelines recommend at least 150 minutes of moderate activity each week. I strongly recommend that you begin to move around more regularly. We always recommend starting from where you are and building up slowly." |
| **Agree** | Co-develop personalized action plan<br>Set specific physical activity goals based on interests and confidence level | Social Support<br><br>"I understand that you have a busy work and family schedule. How do you feel about starting with 20-minute walks for 3 days next week? Maybe you could also use that time to spend with your daughter?" |
| **Assist** | Identify barriers and create strategies to address them<br>Identify resources for physical activity and social support | Community Resources<br><br>"Do you have a gym, park, trail system, or other safe place to be active near your home or workplace?" |
| **Arrange** | Specify plan for follow-up (e.g., visits, phone calls, text messages)<br>Check on progress/ maintenance of physical activity change | Provider/Team<br><br>"We would like to hear about how the walking is going for you. The nurse will call you in one week to check in and see if you have any questions or concerns." |

## Assess

Routine screening of physical activity should be implemented in primary care and psychiatric settings. While it has been suggested that physical activity level should be the fifth vital sign, only a few organizations currently prioritize such screening in a systematic manner (Sallis, 2011). Use of physician time can be optimized through implementation of standardized screening protocols. Screening for physical activity levels can be done at each appointment, by a nurse or medical assistant. By making this a routine "fifth vital sign," the discussion concerning physical activity has begun before the patient arrives in the physician's exam room. Data show that such screening can be completed in less than 1 min (AuYoung et al., 2016).

Lack of routine screening also greatly impacts psychiatrists' ability to deliver physical activity counseling to their patients. Visits to community psychiatrists do not typically include routine vital signs, much less physical activity levels. Multiple studies show a lack of routine metabolic monitoring for persons prescribed atypical antipsychotics, despite national recommendations to do so (the American Diabetes Association, the American Psychiatric Association, the European Psychiatric Association, and the Spanish Societies of Psychiatry and Biological Psychiatry; Ward et al., 2015).

## Advise

The physician should take 2–3 min to counsel patients on their physical activity, reviewing key messages about the importance of physical activity to health, particularly about the patient's conditions or concerns. A physician can provide an exercise prescription in a busy clinical setting using the FITT mnemonic. "F" stands for frequency, and the ideal frequency of exercise is five or more days of the week. "I" stands for intensity, and the recommended intensity of exercise is at the moderate level, which can be gauged by a heart rate that is roughly 50%–70% of maximum. Maximum heart rate can be estimated by subtracting the patient's age from 220. A much simpler way to estimate intensity of exercise is by using the "sing–talk" test (Foster et al., 2008). During moderate exercise, a patient would not be able to sing but should be able to talk. Moderate exercise should not be exceedingly uncomfortable to engage in. The first "T" stands for type of exercise. The type is not too important, as long as the exercise works for large muscle groups and is something that the patient enjoys. The second "T" stands for time spent exercising, which should be 30 min. So, a simple exercise prescription would be to advise the patient to walk 30 min at a brisk pace for 5 days each week.

Patients should understand that although 150 min per week of moderate–vigorous activity is the goal, it does not have to be the starting point (Sallis, 2015). It is important for patients who currently engage in no physical activity to start off slowly, with 1–2 days a week and to gradually try to increase. Studies show that three 10-min bouts of exercise on any given day work just as well to benefit health as 30 sustained min (US Department of Health and Human Services. Physical activity and health: a report of the surgeon general. U.S. Department of Health and Human Services, Centers for Disease Control and Prevention, National Center for Chronic Disease Prevention and Health Promotion; Atlanta, GA: 1996). Any amount of exercise has a positive impact on health, and patients should take every opportunity to engage in physical activity. This may involve parking their car further away or taking the stairs rather than the elevator.

## Agree

Assessment of physical activity by the medical assistant emphasizes to the patient that physical activity is important to one's health. Even if the physician has less than 1 min to offer advice, they can acknowledge patients' current level of activity. Physicians can congratulate patients who are getting the 150 min of moderate–vigorous physical activity per week needed to be healthy and encourage them to continue. Physicians should encourage patients not meeting this threshold to try to become more active by explaining the connections to existing chronic medical conditions and the effect that such conditions have on their overall quality of life. For example, in a patient with obesity and osteoarthritis presenting with a chief complaint of chronic pain, the importance of exercise in decreasing their pain level may be highlighted.

## Assist

If the physician has any additional time for counseling, she/he might assess the patient's readiness for change regarding exercise and ask what the patient would want to do to be more active and what barriers are preventing this from happening. The physician might suggest useful resources such as a pedometer (with a daily goal of 8000 to 10,000 steps), an exercise class at the YMCA, using an exercise DVD, or a local fitness professional.

Walking should be considered the default exercise prescription. It is accessible for all ages and fitness levels and can be done alone or in groups in almost any setting. Walking is low-cost and does not require a gym or specialized equipment. It is also easy to measure walking using a pedometer or a stopwatch or by marking off a specific distance. Walking is the most common form of adult activity and has generally good long-term adherence.

## Arrange

Physicians should be aware of community resources which might support their patients' regular physical activity so that they can make referrals to effective treatment. In addition, technological advances may help overcome some of the barriers to physical activity. State-of-the-art wearable technology is increasingly popular, or patients can use even a basic pedometer to track physical activity at a low cost. Smartphone use is also common, and patients can take advantage of applications that support self-monitoring of activity, instruct on types of physical activity, monitor personal health information, or provide exercise videos. For individuals without a strong social network, virtual support groups can be accessed through websites, apps, and forums (AuYoung et al., 2016).

## Evidence-Based Lifestyle Interventions

Physicians may rely on other health care team members to counsel on physical activity. When available, physicians can refer patients to health coaches or health psychologists within their own practice. Physicians should also take advantage of lifestyle interventions within their organization or within the community. Physicians may identify relevant community resources through local health departments, health-related organizations, or national campaigns for health. Local community or senior centers, churches, and schools may offer free exercise classes or free childcare to allow the caregiver to partake in physical activity. Such community resources can build social networks and address some of the barriers associated with poverty (such as cost of gym membership or safe places to exercise; AuYoung et al., 2016).

Interventions done in group settings may improve engagement, bolster social connections, and reduce attrition (Roberts and Bailey, 2011). Other patient factors can be addressed in the group setting as well. Incentivizing participants with modest rewards (e.g., gift certificates, token systems) can target amotivation (Kemp et al., 2009; Loh et al., 2006; Roberts and Bailey, 2011). Intervention content can be structured to mitigate cognitive deficits, including simplified handout materials, materials in large font sizes, and frequent quizzes to reinforce lessons (Cabassa et al., 2010). The ACHIEVE study tailored their intervention specifically to address cognitive issues by dividing information into smaller sections and utilizing repetition to solidify important concepts (Daumit et al., 2013b). Provider factors can also have a positive effect on patient motivation; and staff can effectively model healthy behaviors alongside patients to improve adherence and solidify therapeutic alliance (Loh et al., 2006).

## Optimizing Pharmacotherapy for Psychosis

Effectively treating the symptoms of mental illness is essential to patients' understanding, processing, and accomplishing physical activity goals. Optimizing psychiatric medication management must be a top priority, and PCPs should consult with psychiatric colleagues to achieve this. Side effects of psychotropic medications (including sedation, extrapyramidal symptoms (EPS), and weight gain) can also interfere with effective physical activity counseling. Sedating effects of medication can be mitigated by timing exercise, and education sessions in the early morning before medications are administered or later in the day when the side effects have had time to wear off. When weight gain occurs as a side effect of psychotropic medications, particularly with use of second-generation antipsychotics, switching to a less metabolically active medication can lead to weight loss and reduction in non-high-density lipoprotein cholesterol

(Stroup et al., 2011). Psychiatrists may elect to make such a medication change in order to target weight gain and obesity, while also weighing the risk of psychiatric decompensation (De Hert et al., 2012).

## Addressing Social Determinants of Health

Low socioeconomic status is associated with decreased likelihood of regular physical activity. Physicians can help patients with limited resources to problem solve their barriers for regular physical activity. For example, walking up and down the stairs in their residence can circumvent an unsafe neighborhood (Lowe and Lubos, 2008). Other options include distributing exercise videos or handouts or providing gym memberships. Multiple reviews report providing YMCA memberships as an effective intervention, and this may be an option for community mental health agencies (Loh et al., 2006; Roberts and Bailey, 2011). In-clinic exercise sessions may also overcome economic barriers to physical activity. For example, Bradshaw et al. discuss the use of in-clinic stationary bicycles (Bradshaw et al., 2005), and Roberts et al. report the use of in-clinic treadmills (Roberts and Bailey, 2011). Providers can investigate free local resources, such as senior centers, as potential sites for fitness activities. Outdoor recreational activities in small groups may have the added benefit of fostering social connectedness (Kemp et al., 2009).

## Barriers: Provider Factors

Provider factors also impede effective physical activity counseling by physicians. Time limitations present a substantial barrier for PCPs, who have increasingly heavy workloads and serve a large volume of patients with ever shorter visit times. Patient complexity in the primary care setting is high, with roughly one in four primary care patients presenting with multimorbidity (Clark, 2011). PCPs address, on average, three medical problems per visit (AuYoung et al., 2016). With many competing priorities, exercise counseling may fall lower on the list. Stigma also impacts physician engagement in counseling their patients with mental illness. Reports from both individuals with SMI and healthcare providers suggest that general practitioners place too much emphasis on the symptoms of mental illness, while medical concerns are given lower priority (McCabe and Leas, 2008). Moreover, medical professionals report that they see mentally ill patients as disruptive and increase the workload of the practice. Feelings of fear and frustration may lead physicians to withdraw from patients, impacting the quality of the service provided (McCabe and Leas, 2008). While there have been no studies on the impact of stigma on rates of physical activity counseling, there is substantial evidence that patients with mental illness receive fewer standard of care interventions for their physical health. For example, patients with psychosis have lower odds of receiving diabetes standard of care monitoring (such as routine eye examination, as well as testing of hemoglobin A1c and lipids; Parks J., 2006).

Despite facing many of the same challenges, there is some evidence that psychiatrists may engage their patients in physical activity counseling at a higher rate than primary care physicians. One study in the United States shows that approximately 60% of health care providers in one community mental health center provided recommendations on physical activity to more than half of their patients (Chwastiak et al., 2013). Psychiatrists are uniquely positioned to deliver physical activity counseling to persons with mental illness, given their familiarity and expertise with the unique needs of this population, and their training in behavioral therapy and counseling may increase comfort and self-efficacy in such interventions. The willingness of psychiatrists to address physical health appears to depend, at least in part, on their general knowledge level (Vanderlip et al., 2016). PCPs similarly may lack skills in counseling on physical activity. This lack of training may lead to a low perceived self-efficacy in their ability to effectively counsel their patients on physical activity.

## TRAINING AND EDUCATION

Physicians perceive a lack of knowledge and training about physical activity as one important barrier to counseling their patients about physical activity (Hebert et al., 2012). Traditionally, neither graduate nor postgraduate medical education has included specific training about nutrition or physical activity, in addition to system-level barriers.

### Current Graduate and Postgraduate Training Programs

Very few medical schools provide education on physical activity in their curricula. A systematic review of behavioral counseling curricula in medical training found that physical activity was the least addressed among all behavioral interventions (Hauer et al., 2012).

With respect to postgraduate training, an analysis of 25 primary care (family medicine, internal medicine, and obstetrics/gynecology) programs in Ohio found that only 10 programs taught techniques for health behavior counseling. Among these, less than 3 h weekly, on average, were spent on didactics related to obesity, nutrition, and physical activity counseling (Antognoli et al., 2016). A separate survey of 115 US pediatric residency programs reported similarly low rates of specific training on the topic: 26% had a curriculum for physical activity counseling (Goff et al.,

2010), and these programs were focused on knowledge, with limited training in counseling skills. Most US psychiatry residency programs do not offer much general medical training beyond the required 4 months in the first year of residency (Annamalai et al., 2014). While a few psychiatry residency programs have developed specialized modules or tracks for teaching preventive care for people with mental illness (Annamalai et al., 2015), there is no published report of training devoted to lifestyle counseling in psychiatry residency curricula.

There is clearly a discrepancy between the emphasis on addressing health behaviors in clinical settings and the education health care providers receive during medical training. To fill this gap, education and training about nutrition and physical activity must be incorporated into multiple levels of medical training. Educators should determine the optimal strategies to teach these skills by reviewing the existing curricula and rigorously evaluating new curricular designs.

## Curricular Content

A systematic review of physical activity counseling in medical education found significant heterogeneity across programs in length and intensity of training. The authors identified certain characteristics of training that increase the likelihood that medical students will provide counseling in visits with patients (Dacey et al., 2014):

1. Medical training that provides opportunities for students to maintain regular physical activity because students who are more physically active are likely to counsel patients on physical activity.
2. A combination of didactics and (either simulated or real) clinical practice experience.
3. Teaching of conceptual frameworks and counseling models that illustrate behavior changes (such as motivational interviewing) are found in the more successful programs.
4. Integration of physical activity counseling into existing programs which address health promotion activities.

In the study of primary care programs, both residents and faculty reported that teaching health behavior techniques was associated with greater counseling self-efficacy (compared with knowledge-based education on nutrition and physical activity). A longer duration of training, increased number of continuity clinic days, and dedicated fellowships for health behavior counseling were all associated with increased counseling self-efficacy (Antognoli et al., 2016). Interestingly, residents in the different disciplines appeared to have different perspectives. Family medicine residents were more likely than internal medicine and obstetrics/gynecology residents to view lifestyle counseling as an integral part of their training. In the study of 115 pediatric programs, the majority of program directors agreed that counseling in physical activity was an important part of training. Directors from those programs which did not have a curriculum were less likely to believe that pediatricians could influence patients' physical activity behavior.

Psychiatry residency programs, in contrast, typically do include education training in motivational interviewing skills and education about counseling—but this training rarely focuses on physical activity. Education about the conceptual framework and practical training in motivational interviewing skills provides a tremendous opportunity for training on lifestyle counseling. Indeed, psychiatric organizations have encouraged psychiatrists to assume a larger a role in their patients' preventive care (APA Position Statement on Accountability for Persons with Serious Mental Illness, 2016).

### Barriers: Systems Factors

Reimbursement for physician counseling on physical activity varies according to health system. In the United States, the Centers for Medicare and Medicaid now offer reimbursement to physicians for obesity counseling (which generally includes counseling on physical activity). However, there continues to be no reimbursement for counseling of nonobese patients or for counseling done in group format or by nonphysicians (AuYoung et al., 2016). Limited resources for outreach to patients who are not engaged in care presents another system-level barrier to PCPs addressing physical activity. Individuals that do not receive regular medical care miss opportunities to receive counseling, and individuals with SMI are less likely to engage in regular primary care (Alakeson and Frank, 2010).

## CONCLUSION/SUMMARY

Physical activity is a very powerful tool to treat and prevent chronic disease, mitigate the harmful effects of obesity, and lower mortality rates. Exercise has a powerful effect on functional capacity and quality of life. Regular physical activity may be particularly important for individuals with SMI, who are more likely to have a sedentary lifestyle and are at increased risk of obesity, diabetes, and CVD. For these reasons, primary care physicians and psychiatrists have a responsibility to assess physical activity habits in their patients, inform them of the risk of being inactive, and provide a proper exercise prescription. Expert consensus panels have provided recommendations for physicians to assess and counsel patients about physical activity that are simple, brief, and effective. There is a need for specific training of medical students and postgraduate trainees in health behavior counseling. Work is also needed to train the existing workforce of physicians in this practice and provide system-level supports to make this screening and assessment part of routine clinical care.

## RECOMMENDATIONS FOR OVERCOMING BARRIERS TO COUNSELING PATIENTS WITH MENTAL ILLNESS ON PHYSICAL ACTIVITY

### Patient Factors

- Optimally treat psychiatric symptoms with pharmacotherapy
- Address side effects of psychotropic medications, such as weight gain or sedation
- Use games, quizzes, repetition, simplified formats, and visual aids to overcome cognitive impairment
- Tailor recommendations to account for poverty and unsafe environments
  - Walking as the default exercise recommendation
- Use group settings to improve engagement and social connections
- Use technological advances (such as smartphone apps) to assist patients in monitoring physical activity and to patients to social support through virtual groups

### Physician Factors

- Set aside 2–3 min in each appointment to counsel for physical activity, using the 5A's (assess, advise, agree, assist, and arrange)
- Give an "exercise prescription" using the FITT pneumonic: frequency, intensity, type, and time.
- Use a team approach to most effectively use the physician's time
  - Nurses or medical assistants screen for exercise at each appointment
  - Refer patients to psychologists or health coaches for counseling
  - Know local resources for group interventions
- Increase training for physicians on counseling for physical activity
  - Should include both didactic and clinical components

### Systems Factors

- Routinely screen for physical activity: make exercise the "fifth vital sign"

# References

Alakeson, V., Frank, R.G., 2010. Health care reform and mental health care delivery. Psychiatr. Serv. 61 (11), 1063. https://doi.org/10.1176/ps.2010.61.11.1063.

Annamalai, A., Rohrbaugh, R.M., Sernyak, M.J., 2014. Status of general medicine training and education in psychiatry residency. Acad. Psychiatry 38 (4), 473—475. https://doi.org/10.1007/s40596-014-0106-y.

Annamalai, A., Rohrbaugh, R.M., Sernyak, M.J., 2015. General medicine training in psychiatry residency. Acad. Psychiatry 39 (4), 437—441. https://doi.org/10.1007/s40596-015-0344-7.

Antognoli, E.L., Seeholzer, E.L., Gullett, H., Jackson, B., Smith, S., Flocke, S.A., 2016. Primary care resident training for obesity, nutrition, and physical activity counseling: a mixed-methods study. Health Promot. Pract. https://doi.org/10.1177/1524839916658025.

AuYoung, M., Linke, S.E., Pagoto, S., Buman, M.P., Craft, L.L., Richardson, C.R., Sheinfeld Gorin, S., 2016. Integrating physical activity in primary care practice. Am. J. Med. 129 (10), 1022—1029. https://doi.org/10.1016/j.amjmed.2016.02.008.

Barnes, P.A., Schoenborn, C.A., 2012. Trends in Adults Receiving a Recommendation for Exercise or Other Physical Activity from a Physician or Other Health Professional. Retrieved from. https://www.cdc.gov/nchs/data/databriefs/db86.htm.

Bartels, S., Desilets R., Health Promotion Programs for People with Serious Mental Illness, 2012, Retrieved from. http://www.narbha.org/includes/media/docs/Health-Promotion-Whilte-Paper-Bartels-Final-Documents.pdf.

Bradshaw, T., Lovell, K., Harris, N., 2005. Healthy living interventions and schizophrenia: a systematic review. J. Adv. Nurs. 49 (6), 634—654. https://doi.org/10.1111/j.1365-2648.2004.03338.x.

Bravata, D.M., Smith-Spangler, C., Sundaram, V., Gienger, A.L., Lin, N., Lewis, R., Sirard, J.R., 2007. Using pedometers to increase physical activity and improve health: a systematic review. Jama 298 (19), 2296—2304. https://doi.org/10.1001/jama.298.19.2296.

Cabassa, L.J., Ezell, J.M., Lewis-Fernandez, R., 2010. Lifestyle interventions for adults with serious mental illness: a systematic literature review. Psychiatr. Serv. 61 (8), 774—782. https://doi.org/10.1176/appi.ps.61.8.774.

Chwastiak, L., Cruza-Guet, M.C., Carroll-Scott, A., Sernyak, M., Ickovics, J., 2013. Preventive counseling for chronic disease: missed opportunities in a community mental health center. Psychosomatics 54 (4), 328—335. https://doi.org/10.1016/j.psym.2012.10.003.

Clark, N.M., 2011. The multiple challenges of multiple morbidities. Health Educ. Behav. 38 (3), 219—221. https://doi.org/10.1177/1090198111410554.

Compton, M.T., Daumit, G.L., Druss, B.G., 2006. Cigarette smoking and overweight/obesity among individuals with serious mental illnesses: a preventive perspective. Harv. Rev. Psychiatry 14 (4), 212—222. https://doi.org/10.1080/10673220600889256.

Consensus development conference on antipsychotic drugs, obesity and diabetes, 2004. Diabetes Care 27 (2), 596—601.

Dacey, M.L., Kennedy, M.A., Polak, R., Phillips, E.M., 2014. Physical activity counseling in medical school education: a systematic review. Med. Educ. Online 19, 24325. https://doi.org/10.3402/meo.v19.24325.

Daumit, G.L., Dickerson, F.B., Appel, L.J., 2013a. Weight loss in persons with serious mental illness. N. Engl. J. Med. 369 (5), 486—487. https://doi.org/10.1056/NEJMc1306994.

Daumit, G.L., Dickerson, F.B., Wang, N.Y., Dalcin, A., Jerome, G.J., Anderson, C.A., Appel, L.J., 2013b. A behavioral weight-loss intervention in persons with serious mental illness. N. Engl. J. Med. 368 (17), 1594—1602. https://doi.org/10.1056/NEJMoa1214530.

De Hert, M., Detraux, J., van Winkel, R., Yu, W., Correll, C.U., 2012. Metabolic and cardiovascular adverse effects associated with antipsychotic drugs. Nat. Rev. Endocrinol. 8 (2), 114—126. https://doi.org/10.1038/nrendo.2011.156.

Druss, B.G., Walker, E.R., 2011. The Synthesis Project: Mental Disorders and Medical Comorbidity. Retrieved from. http://www.ibhpartners.org/wp-content/uploads/2015/12/co-occurring-disorders-Druss.pdf.

Druss, B.G., Zhao, L., Von Esenwein, S., Morrato, E.H., Marcus, S.C., 2011. Understanding excess mortality in persons with mental illness: 17-year follow up of a nationally representative US survey. Med. Care 49 (6), 599−604. https://doi.org/10.1097/MLR.0b013e31820bf86e.

Druss, B.G., von Esenwein, S.A., Glick, G.E., Deubler, E., Lally, C., Ward, M.C., Rask, K.J., 2016. Randomized trial of an integrated behavioral health home: the health outcomes management and evaluation (HOME) study. Am. J. Psychiatry. https://doi.org/10.1176/appi.ajp.2016.16050507.

Elley, C.R., Kerse, N., Arroll, B., Robinson, E., 2003. Effectiveness of counselling patients on physical activity in general practice: cluster randomised controlled trial. BMJ 326 (7393), 793. https://doi.org/10.1136/bmj.326.7393.793.

Estabrooks, P.A., Glasgow, R.E., Dzewaltowski, D.A., 2003. Physical activity promotion through primary care. J. Am. Med. Assoc. 289 (22), 2913−2916. https://doi.org/10.1001/jama.289.22.2913.

EU Physical Activity Guidelines: Recommended Policy Actions in Support of Health-Enhancing Physical Activity, 2008. European Union Working Group "Sport & Health", Brussels.

Foster, C., Porcari, J.P., Anderson, J., Paulson, M., Smaczny, D., Webber, H., Udermann, B., 2008. The talk test as a marker of exercise training intensity. J. Cardiopulm. Rehabil. Prev. 28 (1), 24−30. https://doi.org/10.1097/01.HCR.0000311504.41775.78 quiz 31-22.

Gierisch, J.M., Nieuwsma, J.A., Bradford, D.W., Wilder, C.M., Mann-Wrobel, M.C., McBroom, A.J., Hasselblad, V., Williams Jr., J.W., May 2014. Pharmacologic and behavioral interventions to improve cardiovascular risk factors in adults with serious mental illness: a systematic review and meta-analysis. J. Clin. Psychiatry 75 (5), e424−e440.

WHO, 2010. Global Recommendations on Physical Activity for Health. World Health Organization. Retrieved from. http://www.who.int/dietphysicalactivity/publications/9789241599979/en/.

Goff, S.L., Holboe, E.S., Concato, J., 2010. Pediatricians and physical activity counseling: how does residency prepare them for this task? Teach. Learn. Med. 22 (2), 107−111. https://doi.org/10.1080/10401331003656512.

Grandes, G., Sanchez, A., Sanchez-Pinilla, R.O., Torcal, J., Montoya, I., Lizarraga, K., Group, P., 2009. Effectiveness of physical activity advice and prescription by physicians in routine primary care: a cluster randomized trial. Arch. Intern. Med. 169 (7), 694−701. https://doi.org/10.1001/archinternmed.2009.23.

Hauer, K.E., Carney, P.A., Chang, A., Satterfield, J., 2012. Behavior change counseling curricula for medical trainees: a systematic review. Acad. Med. 87 (7), 956−968. https://doi.org/10.1097/ACM.0b013e31825837be.

Hebert, E.T., Caughy, M.O., Shuval, K., 2012. Primary care providers' perceptions of physical activity counselling in a clinical setting: a systematic review. Br. J. Sports Med. 46 (9), 625−631. https://doi.org/10.1136/bjsports-2011-090734.

Joy, E.L., Blair, S.N., McBride, P., Sallis, R., 2013. Physical activity counselling in sports medicine: a call to action. Br. J. Sports Med. 47 (1), 49−53. https://doi.org/10.1136/bjsports-2012-091620.

Kane, J.M., Robinson, D.G., Schooler, N.R., Mueser, K.T., Penn, D.L., Rosenheck, R.A., Heinssen, R.K., 2016. Comprehensive versus usual community care for first-episode psychosis: 2-year outcomes from the NIMH RAISE early treatment program. Am. J. Psychiatry 173 (4), 362−372. https://doi.org/10.1176/appi.ajp.2015.15050632.

Kemp, V., Bates, A., Isaac, M., 2009. Behavioural interventions to reduce the risk of physical illness in persons living with mental illness. Curr. Opin. Psychiatry 22 (2), 194–199. https://doi.org/10.1097/YCO.0b013e328325a585.

Kilbourne, A.M., McCarthy, J.F., Post, E.P., Welsh, D., Pincus, H.A., Bauer, M.S., Blow, F.C., 2006. Access to and satisfaction with care comparing patients with and without serious mental illness. Int. J. Psychiatry Med. 36 (4), 383–399.

Klein, S., Burke, L.E., Bray, G.A., Blair, S., Allison, D.B., Pi-Sunyer, X., Metabolism, 2004. Clinical implications of obesity with specific focus on cardiovascular disease: a statement from professionals from the American heart association Council on nutrition, physical activity, and metabolism: endorsed by the American College of Cardiology Foundation. Circulation 110 (18), 2952–2967. https://doi.org/10.1161/01.CIR.0000145546.97738.1E.

Lester, H., Tritter, J.Q., England, E., 2003. Satisfaction with primary care: the perspectives of people with schizophrenia. Fam. Pract. 20 (5), 508–513.

Lobelo, F., Stoutenberg, M., Hutber, A., 2014. The exercise is medicine global health initiative: a 2014 update. Br. J. Sports Med. 48 (22), 1627–1633. https://doi.org/10.1136/bjsports-2013-093080.

Loh, C., Meyer, J.M., Leckband, S.G., 2006. A comprehensive review of behavioral interventions for weight management in schizophrenia. Ann. Clin. Psychiatry 18 (1), 23–31. https://doi.org/10.1080/10401230500464646.

Lowe, T., Lubos, E., 2008. Effectiveness of weight management interventions for people with serious mental illness who receive treatment with atypical antipsychotic medications. A literature review. J. Psychiatr. Ment. Health Nurs. 15 (10), 857–863. https://doi.org/10.1111/j.1365-2850.2008.01337.x.

McCabe, M.P., Leas, L., 2008. A qualitative study of primary health care access, barriers and satisfaction among people with mental illness. Psychol. Health Med. 13 (3), 303–312. https://doi.org/10.1080/13548500701473952.

McGinty, E.E., Baller, J., Azrin, S.T., Juliano-Bult, D., Daumit, G.L., 2016. Interventions to address medical conditions and health-risk behaviors among persons with serious mental illness: a comprehensive review. Schizophr. Bull. 42 (1), 96–124. https://doi.org/10.1093/schbul/sbv101.

Muntaner, C., Eaton, W.W., Miech, R., O'Campo, P., 2004. Socioeconomic position and major mental disorders. Epidemiol. Rev. 26, 53–62. https://doi.org/10.1093/epirev/mxh001.

Newcomer, J.W., 2005. Second-generation (atypical) antipsychotics and metabolic effects: a comprehensive literature review. CNS Drugs 19 (Suppl. 1), 1–93.

Osborn, D.P., Nazareth, I., King, M.B., 2007. Physical activity, dietary habits and Coronary Heart Disease risk factor knowledge amongst people with severe mental illness: a cross sectional comparative study in primary care. Soc. Psychiatry Psychiatr. Epidemiol. 42 (10), 787–793. https://doi.org/10.1007/s00127-007-0247-3.

Parks, J.S.D., Singer, P., Foti, M.E., Mauer, B., 2006. Morbidity and Mortality in People with Serious Mental Illness (Alexandria vol. A).

Phutane, V.H., Tek, C., Chwastiak, L., Ratliff, J.C., Ozyuksel, B., Woods, S.W., Srihari, V.H., 2011. Cardiovascular risk in a first-episode psychosis sample: a 'critical period' for prevention? Schizophr. Res. 127 (1–3), 257–261. https://doi.org/10.1016/j.schres.2010.12.008.

Position Statement 16: Health and Wellness for People with Serious Mental Illness, 2012. Retrieved from. http://www.nmha.org/go/position-statements/16 website.

Position Statement on the Role of Psychiatrists in Reducing Physical Health Disparities in Patients with Mental Illness, May 2015. Retrieved from. http://apps.psychiatry.org/pdfs/position-statement-role-of-psychiatrists.pdf.

Powell, L.M., Slater, S., Chaloupka, F.J., Harper, D., 2006. Availability of physical activity-related facilities and neighborhood demographic and socioeconomic characteristics: a national study. Am. J. Public Health 96 (9), 1676–1680. https://doi.org/10.2105/ajph.2005.065573.

Quinn, V.P., Hollis, J.F., Smith, K.S., Rigotti, N.A., Solberg, L.I., Hu, W., Stevens, V.J., 2009. Effectiveness of the 5-As tobacco cessation treatments in nine HMOs. J. Gen. Intern. Med. 24 (2), 149−154. https://doi.org/10.1007/s11606-008-0865-9.

Reichenberg, A., Harvey, P.D., Bowie, C.R., Mojtabai, R., Rabinowitz, J., Heaton, R.K., Bromet, E., 2009. Neuropsychological function and dysfunction in schizophrenia and psychotic affective disorders. Schizophr. Bull. 35 (5), 1022−1029. https://doi.org/10.1093/schbul/sbn044.

Reichert, F.F., Barros, A.J., Domingues, M.R., Hallal, P.C., 2007. The role of perceived personal barriers to engagement in leisure-time physical activity. Am. J. Public Health 97 (3), 515−519. https://doi.org/10.2105/ajph.2005.070144.

Reid, E.L., Morgan, R.W., 1979. Exercise prescription: a clinical trial. Am. J. Public Health 69 (6), 591−595.

Roberts, S.H., Bailey, J.E., 2011. Incentives and barriers to lifestyle interventions for people with severe mental illness: a narrative synthesis of quantitative, qualitative and mixed methods studies. J. Adv. Nurs. 67 (4), 690−708. https://doi.org/10.1111/j.1365-2648.2010.05546.x.

Sallis, R.E., 2009. Exercise is medicine and physicians need to prescribe it! Br. J. Sports Med. 43 (1), 3−4. https://doi.org/10.1136/bjsm.2008.054825.

Sallis, R., 2011. Developing healthcare systems to support exercise: exercise as the fifth vital sign. Br. J. Sports Med. 45 (6), 473−474. https://doi.org/10.1136/bjsm.2010.083469.

Sallis, R., 2015. Exercise is medicine: a call to action for physicians to assess and prescribe exercise. Phys. Sportsmed. 43 (1), 22−26. https://doi.org/10.1080/00913847.2015.1001938.

Stroup, T.S., McEvoy, J.P., Ring, K.D., Hamer, R.H., LaVange, L.M., Swartz, M.S., Schizophrenia Trials, N., 2011. A randomized trial examining the effectiveness of switching from olanzapine, quetiapine, or risperidone to aripiprazole to reduce metabolic risk: comparison of antipsychotics for metabolic problems (CAMP). Am. J. Psychiatry 168 (9), 947−956. https://doi.org/10.1176/appi.ajp.2011.10111609.

Trost, S.G., Owen, N., Bauman, A.E., Sallis, J.F., Brown, W., 2002. Correlates of adults' participation in physical activity: review and update. Med. Sci. Sports Exerc. 34 (12), 1996−2001. https://doi.org/10.1249/01.mss.0000038974.76900.92.

Vanderlip, E.R., Raney, L.E., Druss, B.G., 2016. A framework for extending psychiatrists' roles in treating general health conditions. Am. J. Psychiatry 173 (7), 658−663. https://doi.org/10.1176/appi.ajp.2015.15070950.

Ward, M.C., White, D.T., Druss, B.G., 2015. A meta-review of lifestyle interventions for cardiovascular risk factors in the general medical population: lessons for individuals with serious mental illness. J. Clin. Psychiatry 76 (4), e477−486. https://doi.org/10.4088/JCP.13r08657.

Weil, E., Wachterman, M., McCarthy, E.P., Davis, R.B., O'Day, B., Iezzoni, L.I., Wee, C.C., 2002. Obesity among adults with disabling conditions. J. Am. Med. Assoc. 288 (10), 1265−1268.

Wilcox, S., Castro, C., King, A.C., Housemann, R., Brownson, R.C., 2000. Determinants of leisure time physical activity in rural compared with urban older and ethnically diverse women in the United States. J. Epidemiol. Community Health 54 (9), 667−672.

# 15

# Overview of Mechanisms of Action of Exercise in Psychiatric Disorders and Future Directions for Research

*Chad D. Rethorst*

Psychiatry, UT Southwestern Medical Center, Dallas, TX,
United States

*Exercise-Based Interventions for Mental Illness*
https://doi.org/10.1016/B978-0-12-812605-9.00015-0

285

# EFFECTS OF EXERCISE ON THE SEROTONIN SYSTEM

Initial observations of increased serotonergic activity following exercise came from measurement of serotonin (5-HT) metabolites in blood and cerebrospinal fluid of rats (Chaouloff, 1997, 1985, 1986, 1987, 1989). Technological advances in microdialysis techniques facilitated measurement of neurotransmitter release in specific brain regions in subsequent studies. These studies indicate increases in serotonin in several brain regions in animals following acute bouts of exercise, including the hippocampus (Gomez-Merino et al., 2001; Meeusen et al., 1996; Wilson and Marsden, 1996) and the frontal cortex (Gomez-Merino et al., 2001). Furthermore, exercise results in an acute reduction in 5-HT$_{1B}$ receptor in the ventral–dorsal raphe nuclei of rats (Greenwood et al., 2005). The characteristics of the exercise bout (i.e., bout intensity and duration) appear to influence the serotonergic response to exercise. Otsuka et al. (2016) observed increases c-FOS expression in the 5-HT neurons of the dorsal raphe nucleus following low-intensity exercise. Rats in the low-intensity exercise group also demonstrated improved depression/anxiety-like behaviors in behavioral testing. Conversely the effects on 5-HT and behavior were not observed following acute bouts of high-intensity treadmill running.

Chronic exercise also results in alterations to the serotonergic system in animal models. In a series of experiments, Greenwood et al. (2003, 2005) report increases in 5-HT$_{1A}$ receptor messenger RNA (mRNA) and reduced 5-HTT mRNA in the dorsal and medial raphe nuclei following 3–6 weeks of wheel running. Furthermore, 6 weeks of wheel running attenuated stress-induced activity of 5-HT neurons in the dorsal raphe nucleus following uncontrollable tail shock (Greenwood et al., 2005). Similarly, in a study by Li et al. (2010), 10 weeks of swimming exercise resulted in increases in 5-HT in the hippocampus, and when this exercise was performed prior to chronic mild stress (footshock), exercised rats were resistant to negative behavioral consequences.

Studies in humans also highlight the effects of exercise on serotonergic functioning. Struder (Struder et al., 1999) observed increases in tryptophan and plasma prolactin, along with a reduction in 5-HT$_{2A}$ receptors on platelets following acute bouts of aerobic exercise. Jakeman et al. (1994) noted serum prolactin levels following administration of a serotonergic agonist were lower in trained individuals, suggesting lowered sensitivity of serotonin receptors. Chronically, decreased serum serotonin levels have been observed after exercise, which may be due to increased serotonin reuptake and metabolism (Wipfli et al., 2011). Further supporting the chronic effects of exercise on serotonergic function, 3 weeks of aerobic training in sedentary males increased 5-HTT and 5-HT$_{2A}$ receptors and improved mood. However, this effect is again dependent on exercise intensity and duration as overtraining resulted in a decline in $5\text{-}HT_{2A}$ receptors, declined mood, and increase in central fatigue (Struder and Weicker, 2001; Weicker and Strüder, 2001).

# EXERCISE EFFECTS ON THE DOPAMINERGIC SYSTEM

Substantial evidence supports the effects of chronic exercise on the dopaminergic system in animal models. Four to sixweeks of wheel running increased mRNA expression of tyrosine hydroxylase, the rate-limiting enzyme for dopamine synthesis (Foley and Fleshner, 2008; Kim et al., 2011). Wheel running also reduces $D_2$ autoreceptor mRNA in the substantia nigra pars compacta while increasing $D_2$ postsynaptic receptor mRNA in the caudate putamen (Foley and Fleshner, 2008). Similarly, Chen et al. (2017) found 8 weeks of treadmill exercise increased $D_2$ receptor expression and dopamine levels in the ventral tegmental area (VTA) of mice but did not affect dopamine transporter levels; while Vuckovic et al. (2010) report increased striatal $D_2$ receptor expression in the mouse basal ganglia following 6 weeks of treadmill running.

Studies have linked the changes in dopaminergic functioning described previously to behavioral characteristics. For example, 3 weeks of wheel running resulted in higher dopamine at rest and following exposure to stress (forced swim test) in the medial prefrontal cortex. However, when animals were treated with a $D_2$ receptor antagonist, the antidepressant effects of wheel running were eliminated (Chen et al., 2016). In another study, wheel running resulted in improved cognitive functioning, assessed through performance in a T-maze test. These improvements in cognitive performance, however, were reduced with administration of a $D_2$ receptor antagonist (Eddy et al., 2014).

Early studies implicated the effect of exercise on dopaminergic function in humans through analysis of peripheral markers. For example, Christensen et al. (1976) report increased plasma dopamine levels but decreased urinary excretion of dopamine in humans following an acute bout of exercise. Similarly, dopamine metabolite, homovanillic acid, was found to be increased following acute exercise (Chaouloff et al., 1986). However, a more recent study found no effect of a 30-min acute exercise bout on $D_2$ receptor in the putamen (Wang et al., 2000).

While the effect of acute exercise on dopamine receptors is unclear in humans, chronic exercise has been more consistently associated with increases in $D_2$ receptor. Dang et al. (2017) report age-related $D_2$ receptor loss is attenuated in subjects who are physically active. Two studies have also examined the effect of exercise training on $D_2$ receptor binding potential. Fisher et al. (2013) observed increased $D_2$ receptor binding following 8 weeks of exercise in subjects with early stage Parkinson's disease. Similarly, 8 weeks of exercise increased striatal $D_2/D_3$ receptor binding potential in subjects diagnosed with methamphetamine dependence (Robertson et al., 2016).

Finally, there is some evidence that dopamine is involved in the rewarding aspects of exercise and ultimately the motivation to exercise. Rats bred without $D_2$ receptors have been found to engage in less voluntary wheel running (Beeler et al., 2016). In humans, phenylalanine/tyrosine depletion reduced motivation to exercise in healthy control subjects but not in subjects recovering from anorexia nervosa (O'Hara et al., 2016).

## EFFECTS OF EXERCISE ON HYPOTHALAMIC-PITUITARY-ADRENAL AXIS

In humans a single bout of aerobic exercise (Luger et al., 1987; Rojas Vega et al., 2006) or high-intensity resistance training (McGuigan et al., 2004) results in an acute increase in cortisol levels. Hypothalamic-pituitary-adrenal (HPA) axis function is also affected by chronic exercise, as an 8-week aerobic exercise intervention results in reductions in 24-h cortisol excretion (Nabkasorn et al., 2006). Similarly, in animal studies, corticosterone is increased during initiation of chronic exercise; however, corticosterone levels normalize with continued training (Campbell et al., 2009; Fediuc et al., 2006).

Another line of research has examined exercise-induced alterations in the HPA axis response to stressful stimuli. For example, acute increases in adrenocorticotropic hormone and corticosterone in response to exercise in rats are attenuated with chronic exercise training (Watanabe et al., 1991). Similarly, and perhaps of greater relevance to exercise's utility as a treatment for psychiatric disorders, chronic exercise may alter HPA axis response to stress. Numerous studies have observed a blunted HPA axis response to stress following chronic exercise (Dishman et al., 1998; Fediuc et al., 2006; Droste et al., 2003); however, Chennaoui et al. (2002) found no effect of exercise training on HPA axis response to restraint. In humans, greater physical fitness has been associated with a lower cortisol response to stress (Traustadottir et al., 2005; Rimmele et al., 2007).

## ENDOCANNABINOIDS AND EXERCISE

Activation of the endocannabinoid system produces sedation, anxiolysis, and sense of well-being, and as such, it is posited that endocannabinoids may play a role in the positive mood effects of exercise. Acute aerobic exercise has been shown to activate the endo-cannabinoid system, as Sparling et al. (2003) reported increased plasma anandamide levels following cycling and running at 70%–80% of maximum heart rate for 50 min. This finding has since been replicated in other trials (Heyman et al., 2012; Raichlen et al., 2012). Furthermore, postexercise increases in endocannabinoids are associated with improved mood (Brellenthin et al., 2017). Endocannabinoid production following exercise is dependent on exercise intensity as Raichlen et al. (2012) indicate that moderate to intense exercise is (30 min of running) increased anandamide while no change in anandamide was observed following 30 min of walking.

Long-term effects of exercise on the endocannabinoid system have been observed in animal models. Eight days of wheel running increases anandamide in the rat hippocampus along with an increase in $CB_1$ binding site density (Hill et al., 2010). Contrary to this finding, two trials report extended exercise results in reductions in $CB_1$ receptor density in fat tissue (Yan et al., 2007) and the striatum and hippocampus (Gomes da Silva et al., 2010). This apparent contradiction may suggest that the endocannabinoid system adapts to repeated increases in anandamide with chronic exercise by reducing $CB_1$ receptor density.

Finally, research indicates a role of the endocannabinoid system in neurogenesis following exercise. In humans, increases in anandamide during an acute bout of exercise are correlated with increases in brain-derived neurotrophic factor (BDNF; Heyman et al., 2012). More compel-ling evidence for the role of endocannabinoids in exercise-induced neurogenesis is available in animal models. For example, exercise-induced proliferation of progenitor cells in the hippocampus can be attenuated with administration of a $CB_1$ receptor antagonist (Hill et al., 2010). In further support of the role of endocannabinoids in exercise-induced neurogenesis, Wolf et al. (2010) found that access to a running wheel resulted in increased cell proliferation and decreased neuronal differentiation in $CB_1$-knockout mice.

## BDNF AND EXERCISE

BDNF is consistently associated with exercise-induced neurogenesis. Acute treadmill running upregulates c-fos mRNA in an intensity-dependent manner. BDNF mRNA is increased in low-intensity running, while BDNF mRNA was decreased during moderate-intensity running. These decreases in BDNF mRNA during moderate-intensity exercise were associated with increases in blood lactate and corticosterone levels (Soya et al., 2007). These increases in BDNF expression appear to be the result of exercise-induced HDAC inhibition. For example, beta-hydroxybutyrate, a ketone produced during prolonged exercise, has been shown to promote BDNF mRNA expression through inhibition of HDAC2 and HDAC3 (Sleiman et al., 2016).

Alterations in BDNF expression in the brain are also observed following chronic exercise. These alterations appear to be specific to certain brain regions. Increases in BDNF expression are most consistently observed in the hippocampus (Stranahan et al., 2009; Baj et al., 2012; Russo-Neustadt et al., 2004; Farmer et al., 2004; Adlard et al., 2005) and have also been observed in the ventral tegmental area/substantia nigra (Van Hoomissen et al., 2003), striatum (Vaynman et al., 2004), cerebellum (Klintsova et al., 2004), and motor cortex (Klintsova et al., 2004); while wheel running did not affect BDNF expression in the nucleus accumbens or piriform cortex (Van Hoomissen et al., 2003).

BDNF-induced neurogenesis following chronic exercise results in improved cognition and stress resiliency. A study by Vaynman et al. (2004) implicates BDNF in improved cognition following chronic exercise, finding that blocking the action of BDNF attenuated cognitive benefits (performance in a water maze) of wheel running. Several studies have demonstrated neuroprotective benefits of postexercise BDNF expression. Marais et al. (2009) studied the effects of wheel running in sedentary rats separated from their mothers (early life stress) and subjected to restraint (chronic stress) later in life. Wheel running buffered the negative consequences of the combined stressors, as rats with access to a running wheel demonstrated fewer depressive-like symptoms, and higher levels of BDNF in the striatum compared with rats without access to a running wheel. Similarly, wheel running demonstrated neuroprotective effects following bacterial infection (Barrientos et al., 2011) and corticosterone injection (Yau et al., 2011).

A meta-analysis by Szuhany et al. (2015) has summarized the effects of exercise on BDNF in humans. A moderate increase in peripheral BDNF is observed following an acute bout of aerobic exercise. This acute response is increased following chronic exercise training. Finally, a small, but significant effect is observed in resting BDNF levels, as resting BDNF levels increase following exercise training.

## INFORMING CLINICAL TREATMENT DECISIONS USING BIOLOGICAL MECHANISMS

The ultimate goal in illuminating the neurobiological effects of exercise is to provide clinicians with actionable information that will improve treatment outcomes in psychiatric disorders. To illustrate how this research might eventually guide clinical decision-making, we will use the example of treatment of major depressive disorder (MDD). MDD is a chronic, recurrent disorder that is among the most prevalent psychiatric disorders. As a result, MDD is associated with significant disease burden; in fact, it is estimated that MDD will be the leading cause of global disease burden by the year 2020 (Lopez and Murray, 1998).

A major contributing factor to the burden resulting from MDD is the limited effectiveness of current treatments. The STAR*D trial is the largest trial ($n = 4041$) examining the effectiveness of MDD treatment. In this trial, only one-third of patients achieved disease remission following an initial treatment with an antidepressant medication, and one-third of patients remained depressed even after multiple treatment attempts (Rush et al., 2006; Trivedi et al., 2006). The heterogeneity in treatment response observed in MDD is likely due the heterogeneity in underlying biological causes of depression (Nestler 2002). In real-world clinical settings, this heterogeneity in treatment response results in a "trial and error" approach in which patients may experience multiple treatment switches or augmentations before experiencing remission.

However given the wide-ranging neurobiological effects of exercise (Dishman 2006), the identification of predictors of treatment outcomes is therefore an important step in ultimately matching patients with a treatment that is most likely to elicit a positive treatment outcome. To date, several demographic, clinical, and biological predictors of antidepressant treatments have been identified (Trivedi et al., 2016). Similarly, research has aimed to identify predictors of treatment outcomes following exercise treatment, reviewed by Schuch et al. (2016). The majority of identified predictors are the result of secondary analysis of two trials: Blumenthal et al. (1999) and Trivedi et al. (2011).

Herman et al. (2002) assessed several demographic and clinical factors as potential predictors of treatment outcome in the Blumenthal et al. (1999) study. As would be expected, higher exercise adherence (percentage of sessions attended) was associated with lower depressive symptoms at the end of the 16-week study. In addition, greater life satisfaction, more social support, and higher self-esteem at baseline were also associated with lower depressive symptoms at follow-up. Finally, lower baseline state anxiety was associated with lower depressive symptoms at study end. When these factors were entered into a logistic regression model, only life satisfaction and anxiety were independent predictors of treatment remission.

Predictors of treatment outcome in the TREAD trial (Trivedi et al., 2011) have been reported in multiple articles. Marital status was found to be a significant predictor of treatment outcome, as subjects who were married or cohabitating experienced significantly greater reductions in depressive symptoms (Toups et al., 2011). As in the Herman et al.'s (2002) article, higher quality of life at baseline was associated with lower depressive symptoms at study end (Toups et al., 2011). Subjects with hypersomnia at baseline experienced greater decreases in depressive symptoms during the 12-week exercise program (Rethorst et al., 2013a). Two biological markers were also identified as predictors of treatment outcome in the TREAD study. Subjects with higher baseline levels of BDNF (Toups et al., 2011) and tumor necrosis factor (TNF)-α (Rethorst et al., 2013b) had greater decreases in depressive symptoms. Finally, acute affective response was predictive of treatment outcomes. Greater positive affect following the initial exercise sessions was associated with better treatment outcomes (Suterwala et al., 2016).

The research described previously has identified several clinical and biological factors associated with treatment response to exercise in persons with depression. However, what is unclear is whether these factors uniquely predict treatment response to exercise or whether they are global treatment predictors, meaning that they predict treatment outcome regardless of the treatment modality employed. For example, higher co-morbid anxiety is a commonly identified predictor of poor treatment outcome in medication trials (Fava et al., 2004); therefore the finding by Herman et al. (2002) would suggest that anxiety is a global predictor of treatment outcome. Conversely, elevated pretreatment inflammation has been found to be a predictor of poor treatment outcomes in depression treatment trials (Eller et al., 2008; Lanquillon et al., 2000). In contrast, Rethorst et al. (2013b) found that elevated TNF-α is associated with better treatment outcomes in response to exercise.

This contrast in outcomes is an example of a potential moderator of treatment effect. Kraemer et al. (2002) distinguish between treatment predictors and treatment moderators. While predictors are associated with a treatment outcome regardless of treatment modality, a treatment moderator differentially predicts treatment outcomes of two different treatment modalities. Fig. 15.1A depicts sex as a hypothetical treatment predictor; the effect of sex on treatment outcome is equivalent for both selective serotonin reuptake inhibitor (SSRI) and exercise, as female sex is associated with a better treatment outcome regardless of treatment modality. Conversely, Fig. 15.1B depicts sex as a hypothetical moderator of treatment effect. In this scenario the male sex is predictive of a good treatment outcome to exercise but not SSRI.

This distinction is important, as identification of moderators is necessary to ultimately move clinical practice toward a personalized medicine approach to treatment of depression. Identification of treatment moderators requires trials in which two active treatments are compared. To date, few trials have compared exercise with another active treatment, and of those trials, only one has examined moderators of treatment effects. Herman et al. (2002) report the presence of physical

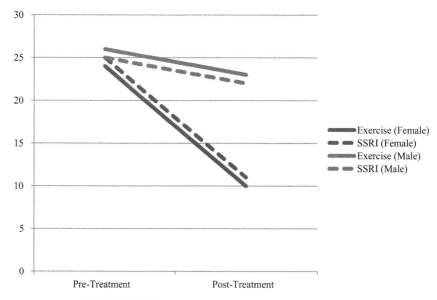

**FIGURE 15.1A**    Sex as a predictor of treatment outcome.

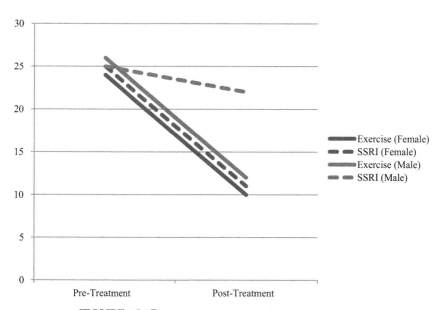

**FIGURE 15.1B**    Sex as a moderator of treatment outcome.

symptoms to moderate treatment response to exercise versus medication (sertraline). Patients achieving remission in the medication group reported lower physical symptoms prior to treatment compared with those who did not achieve remission in the medication group. Conversely, remitted patients in the exercise group reported higher physical symptoms compared with those who did not achieve remission in the exercise group.

Finally, it should be noted that while the identified predictors and moderators are statistically significant, no marker is likely to have a large enough effect to drive clinical decision-making. Therefore studies will need to examine numerous demographic, clinical, and biological markers, and clinical decision tools will need to combine multiple factors to guide treatment decisions. Recent studies have begun to evaluate multiple treatment predictors of other depression treatments (Williams et al., 2011; Dunlop et al., 2012; Trivedi et al., 2016). Likewise, large studies that compare exercise to another established treatment while examining multiple potential treatment moderators are necessary to establish personalized medicine approaches to the use of exercise in the treatment of MDD.

## References

Adlard, P.A., Perreau, V.M., Cotman, C.W., 2005. The exercise-induced expression of BDNF within the hippocampus varies across life-span. Neurobiol. Aging 26, 511−520.

Baj, G., D'alessandro, V., Musazzi, L., Mallei, A., Sartori, C.R., Sciancalepore, M., Tardito, D., Langone, F., Popoli, M., Tongiorgi, E., 2012. Physical exercise and antidepressants enhance BDNF targeting in hippocampal CA3 dendrites: further evidence of a spatial code for BDNF splice variants. Neuropsychopharmacology 37, 1600−1611.

Barrientos, R.M., Frank, M.G., Crysdale, N.Y., Chapman, T.R., Ahrendsen, J.T., Day, H.E., Campeau, S., Watkins, L.R., Patterson, S.L., Maier, S.F., 2011. Little exercise, big effects: reversing aging and infection-induced memory deficits, and underlying processes. J. Neurosci. 31, 11578−11586.

Beeler, J.A., Faust, R.P., Turkson, S., Ye, H., Zhuang, X., 2016. Low dopamine D2 receptor increases vulnerability to obesity via reduced physical activity, not increased appetitive motivation. Biol. Psychiatry 79, 887−897.

Blumenthal, J.A., Babyak, M.A., Moore, K.A., Craighead, W.E., Herman, S., Khatri, P., Waugh, R., Napolitano, M.A., Forman, L.M., Appelbaum, M., Doraiswamy, P.M., Krishnan, K.R., 1999. Effects of exercise training on older patients with major depression. Arch. Intern. Med. 159, 2349−2356.

Brellenthin, A.G., Crombie, K.M., Hillard, C.J., Koltyn, K.F., 2017. Endocannabinoid and mood responses to exercise in adults with varying activity levels. Med. Sci. Sports Exerc. 49 (8), 1688−1696.

Campbell, J.E., Rakhshani, N., Fediuc, S., Bruni, S., Riddell, M.C., 2009. Voluntary wheel running initially increases adrenal sensitivity to adrenocorticotrophic hormone, which is attenuated with long-term training. J. Appl. Physiol. Respir. Environ. Exerc. Physiol. 106, 66−72.

Chaouloff, F., Elghozi, J.L., Guezennec, Y., Laude, D., 1985. Effects of conditioned running on plasma, liver and brain tryptophan and on brain 5-hydroxytryptamine metabolism of the rat. Br. J. Pharmacol. 86, 33–41.

Chaouloff, F., Laude, D., Guezennec, Y., Elghozi, J.L., 1986. Motor activity increases tryptophan, 5-hydroxyindoleacetic acid, and homovanillic acid in ventricular cerebrospinal fluid of the conscious rat. J. Neurochem. 46, 1313–1316.

Chaouloff, F., Laude, D., Serrurier, B., Merino, D., Guezennec, Y., Elghozi, J., 1987. Brain serotonin response to exercise in the rat: the influence of training duration. Biog. Amines 4, 106.

Chaouloff, F., Laude, D., Elghozi, J.L., 1989. Physical exercise: evidence for differential consequences of tryptophan on 5-HT synthesis and metabolism in central serotonergic cell bodies and terminals. J. Neural. Transm. 78, 121–130.

Chaouloff, F., 1997. Effects of acute physical exercise on central serotonergic systems. Med. Sci. Sports Exerc. 29, 58–62.

Chen, C., Nakagawa, S., Kitaichi, Y., An, Y., Omiya, Y., Song, N., Koga, M., Kato, A., Inoue, T., Kusumi, I., 2016. The role of medial prefrontal corticosterone and dopamine in the antidepressant-like effect of exercise. Psychoneuroendocrinology 69, 1–9.

Chen, W., Wang, H.J., Shang, N.N., Liu, J., Li, J., Tang, D.H., Li, Q., 2017. Moderate intensity treadmill exercise alters food preference via dopaminergic plasticity of ventral tegmental area-nucleus accumbens in obese mice. Neurosci. Lett. 641, 56–61.

Chennaoui, M., Gomez Merino, D., Lesage, J., Drogou, C., Guezennec, C.Y., 2002. Effects of moderate and intensive training on the hypothalamo-pituitary-adrenal axis in rats. Acta Physiol. Scand. 175, 113–121.

Christensen, N.J., Mathias, C.J., Frankel, H.L., 1976. Plasma and urinary dopamine: studies during fasting and exercise and in tetraplegic man. Eur. J. Clin. Invest. 6, 403–409.

Dang, L.C., Castrellon, J.J., Perkins, S.F., Le, N.T., Cowan, R.L., Zald, D.H., Samanez-Larkin, G.R., 2017. Reduced effects of age on dopamine D2 receptor levels in physically active adults. Neuroimage 148, 123–129.

Dishman, R.K., Bunnell, B.N., Youngstedt, S.D., Yoo, H.S., Mougey, E.H., Meyerhoff, J.L., 1998. Activity wheel running blunts increased plasma adrenocorticotrophin (ACTH) after footshock and cage-switch stress. Physiol. Behav. 63, 911–917.

Dishman, R.K., Berthoud, H.R., Booth, F.W., Cotman, C.W., Edgerton, V.R., Fleshner, M.R., Gandevia, S.C., Gomez-Pinilla, F., Greenwood, B.N., Hillman, C.H., Kramer, A.F., Levin, B.E., Moran, T.H., Russo-Neustadt, A.A., Salamone, J.D., Van Hoomissen, J.D., Wade, C.E., York, D.A., Zigmond, M.J., 2006. Neurobiology of exercise. Obesity 14, 345–356.

Droste, S.K., Gesing, A., Ulbricht, S., Muller, M.B., Linthorst, A.C., Reul, J.M., 2003. Effects of long-term voluntary exercise on the mouse hypothalamic-pituitary-adrenocortical axis. Endocrinology 144, 3012–3023.

Dunlop, B.W., Binder, E.B., Cubells, J.F., Goodman, M.M., Kelley, M.E., Kinkead, B., Kutner, M., Nemeroff, C.B., Newport, D.J., Owens, M.J., Pace, T.W., Ritchie, J.C., Rivera, V.A., Westen, D., Craighead, W.E., Mayberg, H.S., 2012. Predictors of remission in depression to individual and combined treatments (PReDICT): study protocol for a randomized controlled trial. Trials 13, 106.

Eddy, M.C., Stansfield, K.J., Green, J.T., 2014. Voluntary exercise improves performance of a discrimination task through effects on the striatal dopamine system. Learn. Mem. 21, 334–337.

Eller, T., Vasar, V., Shlik, J., Maron, E., 2008. Pro-inflammatory cytokines and treatment response to escitalopram in major depressive disorder. Prog. Neuro Psychopharmacol. Biol. Psychiatry 32, 445–450.

Farmer, J., Zhao, X., Van Praag, H., Wodtke, K., Gage, F.H., Christie, B.R., 2004. Effects of voluntary exercise on synaptic plasticity and gene expression in the dentate gyrus of adult male Sprague-Dawley rats in vivo. Neuroscience 124, 71–79.

Fava, M., Alpert, J.E., Carmin, C.N., Wisniewski, S.R., Trivedi, M.H., Biggs, M.M., Shores-Wilson, K., Morgan, D., Schwartz, T., Balasubramani, G., 2004. Clinical correlates and symptom patterns of anxious depression among patients with major depressive disorder in STAR* D. Psychol. Med. 34, 1299.

Fediuc, S., Campbell, J.E., Riddell, M.C., 2006. Effect of voluntary wheel running on circadian corticosterone release and on HPA axis responsiveness to restraint stress in Sprague-Dawley rats. J. Appl. Physiol. 100, 1867–1875.

Fisher, B.E., Li, Q., Nacca, A., Salem, G.J., Song, J., Yip, J., Hui, J.S., Jakowec, M.W., Petzinger, G.M., 2013. Treadmill exercise elevates striatal dopamine D2 receptor binding potential in patients with early Parkinson's disease. Neuroreport 24, 509–514.

Foley, T.E., Fleshner, M., 2008. Neuroplasticity of dopamine circuits after exercise: implications for central fatigue. NeuroMol. Med. 10, 67–80.

Gomes DA Silva, S., Araujo, B.H., Cossa, A.C., Scorza, F.A., Cavalheiro, E.A., Naffah-Mazzacoratti Mda, G., Arida, R.M., 2010. Physical exercise in adolescence changes CB1 cannabinoid receptor expression in the rat brain. Neurochem. Int. 57, 492–496.

Gomez-Merino, D., Bequet, F., Berthelot, M., Chennaoui, M., Guezennec, C.Y., 2001. Site-dependent effects of an acute intensive exercise on extracellular 5-HT and 5-HIAA levels in rat brain. Neurosci. Lett. 301, 143–146.

Greenwood, B.N., Foley, T.E., Day, H.E., Campisi, J., Hammack, S.H., Campeau, S., Maier, S.F., Fleshner, M., 2003. Freewheel running prevents learned helplessness/behavioral depression: role of dorsal raphe serotonergic neurons. J. Neurosci. 23, 2889–2898.

Greenwood, B.N., Foley, T.E., Day, H.E., Burhans, D., Brooks, L., Campeau, S., Fleshner, M., 2005. Wheel running alters serotonin (5-HT) transporter, 5-HT1A, 5-HT1B, and alpha 1b-adrenergic receptor mRNA in the rat raphe nuclei. Biol. Psychiatry 57, 559–568.

Herman, S., Blumenthal, J.A., Babyak, M., Khatri, P., Craighead, W.E., Krishnan, K.R., Doraiswamy, P.M., 2002. Exercise therapy for depression in middle-aged and older adults: predictors of early dropout and treatment failure. Health Psychol. 21, 553.

Heyman, E., Gamelin, F.X., Goekint, M., Piscitelli, F., Roelands, B., Leclair, E., Di Marzo, V., Meeusen, R., 2012. Intense exercise increases circulating endocannabinoid and BDNF levels in humans—possible implications for reward and depression. Psychoneuroendocrinology 37, 844–851.

Hill, M.N., Titterness, A.K., Morrish, A.C., Carrier, E.J., Lee, T.T., GIL-Mohapel, J., Gorzalka, B.B., Hillard, C.J., Christie, B.R., 2010. Endogenous cannabinoid signaling is required for voluntary exercise-induced enhancement of progenitor cell proliferation in the hippocampus. Hippocampus 20, 513–523.

Jakeman, P.M., Hawthorne, J.E., Maxwell, S.R., Kendall, M.J., Holder, G., 1994. Evidence for downregulation of hypothalamic 5-hydroxytryptamine receptor function in endurance-trained athletes. Exp. Physiol. 79, 461–464.

Kim, H., Heo, H.I., Kim, D.H., Ko, I.G., Lee, S.S., Kim, S.E., Kim, B.K., Kim, T.W., Ji, E.S., Kim, J.D., Shin, M.S., Choi, Y.W., Kim, C.J., 2011. Treadmill exercise and methylphenidate ameliorate symptoms of attention deficit/hyperactivity disorder through enhancing dopamine synthesis and brain-derived neurotrophic factor expression in spontaneous hypertensive rats. Neurosci. Lett. 504, 35–39.

Klintsova, A.Y., Dickson, E., Yoshida, R., Greenough, W.T., 2004. Altered expression of BDNF and its high-affinity receptor TrkB in response to complex motor learning and moderate exercise. Brain Res. 1028, 92–104.

Kraemer, H.C., Wilson, G.T., Fairburn, C.G., Agras, W.S., 2002. Mediators and moderators of treatment effects in randomized clinical trials. Arch. Gen. Psychiatr. 59, 877–883.

Lanquillon, S., Krieg, J.C., Bening-Abu-Shach, U., Vedder, H., 2000. Cytokine production and treatment response in major depressive disorder. Neuropsychopharmacology 22, 370–379.

Li, N., He, X., Qi, X., Zhang, Y., He, S., 2010. The mood stabilizer lamotrigine produces antidepressant behavioral effects in rats: role of brain-derived neurotrophic factor. J. Psychopharmacol. (Oxf. Engl.) 24, 1772.

Lopez, A.D., Murray, C.C., 1998. The global burden of disease, 1990-2020. Nat. Med. 4, 1241–1243.

Luger, A., Deuster, P.A., Kyle, S.B., Gallucci, W.T., Montgomery, L.C., Gold, P.W., Loriaux, D.L., Chrousos, G.P., 1987. Acute hypothalamic-pituitary-adrenal responses to the stress of treadmill exercise. Physiologic adaptations to physical training. N. Engl. J. Med. 316, 1309–1315.

Marais, L., Stein, D.J., Daniels, W.M., 2009. Exercise increases BDNF levels in the striatum and decreases depressive-like behavior in chronically stressed rats. Metab. Brain Dis. 24, 587–597.

Mcguigan, M.R., Egan, A.D., Foster, C., 2004. Salivary cortisol responses and perceived exertion during high intensity and low intensity bouts of resistance exercise. J. Sports Sci. Med. 3, 8–15.

Meeusen, R., Thorre, K., Chaouloff, F., Sarre, S., De Meirleir, K., Ebinger, G., Michotte, Y., 1996. Effects of tryptophan and/or acute running on extracellular 5-HT and 5-HIAA levels in the hippocampus of food-deprived rats. Brain Res. 740, 245–252.

Nabkasorn, C., Miyai, N., Sootmongkol, A., Junprasert, S., Yamamoto, H., Arita, M., Miyashita, K., 2006. Effects of physical exercise on depression, neuroendocrine stress hormones and physiological fitness in adolescent females with depressive symptoms. Eur. J. Publ. Health 16, 179–184.

Nestler, E.J., Barrot, M., Dileone, R.J., Eisch, A.J., Gold, S.J., Monteggia, L.M., 2002. Neurobiology of depression. Neuron 34, 13–25.

O'hara, C.B., Keyes, A., Renwick, B., Leyton, M., Campbell, I.C., Schmidt, U., 2016. The effects of acute dopamine precursor depletion on the reinforcing value of exercise in anorexia nervosa. PLoS One 11, e0145894.

Otsuka, T., Nishii, A., Amemiya, S., Kubota, N., Nishijima, T., Kita, I., 2016. Effects of acute treadmill running at different intensities on activities of serotonin and corticotropin-releasing factor neurons, and anxiety- and depressive-like behaviors in rats. Behav. Brain Res. 298, 44–51.

Raichlen, D.A., Foster, A.D., Gerdeman, G.L., Seillier, A., Giuffrida, A., 2012. Wired to run: exercise-induced endocannabinoid signaling in humans and cursorial mammals with implications for the 'runner's high'. J. Exp. Biol. 215, 1331–1336.

Rethorst, C.D., Sunderajan, P., Greer, T.L., Grannemann, B.D., Nakonezny, P.A., Carmody, T.J., Trivedi, M.H., 2013a. Does exercise improve self-reported sleep quality in non-remitted major depressive disorder? Psychol. Med. 43, 699–709.

Rethorst, C.D., Toups, M.S., Greer, T.L., Nakonezny, P.A., Carmody, T.J., Grannemann, B.D., Huebinger, R.M., Barber, R.C., Trivedi, M.H., 2013b. Pro-inflammatory cytokines as predictors of antidepressant effects of exercise in major depressive disorder. Mol. Psychiatry 18, 1119–1124.

Rimmele, U., Zellweger, B.C., Marti, B., Seiler, R., Mohiyeddini, C., Ehlert, U., Heinrichs, M., 2007. Trained men show lower cortisol, heart rate and psychological responses to psychosocial stress compared with untrained men. Psychoneuroendocrinology 32, 627–635.

Robertson, C.L., Ishibashi, K., Chudzynski, J., Mooney, L.J., Rawson, R.A., Dolezal, B.A., Cooper, C.B., Brown, A.K., Mandelkern, M.A., London, E.D., 2016. Effect of exercise training on striatal dopamine D2/D3 receptors in methamphetamine users during behavioral treatment. Neuropsychopharmacology 41, 1629–1636.

Rojas Vega, S., Struder, H.K., Vera Wahrmann, B., Schmidt, A., Bloch, W., Hollmann, W., 2006. Acute BDNF and cortisol response to low intensity exercise and following ramp incremental exercise to exhaustion in humans. Brain Res. 1121, 59–65.

Rush, A.J., Trivedi, M.H., Wisniewski, S.R., Nierenberg, A.A., Stewart, J.W., Warden, D., Niederehe, G., Thase, M.E., Lavori, P.W., Lebowitz, B.D., Mcgrath, P.J., Rosenbaum, J.F., Sackeim, H.A., Kupfer, D.J., Luther, J., Fava, M., 2006. Acute and longer-term outcomes in depressed outpatients requiring one or several treatment steps: a STAR*D report. Am. J. Psychiatry 163, 1905–1917.

Russo-Neustadt, A.A., Alejandre, H., Garcia, C., Ivy, A.S., Chen, M.J., 2004. Hippocampal brain-derived neurotrophic factor expression following treatment with reboxetine, citalopram, and physical exercise. Neuropsychopharmacology 29, 2189–2199.

Schuch, F.B., Dunn, A.L., Kanitz, A.C., Delevatti, R.S., Fleck, M.P., 2016. Moderators of response in exercise treatment for depression: a systematic review. J. Affect. Disord. 195, 40–49.

Sleiman, S.F., Henry, J., AL-Haddad, R., EL Hayek, L., ABOU Haidar, E., Stringer, T., Ulja, D., Karuppagounder, S.S., Holson, E.B., Ratan, R.R., Ninan, I., Chao, M.V., 2016. Exercise promotes the expression of brain derived neurotrophic factor (BDNF) through the action of the ketone body beta-hydroxybutyrate. Elife 5.

Soya, H., Nakamura, T., Deocaris, C.C., Kimpara, A., Iimura, M., Fujikawa, T., Chang, H., Mcewen, B.S., Nishijima, T., 2007. BDNF induction with mild exercise in the rat hippocampus. Biochem. Biophys. Res. Commun. 358, 961–967.

Sparling, P.B., Giuffrida, A., Piomelli, D., Rosskopf, L., Dietrich, A., 2003. Exercise activates the endocannabinoid system. Neuroreport 14, 2209–2211.

Stranahan, A.M., Lee, K., Martin, B., Maudsley, S., Golden, E., Cutler, R.G., Mattson, M.P., 2009. Voluntary exercise and caloric restriction enhance hippocampal dendritic spine density and BDNF levels in diabetic mice. Hippocampus 19, 951–961.

Struder, H.K., Weicker, H., 2001. Physiology and pathophysiology of the serotonergic system and its implications on mental and physical performance. Part II. Int. J. Sports Med. 22, 482–497.

Struder, H.K., Hollmann, W., Platen, P., Wostmann, R., Weicker, H., Molderings, G.J., 1999. Effect of acute and chronic exercise on plasma amino acids and prolactin concentrations and on [3H]ketanserin binding to serotonin2A receptors on human platelets. Eur. J. Appl. Physiol. Occup. Physiol. 79, 318–324.

Suterwala, A.M., Rethorst, C.D., Carmody, T.J., Greer, T.L., Grannemann, B.D., Jha, M., Trivedi, M.H., 2016. Affect following first exercise session as a predictor of treatment response in depression. J. Clin. Psychiatry 77, 1036–1042.

Szuhany, K.L., Bugatti, M., Otto, M.W., 2015. A meta-analytic review of the effects of exercise on brain-derived neurotrophic factor. J. Psychiatr. Res. 60, 56–64.

Toups, M.S., Greer, T.L., Kurian, B.T., Grannemann, B.D., Carmody, T.J., Huebinger, R., Rethorst, C., Trivedi, M.H., 2011. Effects of serum brain derived neurotrophic factor on exercise augmentation treatment of depression. J. Psychiatr. Res. 45, 1301–1306.

Traustadottir, T., Bosch, P.R., Matt, K.S., 2005. The HPA axis response to stress in women: effects of aging and fitness. Psychoneuroendocrinology 30, 392–402.

Trivedi, M., Fava, M., Wisniewski, S., Thase, M., Quitkin, F., Warden, D., Ritz, L., Nierenberg, A., Lebowitz, B., Biggs, M., 2006. Medication augmentation after the failure of SSRIs for depression. N. Engl. J. Med. 354, 1243.

Trivedi, M.H., Greer, T.L., Church, T.S., Carmody, T.J., Grannemann, B.D., Galper, D.I., Dunn, A.L., Earnest, C.P., Sunderajan, P., Henley, S.S., Blair, S.N., 2011. Exercise as an augmentation treatment for nonremitted major depressive disorder: a randomized, parallel dose comparison. J. Clin. Psychiatry 72, 677–684.

Trivedi, M.H., Mcgrath, P.J., Fava, M., Parsey, R.V., Kurian, B.T., Phillips, M.L., Oquendo, M.A., Bruder, G., Pizzagalli, D., Toups, M., Cooper, C., Adams, P., Weyandt, S., Morris, D.W., Grannemann, B.D., Ogden, R.T., Buckner, R., Mcinnis, M., Kraemer, H.C., Petkova, E., Carmody, T.J., Weissman, M.M., 2016. Establishing moderators and biosignatures of antidepressant response in clinical care (EMBARC): rationale and design. J. Psychiatr. Res. 78, 11−23.

Van Hoomissen, J.D., Chambliss, H.O., Holmes, P.V., Dishman, R.K., 2003. Effects of chronic exercise and imipramine on mRNA for BDNF after olfactory bulbectomy in rat. Brain Res. 974, 228−235.

Vaynman, S., Ying, Z., Gomez-Pinilla, F., 2004. Hippocampal BDNF mediates the efficacy of exercise on synaptic plasticity and cognition. Eur. J. Neurosci. 20, 2580−2590.

Vuckovic, M.G., Li, Q., Fisher, B., Nacca, A., Leahy, R.M., Walsh, J.P., Mukherjee, J., Williams, C., Jakowec, M.W., Petzinger, G.M., 2010. Exercise elevates dopamine D2 receptor in a mouse model of Parkinson's disease: in vivo imaging with [(1)(8)F]fallypride. Mov. Disord. 25, 2777−2784.

Wang, G.J., Volkow, N.D., Fowler, J.S., Franceschi, D., Logan, J., Pappas, N.R., Wong, C.T., Netusil, N., 2000. PET studies of the effects of aerobic exercise on human striatal dopamine release. J. Nucl. Med. 41, 1352−1356.

Watanabe, T., Morimoto, A., Sakata, Y., Wada, M., Murakami, N., 1991. The effect of chronic exercise on the pituitary-adrenocortical response in conscious rats. J. Physiol. 439, 691−699.

Weicker, H., Strüder, H.K., 2001. Influence of exercise on serotonergic neuromodulation in the brain. Amino Acids 20, 35−47.

Williams, L.M., Rush, A.J., Koslow, S.H., Wisniewski, S.R., Cooper, N.J., Nemeroff, C.B., Schatzberg, A.F., Gordon, E., 2011. International Study to Predict Optimized Treatment for Depression (iSPOT-D), a randomized clinical trial: rationale and protocol. Trials 12, 4.

Wilson, W.M., Marsden, C.A., 1996. In vivo measurement of extracellular serotonin in the ventral hippocampus during treadmill running. Behav. Pharmacol. 7, 101−104.

Wipfli, B., Landers, D., Nagoshi, C., Ringenbach, S., 2011. An examination of serotonin and psychological variables in the relationship between exercise and mental health. Scand. J. Med. Sci. Sports 21, 474−481.

Wolf, S.A., Bick-Sander, A., Fabel, K., Leal-Galicia, P., Tauber, S., Ramirez-Rodriguez, G., Muller, A., Melnik, A., Waltinger, T.P., Ullrich, O., Kempermann, G., 2010. Cannabinoid receptor CB1 mediates baseline and activity-induced survival of new neurons in adult hippocampal neurogenesis. Cell Commun. Signal. 8, 12.

Yan, Z.C., Liu, D.Y., Zhang, L.L., Shen, C.Y., Ma, Q.L., Cao, T.B., Wang, L.J., Nie, H., Zidek, W., Tepel, M., Zhu, Z.M., 2007. Exercise reduces adipose tissue via cannabinoid receptor type 1 which is regulated by peroxisome proliferator-activated receptor-delta. Biochem. Biophys. Res. Commun. 354, 427−433.

Yau, S.Y., Lau, B.W., Tong, J.B., Wong, R., Ching, Y.P., Qiu, G., Tang, S.W., Lee, T.M., So, K.F., 2011. Hippocampal neurogenesis and dendritic plasticity support running-improved spatial learning and depression-like behaviour in stressed rats. PLoS One 6, e24263.

# Research and Evaluation in Exercise and Mental Health

*Simon Rosenbaum[1,2], Brendon Stubbs[3,4], Davy Vancampfort[5,6]*

[1] School of Psychiatry, Faculty of Medicine, University of New South Wales, Sydney, Australia; [2] The Black Dog Institute, Sydney, Australia; [3] Institute of Psychiatry, Psychology and Neuroscience, King's College London and Head of Physiotherapy, South London and Maudsley NHS Foundation Trust, London, United Kingdom; [4] Physiotherapy Department, South London and Maudsley NHS Foundation Trust, London, United Kingdom; [5] KU Leuven, Department of Rehabilitation Sciences, Leuven, Belgium; [6] KU Leuven, University Psychiatric Center KU Leuven, Leuven-Kortenberg, Belgium

*Exercise-Based Interventions for Mental Illness*
https://doi.org/10.1016/B978-0-12-812605-9.00016-2

# INTRODUCTION

The concept of evidence-based medicine refers to *"integrating individual clinical expertise with the best available external clinical evidence from systematic* research" (Sackett, 1997). Applying the principles of evidence-based medicine to the prescription of exercise for people with mental illness and indeed to exercise prescription more broadly underpins the potential success of any intervention and ensures practitioners are guided by "tried and tested" strategies. For many undergraduate students and clinically focused practitioners, the term "research" often evokes negative emotions and may seem inextricably linked to complicated statistics. While some types of research and evaluation may require complicated statistical approaches, simple evaluation often embedded as part of usual care is not only good practice but can be a powerful tool from which small, local services can be replicated and scaled. Health professionals, exercise practitioners, and physical therapists have an ethical obligation to critically appraise the scientific literature to ensure they are up to date on the latest scientific findings (Ekkekakis et al., 2018). The science guiding exercise interventions for people living with mental illness has seen considerable progress since the second half of the 20th century with an exponential increase in the number of scientific articles including clinical trials, systematic reviews, and clinical practice guidelines. Indeed, the clinical application of physical activity as a treatment for mental illness can be traced back to the 1960s and the creation of dedicated physical therapy training programs in mental health (Probst, 2012) and randomized controlled trials from 1975 (Clark et al., 1975) to the present day. From an implementation perspective, as allied health clinicians trained in exercise prescription, physical therapists, and exercise physiologists are commonly utilized in both research and clinical settings to design, deliver, and evaluate exercise interventions for people with mental illness (Probst, 2012; Stanton et al., 2017; Lederman et al., 2016; Stubbs et al., 2014).

# DESIGNING AN EVALUATION FRAMEWORK: BEYOND THE RANDOMIZED CONTROLLED TRIAL

According to the hierarchy of evidence pyramid, of all experimental studies, randomized controlled trials (RCTs) are considered as the gold standard method for determining the efficacy of an intervention. In an RCT, participants are randomly allocated to either the experimental group receiving the treatment under investigation or to a control condition (e.g., usual care or a wait-list control). Data from RCTs are then combined qualitatively in systematic reviews and quantitatively through meta-analyses, which are considered the highest level of evidence. In the exercise and mental health field, numerous systematic reviews have demonstrated a consistent antidepressive (Schuch et al., 2016c; Rebar et al., 2015), anxiolytic (Stubbs et al., 2017), and positive effect on reducing symptoms of other mental disorders (Firth et al., 2015; Rosenbaum et al., 2014). Indeed, there have been numerous calls for greater academic focus on translation efforts to ensure better application of the evidence to routine clinical practice (Vancampfort et al., 2015b; Vancampfort and Faulkner, 2014; Rebar and Taylor, 2017).

An important distinction to make before conducting or planning any evaluation is the primary purpose of the evaluation. An important step in planning any evaluation is deciding on whether the primary aim of interest is *efficacy* or *effectiveness* (Vancampfort et al., 2015c). While *efficacy* refers to the fundamental question of "does an intervention work," often under ideal conditions, *effectiveness* refers to how well an intervention works under real-world conditions. Increasingly, examples of effectiveness research within the exercise and mental health field are being conducted which help inform the design and delivery of exercise interventions. Examples of when an *efficacy*-based approach would be appropriate include RCTs aiming to elucidate mechanistic effects of exercise interventions, which may include costly, technical assessments such as neuroimaging and biochemistry. On the other hand, examples of *effectiveness* research might include quality improvement evaluations of services which may also include process-based measures, including feasibility and acceptability (i.e., percentage of total sessions attended, referral pathways, and percentage of all potential participants eligible for referral who take up the intervention). Other assessment outcomes may include symptoms, anthropometry, and quality of life (QoL).

Practitioners and researchers must ensure that the methodological approach used in any evaluation is appropriate for answering the desired question. For example, at a fundamental level, practitioners must decide on whether to utilize *quantitative*, *qualitative*, or *mixed-methods* approaches.

*Quantitative* research involves research using numbers and often but not limited to continuous outcomes, for example, symptoms, waist circumference, and QoL. Examples of *quantitative* research may include assessing the impact of a 12-week inpatient exercise program on the waist circumference of inpatients with schizophrenia, taking antipsychotic medication. *Qualitative* research uses different methodologies such as focus groups and 1:1 interviews in order to gain a more complete or holistic understanding of how participants may *feel* about an intervention or program. Continuing the previously mentioned example, a *qualitative* approach may be to conduct focus groups with participants at various time points throughout and/or following the intervention. Outcomes that may be of interest include how the participants felt about the program, were there any barriers or motivating factors, and how could the intervention be improved in the future. When both *quantitative* and *qualitative* methodologies are used, the evaluation is said to be employing a *mixed-methods* approach. A key gap in the existing exercise and mental health literature, which is pivotal to affecting change in policy is *economic evaluations* of interventions. Economic evaluations such as *cost-effectiveness* research aim to quantify the cost and potential savings of interventions. There are various approaches to economic analyses that are beyond the scope of this chapter; however, basic economic analysis can often be conducted in services where the costs of providing interventions can easily be calculated. In addition, adding simple measures of QoL can often provide cost-utility data that can be converted into standardized units (e.g., QALYs or *quality-adjusted life years*).

Typically, all research conducted with human subjects requires review and approval by an ethics committee or institutional review board (IRB). Completing the documentation required by such committees also ensures that detailed protocols have been written, the project is methodologically sound, and most importantly, does not pose any significant or unnecessary risks to potential participants. Several ethical considerations must be taken into account including the type of data to be collected, participant confidentiality, any risk of coercion, participant reimbursement, recruitment process, and capacity to provide written informed consent. In addition, prior to submitting applications for ethical review, researchers/ practitioners must decide on the level of risk associated with the project which in many cases will determine the type of form the be completed. For example, clinical trials require a high level of scrutiny and detail, and participants will nearly always have to provide written informed consent after being given a participant information statement and consent form. In specific cases, alternatives to individual level written informed consent may be appropriate, for example, conducting a file audit of routinely collected clinical data may be approved under a low-negligible risk application providing all data are deidentified, and all patient confidentiality and ethical obligations are met. Regardless of the methodology, all human research requires review and approval from an appropriate ethical committee/IRB, and failure to seek such approval could result in serious consequences, including academic misconduct charges. It is therefore advised to always seek guidance from the committee prior to conducting any evaluation.

# WHAT TO MEASURE? SELECTING APPROPRIATE OUTCOMES

Choosing appropriate outcome measures is a fundamental component of any evaluation. Exercise programs for people living with mental illness may be associated with positive changes across a broad range of outcomes including physical and mental health, psychosocial functioning, QoL, and clinical service utilization. No single outcome measure will cover all of the previously mentioned constructs, and therefore understanding and deciding on the purpose of the evaluation are critical to informing decisions around the most appropriate outcome to use. Selecting outcome measures can be considered as a compromise between several factors. For example, with increasing precision often comes increased cost. Costs include not only those required to purchase equipment (e.g., ergometers or physical activity measurement devices) but also the cost of relevant human resources (e.g., cost of hiring mental health clinicians to conduct structure clinical interviews) and also participant burden (e.g., transport to and from testing facilities and reimbursement for time). All these factors should be considered when selecting appropriate outcome measures.

## Objective Versus Subjective Assessments

Objective measures refer to those that are assessed directly and are less susceptible to recall bias. Accelerometers to measure physical activity, clinician-rated symptom scales, and costs associated with service utilization and biochemical/anthropomorphic assessments, including cholesterol, blood pressure, and body weight are all examples of objective measures.

Subjective measures tend to measure patient factors and are based on or influenced by personal feelings or opinions. Examples of subjective measures include self-reported symptoms, physical activity levels, diet, and sleep quality. Subjective measures are an important tool and are highly accessible through structured and often validated self-report tools.

Commonly used self-report tools that have been validated in people with mental illness and used in exercise research include:

|  | Objective | Subjective |
|---|---|---|
| Physical activity | Heart rate monitoring<br>Pedometers<br>Accelerometers<br>Indirect calorimetry<br>Doubly labeled water | Questionnaires<br>Self-report |
| Sleep | Polysomnography | Questionnaires<br>Self-report |
| Fitness | Maximal<br><br>Astrand<br><br>YMCA<br><br>6MWT<br><br>Eurofit | Questionnaires<br>Self-report |

## Measuring Physical Activity Participation and Sedentary Behavior

Increasing the overall volume of physical activity that participants engage in is in most cases the primary purpose of exercise therapy, regardless of whether the desired benefits are primarily physical (e.g., improve body composition and fitness), mental (e.g., reduce depressive symptoms), or both. Therefore being able to quantitatively demonstrate increases in physical activity participation in response to interventions is of high clinical interest. A potential barrier to the routine implementation of physical activity programs within mental health settings is the difficulty in applying routine measurement that enables evaluation of intervention effectiveness (Warren et al., 2010). The measurement of physical activity among people with mental illness presents unique challenges, given the diverse diagnoses and wide range of symptoms profiles among psychiatric patients (Vancampfort et al., 2013). For example, clinical variability in mood may influence the ability to accurately respond to self-report questionnaires, especially among people who experience symptom fluctuation such as rapid cycling bipolar disorder (Jabben et al., 2012; Köhler et al., 2015). Psychotic symptoms, grandiosity, and severe symptoms of depression and anxiety are also likely to influence the utility of self-report measures (Linden and Godemann, 2007). In addition, people with mental illness may have unique difficulties accessing exercise facilities, and some may be hospitalized and have restrictions on their opportunities to engage in physical activity. This section will briefly summarize and discuss some of the key issues around physical activity measurement within mental health settings.

Physical activity can be assessed through both objective and self-report measures, with ease of measurement, precision, and cost factors influencing the choice of measurement tool (Warren et al., 2010). The conceptualization of physical activity into dimensions and domains (recreational, domestic, vocational, and transport) also has significant implications for the design and selection of physical activity measurement tools, with an ideal measure covering all domains and providing data on both structured and unstructured physical activity participation. The importance of accurately assessing total sedentary behavior has also been well established (Kohl et al., 2012; Owen et al., 2009). Various measurement options are available including direct measurement through invasive and time-consuming procedures such as direct calorimetry and doubly labeled water which although maximize precision have been used previously in only very small pilot studies in people with mental illness (Sharpe et al., 2006; Bossu et al., 2007) and are not feasible for use in routine clinical practice. Accelerometers (small, waist, or wrist-worn monitors) are a common objective measure of physical activity that are increasingly used for research purposes in people with mental illness (Chapman et al., 2015). Accelerometers have been extensively used for research purposes within psychiatric settings, and in one study were shown to be more feasible for assessing sedentary behavior compared with questionnaires, however (Jerome et al., 2009), may be too expensive and resource intensive for routine clinical use (Gorczynski et al., 2014; Strath et al., 2013; Rosenbaum et al., 2016). In addition, older age, current employment, tertiary education, nonsmoking, and high self-reported health are associated with increased adherence to accelerometer protocols in the general population (Lee et al., 2013). Given that many of these adherence factors are underrepresented in psychiatric patients, adherence may be suboptimal.

Self-report questionnaires provide a feasible, cost-effective alternative to objective measures, with varying levels of agreement and correlation with objective measures (Strath & et al., 2013). Soundy et al. (2014) conducted a comprehensive review of the selection, use, and psychometric properties of physical activity measures used in studies evaluating physical activity in people with severe mental illness, highlighting methodological limitations in the few studies reporting validity coefficients for self-report questionnaires. The review identified six unique self-report questionnaires that were used to assess physical activity across seven different studies of participants with mental illness

(Soundy et al., 2014). The number of different questionnaires used highlights the absence of a standardized measure, and a lack of agreement between researchers investigating the relationship between physical activity and mental illness as to the most appropriate questionnaire for use in psychiatric populations, which limits cross-study comparison. This lack of agreement can also be seen in other domains of physical activity research (Shephard, 2003), but the disparity in physical health outcomes among people experiencing mental illness highlights the unique need for consensus in this area.

Three key psychometric concepts must be understood when considering the accuracy and precision of a physical activity assessment tool, that is, reliability, validity, and responsiveness. Reliability refers to the consistency of a measure to produce similar results under comparable conditions or within the same subject (Vanhees et al., 2005). A 2012 systematic review of the reliability and validity of physical activity questionnaires found that reliability was generally acceptable with median intraclass correlation coefficients ranging from 0.62 to 0.76 (Helmerhorst et al., 2012). The same review found that the validity of existing physical activity questionnaires (the extent to which the questionnaires measure what is claimed, often assessed via comparison with an objective measure) was less convincing with intraclass correlation coefficients ranging from 0.25 to 0.41 (Helmerhorst et al., 2012). Responsiveness refers to the capacity of a tool to capture change over time, for example, in response to an intervention (Warren et al., 2010; Vanhees et al., 2005). In order for a tool to be considered responsive, it must both detect meaningful change when change has occurred, yet remain stable in the absence of any significant change.

## International Physical Activity Questionnaire

One commonly used self-report measure of physical activity in people with mental illness is the International Physical Activity Questionnaire (IPAQ), particularly the five-item IPAQ-short form (IPAQ-SF; Faulkner et al., 2006; Lee et al., 2011; Craig et al., 2003). The original 2006 validation study of the IPAQ-SF in people with schizophrenia found correlation coefficients of 0.68 for reliability and 0.37 for criterion validity for total reported minutes of physical activity (Faulkner et al., 2006). Coupled with results from a larger 2016 study which included 4-week reliability data from the same research group, the authors conclude that although not without limitations, the IPAQ-SF exhibits measurement properties comparable to those reported in the general population and therefore can be considered as an appropriate surveillance tool to assess levels of physical activity in people with schizophrenia (Faulkner et al., 2006; Duncan et al., 2017). A 2017 study using UK Biobank data found that people with schizophrenia self-reported the same physical activity levels as those without as assessed with the IPAQ-SF, however, accelerometer data revealed a large and statistically significant reduction in physical activity in schizophrenia (Firth et al., 2017). The study reported that people with schizophrenia, on average, engaged in less physical activity than 80% of the general population, with the authors concluding that self-report measures in epidemiological studies fail to capture the reduced activity levels in schizophrenia. The sensitivity of the IPAQ-SF to change in physical activity minutes, in response to interventions, and therefore its appropriateness as a clinical measure have also been questioned (Bauman et al., 2009), further highlighting the importance of determining the primary aim and purpose of any evaluation and selecting appropriate outcome measures that.

## Physical Activity as a Vital Sign

Leading physical activity researchers have argued that health-care providers should obtain a "physical activity vital sign" on every patient they see, given that there is "no better indicator of a person's health and likely longevity" than their level of physical activity (Sallis, 2011). The notion of a community of practice or a "movement for movement" in which every contact with health professionals is seen as an opportunity for brief advice around the importance of regular physical activity (Gates et al., 2017) is also increasingly gaining momentum within clinical services, including mental health facilities (Lederman et al., 2017).

The physical activity as a vital sign (PAVS) method involves a single item and provides a quick method of determining compliance with international physical activity guidelines of 150 min of moderate−vigorous physical activity per week (Sallis, 2011). The PAVS has been used in various psychiatric populations including in people with schizophrenia (Vancampfort et al., 2016d), bipolar disorder (Vancampfort et al., 2016c), and in a mixed sample of in- and out-patients with serious mental illness in a low-resource setting (Uganda; Vancampfort et al., 2018). Across all studies, the PAVS was deemed to be an effective tool to assess cardiometabolic risk in psychiatric patients. Given the relative brevity of the tool (single item), low participant burden, and high feasibility and acceptability, there have been calls for the PAVS to be integrated as a routine assessment tool. Similarly, to the IPAQ-SF, the sensitivity of the PAVS to change in response to interventions has not been established.

## The Simple Physical Activity Questionnaire

An international multidisciplinary working group comprising psychiatrists, psychologists, physical therapists, exercise physiologists, and epidemiologists has aimed to address the limitations of existing physical activity tools, in reference to clinical populations at risk of engaging in high levels of sedentary behavior (such as people living with mental illness; Rosenbaum et al., 2016). The aim of the Simple Physical Activity Questionnaire (SIMPAQ) project was to develop a self-report physical activity tool that is sensitive to change and appropriate for use within routine clinical services. Between 2014 and 2016, the international working group developed the five-item SIMPAQ as an instrument to assess physical activity and sedentary behavior among clinical populations. During 2016–17, 40 centers from 23 countries collected reliability and validity data on the SIMPAQ from patients with mental illness including test–retest repeatability assessed 1-week apart. Criterion SIMPAQ validity was assessed against the Actigraph Gt3x accelerometer. Differences between the SIMPAQ and existing tools such as the IPAQ-SF include recommendation that the tool be used as a structured interview, features allowing for participant responses to be checked to minimize risk of significant under- and over-reporting, removal of reference to physical activity intensity, and inclusion of dedicated napping question, given the high clinical relevance of day-time sleep to the functional recovery of people living with mental illness. In addition, contrary to the IPAQ-SF, the SIMPAQ aims to capture very low levels of physical activity, given the established acute benefits of even small amounts of activity for people with mental illness (as opposed to minimum 10-min bouts assessed by the IPAQ-SF).

## Cardiorespiratory Fitness and Exercise Capacity

People living with mental illness have significantly reduced fitness (aerobic exercise capacity) compared with the general population, which is a key contributing factor to the high rates of premature mortality in this population (Kennedy et al., 2018; Vancampfort et al., 2016a, 2017b). In a review of prospective cohort studies, data from 1,142,699 people found that, among both men and women, poor cardiorespiratory fitness was linked to a higher risk of developing depression, with low fitness levels associated with a 75% increased risk of depression, while those with medium fitness levels had an increased risk of approximately 23% (Schuch et al., 2016a). In a long-term prospective cohort study, cardiorespiratory fitness was shown to be associated with a reduced risk of future psychosis in roughly graded dose–response pattern among middle-aged Caucasian men (Kunutsor et al., 2018). Clearly, the prognostic value of fitness for future mental health risk requires further methodologically robust investigation. A subsequent study with over one million Swedish males also found that lower fitness in late adolescent males was associated with an increased risk of serious nonaffective mental disorders in adulthood (Nyberg et al., 2017). In a sample of 70 patients experiencing first-episode schizophrenia in the United States, muscular strength and endurance, muscular flexibility, and cardiorespiratory fitness were assessed using the Young Men's Christian Association standardized fitness test, with most scores below the 50th percentile compared with national norms (Gretchen-Doorly et al., 2012). Furthermore, patients with a higher body mass index and those who smoked had even poorer results, with a nonsignificant trend indicating that patients with a longer duration of illness had a further reduced exercise capacity (Gretchen-Doorly et al., 2012). In another sample of 60 desired weight and overweight patients with schizophrenia, exercise capacity and self-reported physical activity levels were assessed via the 6-min walk test and Baecke questionnaire (Vancampfort et al., 2011). Compared with healthy controls, patients with schizophrenia walked a significantly shorter distance ($P < .001$; Vancampfort et al., 2011).

Improved fitness in response to exercise interventions is also an important outcome for exercise professionals to promote to mental health professionals. A common misconception among health professionals and the general population is that the primary reason people with a mental illness (and indeed the general population) should engage in exercise is for weight management, despite strong, consistent evidence that (1) exercise alone in the absence of dietary modification is an ineffective weight loss strategy, with low probability of obese individuals achieving normal weight status (Donnelly et al., 2009) and (2) changes in psychiatric symptomatology in response to exercise occur independently (and even in the absence) of weight loss (Firth et al., 2015). Exercise-based interventions targeting people experiencing mental illness significantly improve cardiorespiratory fitness, typically over a relatively short period of time (typically 12 weeks; Stubbs et al., 2016a; Vancampfort et al., 2015a). Improvements are greater following interventions incorporating high-intensity activity, those with a higher frequency of exercise (at least three times per week) and those interventions that are supervised by qualified personnel (i.e., physical therapists and exercise physiologists; Stubbs et al., 2016a; Vancampfort et al., 2015a).

Similarly to physical activity levels, there are a number of commonly utilized methods to assess cardiorespiratory fitness, ranging from direct measurement through resource-intensive ergometers and metabolic carts to extrapolating heart rate response to a given exercise workload. As previously stated, the choice of assessment tool should be informed by the purpose of the evaluation. For example, maximal exercise tests (assessing maximal oxygen uptake; $VO_2max$) are unlikely to be feasible or acceptable for routine use within clinical mental health facilities. Maximal exercise tests require not only trained professionals and dedicated infrastructure but also a considerable level of participant motivation to achieve physiological maximum (Noonan and Dean, 2000). Submaximal exercise tests including protocols such as the YMCA (American College of Sports Medicine, 2013) and Astrand-Rhyming (Astrand and Rhyming, 1954) tests offer a feasible alternative to maximal tests and have been used extensively among people with mental illness (Vancampfort et al., 2014; Rosenbaum et al., 2015). Another feasible option for assessing functional exercise capacity that has been used among people with mental illness is the 6-min walk test (Bernard et al., 2015). The 8-item Eurofit battery has also been shown to be feasible and acceptable to measure various aspects of exercise capacity (whole body balance, speed of limb movement, flexibility, explosive strength, static strength, abdominal muscular endurance, running speed, and cardiovascular endurance) in adolescents taking antipsychotic medication (Vancampfort et al., 2016b).

## Quality of Life

Another important outcome for practitioners to consider is QoL (Katschnig, 2000). Physical activity interventions can have a significant effect on improving QoL among people with a mental illness (Rosenbaum et al., 2014; Vancampfort et al., 2017a; Schuch et al., 2016b). Various tools exist by which QoL can be assessed through self-report including but not limited to the SF-36 (Jenkinson et al., 1993), SF-12 (Ware et al., 1995), and the World Health Organization Quality of Life instrument (WHOQOL) and World Health Organization Quality of Life instrument and brief version (WHOQOL-BREF) (Group W, 1998). The ability to conduct economic analyses using QoL data is another benefit of assessing QoL as part of any evaluation.

## Sleep Behavior

People living with mental illness often experience poorer overall sleep quality in comparison to the general population. Poor sleep quality can exacerbate symptoms of mental illness and contribute to the high prevalence of poor physical health (Stubbs et al., 2016b). Physical activity may serve as an effective nonpharmacological strategy for managing poor sleep behavior and therefore assessing sleep behavior through objective (e.g., polysomnography) or self-report tools (Pittsburgh Sleep Quality Index; Buysse et al., 1989) may be warranted.

# PUTTING IT ALL TOGETHER: PLANNING FOR AND CONDUCTING AN EVALUATION

## Asking the Right Question

As discussed previously, the steps involved in conducting an evaluation include firstly deciding what the research question is that you want to be answered. Often one of the biggest challenges facing researchers is narrowing their primary question down to a single, feasible, and realistic aim. An important skill for practitioners is the ability to ask research questions that will simultaneously enhance service delivery while also contributing to knowledge in a progressive "step-by-step- manner." Having access to mentors with research experience who can not only guide practitioners through the practical research process but also help to narrow ideas is a fundamental part of the overall research experience.

## Ensuring the Method Matches the Aim

Once the aim of the project has been decided, it is imperative that the chosen methodology is appropriate to answer the specific question. For example, qualitative research methods may not be appropriate to answer questions related to the efficacy of an intervention in improving cholesterol but may be appropriate in helping to understand why a participant did or did not attend an exercise program.

## Choosing the Right Outcome Measure

Although it may be tempting to use lots of different measures, there are a number of factors to consider including the participant burden associated with completing the assessments (i.e., how long it takes for the participant to complete). In addition, measuring lots of different outcomes naturally increases the probability of a significant finding (i.e., rejecting the null hypothesis or *type 1 error*). Regularly referring back to the aim and chosen methodology can help to ensure that the outcomes are appropriate, given the desired aims of the evaluation. Another important consideration is the access to relevant resources (including human resources) and funds, given the impact that both can have on the complexity of any outcome. For example, in well-funded evaluations such as clinical trials, it may be realistic to use neuroimaging such as magnetic resonance imaging, whereas a service evaluation auditing existing clinical data may rely on a routinely assessed outcome such as blood pressure.

## Developing a Protocol and Submitting for Ethical Review

Once the aim, methodology, and outcomes have been decided, developing a detailed research protocol is necessary to maintain quality, fidelity, reproducibility, and for audit purposes. A detailed research protocol is a required component of any submission to an ethical review board and the development of which can also help refine the evaluation.

## Data Collection, Analysis, and Dissemination

While the specifics of data collection and statistical analysis are beyond the scope of this chapter, this can certainly be a frustrating time for people trying to conduct clinical research. Delays in participant recruitment, logistical issues with clinical facilities, referral problems, and resourcing limitations such as change in budgets/staffing are all common challenges faced by those conducting pragmatic evaluation within clinical settings. A part of the research process that is often overlooked, yet vital for progress is the need to dissemination results (i.e., communicate the findings). Be it through departmental presentations, conferences, social media (if ethically approved and appropriate), or publication in peer-reviewed journals, dissemination can take place through a number of ways and is arguably as important as the other steps involved in the research process. In addition to peer review, dissemination and knowledge translation are fundamental to ensuring that results can have real-world impact and contribute to the constantly evolving interrelationship between evidence and practice.

## References

American College of Sports Medicine, 2013. ACSM's Guidelines for Exercise Testing and Prescription, ninth ed. Lippincott Williams & Wilkins, Philadelphia.

Astrand, P., Rhyming, I., 1954. A nomogram for calculation of aerobic capacity (Physical Fitness) from pulse rate during submaximal work. J. Appl. Physiol. 7, 218−221.

Bauman, A., et al., 2009. Progress and pitfalls in the use of the International Physical Activity Questionnaire (IPAQ) for adult physical activity surveillance. J. Phys. Activ. Health 6 (1), S5.

Bernard, P., et al., 2015. Six minutes walk test for individuals with schizophrenia. Disabil. Rehabil. 37 (11), 921−927.

Bossu, C., et al., 2007. Energy expenditure adjusted for body composition differentiates constitutional thinness from both normal subjects and anorexia nervosa. Am. J. Physiol. Endocrinol. Metabol. 292 (1), E132−E137.

Buysse, D.J., et al., 1989. The Pittsburgh Sleep Quality Index: a new instrument for psychiatric practice and research. Psychiatry Res. 28 (2), 193−213.

Chapman, J.J., et al., 2015. The feasibility and acceptability of questionnaires and accelerometry for measuring physical activity and sedentary behaviour in adults with mental illness. J. Ment. Health 24 (5), 299−304.

Clark, B.A., et al., 1975. Response of institutionalized geriatric mental patients to a twelve-week program of regular physical activity. J. Gerontol. 30 (5), 565–573.

Craig, C.L., et al., 2003. International physical activity questionnaire: 12-country reliability and validity. Med. Sci. Sports Exerc. 35.

Donnelly, J.E., et al., 2009. American College of Sports Medicine Position Stand. Appropriate physical activity intervention strategies for weight loss and prevention of weight regain for adults. Med. Sci. Sports Exerc. 41 (2), 459–471.

Duncan, M.J., et al., 2017. Revisiting the international physical activity questionnaire (IPAQ): assessing physical activity among individuals with schizophrenia. Schizophr. Res. 179, 2–7.

Ekkekakis, P., Hartman, M.E., Ladwig, M.A., 2018. Mass media representations of the evidence as a possible deterrent to recommending exercise for the treatment of depression: lessons five years after the extraordinary case of TREAD-UK. J. Sports Sci. 1–12.

Faulkner, G., Cohn, T., Remington, G., 2006. Validation of a physical activity assessment tool for individuals with schizophrenia. Schizophr. Res. 82, 225–231.

Firth, J., et al., 2015. A systematic review and meta-analysis of exercise interventions in schizophrenia patients. Psychol. Med. 45 (7), 1343–1361.

Firth, J., et al., 2017 Oct 24. The validity and value of self-reported physical activity and accelerometry in people with schizophrenia: a population-scale study of the UK Biobank. Schizophr. Bull. https://doi.org/10.1093/schbul/sbx149 [Epub ahead of print].

Gates, A.B., et al., 2017. Movement for movement: exercise as everybody's business? Br. J. Sports Med. 51, 767–768.

Gorczynski, P., et al., 2014. Examining strategies to improve accelerometer compliance for individuals living with schizophrenia. Psychiatr. Rehabil. J. 37 (4), 333–335.

Gretchen-Doorly, D., et al., 2012. Cardiorespiratory endurance, muscular flexibility and strength in first-episode schizophrenia patients: use of a standardized fitness assessment. Early Intervention Psychiatry 6 (2), 185–190.

Helmerhorst, H.J., et al., 2012. A systematic review of reliability and objective criterion-related validity of physical activity questionnaires. Int. J. Behav. Nutr. Phys. Act. 9 (1), 103.

Jabben, N., et al., 2012. Cognitive processes and attitudes in bipolar disorder: a study into personality, dysfunctional attitudes and attention bias in patients with bipolar disorder and their relatives. J. Affect. Disord. 143 (1–3), 265–268.

Jenkinson, C., Coulter, A., Wright, L., 1993. Short form 36 (SF36) health survey questionnaire: normative data for adults of working age. Bmj 306 (6890), 1437–1440.

Jerome, G.J., et al., 2009. Physical activity levels of persons with mental illness attending psychiatric rehabilitation programs. Schizophr. Res. 108 (1–3), 252–257.

Katschnig, H., 2000. Schizophrenia and quality of life. Acta Psychiatr. Scand. 102 (s407), 33–37.

Kennedy, A., Lavie, C.J., Blair, S.N., 2018. Fitness or fatness: which is more important? J. Am. Med. Assoc. 319 (3), 231–232.

Kohl, H.W., et al., 2012. The pandemic of physical inactivity: global action for public health. Lancet 380 (9838), 294–305.

Köhler, S., et al., 2015. Dysfunctional cognitions of depressive inpatients and their relationship with treatment outcome. Compr. Psychiatry 58, 50–56.

Kunutsor, S.K., Laukkanen, T., Laukkanen, J.A., 2018. Cardiorespiratory fitness is associated with reduced risk of future psychosis: a long-term prospective cohort study. Schizophr. Res. 192, 473–474.

Lederman, O., et al., 2016. Consensus statement on the role of Accredited Exercise Physiologists within the treatment of mental disorders: a guide for mental health professionals. Australas. Psychiatry 24 (4), 347–351.

Lederman, O., et al., 2017. Embedding exercise interventions as routine mental health care: implementation strategies in residential, inpatient and community settings. Australas. Psychiatry 25 (5), 451–455.

Lee, P., et al., 2011. Validity of the international physical activity questionnaire short form (IPAQ-SF): a systematic review. Int. J. Behav. Nutr. Phys. Act. 8 (115).

Lee, P.H., Macfarlane, D.J., Lam, T.H., 2013. Factors Associated with Participant Compliance in Studies Using Accelerometers. Gait Posture vol. 38 (4), 912—917.

Linden, M., Godemann, F., 2007. The differentiation between 'lack of insight' and 'dysfunctional health beliefs' in schizophrenia. Psychopathology 40 (4), 236—241.

Noonan, V., Dean, E., 2000. Submaximal exercise testing: clinical application and interpretation. Phys. Ther. 80 (8), 782—807.

Nyberg, J., et al., 2017. Cardiovascular fitness in late adolescent males and later risk of serious non-affective mental disorders: a prospective, population-based study. Psychol. Med. 1—10.

Owen, N., Bauman, A., Brown, W., 2009. Too much sitting: a novel and important predictor of chronic disease risk? Br. J. Sports Med. 43 (2), 81—83.

Probst, M., 2012. The international organization of physical therapists working in mental health (IOPTMH). Mental Health Phys. Act. 5 (1), 20—21.

Rebar, A.L., et al., 2015. A Meta-Meta-Analysis of the effect of physical activity on depression and anxiety in non-clinical adult populations. Health Psychol. Rev. 9 (3), 1—78.

Rebar, A.L., Taylor, A., 2017. Physical activity and mental health; it is more than just a prescription. Mental Health Phys. Act. 13, 77—82.

Rosenbaum, S., et al., 2014. Physical activity interventions for people with mental illness: a systematic review and meta-analysis. J. Clin. Psychiatry 75 (9), 964—974.

Rosenbaum, S., et al., 2015. Aerobic exercise capacity: an important correlate of psychosocial function in first episode psychosis. Acta Psychiatr. Scand. 131 (3), 234.

Rosenbaum, S., Ward, P.B., International Working, G., 2016. The simple physical activity questionnaire. Lancet Psychiatry 3 (1), e1.

Sackett, D.L., 1997. Evidence-based medicine. In: Seminars in Perinatology. Elsevier.

Sallis, R., 2011. Developing healthcare systems to support exercise: exercise as the fifth vital sign. Br. J. Sports Med. 45 (6), 473—474.

Schuch, F.B., et al., 2016a. Are lower levels of cardiorespiratory fitness associated with incident depression? A systematic review of prospective cohort studies. Prev. Med. 93, 159—165.

Schuch, F.B., et al., 2016b. Exercise improves physical and psychological quality of life in people with depression: a meta-analysis including the evaluation of control group response. Psychiatry Res. 241, 47—54.

Schuch, F.B., et al., 2016c. Exercise as a treatment for depression: a meta-analysis adjusting for publication bias. J. Psychiatr. Res. 77, 42—51.

Sharpe, J.K., et al., 2006. Energy expenditure and physical activity in clozapine use: implications for weight management. Aust. N. Z. J. Psychiatr. 40 (9), 810—814.

Shephard, R.J., 2003. Limits to the measurement of habitual physical activity by questionnaires. Br. J. Sports Med. 37 (3), 197—206 discussion 206.

Soundy, A., et al., 2014. Selection, use and psychometric properties of physical activity measures to assess individuals with severe mental illness: a narrative synthesis. Arch. Psychiatr. Nurs. 28 (2), 135—151.

Stanton, R., et al., 2017. Implementation in action: how Australian Exercise Physiologists approach exercise prescription for people with mental illness. J. Ment. Health 1—7.

Strath, S.J., et al., 2013. Guide to the assessment of physical activity: clinical and research applications: a scientific statement from the American Heart Association. Circulation 128 (20), 2259—2279.

Stubbs, B., et al., 2014. Physiotherapists can help implement physical activity programmes in clinical practice. Br. J. Psychiatry 204 (2), 164.

Stubbs, B., et al., 2016a. Exercise improves cardiorespiratory fitness in people with depression: a meta-analysis of randomized control trials. J. Affect. Disord. 190, 249—253.

Stubbs, B., et al., 2016b. The prevalence and predictors of obstructive sleep apnea in major depressive disorder, bipolar disorder and schizophrenia: a systematic review and meta-analysis. J. Affect. Disord. 197, 259–267.

Stubbs, B., et al., 2017. An examination of the anxiolytic effects of exercise for people with anxiety and stress-related disorders: a meta-analysis. Psychiatry Res. 249, 102–108.

Vancampfort, D., et al., 2011. Relationships between obesity, functional exercise capacity, physical activity participation and physical self-perception in people with schizophrenia. Acta Psychiatr. Scand. 123 (6), 423–430.

Vancampfort, D., et al., 2013. A review of physical activity correlates in patients with bipolar disorder. J. Affect. Disord. 145 (3), 285–291.

Vancampfort, D., et al., 2014. Reliability and clinical correlates of the Astrand-Rhyming submaximal exercise test in patients with schizophrenia or schizoaffective disorder. Psychiatry Res. 220 (3), 778–783.

Vancampfort, D., et al., 2015a. Exercise improves cardiorespiratory fitness in people with schizophrenia: a systematic review and meta-analysis. Schizophr. Res. 169 (1–3), 453–457.

Vancampfort, D., et al., 2015b. Integrating physical activity as medicine in the care of people with severe mental illness. Aust. N. Z. J. Psychiatry 49 (8), 681–682.

Vancampfort, D., et al., 2015c. Why moving more should be promoted for severe mental illness. Lancet Psychiatry 2 (4), 295.

Vancampfort, D., et al., 2016a. Cardiorespiratory fitness in severe mental illness: a systematic review and meta-analysis. Sports Med. 1–10.

Vancampfort, D., et al., 2016b. Impact of antipsychotic medication on physical activity and physical fitness in adolescents: an exploratory study. Psychiatry Res. 242, 192–197.

Vancampfort, D., et al., 2016c. Physical activity as a vital sign in patients with bipolar disorder. Psychiatry Res. 246, 218–222.

Vancampfort, D., et al., 2016d. Physical activity as a vital sign in patients with schizophrenia: evidence and clinical recommendations. Schizophr. Res. 170 (2–3), 336–340.

Vancampfort, D., et al., 2017a. Physical activity is associated with the physical, psychological, social and environmental quality of life in people with mental health problems in a low resource setting. Psychiatry Res. 258, 250–254.

Vancampfort, D., et al., 2017b. Sedentary behavior and physical activity levels in people with schizophrenia, bipolar disorder and major depressive disorder: a global systematic review and meta-analysis. World Psychiatr. 16 (3), 308–315.

Vancampfort, D., et al., 2018. Adherence to physical activity recommendations and physical and mental health risk in people with severe mental illness in Uganda. Psychiatry Res. 260, 236–240.

Vancampfort, D., Faulkner, G., 2014. Physical activity and serious mental illness: a multidisciplinary call to action. Mental Health Phys. Act. 3 (7), 153–154.

Vanhees, L., et al., 2005. How to assess physical activity? How to assess physical fitness? Eur. J. Cardiovasc. Prev. Rehabil. 12 (2), 102–114.

Ware, J.E., Keller, S.D., Kosinski, M., 1995. SF-12: How to Score the SF-12 Physical and Mental Health Summary Scales. Health Institute, New England Medical Center.

Warren, J.M., et al., 2010a. Assessment of physical activity—a review of methodologies with reference to epidemiological research: a report of the exercise physiology section of the European Association of Cardiovascular Prevention and Rehabilitation. Eur. J. Cardiovasc. Prev. Rehabil. 17 (2), 127–139.

Whoqol Group, 1998. Development of the world health organization WHOQOL-BREF quality of life assessment. Psychol. Med. 28 (3), 551–558.

## CHAPTER

# 17

# Research to Practice: Case Studies[*]

*Paul Gorczynski[1], Solfrid Bratland-Sanda[2], Oscar Lederman[3], Javier Bueno-Antequera[4], Diego Munguía-Izquierdo[4]*

[1] Department of Sport and Exercise Science, University of Portsmouth, Hampshire, United Kingdom; [2] University College of Southeast Norway, Bø, Norway; [3] University of New South Wales, Sydney, Australia; [4] Universidad Pablo de Olavide, Seville, Spain

[*] This whole chapter was edited by Simon Rosenbaum, University of New South Wales, Sydney, Australia

*Exercise-Based Interventions for Mental Illness*
https://doi.org/10.1016/B978-0-12-812605-9.00017-4

**319**

Exercise interventions for people living with mental illness are delivered in a variety of ways, by a range of professionals, across different clinical and nonclinical environments. The aim of this chapter was to provide examples of real-world case studies which demonstrate how exercise has been used across a diverse range of diagnoses and settings. This chapter describes case studies from four different settings, including

- a 25-year-old inpatient with schizophrenia in the United Kingdom
- a 27-year-old female outpatient with anorexia nervosa in Norway
- a 19-year-old male with the first-episode psychosis (FEP) living in the community in Australia
- a 39-year-old female outpatient with bipolar disorder in Spain

Details of the clients, pathology, and treatment plan have been provided along with information regarding the education of the supervisor and the context in which the intervention was delivered. All four case studies represent real experiences of the author.

# EXERCISE COUNSELLING FOR PEOPLE LIVING WITH A DIAGNOSIS OF SCHIZOPHRENIA: A CASE STUDY

**Dr Paul Gorczynski, University of Portsmouth, UK.**

| | |
|---|---|
| Country | United Kingdom |
| Professional background/discipline | Exercise Science, Exercise Psychology |
| Qualification/experience | PhD Exercise Science, British Psychological Society Chartered Psychologist |
| Occupation | Senior Lecturer, University of Portsmouth |

**1. Client/patient demographics**

| | |
|---|---|
| Occupation | Unemployed |
| Sex | Female |
| Age | 25 years |
| Diagnosis | Schizophrenia |
| Medical history | Length of illness 13 years |
| Current medication | Clozapine, Benztropine, Orlistat |
| Setting | Group home residence where meals are provided; treatment provided at outpatient clinic |
| Social context | No currently working, living in group facility |
| Patient complaint(s) | None |

**2. Assessment(s)**

| | |
|---|---|
| Objective | Accelerometer |
| Self-report | Readiness to become active, self-efficacy, physical activity (International Physical Activity Questionnaire [IPAQ]) |

Kristen was a 25-year-old, single woman living with a diagnosis of schizophrenia for the past 13 years. Kristen was not working and lived in an in-patient setting where meals were provided. Her medication regimen included Clozapine, Benztropine, and a weight reduction medication. She had a body mass index (BMI) of 31.9 $kg/m^2$ and described herself as being physically inactive, but thinking about becoming active in the next 3—6 months. Kristen had agreed to take part in exercise counseling to improve and sustain her overall levels of physical activity (Gorczynski et a., 2014).

The exercise counseling intervention consisted of four 60-min individual sessions over the course of 1 month with a trained exercise professional. The exercise professional was trained in motivational interviewing and sport and exercise psychology. Baseline measurements were conducted 1 and 2 weeks prior to the session, and identical follow-up measurements were conducted 4 and 5 weeks after the last session. Measurements included the Physical Activity Questionnaire, physical activity self-efficacy, and perceived benefits of and barriers to physical activity (Craig et al., 2003; Long et al., 1996).

The exercise counseling sessions were based on motivational interviewing techniques and reinforced its five core principles: expressing empathy through reflective listening; developing discrepancy between current behavior and future goals; avoiding argumentation; working with resistance; and strengthening self-efficacy (Carey et al., 2007; Miller and Rollnick, 2002). The overall goal of the exercise counseling was to help patients increase their levels of physical activity by strengthening their physical activity self-efficacy and improving their perceptions of living an active life.

## Session 1: Build Rapport and Gather Knowledge

The first session aimed to establish a therapeutic alliance between Kristen and the exercise professional and assess her readiness to become active. Past and present physical activity behaviors were examined as well as her future physical activity interests. Kristen was asked to complete a decisional balance that assessed her positive and negative perceptions of becoming active, with an encouragement to think positively about the benefits of physical activity. Lastly, Kristen was asked how confident she was to become active and how important it was for her to do so. Overall, Kristen indicated that she felt fairly confident about becoming active and that it was important to her. She also indicated that she didn't think anything could get in her way.

## Session 2: Goal Setting

The second session aimed to help Kristen establish an action plan to become active. Specifically, the session was designed around setting a particular physical activity goal, describing it's importance, creating a series of steps to achieve it, and listing possible support structures to help her achieve it. Additionally, Kristen was asked about potential barriers and how she would address them. The techniques used in this session were designed to help Kristen feel confident in becoming active by strengthening her overall physical activity self-efficacy and barriers self-efficacy through verbal persuasion. Additionally, the session allowed Kristen to autonomously choose an activity she would like to pursue and to do so in a competent manner, knowing there would be support for her should she need it. During the session, Kristen indicated she wanted to walk more and begin riding her bike in the community. Kristen aimed to walk daily for 30 min and ride her bike two times per week. She indicated she kept in regular contact with family members, and that they would be willing to help her if necessary.

## Sessions 3 and 4: Evaluate, Revise, Inform

The third and fourth sessions aimed to help Kristen stay on top of her physical activity goals by evaluating her progress and adjusting to un-foreseen challenges. Throughout the sessions, Kristen was reminded of her support structures and how to rely on them for help when needed. During the weeks in between sessions 3 and 4, Kristen indicated she struggled with getting out of bed, feeling very unmotivated toward being active. She also lost the key to her bicycle lock. Kristen relied on her support networks to help her manage throughout the intervention. She called on a family friend who helped her get out of bed and walk daily. Given that Kristen was not able to locate her bike lock key, she decided to increase her daily walking route.

Overall, Kristen's self-efficacy improved from baseline ($M = 2.7$, standard deviation [SD] $= 0.24$) throughout the intervention ($M = 2.9$, $SD = 0.44$), to follow-up ($M = 3.2$, $SD = 0.0$). Although there was no change in Kristen's perceived benefits of physical activity from baseline ($M = 3.6$, $SD = 0.35$) to follow-up ($M = 3.6$, $SD = 0.35$), Kristen perceived there to be fewer barriers with being regularly active from baseline ($M = 2.2$, $SD = 0.24$) to follow-up ($M = 1.1$, $SD = 0.12$). Despite changes in these determinants of physical activity, Kristen's daily moderate and vigorous physical activity levels fell throughout the intervention from 8.2 min at baseline to 4.3 min at follow-up.

Future efforts need to be made to ensure patients can deal effectively with unexpected personal and environmental challenges that may threaten their overall physical activity. In a sense, counselors need to be mindful of how to help patients deal with physical activity lapses and negative thinking to prevent full relapses. Counselors need to ensure patients have realistic action plans, support networks, and opportunities to continue to strengthen their physical activity self-efficacy and barriers self-efficacy.

# MAXIMAL STRENGTH TRAINING IN RECOVERY OF EATING DISORDERS

## A/Prof Solfrid Bratland-Sanda, University College of Southeast Norway.

| | |
|---|---|
| Country | Norway |
| Professional background/discipline | Clinical Exercise Physiologist/Sport Science |
| Qualification/experience | PhD in sport science |
| Occupation | Associate professor at USN, Norway |

### 1. Client/patient demographics

| | |
|---|---|
| Occupation | Physiotherapist |
| Sex | Female |
| Age | 27 years |
| Diagnosis | DSM-5 Anorexia nervosa |
| Medical history | BMI: 18.4 at baseline<br>Onset of eating disorder: 19 years<br>Treatment: approximately 8 years as both an inpatient and outpatient<br>Normal menstrual cycle at baseline, but with history of amenorrhea |
| Current medication | None |
| Setting | Outpatient |
| Social context | Exercise was supervised by a female instructor with competence in clinical exercise physiology. The participant had sporadically counselling sessions with a psychiatrist during the strength training intervention. She was also encouraged to have contact with her GP whenever she needed. |

### 2. Assessment(s)

| | |
|---|---|
| Objective | Muscle strength, muscle power, body weight, body composition, bone mineral density |
| Self-report | Eating Disorder Examination (EDE) clinical semistructured interview, 4-day food diary |

BMI, body mass index; DSM-5, Diagnostic and Statistical Manual of Mental Disorders; GP, general practitioner; USN, University College of Southeast Norway.

"Anna" was a 27-year-old single woman with an 8-year history of anorexia nervosa and atypical anorexia nervosa. She was currently diagnosed with anorexia nervosa with mild severity (due to BMI higher than 17.5 kg/m$^2$; APA, 2013). The client completed a 16-week maximal strength training program (three sets of 5RM with 2−3 min breaks in between each set, exercises: squats, dead lift, seated rowing, bench press). Sessions were supervised and guided by an experienced clinical exercise physiologist.

She attended 88% (43 out of 48) of all sessions. Energy intake remains unchanged as did body weight and BMI. Improvements were found for upper body (17%) and lower body (13%) muscle strength. Muscle power increased by 22%, and muscle mass increased by 4%. Lumbar spine bone mineral density (BMD) also increased by 3%. As increase in BMD is difficult to achieve, and due to error estimates, this cannot be considered clinically significant (Nguyen et al., 2000). To classify osteopenia and osteoporosis, a T-score is developed (Leib et al., 2004). A T-score higher than −0.99 indicates normal BMD values. Osteopenia, or reduced BMD, is defined as T-score of −1.0 to −2.5. A T-score lower than −2.5 is classified as osteoporosis. Lumbar spine T-score improved from −1.4 to −1.2, indicating that she still had osteopenia after the training intervention. Although her bone health was not clinically significant improved, it was neither deteriorated. This indicates that maximal strength training is tolerable when nutrition is adequate.

The Eating Disorder Examination (EDE) global score was reduced from 2.73 (i.e., score within pathological values) at baseline to 1.97 (i.e., score within normal values, no symptoms of and ED) at posttest (Fairburn, Cooper and O'Connor, 2008). She was temporary amenorrheic during the intervention.

She felt insecure about her lifting technique at pretest and believed that the instructor had inadequate focus on this. This insecurity made her afraid to ask the instructor for help. The training protocol focused on proper technique, and the instructor was carefully spotting Anna's technique during all lifts and all exercises. However, this spotting of technique should have been communicated better to her during the session.

In addition, there was a lack of habituation to the exercises in the testing procedure. Anna considered this a failure, and it impaired her confidence in the training protocol. As ambivalence, fright/anxiety, reluctance to change, and low self-efficacy are common features in anorexia nervosa, the instructor used techniques from motivational interviewing to improve her therapeutic rapport with Anna. During the intervention, Anna therefore became more confident in the communication with the instructor. She also experienced that thoughts related to the eating disorder were in conflict with the training. However, she challenged these thoughts and experienced how the increase in muscle strength made her feel stronger and able to *"take more space"*: *"I feel stronger and more upright. To be able to lift the heavy weights, I had to straighten up and improve my posture. When I did that, something happened to me inside. I was able to take more space. [ …. ] When I straightened up, I had to fight some of my thoughts, if I did not they would have influenced and disturbed me. After that, bit by bit, I straightened up both outside and inside."* Strengthen of self-worth is important in treatment of eating disorders, and the possible psychological effects from maximal strength training exercises on eating disorder psychopathology warrant further research.

Furthermore, she experienced that the recovery breaks between the sets of resistance exercises prompted her to consider taking breaks in other areas of life (during work, at home etc.): *"I have learned the value of taking breaks. Not just in the training settings, but I have transferred this to other situations in the daily life."*

The importance of close follow-up by a competent instructor, and the rapport they developed were emphasized: *"It took a long time before I was comfortable with the long breaks. I felt I got close follow-up during the 16-week. It was easiest to rest when we talked about things other than exercise."* Educated as a physiotherapist, she addressed lack of posture correction and adaptation to the exercises at baseline.

She reported that she would have wanted more of a focus on the nutrition in addition to the exercise. She felt three strength training sessions per week were excessive: *"Three sessions per week felt a lot (…) Will my body get enough recovery time? I still struggled with eating and I lost my period during the study, in addition, it was difficult to control the exercise I did on my own. (…) It is no good to just exercise, if you don't have resources for the recovery. Me losing my period felt like a clear signal of inadequate recovery, and I call for action when menstrual disorders occur. I wish I had two instead of three sessions per week."*

Six months after the intervention, she still performed strength training on regular basis. She reported improvements in muscle strength and the modality with long recovery breaks between the sets as important reasons for continuing to engage in strength training.

Lessons learned from this case are the importance of open communication with the patient. In addition, possible therapeutical benefits of strength training must be explored together with the patient, and other therapists involved in the treatment to ensure awareness and competence about the role and possibilities of exercise in their recovery.

# INCLUDING EXERCISE IN EARLY INTERVENTION FOR YOUNG PEOPLE WITH A FIRST-EPISODE PSYCHOSIS: A CASE STUDY

Oscar Lederman, UNSW Sydney and South Eastern Sydney Local Health District, Sydney, Australia.

| | |
|---|---|
| **1. Case study title** | Early psychosis and clozapine |
| **2. Author details** | |
| Name | Oscar Lederman |
| Country | Australia |
| Professional background/ discipline | Exercise Physiology, Exercise Science, Mental Health Research |
| Occupation | Exercise Physiologist, South Eastern Sydney Local Health District, PhD Candidate, UNSW, Sydney, Australia |
| **3. Client/Patient** demographics | Name: Elliot |
| Occupation | Student |
| Sex | Male |
| Age | 19 years |
| Diagnosis | First-episode psychosis |
| Medical history | Longstanding autistic spectrum disorder |
| Current medication | Clozapine 300 mg nocte oral<br>Lithium Carbonate MR 900 mg nocte oral<br>Aripiprazole 10 mg mane |
| Setting | Community mental health |

Elliot is a 19-year-old male who lives with family and attends college, studying art. Elliot presented initially to the mental health service with auditory hallucinations, mania, and a decline in function, resulting in dropping out of his studies. He was brought into hospital by family due to concerns for his safety as Elliot was demonstrating uncharacteristic behavior.

While in hospital, Elliot was diagnosed with a FEP and prescribed medication. While an inpatient Elliot attended one session with the exercise physiologist in which he was unable to complete a structured exercise session due to mania and being constantly distracted, exercising at dangerous intensities and constantly getting on and off the equipment. Over the following 2 weeks, his mental state continued to deteriorate despite treatment, and he was admitted to an inpatient rehabilitation ward, where he remained for 5 months. Symptoms persisted during his hospital admission, and he was trialed on two types of antipsychotic medications, both of which had no therapeutic effect. The treating psychiatrist then prescribed clozapine (antipsychotic for treatment-resistant psychosis). Once stable, Elliot was discharged from hospital and referred to the local early psychosis team at the community mental health center.

In the community, Elliot had a gym membership and intended to go with his brother however he had not been in over 8 months and his mother had considered cancelling the membership. The community case manager rereferred Elliot to the physical health team (Keeping the Body in Mind program) due to concerns over weight gain, high levels of sedentary behavior, reduced perceived fitness, and increases in blood sugar levels. Elliot also complained about his increased central adiposity which had negatively affected his confidence. The physical health team included an exercise physiologist (Lederman & et al., 2016), dietitian, and metabolic nurse.

## Prescreening

Elliot was medically cleared to participate in an exercise intervention by his general practitioner. No contraindications to exercise were identified as determined by the preexercise screening tool, the Physical Activity Readiness Questionnaire; however, a family history of hypertension was noted.

The initial exercise physiology assessment included objective measures of fitness and a subjective physical activity questionnaire. Results are described below.

Anthropometric and metabolic measures included the following:

Waist circumference: 94 cm (6 cm increase following 3-month hospital admission), weight: 83 kg (8 kg increase following 3-month hospital admission), blood pressure: 132/72, height: 170 cm, BMI: 28.72, BSL Random (point of care testing kit): 7.0 mmol/L.

Keeping the Body in Mind fitness assessment (Curtis & et al., 2016);

1. Aerobic capacity (cardiovascular fitness)—Astrand-Rhyming protocol for sub-$VO_{2max}$ = 38.2 mL/kg/min (poor)
2. Upper body strength assessment—YMCA push-up test (number of push-ups until failure) = 20 reps (fair)
3. Forearm strength—Dynamometer hand-grip strength = R-39 kg, L-37 kg (average)
4. Hamstring flexibility test—sit and reach = −18 cm (poor)
5. Core endurance—YMCA 1-min crunch test = 38 reps (good)

Self-reported physical activity in the past week was measured using the Simple Physical Activity Questionnaire—Short Form (Rosenbaum and Ward, 2016).

Average hours in bed per night: 12.

Average hours sedentary per day: 9 (mainly video games, TV, and reading).

Average minutes walking per day: 40 min.

Average minutes sport/exercise per day: 20 min.

Average time of other activities per day: 15 min.

Napping: 0.

Elliot previously attended a local gym where he enjoyed doing occasional sessions with his brother. These sessions were self-guided and generally included jogging on treadmill and two strength exercises (chest press and lat pull-downs). Elliot also played team sport at school which he enjoyed but had not participated in since leaving school 2 years prior.

Following the initial exercise assessment, the exercise physiologist (EP) met with Elliot for the initial consultation which included an introduction by the case manager and prioritizing rapport building. This was achieved by discussing hobbies, his physical activity history, his current physical activity and barriers to exercise, strategies to overcome the identified barriers, and Specific Measureable Achievable Realistic and Time-Specific goal setting.

Education was provided regarding the differences between structured exercise and sedentary activity. Goals were set that focused on decreasing sedentary activity using an activity planner and a pedometer to achieve a daily minimum of 5000 steps.

## Session 2

Initial exercise assessment and baseline metabolic measures were conducted. Elliot was encouraged to attend "*Sports Group*," to which he was agreeable. "*Sports Group*" is a weekly exercise physiology-led group ran through the mental health service that aims to promote physical activity through social, noncompetitive sport, for example, soccer, tennis, netball, and basketball. Utilizing individual and group-based approaches facilitates engagement in exercise programs and in combination with individual intervention strategies has been show to maximize adherence and attendance (Ward et al., 2015).

## Session 3

Interpreted results from the fitness assessment reviewed goals and had initial discussions of designing a gym-based program for Elliot, assessing

Elliot's "readiness to change" in accordance with the self-determination theory (Vancampfort & et al., 2013).

## Session 4: Motivational Interviewing

Elliot identified he was finding it difficult to initiate his home-based walking (one of his goals); hence, a session of motivational interviewing was conducted. Here, the EP used techniques including "decision balance," "reflective listening" and "rolling with resistance" to discuss Elliot's barriers to achieving his desired goals. Elliot and the EP mutually developed a home-based exercise program which was in line with his goals, strengths, and physical capacity. Allowing choice with the exercises helped to increase a sense of autonomy and choosing exercises that Elliot was familiar with made the program more relatable. Targeting the program at a level that was in line with his ability allowed Elliot to feel a sense of competency. Addressing these three psychological needs when developing the program helped to increase Elliot's intrinsic (or autonomous) motivation (Vancampfort et al., 2015), which is associated with exercise behavior long-term.

## Outcome

Twelve weeks following the initial assessment with the EP, Elliot achieved his goals of reducing his sitting time from 11.5 to 9 h per day. This was achieved by incorporating small 10-min walks every 3 hours of sitting and walking to the shops as opposed to getting a lift (a goal set by Elliot initially). Elliot was reluctant about using his local gym due to paranoia and a level of self-consciousness about his reduced strength and fitness from when he was attending the gym before becoming unwell. Elliot and the EP collaboratively developed a plan to start a home-based exercise program that aimed to build his confidence and physical strength, which could then progress to a gym-based program. Elliot's weight remained neutral 3 weeks into the intervention; however, his physical activity levels increased, and Elliot reported benefits of the exercise on improving his energy levels, mood, and his sleep quality.

For young people presenting to mental health services for the first time, it can be a daunting and often overwhelming experience. Promoting healthy lifestyle choices at the earliest stage can prevent the physical health decline that is commonly seen. A collaborative and patient-centered approach that aims to increase intrinsic motivation and focuses on the individual's goals, strengths, and physical capacity can lead to long-term maintenance goals and promote healthy and active lives.

# LIFESTYLE CHANGES AND CARDIOVASCULAR HEALTH IN A WOMAN WITH BIPOLAR DISORDER: A CASE STUDY OF THE PSYCHOACTIVE PROJECT

**Javier Bueno-Antequera and Prof Diego Munguía-Izquierdo. Universidad Pablo de Olavide, Seville, Spain.**

| | |
|---|---|
| Country | Spain |
| Professional background/discipline | Exercise Science |
| Qualification/experience | MS Exercise Science |
| Occupation | PhD Exercise Science, supported by the Spanish Ministry of Education (grant number FPU13/05130) |
| **1. Client/patient demographics** | |
| Occupation | Unfit to work |
| Sex | Female |
| Age | 39 years |
| Diagnosis | Bipolar disorder |
| Medical history | Length of illness 5 years |
| Current medication | Combination of first- and second-generation antipsychotics, antidepressant, benzodiazepine, anticholinergic, mood stabilizer, antihypertensive, and lipid-lowering medication |
| Setting | Outpatient |
| Social context | No currently working, living with her family and two sons |
| **2. Assessment(s)** | |
| Objective | Physical activity, sedentary behavior, body mass index, total cholesterol, fasting glucose, blood pressure, fitness |
| Self-report | Smoking status, diet, symptom severity |

Silvia is a 39-year-old woman with a medical history of bipolar disorder for 5 years, fibromyalgia, osteoporosis, early menopause, hypothyroidism, thalassemia minor, who smokes approximately 40 cigarettes per day with comorbid obesity and persistent back pain, medically unfit to work and who lives independently with her family.

She had agreed to participate voluntarily and without economic compensation in the PsychoActive project that includes cross-sectional and intervention multicenter studies as an integrated approach to positive health behavior and healthy lifestyle from people with severe mental illness from Spain.

The intervention involved primarily increasing time engaged in physical activity (walking) and encouraging healthier eating (replacing fat intake with fruits and vegetables and replacing breakfast and dinner with liquid supplementation).

Baseline assessment included the seven ideal components of cardio-vascular health defined by the American Heart Association (Lloyd-Jones et al., 2010), including sedentary behavior, fitness, and severity of psychiatric symptoms. Follow-up measurements were conducted 18 months following the intervention. At both times, Silvia was clinically stable and prescribed second-generation antipsychotic medication.

## RESULTS

Table 17.1 summarizes Silvia's characteristics at both time points. 18 months after commencing basic lifestyle changes, Silvia was engaged in more active and less sedentary activities and showed increased adherence to a Mediterranean diet, achieving five of the seven ideal cardiovascular health (CVH) metrics, which is associated with a lower risk of all-cause and cardiovascular mortalities (Younus et al., 2016). Improvements in anthropometric data (e.g., reduced body mass from 108 to 79 kg), fitness, and reductions in severity of psychiatric symptoms and medication use were also found.

## DISCUSSION

Our single-study case demonstrated substantial improvements in cardiovascular health, anthropometric data, and fitness, which were accompanied by reductions in severity of psychiatric symptoms and medication use, in response to a simple healthy lifestyle intervention.

At follow-up, Silvia was engaged in more active and less sedentary activities and had increased adherence to Mediterranean diet over the study period. These healthy lifestyle choices are related to improvements in cardiovascular health (Same et al., 2016; Alves et al., 2016; Sofi et al., 2014). In addition to the notable weight loss (29 kg), the significant improvements in fitness should be also considered as a key outcome following the intervention, given that high levels of physical fitness are known to be protective against cardiovascular disease morbidity and mortality (Zomer et al., 2016; Barry et al., 2014). The reduction in upper-limb strength may be a result of the physical activity modality selected

TABLE 17.1   Silvia's Characteristics

| Variable | Baseline | Follow-Up |
|---|---|---|
| **Cardiovascular Health** | | |
| Smoking | current | current |
| Body mass index (kg/m$^2$) | 38.7 | 28.0 |
| Physical activity (min/week) | 375 | 533 |
| Healthy diet pattern (MEDA score) | 6 | 10 |
| Total cholesterol (mg/dL) | 183 | 190 |
| Systolic/diastolic blood pressure (mm Hg) | 128/83 | 102/71 |
| Fasting plasma glucose (mg/dL) | 100 | 78 |
| Number of ideal criteria fulfilled[a] (n) | 2 | 5 |
| Sedentary time (h/day, % of waking time) | 12.0 (82) | 7.4 (47) |
| **Fitness** | | |
| 30-s arm curl (repetitions) | 27 | 23 |
| 30-s chair timed stand (repetitions) | 16 | 20 |
| 6-minute walking (m) | 487 | 573 |
| Severity of psychiatric symptoms[b] (0–72) | 40 | 24 |
| Chlorpromazine equivalent dose (mg/day) | 630 | 150 |
| **No antipsychotic medication (−/use)** | | |
| Antidepressant | use | − |
| Benzodiazepine | use | use |
| Anticholinergic | use | − |
| Mood stabilizer | use | − |
| Antidiabetic | − | − |
| Antihypertensive | use | − |
| Lipid-lowering medication | use | − |

[a]*Following the American Heart Association ideal cardiovascular health definition, ideal criteria were smoking: never or quit >12 month ago; body mass index: <25 kg/m$^2$; physical activity: ≥ 150 min/week moderate–vigorous physical activity accumulated in bouts of ≥10 min (SenseWear Pro3 Armband); healthy diet pattern (adherence to the Mediterranean diet with scores ≥ 10 in the 14-item Mediterranean Diet Tool (Martinez-Gonzalez et al., 2012); total cholesterol: <200 mg/dL; blood pressure: <120/<80 mm Hg; fasting plasma glucose: <100 mg/dL.*
[b]*Severity of psychiatric symptoms was assessed using the Spanish version of the Brief Symptoms Inventory-18, with a higher score indicating high severity.*

by Silvia which was predominately walking, involving the lower limb muscles. The reductions in severity of psychiatric symptoms and medication use are also of clinical and public health interest suggesting that lifestyle change interventions may potentially have utility in reducing the overall number of services and hence the cost of medical care for people with bipolar disorder. In summary, the single-case study highlights that lifestyle change interventions are a feasible, effective, and acceptable adjunct to usual care and may protect the cardiovascular health of people with bipolar disorder.

# References

Alves, A.J., Viana, J.L., Cavalcante, S.L., et al, 2016. Physical activity in primary and secondary prevention of cardiovascular disease: overview updated. World J. Cardiol. 8 (10), 575–583.

APA., 2013. Diagnostic and Statistical Manual of Mental Disorders, fifth ed. American Psychiatric Publishing, Arlington, VA.

Barry, V.W., Baruth, M., Beets, M.W., Durstine, J.L., Liu, J., Blair, S.N., 2014. Fitness vs. fatness on all-cause mortality: a meta-analysis. Prog. Cardiovasc. Dis. 56 (4), 382–390.

Carey, K.B., Leontieva, L., Dimmock, J., Maisto, S.A., Batki, S.L., 2007. Adapting motivational interviewing for comorbid schizophrenia and alcohol use disorders. Clin. Psychol. Sci. Pract. 14 (1), 39e57. https://doi.org/10.1111/j.1468-2850.2007.00061.x.

Craig, C.L., Marsha, A.L., Sjostrom, M., Bauman, A.E., Booth, M.L., Ainsworth, A.E., et al., 2003. International physical activity questionnaire: 12-country reliability and validity. Med. Sci. Sports Exerc. 35 (8), 1381–1395.

Curtis, J., et al, 2016. Evaluating an individualized lifestyle and life skills intervention to prevent antipsychotic-induced weight gain in first-episode psychosis. Early Interv. Psychiatry 10 (3), 267–276.

Fairburn, C., Cooper, Z., O'Connor, M., 2008. The Eating disorder Examination (16.0D). In: Fairburn, C. (Ed.), Cognitive Behavior Therapy and Eating Disorders. Guilford Press, New York, pp. 265–308.

Gorczynski, P., Faulkner, G., Cohn, T., Remington, G., 2014. Examining the efficacy and feasibility of exercise counseling in individuals with schizophrenia: a single-case experimental study. Mental Health Phys. Act. 7 (3), 191–197.

Lederman, O., et al, 2016. Consensus statement on the role of accredited exercise physiologists within the treatment of mental disorders: a guide for mental health professionals. Australas. Psychiatr. 24 (4), 347–351.

Leib, E.S., Lewiecki, E.M., Binkley, N., Hamdy, R.C., 2004. Official positions of the international society for clinical densitometry. J. Clin. Densitom. 7 (1), 1–6.

Lloyd-Jones, D.M., Hong, Y., Labarthe, D., et al., 2010. Defining and setting national goals for cardiovascular health promotion and disease reduction: the American Heart Association's strategic impact goal through 2020 and beyond. Circulation 121 (4), 586–613.

Long, B.J., Calfas, K.J., Wooten, W., Sallis, J.F., Patrick, K., Goldstein, M., et al., 1996. A multisite field test of the acceptability of physical activity counseling in primary care: project PACE. Am. J. Prev. Med. 12 (2), 73e81.

Martinez-Gonzalez, M.A., Garcia-Arellano, A., Toledo, E., et al., 2012. A 14-item Mediterranean diet assessment tool and obesity indexes among high-risk subjects: the PREDIMED trial. PLoS One 7 (8), e43134.

Miller, W.R., Rollnick, S., 2002. Motivational Interviewing: Preparing People for Change, second ed. Guilford, New York.

Nguyen, T.V., Pocock, N., Eisman, J.A., 2000. Interpretation of bone mineral density measurement and its change. J. Clin. Densitom. 3 (2), 107–119.

Rosenbaum, S., Ward, P.B., 2016. The simple physical activity questionnaire. Lancet Psychiatry 3 (1), e1.

Same, R.V., Feldman, D.I., Shah, N., et al., 2016. Relationship between sedentary behavior and cardiovascular risk. Curr. Cardiol. Rep. 18 (1), 6.

Sofi, F., Macchi, C., Abbate, R., Gensini, G.F., Casini, A., 2014. Mediterranean diet and health status: an updated meta-analysis and a proposal for a literature-based adherence score. Public Health Nutr. 17 (12), 2769–2782.

Vancampfort, D., et al., 2013. The importance of self-determined motivation towards physical activity in patients with schizophrenia. Psychiatr. Res. 210 (3), 812–818.

Vancampfort, D., et al., 2015. Adopting and maintaining physical activity behaviours in people with severe mental illness: the importance of autonomous motivation. Prev. Med. 81, 216–220.

Ward, M.C., White, D., Druss, B.G., 2015. A meta-review of lifestyle interventions for cardiovascular risk factors in the general medical population: lessons for individuals with serious mental illness. J. Clin. Psychiatr. 76 (4) e477-86.

Younus, A., Aneni, E.C., Spatz, E.S., et al., 2016. A systematic review of the prevalence and outcomes of ideal cardiovascular health in US and non-US populations. Mayo Clin. Proc. 91 (5), 649–670.

Zomer, E., Gurusamy, K., Leach, R., et al., 2016. Interventions that cause weight loss and the impact on cardiovascular risk factors: a systematic review and meta-analysis. Obes. Rev. 17 (10), 1001–1011.

# Index

CPI Antony Rowe

Chippenham, UK

2019-02-28 18:11